Hybrid Threats and the Law of the Sea

International Straits of the World

Series Editor

Nilufer Oral

VOLUME 19

The titles published in this series are listed at *brill.com/insw*

Hybrid Threats and the Law of the Sea

Use of Force and Discriminatory Navigational Restrictions in Straits

By

Alexander Lott

BRILL
NIJHOFF

LEIDEN | BOSTON

This project received funding from the European Union's Horizon 2020 research and innovation programme under the Marie Sklodowska-Curie grant agreement No 101018998. This book reflects only the author's view and the European Research Executive Agency is not responsible for any use that may be made of the information it contains.

The publication charges for this book have been funded by a grant from the publication fund of UiT–The Arctic University of Norway.

Library of Congress Cataloging-in-Publication Data

Names: Lott, Alexander, author.
Title: Hybrid threats and the Law of the Sea : use of force and discriminatory navigational restrictions in straits / by Alexander Lott.
Description: Leiden ; Boston : Brill Nijhoff, [2022] | Series: International straits of the world, 0924-4867 ; volume 19 | Includes bibliographical references and index. | Identifiers: LCCN 2022025798 (print) | LCCN 2022025799 (ebook) | ISBN 9789004509351 (hardback) | ISBN 9789004509368 (ebook)
Subjects: LCSH: Straits. | Law of the sea. | War, Maritime (International law)
Classification: LCC KZ3760 .L68 2022 (print) | LCC KZ3760 (ebook) | DDC 341.4/46–dc23/eng/20220801
LC record available at https://lccn.loc.gov/2022025798
LC ebook record available at https://lccn.loc.gov/2022025799

Typeface for the Latin, Greek, and Cyrillic scripts: "Brill". See and download: brill.com/brill-typeface.

ISSN 0924-4867
ISBN 978-90-04-50935-1 (hardback)
ISBN 978-90-04-50936-8 (e-book)

This book is printed on acid-free paper and produced in a sustainable manner.

To Mare L.

Contents

Preface

The current study approaches the legal regime of straits mostly through the prism of maritime security law and has a relatively wide geographical scope. It covers straits located in the Baltic Sea, the Black Sea, the Red Sea, the Persian Gulf, and the South China Sea. The focus of the book is not only on doctrinal research (particularly on the law of the sea and international security law), but also on international relations, conflict studies (naval hybrid warfare/conflict), and the historical background of recent maritime incidents.

Thus, the book embraces to some extent the law in context approach, which is an interdisciplinary concept that draws on, e.g., political and historical theories while at the same time seeking to "broaden the study of law from *within*".[1] The present study first identifies the challenges that hybrid threats pose to maritime security law and the legal regime of straits. It proceeds by adopting a regional approach for identifying straits that are impacted by hybrid threats and for carrying out case studies of specific maritime incidents in the Baltic Sea, the Black Sea, the waters around the Arabian Peninsula, and the South China Sea. On this basis, this study finally draws broader conclusions on the interaction between the law of the sea, international security law, humanitarian law, and hybrid threats. It seeks to reach general conclusions about how the law of the sea and international security law operate in hybrid conflicts.

The research results of this monograph are disseminated in a somewhat 'hybrid' manner. This manuscript includes both unpublished text as well as analysis that I have published in journal articles and blog posts, but parts of which have now been turned into a book. In other words, while this monograph incorporates many new and unpublished chapters, it also builds on my previous publications on navigational regimes.

Chapter 13 in Part 4, Chapter 4.8.4 of Part 2 and Chapter 7 of Part 2 are partly based on my article that appeared in the French review *Stratégique*.[2] Its editor Matthieu Chillaud kindly gave his permission for translating parts of that article for incorporating it into this manuscript. In addition, Chapter 4 of Part 2 as well as Chapters 10 and 11 of Part 3 are based on my articles 'The (In) applicability of the Right of Innocent Passage in the Gulf of Finland – Russia's Return to a *Mare Clausum*?'[3] and 'The Passage Regimes of the Kerch Strait – To

1 W Twining, *Jurist in Context: A Memoir* (Cambridge University Press, Cambridge, 2019) 162.
2 'Le régime légal de la partie septentrionale de la mer Baltique dans le contexte des récents développements de sécurité', *Stratégique* 2019(1–2).
3 Published in *The International Journal of Marine and Coastal Law* (2021) 36(2).

Each Their Own?'.[4] Chapter 6 of Part 2 is based on an extended version of my post that appeared in June 2021 in the NCLOS blog under the title 'Maritime Security Threats and the Passage Regime in the Bab el-Mandeb' and it also incorporates some fragments of my article 'The Tagliavini Report Revisited: Jus ad Bellum and the Legality of the Russian Intervention in Georgia'.[5] Chapter 8 of Part 3 adapts my part of an article co-authored with Shin Kawagishi on the legal regime of the Strait of Hormuz and the passage of oil tankers from a law of the sea and *jus ad bellum* perspective.[6] Chapter 12 of Part 4 is partly based on my journal article 'Marine Environmental Protection and Transboundary Pipeline Projects: A Case Study of the Nord Stream Pipeline'.[7]

I have also adapted my blog post 'Implications of Hybrid Threats for the Order of the Oceans' to this manuscript. It was published by the Center for International Maritime Security in 2020 and cross-posted in The National Interest blog (under the title 'What Does Hybrid Warfare Mean for Maritime Security?') and EURISLES (in French, under the title 'Implications de la guerre hybride pour l'ordre des océans'). I have now mixed it with the rest of the text in Chapters 1 and 3.3 of Part 1 and Chapter 15 of Part 5. Chapter 18 of Part 5 incorporates my blog post 'Guidelines for Grey Zone Naval Incidents: Distinguishing between the Rules of Armed Conflict and Law Enforcement' that was published in the NCLOS Blog in 2022. Chapter 4.8.2 of Part 2 is partly based on my post 'Russia's Blockade in the Sea of Azov: A Call for Relief Shipments for Mariupol' that appeared in EJIL: Talk! in 2022. An updated version of Chapter 5.3.1 of Part 2 appeared on Brill's blog 'Humanities Matter' in August 2022 soon after the publication of the arbitral award on the preliminary objections of the Russian Federation in the case concerning the Kerch Strait incident.

Most of these papers have been published during my fellowship at the Norwegian Centre for the Law of the Sea. The editors of the journals have confirmed that the relevant publication licences allow me to adapt, republish or mix these previously published articles in this monograph. I thank the editors as well as the anonymous reviewers for their work on the relevant manuscripts.

4 Published in *Ocean Development & International Law* (2021) 52(1).
5 Published in *Utrecht Journal of International and European Law* (2012) 28.
6 Published in *Ocean Development & International Law* (2022) 53(2).
7 Published in *Utrecht Journal of International and European Law* (2011) 27.

Acknowledgements

This manuscript is the result of my research stay at the Norwegian Centre for the Law of the Sea (NCLOS), University of Tromsø. My project on the law of the sea and hybrid warfare (LOSFARE) forms one of the sub-projects at the Centre. I extend my gratitude to the founder of the Centre Tore Henriksen for his comments and suggestions on an earlier draft of this work. I would also like to thank other members of the Centre, in particular its current leader Ingvild Ulrikke Jakobsen and senior advisor Christin Skjervold, for their support to this project. Working in the vibrant and multicultural environment and collaboration as a member of the Centre's group on the overarching issues of the law of the sea added breadth and new knowledge to the project. *Tusen takk!*

This research benefitted substantially from the feedback of the series editor Nilüfer Oral who devoted her time to commenting on this work. Marie Sheldon and her team at Brill showed much hospitality during the publishing process.

I would like to thank Erik Molenaar, Karen Scott, Magne Frostad, Shin Kawagishi, Jan Solski, Endalew Lijalem Enyew, Iva Parlov, Pierre Thévenin, Susan Rolston, Dmitry Filipoff, and the anonymous reviewers for their comments on my previously published works that I have adapted to this manuscript. Any errors and omissions remain my own responsibility. I am also grateful to my colleagues at the School of Law, University of Tartu, in particular the head of our institute Lauri Mälksoo, for backing my research stay in the Arctic, far away from the classrooms where I ought to have lectured on various courses of law had I not been invited to join the NCLOS team.

This study was possible thanks to my wife Kati who enabled me to take occasional breaks from my family responsibilities while being away in the world's northernmost university. *Suur aitäh* for your trust and support.

Illustrations

Maps

Figures

Tables

Abbreviations and Euphemisms

ADIZ	air defence identification zone
EEZ	exclusive economic zone
EU	European Union
ICJ	International Court of Justice
ICRC	The International Committee of the Red Cross
ICTY	The International Criminal Tribunal for the Former Yugoslavia
IMO	International Maritime Organization
ITLOS	International Tribunal for the Law of the Sea
international strait	a natural sea passage used for international navigation between two larger maritime areas and which is not more than 24 NM wide as measured from coast to coast or from baseline to baseline and where international navigation is safeguarded under the Convention.
long-standing internal waters	where the first establishment of a straight baseline in accordance with the method set forth in Article 7 of LOSC has the effect of enclosing as internal waters areas which had also previously been considered as internal waters.
LNG	liquefied natural gas
LOSC/Convention	1982 United Nations Convention on the Law of the Sea
NM	nautical mile
NATO	North Atlantic Treaty Organization
strait State	coastal State of a strait
TSS	traffic separation scheme
UN	United Nations
VCLT	Vienna Convention on the Law of Treaties
VTS	vessel traffic service

PART 1

The Meaning of Straits and Hybrid Threats

CHAPTER 1

The Implications of Hybrid Threats to the Maritime Domain

John Allen, Ben Hodges, and Julian Lindley-French begin their recent book on future war with the thesis that a new comprehensive concept of security is essential for an effective deterrence against a mixture of threats "that stretches across a complex and interlocking mosaic of hybrid, cyber, and hyper-warfare".[1] Against this backdrop, this book focuses on the use of force and the practice of States in imposing navigational restrictions on foreign ships and aircraft in densely navigated straits in the context of hybrid warfare and hybrid conflicts.

In recent years, the significance of straits for maritime security has been underlined by, e.g.,

- limpet mine attacks, sabotage, and arrest of ships in and near the Strait of Hormuz and the Bab el-Mandeb;
- incursions of foreign submarines and aircraft to coastal States' sovereign territories in the Baltic straits;
- coastal State's use of force against foreign warships in the Kerch Strait;
- the blockade of the Sea of Azov by denying foreign ships passage through the Kerch Strait;
- Turkey's refusal to permit the passage of Russian warships through the Turkish Straits in the wake of the Russian invasion of Ukraine;
- freedom of navigation operations in the Taiwan Strait by the United States warships and its allies;
- a Chinese-Russian joint operation that involved their warships passing through Japanese Straits under the freedom of navigation.

The somewhat ambiguous character of the concept of hybrid conflict implies that there is a risk of wrongly characterising a particular incident as forming a hybrid conflict. This risk is also embedded in the present study. Yet this research seeks to address this problem by way of openly debating the 'quasi-legal' classification of recent naval incidents between the concepts of hybrid warfare and hybrid conflict in their broader geopolitical context. Such classification concerns maritime incidents in or near the straits of the Baltic Sea, the

1 JR Allen, FB Hodges, J Lindley-French, *Future War and the Defence of Europe* (Oxford University Press, Oxford 2021), preface.

Black Sea, the Persian Gulf, the Red Sea, and the South China Sea based on the context and the nature of the discriminatory measures or coercion used by the adversary in its capacity as either a flag, port, or coastal State. In general, these categorisations are made in a somewhat inconclusive manner and without the ambition to provide a definite judgment over the nature of these incidents.

The previous examples are chosen in this book to serve as the basis of some case studies that serve the purpose of exemplifying and helping to draw a line between situations of normal peacetime measures, hybrid conflict, hybrid naval warfare, and naval warfare (armed conflict). This enables to reflect on the implications of hybrid conflicts to international security law and maritime security law. Thus, the present study purports to contribute to the debate over the nature of hybrid threats and explore both widely acknowledged and lesser-known maritime incidents that meet the characteristics of hybrid warfare or hybrid conflict. In so doing, this research approaches hybrid naval conflicts from a specific angle, i.e., the interrelationship between discriminatory navigational restrictions, coercion, armed attack, law enforcement, and the legal regime of straits.

In times of increased tension between States, coastal States tend to use their security considerations as an argument – legitimate or not – to adopt measures that restrict navigational rights under the law of the sea. Many States have adopted also permanent arrangements that restrict navigational rights and freedoms in their maritime zones due to *inter alia* security considerations, e.g., China's asserted control over foreign military activities in its exclusive economic zone (hereafter EEZ),[2] the Russian Federation's permit-based regime of innocent passage through its territorial sea in the Gulf of Finland and the Kerch Strait,[3] etc. Irrespective of whether these restrictive requirements are permanent or temporary, they tend to have the effect of contributing to the escalation of so-called grey zone conflicts, as examined below based on the examples of recent incidents in the Kerch Strait and the Strait of Hormuz.[4] This may occur by restricting navigation through important chokepoints of maritime commerce by, for example, subjecting transiting ships or aircraft to the requirements of prior notification or authorisation or even the use of force or coercion by the coastal State of the strait (hereafter strait State).

Such practices contradict the aims to keep commercial trade routes open and ensure the rule of law also in the maritime domain. In 2018 and 2019, the volume of seaborne trade reached over 11 billion tons which accounts for

2 See *infra* Chapter 5.3 of Part 2. See also, e.g., R Pedrozo, 'Close Encounters at Sea: The USNS *Impeccable* Incident', (2009) 62(3) *Naval War College Review*, 101–110.

3 See *infra* Chapter 1 of Part 2, Chapters 10–4 of Part 3.

4 See *infra* Chapter 1 of Part 2 and Chapter 8 of Part 3.

approximately 90 percent of global trade.[5] Hybrid conflicts and discriminatory navigational restrictions are a hindrance to navigation in important maritime routes. They conflict with the strategic interest of maintaining the stability of global commerce. For example, the strategic maritime security interests of the European Union (hereafter EU) and its Member States are, *inter alia*, "the preservation of freedom of navigation, the protection of the global EU supply chain and of maritime trade, the right of innocent and transit passage of ships and the security of their crew and passengers".[6] The United States shares these interests and, in pursuance of these aims, operates the freedom of navigation program for the protection of navigation rights globally.

This study focuses on the challenges that a hybrid conflict poses for the rights of navigation and thus for the stability of the law of the sea. It seeks to determine how the law of the sea and maritime security law can contribute to ensuring the rule of law in major commercial shipping routes that are impacted by hybrid conflicts. The primary objects of this research are restrictions of passage rights in straits, incl. arrest of ships and threat and use of force against commercial and naval vessels. The meaning of the legal concept of strait and various legal categories of straits that serve as the basis of the following analysis are examined next.

5 UN Conference on Trade and Development, '2019 e-Handbook of Statistics', Geneva, 2019. UN Conference on Trade and Development, 'Review of Maritime Transport 2020', Geneva, 2020, 11.

6 Council of the European Union, 'European Union Maritime Security Strategy', Brussels 2014, 6–7.

CHAPTER 2

The Legal Concept and Classification of Straits

2.1 The Legal Concept of a Strait

The meaning of the terms "strait" and "strait used for international navigation" (hereafter as a euphemism "international strait") are left undefined in the 1982 United Nations Convention on the Law of the Sea[1] (hereafter LOSC or Convention). Under the present author's interpretation of LOSC, an international strait is a natural sea passage that is used for international navigation between two larger maritime areas, and which is not more than 24 nautical miles (hereafter NM) wide as measured from coast to coast or from baseline to baseline and, in respect of which, international navigation is safeguarded under the Convention. In Europe alone, over 30 natural sea passages meet the criteria of an international strait (see Map 1).

The 24-NM-limit follows from the teleological interpretation of Part III of the LOSC that was designed to safeguard passage rights in and above straits in the context of the extension of the maximum outer limit of territorial sea to 12 NM. This means that straits which include an EEZ or the high seas corridor (so-called Article 36-category of straits) still meet the legal definition of strait provided that they are up to 24 NM wide. This follows from Article 35(b) of LOSC which stipulates that nothing in Part III of the Convention affects the legal status of the waters beyond the territorial seas of States bordering straits as EEZs or high seas.

Hence, the EEZ or high seas corridor in the Article 36-type of international strait could be established by strait States by means of voluntarily limiting the width of the outer limits of their territorial sea. As examined below, this method has been used by Japan in respect of many straits that would be otherwise located entirely in its territorial sea or internal waters and by the Baltic strait States in respect of, *inter alia*, the Kadet and Femer straits,[2] Bornholmsgat[3]

1 United Nations Convention on the Law of the Sea, adopted 10 December 1982, entered into force 16 November 1994, 1833 UNTS 397.

2 Section 1 of the Proclamation by the Government of the Federal Republic of Germany concerning the extension of the breadth of the German territorial sea, adopted 11 November 1994, entered into force 1 January 1995, available http://www.un.org/depts/los/LEGISLATIONANDTREATIES/PDFFILES/deu_1994_territorial_proclamation.pdf; accessed 30 October 2021.

3 Exchange of Notes Constituting an Agreement between Denmark and Sweden concerning the Delimitation of the Territorial Waters between Denmark and Sweden, adopted 25

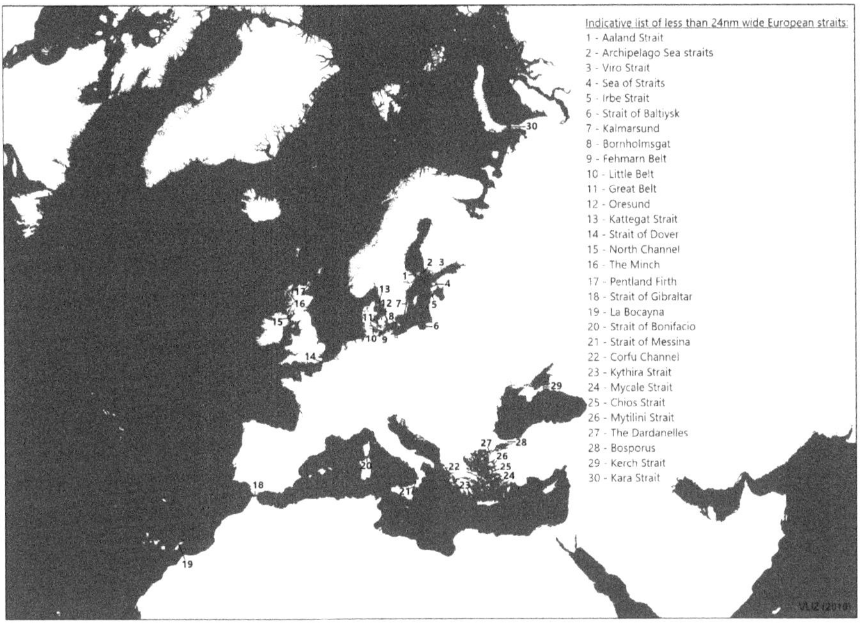

MAP 1 European Straits
SOURCE: BASE MAP IS CREATED BY MARINEREGIONS.ORG, 'EUROPE', FLANDERS MARINE INSTITUTE (VLIZ), 2010, AVAILABLE HTTPS://WWW.MARINEREGIONS.ORG/MAPS.PHP?ALBUM=3753&PIC=64923; ACCESSED 5 APRIL 2021. THE INDICATIVE LIST OF LESS THAN 24-NM-WIDE STRAITS IN EUROPE IS CREATED BY THE AUTHOR AND THE BASE MAP IS MODIFIED BY THE AUTHOR TO INCLUDE THEIR LOCATIONS. THE BASE MAP IS ALSO TURNED INTO BLACK AND WHITE BY THE AUTHOR.

and the Viro Strait.[4] However, as an exception to the 24-NM-rule, if the strait is only a couple of NM wider than 24 NM,[5] as a result of which there exists a very narrow EEZ corridor, the straits regime still applies if the EEZ corridor is not of similar convenience with respect to navigational and hydrographical characteristics as the rest of the strait (Art 36 of LOSC).

June 1979, entered into force 21 December 1979, available http://www.un.org/depts/los/LEGISLATIONANDTREATIES/PDFFILES/TREATIES/DNK-SWE1979TW.PDF; accessed 30 October 2021.

4 Exchange of Notes Constituting an Agreement on the Procedure to be followed in the Modification of the Limits of the Territorial Waters in the Gulf of Finland, adopted 4 May 1994, entered into force 31 July 1995, 1887 UNTS 223.

5 E.g., the western part of the Strait of Hormuz in the Persian Gulf, see *infra* Chapter 8.2 of Part 3.

Geographical limits of a strait often overlap with its legal scope. For example, in respect of the Strait of Singapore, Part III of LOSC is applicable throughout the maritime area that is commonly understood as forming the strait.[6] Yet it is equally possible that what is generally referred to as a strait is not a strait legally. For example, of the straits that form the object of this research, the Taiwan Strait meets the geographical and functional criteria of a strait (in fact, being the busiest strait globally). Still, the Taiwan Strait is not subject to the legal regime of straits, since the freedom of international navigation through the Taiwan Strait is not threatened by the overlapping territorial sea.[7] In some cases, the opposite is true – a maritime area is perceived by the general public as well as the relevant coastal and user States as not forming a strait, while it is actually subject to the legal regime of straits under the Convention (e.g., the Viro Strait/Gulf of Finland). Similar to, for example, the Taiwan Strait, an EEZ corridor exists in the Viro Strait (the Gulf of Finland), but different from the Taiwan Strait, the EEZ corridor can be abolished by the strait States Estonia and Finland if they decide to extend the outer limits of their territorial sea to the 12-NM-wide maximum extent. In this case, the legal regime of straits under the Convention would still safeguard international maritime and air navigation in and over the strait as the Viro Strait would be subject to the regime of transit passage.[8]

In addition, there are cases where the legal regime of a strait is applicable to a strait only in a small part of a strait's geographical limits, e.g., the Strait of Malacca,[9] or Part III of LOSC has extended the spatial limits of a strait as compared to its commonly accepted geographical borders, e.g., the Bab el-Mandeb.[10] These examples show that law is redefining our long-held (geographic) understandings of what constitutes a strait.

2.2 The Legal Classification of Straits

LOSC recognises various navigational regimes, including the freedom of navigation and overflight, transit passage, archipelagic sea lanes passage, suspendable and non-suspendable innocent passage, special passage regimes, and passage subject to the coastal State's authorisation. Nearly half of them are

6 *Infra* Chapter 14 of Part 4.
7 *Infra* Chapter 9 of Part 3.
8 *Infra* Chapter 7 of Part 2.
9 *Infra* Chapter 14 of Part 4.
10 *Infra* Chapter 6.1 of Part 2.

such passage regimes that only apply in straits: the regimes of transit passage, non-suspendable innocent passage and special passage regimes that have been drafted under treaties that regulate navigation through specific straits. In addition, the legal categories of straits also rely on general navigational regimes, including the freedom of navigation and overflight (Art 36 of LOSC) as well as archipelagic sea lanes passage (Art 54 of LOSC) and permit-based passage (Art 35(a) of LOSC).

There is no generally agreed list of the legal categories of straits. Numerous authors have provided their accounts of the legal categories of straits that, according to most authors' interpretation of the Convention, includes up to five or six types of straits. For example, Kraska and Pedrozo have found that:

> There are six types of international straits: (1) geographic straits through which a high-seas corridor exists (such as the Taiwan Strait or some of the Japanese straits); (2) straits governed by long-standing conventions (such as the afore-mentioned Strait of Magellan and the Turkish Straits, as well as the Danish Straits); (3) straits with routes through the high seas or EEZ that are of similar convenience; (4) straits formed by islands (e.g., the Messina Strait); (5) archipelagic straits governed by archipelagic sea lanes passage, and (6) dead end straits. Each archetype has unique characteristics.[11]

Under the present author's interpretation of the Convention, it is possible to distinguish also numerous other legal categories of straits, some of which are based on a provision of LOSC that falls outside Part III of the Convention that is specifically devoted to the legal regime of straits. Based on a systemic interpretation of the Convention, the legal categories of straits and the corresponding navigational regimes are systemized in the table below (see Table 1).

This book centres around the above-listed legal categories of straits when examining the legality of navigational restrictions in hybrid conflicts and hybrid warfare. In this context, particular emphasis lies on studying such complex situations where navigation through a strait is governed by parallel passage regimes. This occurs where the strait States or the strait State and user States disagree on the passage regime that applies to a particular strait. It results in a 'grey area' in relation to the governance of a strait, since strait State(s) and

11 J Kraska, R Pedrozo, *International Maritime Security Law* (Martinus Nijhoff, Leiden/Boston, 2013), 224.

TABLE 1 Legal categories of Straits[a]

Legal basis	Category of straits	Passage regime	Examples
International straits			
Art 37 LOSC	Strait linking two parts of an EEZ or the high seas	Transit passage	The straits of Dover, Gibraltar, Malacca, Hormuz, Bab el-Mandeb
Art 38(1) LOSC	Strait formed by an island of a strait State and its mainland coast	Non-suspendable innocent passage	The Strait of Messina Kalmarsund Corfu Channel
Art 45(1)(b) LOSC	Strait linking EEZ/high seas with a foreign State's territorial sea	Non-suspendable innocent passage	The Strait of Tiran (prior to the 1979 Treaty) Head Harbour Passage
Art 53 LOSC	Strait in the archipelagic waters	Archipelagic Sea Lanes Passage	Sunda Strait Lombok Strait Makassar Strait
Art 36 LOSC	Strait that includes an EEZ or the high seas corridor	Freedom of Navigation & Overflight	Femer Belt, Kadet, Viro Strait (Gulf of Finland), Tsugaru, Osumi, Soya, Bornholmsgat
Art 311(2) LOSC	*Sui generis* strait	Specific passage regime	The Strait of Tiran (1979 Treaty) The Kerch Strait (2003 Treaty) The Baltiysk Strait (2009 Treaty)
Art 35(c) LOSC	Strait regulated by a long-standing international convention	Specific passage regime	The Danish Straits The Åland Strait The Strait of Magellan The Turkish Straits
Art 234 LOSC	Potentially/contested: ice-covered strait	Specific passage regime	The Northwest Passage The Northern Sea Route
Non-international straits			
Art 35(a) LOSC	Strait in long-standing internal waters	Permit-based passage	The Sea of Straits The Archipelago Sea straits

TABLE 1 Legal categories of Straits (*cont.*)

Legal basis	Category of straits	Passage regime	Examples
Art 34 LOSC	Non-navigable strait	Presence of barriers, e.g., causeways	The Canso Strait The Johor Strait *Väike väin* (the Small Strait)

a This categorisation is based on the present author's systemic interpretation of LOSC. For comments and literature review, see A Lott, *The Estonian Straits: Exceptions to the Strait Regime of Innocent or Transit Passage* (Brill, Leiden/Boston, 2018), 5–46.

user States are unwilling to agree on a uniform set of rules for the regulation of passage of foreign ships and aircraft in and above the relevant strait.

Parallel legal regimes of a strait may be caused, e.g., by a user State's note of diplomatic protest to the strait State's domestic legal act that regulates passage in a particular strait (e.g., the United States objections to the Russian Federation's domestic regulations on the Northern Sea Route). A strait may be subject to different regimes also because of another State's objection to State continuity (e.g., the Estonian Straits) or the non-recognition of an unlawful territorial annexation (e.g., the Kerch Strait). Furthermore, the legal regime of the Strait of Hormuz illustrates that a parallel legal regime of a strait may be the consequence of partial non-applicability of LOSC to the regulation of navigation in a strait due to, e.g., the strait State's objection to the regime of transit passage as well as its or user State's decision to abstain from becoming a party to the LOSC (see *infra* Chapter 8.4 of Part 3).

The parallel legal regimes may result in situations where parties to a dispute may be in diametrically opposing positions over whether international navigation through a particular strait is regulated by the right of transit passage, non-suspendable innocent passage, specific treaty regime or permit-based passage. This results in legal uncertainty over passage rights which, in turn, is a fertile ground for the escalation of hybrid conflicts. Such disputes often lead to actual maritime incidents and conflicts between the parties as illustrated by the naval incidents in the Kerch Strait and the Strait of Hormuz. Ukraine claims that passage through the Kerch Strait is regulated by the regime of transit passage, whereas the Russian Federation considers that the Kerch Strait is subject to a specific treaty regime. Similarly, the United States considers that the regime of transit passage applies to its ships and aircraft in and over the Strait of Hormuz, while Iran recognises the applicability of the right of innocent passage.

It is argued below that the parallel legal regimes of a strait are the crux of the problem that has led to conflicts in the Strait of Hormuz and the Kerch Strait between the strait States and user States (see *infra* Chapter 4.7 of Part 2 and Chapter 8.4 of Part 3). This book seeks to assess such incidents and asks if the law of the sea and general international law can accommodate the legality of the conflicting approaches to a strait's legal regime on such occasions. Other instances that give rise to parallel passage regimes in a particular strait are due to the law of naval warfare and, in particular, the law of neutrality, as examined next.

2.3 The Law of Naval Warfare in Straits and Its Relation to the Law of the Sea

LOSC does not regulate matters of war. Instead, pursuant to the meaning of its preamble, naval warfare is regulated by the rules and principles of general international law. Yet this does not mean that LOSC loses its significance in an armed conflict. The legal framework and the rules stipulated in the LOSC in respect of various maritime zones and activities therein largely continue to apply in times of war, both in respect of neutral as well as belligerent States.[12] Furthermore, as argued by Heintschel von Heinegg, the violation by a foreign warship of the rules of (non-suspendable) innocent passage or transit passage in straits and by not complying with the coastal State's order to leave its territorial sea might potentially *per se* amount to the use of force under Article 2(4) of the United Nations (hereafter UN) Charter that triggers the applicability of *jus in bello*.[13]

Straits gain an increased significance in an armed conflict as the control over these vital sea lanes is of strategic importance for the belligerent war efforts. At the same time, navigation through straits in times of war is threatened not only from the presence of belligerent warships patrolling these narrow waterways, but also from attacks launched from adjacent coasts and

12 See Kraska and Pedrozo, *op. cit.*, 864. N Klein, *Maritime Security and the Law of the Sea* (Oxford University Press, Oxford 2013), 259. W Heintschel von Heinegg, 'The Law of Armed Conflict at Sea', in D Fleck (ed.), *The Handbook of International Humanitarian Law* (2nd Ed, Oxford University Press, Oxford, 2009), 476ff. H Caminos, VP Cogliati-Bantz, *The Legal Regime of Straits: Contemporary Challenges and Solutions* (Cambridge University Press, Cambridge, 2014), 11–12.

13 W Heintschel von Heinegg, 'The difficulties of conflict classification at sea: Distinguishing incidents at sea from hostilities', (2016) 98(2) *International Review of the Red Cross*, 457–459.

particularly from mine warfare. For example, one of the deadliest naval battles was fought in late August 1941 in the Viro Strait during the evacuation of the Soviet Union's Baltic fleet from Tallinn to St Petersburg (also known as the Soviet Dunkirk). The Soviet fleet was *en route* to St Petersburg when it suffered heavy losses in the Finnish and German minefields in the Viro Strait as well as from German and Finnish naval and air attacks complemented with the German artillery fire from the Estonian northern coast (Juminda Peninsula).[14]

The rules of customary international law applicable to naval warfare in international straits is largely reflected in Section II of the San Remo Manual. According to the San Remo Manual, ships and aircraft retain in an armed conflict their rights of transit and archipelagic sea lanes passage through, under or over neutral international straits, but, at the same time, transiting ships must not jeopardize the neutrality of the strait State.[15] Furthermore, belligerent ships, submarines and aircraft have the rights of transit passage and archipelagic sea lanes passage also in non-neutral straits ('through, under, and over all straits') to which these rights generally apply.[16] Yet they can be subject to belligerent attacks while navigating in or over such straits.[17] Caminos and Cogliati-Bantz note that: "It is beyond doubt that a belligerent State bordering a strait is not obliged to respect the right of transit of enemy vessels."[18] By contrast, ships and aircraft of neutral States retain their passage rights and cannot be attacked while transiting belligerent straits.[19]

The foregoing also applies to the right of non-suspendable innocent passage in international straits in an armed conflict.[20] Unlike the coastal State's general right to temporarily suspend innocent passage through its territorial sea on, e.g., security grounds, the right of innocent passage through international straits cannot be suspended under customary international law. This was recognised by the International Court of Justice (hereafter ICJ) in the

14 See M Õun, *Juminda miinilahing 1941 – maailmasündmus meie koduvetes* (Juminda Sentinel, Juminda, 2006).

15 San Remo Manual on International Law Applicable to Armed Conflicts at Sea, 12 June 1994, Rules 23–25, 27. Available: https://ihl-databases.icrc.org/ihl/INTRO/560; accessed 1 October 2021.

16 Ibid., Rules 27–28.

17 W Heintschel von Heinegg, 'The Law of Naval Warfare and International Straits' (1998) 71 *International Law Studies*, 265.

18 Caminos and Cogliati-Bantz, *op. cit.*, 21.

19 San Remo Manual, *op. cit.*, Rule 26.

20 Ibid., Rule 33.

1949 judgment of the *Corfu Channel case* according to which the right of non-suspendable innocent passage applies in straits that connect two parts of the high seas.[21]

In the Corfu Channel incident, the warships of the United Kingdom struck Albanian mines while navigating the Corfu Channel. The ICJ noted that at the time Greece considered herself as being 'technically' in an armed conflict with Albania, and that Albania, "in view of these exceptional circumstances, would have been justified in issuing regulations in respect of the passage of warships [of neutral States] through the Strait, but not in prohibiting such passage or in subjecting it to the requirement of special authorization."[22] Consequently, the Court upheld the right of non-suspendable innocent passage through an international strait that cannot be denied for neutral shipping even in times of war.

By now, similar conclusions can be drawn in respect of the right of transit passage. Heintschel von Heinegg maintains that: "Recent state practice also indicates the existence of a rule prohibiting the suspension of the right of transit passage, even during an international armed conflict."[23] Similar to the San Remo Manual, he finds that the right of transit passage and non-suspendable innocent passage cannot be denied by belligerents in respect of neutral States.[24]

The extent of the right of innocent passage of warships was at the time of the *Corfu Channel case* still unclear, particularly in the context of an international armed conflict between the strait State and another State. Equally, it was disputed whether the Corfu Channel constitutes such narrow sea passage through which international navigation needs to be safeguarded under international law. Albania maintained in the *Corfu Channel case* that by sending its warships through the Albanian territorial sea in the Corfu Channel, the United Kingdom violated its sovereignty and that Albania was entitled, in such exceptional circumstances, to regulate the passage of foreign warships through its territorial sea by requiring that foreign warships apply for a prior authorisation.[25] Albania also alleged that the passage of the Royal Navy's warships through its territorial sea was not of an innocent character.[26] The ICJ rejected the Albanian claims.[27]

21 Corfu Channel Case (United Kingdom v. Albania), Judgment, I.C.J. Reports 1949, 28.
22 The Corfu Channel Case, *op. cit.*, 29.
23 Heintschel von Heinegg 1998, *op. cit.*, 265.
24 Ibid., 266.
25 The Corfu Channel Case, *op. cit.*, 12.
26 Ibid.
27 Ibid., 29.

Based on the underlying logic of the judgment in the *Corfu Channel case*, a strait State, nor any other party, is not entitled to temporarily close, e.g., by means of laying minefields or a blockade, an international strait for the navigation of neutral ships or aircraft in an armed conflict. Caminos and Cogliati-Bantz refer to the San Remo Manual and the International Law Association's position in arguing that a "complete closure of the strait because of the existence of minefields, which render passage impossible, would be illegal".[28] In particular, the San Remo Manual stipulates that: "Transit passage through international straits and passage through waters subject to the right of archipelagic sea lanes passage shall not be impeded unless safe and convenient alternative routes are provided."[29] Thus, where the strait State closes parts of a strait for international navigation in an armed conflict, e.g. by mining the strait or by means of a blockade, it still needs to ensure the expeditious transit of neutral ships via safe corridors.[30]

However, there are, arguably, exceptions to this rule. First, as noted by Heintschel von Heinegg as well as Caminos and Cogliati-Bantz, a strait State might be entitled to close the airspace for overflight of neutral aircraft, let alone belligerent aircraft, in an armed conflict due to its security considerations.[31] Furthermore, as Caminos and Cogliati-Bantz point out, it is open to interpretation whether the strait State is entitled to completely close an international strait subject to military necessity and if 'justified by the gravest of circumstances'.[32] Similarly, for Heintschel von Heinegg this question 'is a matter of dispute'.[33]

---

28 Caminos and Cogliati-Bantz, *op. cit.*, 27.

29 San Remo Manual, *op. cit.*, Rule 89.

30 Caminos and Cogliati-Bantz, *op. cit.*, 25–27.

31 Heintschel von Heinegg 1998, *op. cit.*, 267, 270. Caminos and Cogliati-Bantz, *op. cit.*, 29.

32 Caminos and Cogliati-Bantz, *op. cit.*, 30.

33 Heintschel von Heinegg 1998, *op. cit.*, 265. Based on a detailed examination of the applicable law and State practice in the 20th century, the author notes that 'it is far from clear' in which cases the right of transit passage may be restricted in respect of neutral shipping. Ibid., 266.

CHAPTER 3

The Concept of Hybrid Threats

Hybrid threats stem from hybrid conflicts and hybrid warfare (see Figure 1). The meaning of these two concepts is explained next. Legally speaking, the phenomenon of hybrid warfare appears to be intertwined with the question of the threshold for the applicability of the laws of armed conflict. As explained below, in situations of hybrid warfare, it tends to be unclear whether the legality of the use of force or direct coercion at sea should be assessed based on the legal framework applicable to naval warfare or law enforcement. For unpacking the concept of hybrid warfare, the following analysis addresses the distinction between the concepts of peacetime law enforcement and naval warfare, since by its very nature, hybrid warfare takes advantage of the grey zone between the laws of peace and war. Yet first it is examined how a hybrid conflict differs from hybrid warfare.

3.1 The Meaning of Hybrid Conflicts

Hybrid conflicts are understood to constitute "a situation in which parties refrain from the overt use of armed forces against each other, relying instead on a combination of military intimidation (falling short of an attack), exploitation of economic and political vulnerabilities, and diplomatic or technological means to pursue their objectives."[1] Hybrid conflicts do not need to involve a direct military dimension which, instead, is rather characteristic of hybrid warfare. Thus, for the purposes of this study, the term *hybrid conflict* is not synonymous to the concept of *hybrid warfare* that implies a greater degree of aggression (see *infra* Chapter 3.3 of Part 1).[2]

For example, were a particular State to facilitate actively the flow of massive illegal migration from one State to a third State, e.g., by means of logistically and financially supporting the creation of a transport corridor by air or sea routes, it would enable to trigger political unrest and destabilize the internal public order in the victim State. In such scenario, the State that triggers the

1 European Parliament Research Service, 'At a glance – Understanding hybrid Threats', Brussels 2015, 1.

2 On the comparison between the two concepts, see, e.g., R Värk, 'Legal Complexities in the Service of Hybrid Warfare' (2020) 6 *Kyiv-Mohyla Law and Politics Journal*, 31.

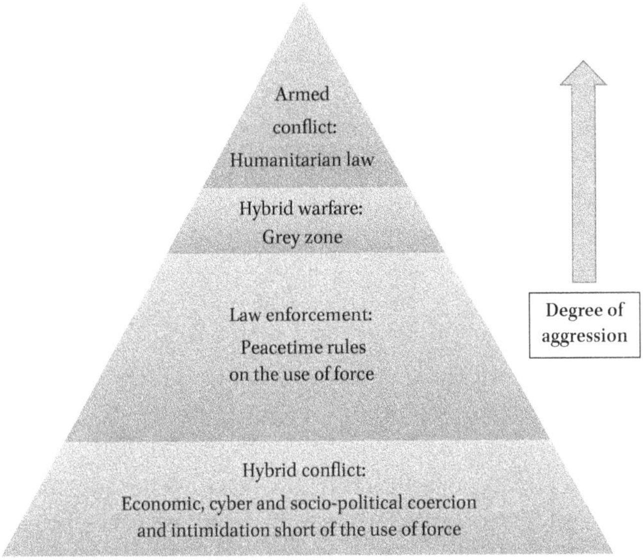

FIGURE 1 The relationship of hybrid conflicts and hybrid warfare with the armed conflict and peacetime law enforcement paradigms

migrant crisis employs means of socio-political coercion and intimidation short of the use of force and military means. In response to the massive inflow of illegal migration, the targeted State presumably would use law enforcement measures to ensure effective border control and handling of the crisis.

In the context of the maritime domain, *hybrid conflict* can be understood as a broad term that encapsulates a combination of economic and socio-political coercion and intimidation (e.g., discriminatory arrests of ships and prohibitions of passage), including in the cyber domain (e.g., grey maritime networks, manipulations with the cyber systems of ships or aircraft).

The foregoing does not mean that from the scope of hybrid conflicts are excluded incidents that have a military dimension. Yet, in this study, hybrid conflicts are understood to include only such military activities where the States involved abstain from the use of force against each other (e.g., passage of warships or military aircraft, military research activities, military build-up near borders, etc). The use of force by one State against another State is indicative of the existence of a situation of hybrid warfare where it is unclear if the use of force amounts to an armed attack under Article 51 of the UN Charter.[3] For

3 Charter of the United Nations, adopted 26 June 1945, entered into force 24 October 1945, 1 UNTS XVI.

example, such examples include illegal incursions into the sovereign airspace or maritime areas (e.g., by military aircraft or submarines). Hybrid warfare may also include dangerous approaches to warships, as practiced by the Iranian and Russian navies.[4] By contrast, where the use of force by one State against another State clearly constitutes an armed attack under Article 51 of the UN Charter, the laws of armed conflict apply.

Albeit a lot has been written on navigational regimes and coastal State's rights to regulate navigation in general, the existing legal literature has not so far focused on the challenges that a hybrid conflict poses for navigation. Geopolitical tensions between a coastal and a flag State have had a direct adverse impact on the passage rights of ships in various straits of the world. Four case studies on discriminatory restrictions on the passage rights of commercial ships in straits are selected for that purpose. Chapter 8 of Part 3 scrutinizes the arrest of the United Kingdom-flagged tanker *Stena Impero* by Iran in the Strait of Hormuz in 2019. Chapter 9 of Part 3 addresses tensions in and over the Taiwan Strait with a focus on China's rules on the passage rights of foreign ships in its maritime areas. Chapter 10 of Part 3 analyses the legal complexities of the delays caused by the Russian Federation to foreign commercial ships' passage through the Kerch Strait.

In contrast to the Black Sea context, the Russian Federation's practice in relation to passage rights of foreign ships and aircraft in, above and near its maritime areas in the Baltic Sea (such as the eastern part of the Gulf of Finland and adjacent to the Kaliningrad enclave) has largely remained unnoticed in legal research. Chapter 11 of Part 3 examines the *Vironia* incident in the Gulf of Finland in which case the Russian Federation declined to give its authorisation for crossing its territorial sea under the right of innocent passage to the Estonian-flagged commercial ship *Vironia*. This occurred in the immediate aftermath of the 2007 riots and large-scale cyber-attacks against Estonia, which were sparked in the Russian-speaking minority in Tallinn due to the relocation of the Soviet Bronze Soldier monument. *Vironia* transported goods and passengers in the eastern Gulf of Finland that borders the Viro Strait between the Estonian Sillamäe Port and the Finnish Kotka Port. It is explained below that due to its refusal to grant permission for exercising the right of innocent passage, the Russian Federation effectively caused the closure of the ferry line.

Hybrid conflicts that are triggered by economic intimidation may involve, for example, industrial projects that cause ecological destruction, pose

4 For a definition of warship, see Art 29 of the LOSC.

security threats in the maritime domain and enable to exert economic coercion. Notable examples include the construction of the Kerch Strait Bridge in the Black Sea and the artificial islands in the South China Sea. To this list may also be added the Nord Stream pipelines in the Baltic Sea. Chapter 12 of Part 4 elaborates on the maritime incidents between Estonia and the Russian Federation in the context of the Nord Stream project. These incidents were due to the States' conflicting interpretations of the legal regime of marine scientific research and navigational freedoms and the chapter takes a detailed look on unconsented-to research activities of Russian ships in the Estonian maritime area.

Major industrial projects can be 'weaponized' to advance a State's strategic aims. Furthermore, such projects as the Kerch Strait Bridge, artificial islands in the South China Sea, and the Nord Stream pipelines enable to create a sphere of influence and project a State's armed force in an extensive maritime area outside the relevant State's own maritime zones. For the protection of the relevant installations and constructions, a safety zone of up to 500 meters around them can be established by the coastal State in its EEZ under Article 60(4–7) of LOSC.

Indicative of the categorisation of the Nord Stream project as a threat to the Baltic Sea region's security is the United States Secretary of State's characterisation of the objective of the Nord Stream project: "As multiple U.S. administrations have made clear, this pipeline is a Russian geopolitical project intended to divide Europe and weaken European energy security."[5] The defence minister of Finland has considered the Nord Stream project as a potential threat to Finland's national security,[6] while these concerns are largely shared by Ukraine, the Baltic States, and Poland.

Such projects may also enable to exert economic and political pressure against the coastal States that are impacted by the industrial projects. For example, the Nord Stream project enables to cut off Ukraine from the transit of Russian natural gas to Europe, thereby significantly increasing Ukraine's vulnerability to political manipulation. These projects have also created new challenges for the rights of navigation in the relevant maritime areas and thus for the stability of the law of the sea. This is demonstrated by the Russian Federation's blocking of the Kerch Strait in 2018 by means of placing a commercial ship under the Kerch Strait Bridge, Russia's blockade in the same area

5 Secretary of State AJ Blinken, 'Nord Stream 2 and Potential Sanctionable Activity', Press Statement, 18 March 2021, available https://www.state.gov/nord-stream-2-and-potential-sanctionable-activity; accessed 1 June 2021.

6 See *infra* Chapter 12.1 of Part 4.

in 2022, and the creation of Chinese military bases on artificial islands in the South China Sea where the United States has repeatedly conducted Freedom of Navigation operations.

3.2 Differences between the Rules on the Use of Force in Maritime Law Enforcement Operations and Armed Conflicts

Problems in the classification of naval incidents between peacetime law enforcement and humanitarian law paradigms underline many contemporary inter-State naval conflicts, e.g., the Kerch Strait incident (see *infra* Chapters 4 and 5 of Part 2), attacks against ships in the 'shadow war' between Iran and Israel (see *infra* Chapter 6.5 of Part 2) and the 'spillover' of the Yemeni armed conflict in the Red Sea as manifested by attacks against foreign ships passing through that important waterway (*supra* Chapter 6.4 of Part 2). In the Baltic Sea region, there have been repeated incursions of suspected Russian submarines into the territorial seas of Sweden and Finland and multiple violations of Russia's neighbouring States' airspace by Russia's military aircraft. These are all instances that merit further attention in the context of hybrid warfare in the Baltic Sea region (see *infra* Chapter 7 of Part 2 and Chapter 13 of Part 4).

As these examples demonstrate, it is not entirely clear to what extent the law of the sea applies in hybrid warfare. This is intertwined with the question of whether the rules of naval warfare or law enforcement should be applied in so-called grey zones to assess the legality of the coastal State's use of force or direct coercion at sea. The Annex VII Arbitral Tribunal has found that "[l]aw enforcement forces ... are generally authorised to use physical force without their activities being considered military for that reason."[7] In this context, Gill and Fleck also note that:

> Forces involved in contemporary military operations are often called upon to assume functions both of law enforcement and of hostilities, each of which are governed by different legal standards. It is therefore important to distinguish between these two concepts, identify potential

7 Annex VII Arbitral Tribunal, *Dispute Concerning Coastal State Rights in the Black Sea, Sea of Azov, and Kerch Strait (Ukraine v. the Russian Federation)*, Award Concerning the Preliminary Objections of the Russian Federation, 21 February 2020, para 21, available https://pca-cpa.org/en/cases/149/; accessed 5 April 2021.

> overlaps between them, and determine how the respective legal paradigms governing each type of operation interrelate.[8]

It has been observed that the use of arms in peacetime law enforcement operations is not sufficiently regulated under international law, including in the LOSC,[9] and that the rules on the use of force at sea stem mainly from customary international law,[10] particularly from human rights law.[11] Law enforcement operations traditionally fall under the legal framework of domestic administrative law. Under administrative law, law enforcement measures need to have, *inter alia*, a clear legal basis in the relevant domestic legal acts and cannot amount to an abuse of discretion. In a law enforcement operation, a State is required to observe the principle of proportionality within the scope of which is included the principle of necessity.

Based on the case law of international courts and tribunals, analogous criteria apply when assessing the legality of law enforcement measures under international law. The Annex VII Arbitral Tribunal stated in the arbitration between Guyana and Suriname that when force is used in law enforcement activities, recourse to force must be unavoidable, reasonable and necessary.[12] This was confirmed in the *Arctic Sunrise Case* where the Annex VII Arbitral Tribunal explained that:

> To assess the lawfulness of measures taken by a coastal State in response to protest actions within its EEZ, the Tribunal considers it necessary to determine whether: (i) the measures had a basis in international law; and (ii) the measures were carried out in accordance with international law, including with the principle of reasonableness. Where such measures involve enforcement measures they are subject to the general principles of necessity and proportionality.[13]

8 TD Gill, D Fleck, 'Conceptual Distinction and Overlaps between Law Enforcement and the Conduct of Hostilities', in TD Gill, D Fleck (eds), *The Handbook of the International Law of Military Operations* (Oxford University Press, Oxford, 2015), 63.

9 A Kanehara, 'The Use of Force in Maritime Security and the Use of Arms in Law Enforcement under the Current Wide Understanding of Maritime Security' (2019) 3(2) *Japan Review*, 53.

10 C Moore, 'The Use of Force', in R Warner, S Kaye (eds.), *Routledge Handbook of Maritime Regulation and Enforcement* (Routledge, New York/Abingdon, 2018), 27.

11 Gill and Fleck, *op. cit.*, 69.

12 Annex VII Arbitral Tribunal, Matter of an Arbitration between Guyana and Suriname, Award of 17 September 2007, para 445.

13 Arctic Sunrise Arbitration (the Netherlands v. the Russian Federation). Award of the LOSC Annex VII Tribunal, 14 August 2015, para 222.

The Tribunal found that the boarding, seizure, and detention of the Greenpeace ship *Arctic Sunrise* by the Russian Federation near a Russian offshore oil platform in the Russian EEZ in the Pechora Sea violated the Netherlands' exclusive jurisdiction over the *Arctic Sunrise*. The Tribunal concluded that the Russian law enforcement measures lacked a legal basis in international law and thus did not consider it relevant to assess the reasonableness, necessity, and proportionality of those measures.[14]

The above-referred practice of the Annex VII Arbitral Tribunal conforms with the 1999 position of the ITLOS which found in the *M/V Saiga case* that:

> [T]he use of force must be avoided as far as possible and, where force is unavoidable, it must not go beyond what is reasonable and necessary in the circumstances.... The normal practice used to stop a ship at sea is first to give an auditory or visual signal to stop, using internationally recognized signals. Where this does not succeed, a variety of actions may be taken, including the firing of shots across the bows of the ship. It is only after the appropriate actions fail that the pursuing vessel may, as a last resort, use force. Even then, appropriate warning must be issued to the ship and all efforts should be made to ensure that life is not endangered.[15]

The so-called *Saiga* principles have been considered to form part of customary international law.[16] These criteria were developed on the basis of the 1929 *I'm Alone* and the 1961 *Red Crusader* incidents that led the relevant commissions to conclude that an intentional sinking of a ship violates peacetime law enforcement rules,[17] and that the legitimate use of force requires that the measures employed for stopping a ship do not create danger to human life on board a ship without proven necessity.[18] In a similar vein, Article 225 of LOSC stipulates that: "In the exercise under this Convention of their powers of enforcement against foreign vessels, States shall not endanger the safety of navigation or

14 Ibid., para 333. See also para 401.

15 M/V "SAIGA" (No. 2) (Saint Vincent and the Grenadines v. Guinea), Judgment, ITLOS Reports 1999, p. 10, paras. 155–156.

16 Moore, *op. cit.*, 38.

17 Claim of the British Ship "I'm Alone" *v.* United States, 'Reports of the Commissioners' (1935) 29(2) *American Journal of International Law*, 330.

18 *Investigation of certain incidents affecting the British trawler Red Crusader*, Denmark v United Kingdom, Report of 23 March 1962 of the Commission of Enquiry established by the Government of the United Kingdom of Great Britain and Northern Ireland and the Government of the Kingdom of Denmark on 15 November 1961, 1962 (24) *Reports of International Arbitral Awards*, 538.

otherwise create any hazard to a vessel, or bring it to an unsafe port or anchorage, or expose the marine environment to an unreasonable risk." However, Moore has pointed out that considering the placement of this provision within Part XII of the Convention that regulates the protection and preservation of the marine environment, there may still occur exceptional cases even in the field of the protection of marine environment where a ship needs to be destroyed in the course of a law enforcement operation, such as in the case of the *MV Torrey Canyon* incident in which case the Royal Air Force bombed an abandoned tanker in light of the threat that the ship posed to the marine environment.[19]

The limits on the use of arms are narrower in the general ramifications of law enforcement operations (administrative law) as compared to the rules of self-defence and humanitarian law.[20] This difference can be exploited by the aggressor State in hybrid warfare, as examined below based on the relevant case law and, in particular, the circumstances of the Kerch Strait incident (see *infra* Chapters 4.1 and 5.3.1 of Part 2). This is due to ambiguity regarding the threshold that determines whether the use of force by one State against another State should be categorised as an armed attack against which the targeted State can use its inherent right of self-defence under Article 51 of the UN Charter. In other words, the threshold of an armed conflict is unclear, and its limits are sometimes intentionally stretched by aggressor States in a hybrid naval warfare.

Common Article 2 of the Geneva Conventions stipulates that the laws of humanitarian law "apply to all cases of declared war or of any other armed conflict which may arise between two or more of the High Contracting Parties, even if the state of war is not recognized by one of them."[21] Contemporary conflicts rarely involve declared wars and the existence of an armed conflict needs to be determined based on the objective facts. In a hybrid warfare, a belligerent tends to deny the existence of an armed conflict, which, however, "within the

19 Moore, *op. cit.*, 36.

20 See also M Fink, *Maritime Interception and the Law of Naval Operations: A Study of Legal Bases and Legal Regimes in Maritime Interception Operations* (TMC Asser Press, The Hague, 2018), 204–205.

21 Convention (I) for the Amelioration of the Condition of the Wounded and Sick in Armed Forces in the Field, adopted 12 August 1949, entered into force 21 October 1950. Convention (II) for the Amelioration of the Condition of Wounded, Sick and Shipwrecked Members of Armed Forces at Sea, adopted 12 August 1949, entered into force 21 October 1950. Convention (III) relative to the Treatment of Prisoners of War, adopted 12 August 1949, entered into force 21 October 1950. Convention (IV) relative to the Protection of Civilian Persons in Time of War, adopted 12 August 1949, entered into force 21 October 1950.

meaning of Article 2(1) in a particular situation does not prevent it from being legally classified as such."[22] The International Criminal Tribunal for the Former Yugoslavia (hereafter ICTY) has found that:

> [A]n armed conflict exists whenever there is a resort to armed force between States or protracted armed violence between governmental authorities and organized armed groups or between such groups within a State.[23]

This so-called *Tadić test* serves as one of the primary sources for defining the existence of an armed conflict. These criteria are relevant for differentiating armed conflicts from *inter alia* terrorist activities and law enforcement operations.[24] They are also particularly significant for drawing a distinction between maritime law enforcement operations and naval warfare in view of the lack of an established case law that would draw a clear and systemic distinction between these two legal concepts.[25]

While the ICTY's case law provides a clear threshold for the existence of an armed conflict, problems arise in distinguishing a law enforcement operation from an armed conflict in light of the ICJ's relevant case law. According to the ICJ's position, the resort to use of force between States also needs to be of sufficient gravity. Based on the objective facts of the relevant case, the Court decides if the level of aggression reached the degree of sufficient gravity that either permitted or did not entitle the victim State to use its inherent right of self-defence to counter an aggression. Chapter 5 of Part 2 is devoted to addressing this dilemma in the context of hybrid warfare and it is concluded that the ICJ's gravity threshold contributes, from a legal point of view to the core element of the grey zone on which hybrid warfare relies upon.

Similar to law enforcement operation, the use of force in an armed conflict is subject to the limitations of necessity and proportionality.[26] Yet, as Gill and Fleck explain, the principle of necessity implies in law enforcement operations

22 ICRC, *Commentary on the First Geneva Convention: Convention (I) for the Amelioration of the Condition of the Wounded and Sick in Armed Forces in the Field*, 2nd edition, 2016, Art. 2, para 213.

23 *Prosecutor v Tadić*, Jurisdiction, ICTY Case No IT-94-1-AR72, 2 October 1995, para 70.

24 See, e.g., *Prosecutor v Tadić*, Opinion and Judgment, ICTY Case No. IT-94-1-T, 7 May 1997, para 562. See also *Prosecutor v Kordić and Čerkez*, Judgment, ICTY Case No. IT-95-14/2-A, 17 December 2004, para 341.

25 See Kanehara, Japan Review, *op. cit.*, 46.

26 San Remo Manual, *op. cit.*, Rules 3-5. In the context of *jus ad bellum*, see also *Legality of the Threat or Use of Nuclear Weapons*, Advisory Opinion, ICJ Reports 1996, p. 226, para 41.

that even if there is a legitimate purpose, the destruction of life is prohibited (except for extreme situations), whereas enemy combatants are legitimate targets in an armed conflict.[27] Commentary to Article 3 of the UN Code of Conduct for Law Enforcement Officials provides that:

> The use of firearms is considered an extreme measure. Every effort should be made to exclude the use of firearms, especially against children. In general, firearms should not be used except when a suspected offender offers armed resistance or otherwise jeopardizes the lives of others and less extreme measures are not sufficient to restrain or apprehend the suspected offender. In every instance in which a firearm is discharged, a report should be made promptly to the competent authorities.[28]

Combatants are not subject to the stringent checks and balances that are designed to ensure the legality of peacetime use of arms in law enforcement operations.[29] In addition, the legality of incidental harm as well as civilian death or injury or damage to civilian objects is assessed based on different standards under international humanitarian law and law enforcement operations.[30] To sum up, Gaggioli lists the following main differences between the two paradigms: the principles of necessity, proportionality, and precaution.[31]

Overall, there is no clear-cut criteria for differentiating between whether a particular incident falls under the legal framework of humanitarian law or law enforcement. Law enforcement operations may take place also within armed conflicts and human rights law may apply to a particular maritime incident in parallel with humanitarian law.[32] In practice, this makes it occasionally

27 Gill and Fleck, *op. cit.*, 70, 77. See also, e.g., G Gaggioli, *The Use of Force in Armed Conflicts: Interplay between the Conduct of Hostilities and Law Enforcement Paradigms* (ICRC, Geneva, 2013), 1.

28 UN Code of Conduct for Law Enforcement Officials, Adopted by General Assembly resolution 34/169 of 17 December 1979, Article 3, Commentary, available https://www.ohchr.org/en/professionalinterest/pages/lawenforcementofficials.aspx; accessed 28 November 2021.

29 Gill and Fleck, *op. cit.*, 77.

30 Ibid. Gaggioli, *op. cit.*, 2.

31 Gaggioli, *op. cit.*, 9.

32 Ibid., 1. Gill and Fleck, *op. cit.*, 79. Fink, *op. cit.*, 218–219. See also PJ Kwast, 'Maritime Law Enforcement and the Use of Force: Reflections on the Categorisation of Forcible Action at Sea in the Light of the Guyana/Suriname Award' (2008) 13(1) *Journal of Conflict & Security Law*, 90. Kwast concludes that the case law and State practice 'tend to be anecdotal and lacking a coherent framework' for differentiating between law enforcement and humanitarian law paradigms, while at the same time noting that 'the legal conceptualisation of the matters involved seems warranted as well as possible.'

difficult, particularly in the context of non-international armed conflicts, to distinguish between these two legal frameworks.[33]

Yet the primary criteria for the differentiation between the two paradigms are "the status, function or conduct of the person against whom force may be used".[34] In that context, the status of the State-owned ships that resort to the use of force is significant, albeit far from decisive. Both warships and coast guard vessels, as well as other government ships are entitled under the LOSC to perform law enforcement operations and in that capacity can resort to the use of force.[35] Against this background, the Annex VII Arbitral Tribunal has found that "the mere involvement of military vessels or personnel in an activity does not *ipso facto* render the activity military in nature."[36] Hence, Tanaka has observed that for deciding on whether a dispute concerns military activities, "the type of vessels involved constitutes only one of the relevant factors."[37] Nonetheless, it is of great relevance whether the use of force is targeted against a foreign warship or not, since "a warship is an expression of the sovereignty of the State whose flag it flies."[38] Kwast has concluded that:

> [I]t is clear that forcible actions against vessels with a sovereign status—such as the U.S.S. Pueblo and U.S.S. Samuel B. Roberts—are to be considered within the framework of the law on the use of force in international relations. This provides further delineation of the distinction between armed force and police force in the sense that the resort to force against 'sovereign' ships is evidently beyond the scope of states' police powers and commonly accepted policing purposes. As such, they cannot reasonably be understood to be of a law enforcement nature. ... While the sovereign status of a foreign public ship (threatened to be) subjected to forcible action will in principle prevent any classification of the action as law enforcement, the absence of such a status will also not necessarily

33 Gaggioli, *op. cit.*, 1.

34 Ibid., 59. See also Gill and Fleck, *op. cit.*, 79. See also Kwast, *op. cit.*, 54.

35 See, e.g., Articles 107, 111(5), and 224 of LOSC. See further, e.g., Kwast, *op. cit.*, 72–73.

36 *Dispute Concerning Coastal State Rights*, 2020 Award on Preliminary Objections, *op. cit.*, para 340.

37 Y Tanaka, 'Release of a Detained Warship and Its Crew through Provisional Measures: A Comparative Analysis of the ARA Libertad and Ukraine v. Russia Cases' (2020) 96 *International Law Studies*, 232.

38 "ARA Libertad" (Argentina v. Ghana), Provisional Measures, Order of 15 December 2012, ITLOS Reports 2012, p. 332, para 94.

establish the measures to be police action rather than the use of force in international relations.[39]

For distinguishing between maritime law enforcement operations and military operations, the Annex VII Arbitral Tribunal's award in the *Guyana v. Suriname arbitration* is indicative. Based on the facts of that case, the Suriname's Navy had ordered a private company's oil rig and drill ship *C.E. Thornton* to leave the disputed area in 12 hours, issuing a warning that if this order was not complied with, "the consequences will be yours."[40] The Suriname's Navy was acting in response to Guyana's unilateral exploitation of natural resources in a disputed maritime area. It has been argued, in the context of disputed maritime areas,[41] that particularly after the award in the *Guyana v. Suriname arbitration*, "the pendulum has swung more towards a prohibition on unilateral drilling becoming a customary rule."[42] From the perspective of a coastal State claiming its title over a particular disputed maritime area, its unilateral activities similar to the ones that were challenged before the Annex VII Arbitral Tribunal in the *Guyana v. Suriname arbitration* may usually be categorized as falling within the scope of law enforcement operations that the relevant coastal State carries out (enforces its jurisdiction) in a disputed maritime area.[43] But as observed by Ruys, the award of the Annex VII Arbitral Tribunal shows that "even relatively small-scale forcible measures against merchant vessels do not necessarily escape the scope of Article 2(4) [of the UN Charter]."[44]

The Annex VII Arbitral Tribunal provided scarce reasoning on why it reached such conclusion. It found, "that the order given by Major Jones to the rig constituted an explicit threat that force might be used if the order was not complied with."[45] The threat to use force was unlawful, since any actual use of force against the rig and the commercial ship would have violated the UN Charter.[46] Since it was a border-line incident falling between the laws of peace

39 Kwast, *op. cit.*, 85.
40 Annex VII Arbitral Tribunal, *Guyana v. Suriname Award, op. cit.*, para 433.
41 For a definition of disputed maritime areas, see Y-C Chang, 'The use of force during law enforcement in disputed maritime areas' (2021) 124 *Marine Policy*, 2.
42 Y Van Logchem, *The Rights and Obligations of States in Disputed Maritime Areas* (Cambridge University Press, Cambridge, 2021), 299.
43 Ibid., 314.
44 T Ruys, 'The Meaning of 'Force' and The Boundaries of The Jus Ad Bellum: Are 'Minimal' Uses of Force Excluded from UN Charter Article 2(4)?' (2014) 108(2) *The American Journal of International Law*, 205.
45 Annex VII Arbitral Tribunal, *Guyana v. Suriname Award, op. cit.*, para 439.
46 Ibid. *Case Concerning Military and Paramilitary Activities in and against Nicaragua (Nicaragua v. United States of America), Judgment,* ICJ Reports 1986, p. 111, para 47.

and *jus ad bellum*,[47] the Tribunal's conclusion that the measures used exceeded the limits of a law enforcement operation is indicative for the categorisation of similar borderline incidents within the hybrid warfare context.

3.3 The Meaning of Hybrid Warfare

Hybrid naval warfare is based on the problem of so-called grey zone. For the purposes of the present study, a grey zone refers to a situation in which it is unclear whether the law of naval warfare or the legal framework of law enforcement should be applied to assess the legality of the coastal State's use of force or direct coercion at sea.[48] The so-called grey zone can be understood as a space short of clear-cut military attack wherein the aggressor creates enough ambiguity (incl. via an information campaign) for reaching its strategic objectives without engaging in an open offensive.[49]

The aggressor usually uses such grey zones to complicate decision-making on the (il)legality of its actions in conflict situations and, from other States' perspective, make it more difficult to take resolute steps in response to them. Such grey zones complicate both military as well as judicial responses to the aggressor State's use of force. The latter is due to the fact that the aggressor State may claim before the international courts and tribunals that it used force under the military activities paradigm (though outside the limits of an armed conflict), thereby triggering the exception to the compulsory dispute settlement procedure.[50] In such circumstances, one of the most challenging questions for the judicial body to decide upon is the categorisation of the dispute between the law enforcement or military activities paradigms. These may be referred to as so-called mixed disputes since, as pointed out by Tanaka, "they may concern both military and law enforcement activities occurring at the same time".[51]

According to Frank Hoffman, "hybrid wars incorporate a range of different modes of warfare including conventional capabilities, irregular tactics and formations, terrorist acts including indiscriminate violence and coercion, and

47 See further, Kwast, *op. cit.*, 82–83.

48 On the differentiation between naval warfare and law enforcement operations, see *infra* Chapter 5.3 of Part 2.

49 See J Stavridis, 'Maritime Hybrid Warfare is Coming' (2016) 142(12) *US Naval Institute Proceedings*.

50 See further, e.g., *infra* Chapter 4.1 of Part 2.

51 Tanaka, *op. cit.*, 238.

criminal disorder."[52] Western scholars have characterised it as a Hobbesian 'war of all against all' that is "tailored for use against democratic adversaries with open societies and multiple communities with a myriad of identities."[53] But it is at least doubtful that hybrid warfare is a method that is developed and employed only by non-democratic States.

In her seminal work on maritime security law that shortly predated, for example, the annexation of Crimea, Yemeni armed conflict and the hybrid naval warfare between Iran and Israel, Natalie Klein makes a brief reference to the concept of hybrid warfare and grey zone. She uses this concept in the context of the United States actions in the 'war on terror' when debating the emerging trends in the laws of armed conflict and naval warfare. Klein comments that:

> The so-called 'war on terror' following the September 11 attacks has both highlighted and contributed to the increasing obfuscation between law enforcement, Security Council action, the right of self-defence, and the law of naval warfare. The Obama Administration's embrace of the notion of 'hybrid warfare' will no doubt perpetuate this difficulty.[54]

Thus, at the time of writing, Klein associated the phenomenon of hybrid warfare mainly with the United States' 'war on terror' and pointed to the lack of clarity for differentiating between the thresholds of peacetime law enforcement measures and the laws of naval warfare.[55] This problem remains pertinent also in the contemporary security environment that is no longer framed in the dubious concept of 'war on terror' but has instead shifted back to inter-State conflicts as demonstrated most clearly by the Ukraine-Russia international armed conflict and tensions between the United States and China. Difficulties in distinguishing between peacetime law enforcement measures and the law of naval warfare complicate the legal assessment of various maritime incidents that have emerged since 2018, including the Russian Federation's use of force against the Ukrainian warships in the Kerch Strait, the missile and mine attacks against commercial ships in or near the Strait of Hormuz and the Bab el-Mandeb, the hybrid naval warfare between Iran and Israel, and the

---

52 FG Hoffman, *Conflict in the 21st Century: The Rise of Hybrid Wars* (Potomac Institute for Policy Studies, Arlington 2007), 29.

53 Allen, Hodges, Lindley-French, *op. cit.*, 92.

54 Klein, *op. cit.*, 298.

55 Ibid., 258, 260.

incursions of suspected Russian submarines as well as military aircraft to the territory of its neighbouring States in the Baltic Sea.

In her recent address to the UN Security Council, the Chef de Cabinet to the UN Secretary General noted that, "maritime security is being undermined at alarming levels" and in this context referred to "armed attacks and crimes at sea, such as piracy, robbery and terrorist acts, as well as use of limpet mines and drones."[56] The head of the French Navy admiral Pierre Vandier has commented that future conflicts will probably be fought in the maritime and cyber domains.[57]

The North Atlantic Treaty Organization (hereafter NATO) has characterised hybrid warfare as a phenomenon "where a wide range of overt and covert military, paramilitary, and civilian measures are employed in a highly integrated design",[58] potentially triggering the applicability of collective self-defence "as in the case of armed attack".[59] The heads of State of the NATO alliance have noted in 2021 that "[w]e are increasingly confronted by cyber, hybrid, and other asymmetric threats, including disinformation campaigns, and by the malicious use of ever-more sophisticated emerging and disruptive technologies."[60] The means of hybrid naval warfare include *inter alia* threats of force, the use of firearms and explosives by paramilitaries or their concealed use by States (e.g., limpet mines and drone attacks), and cyber capabilities (e.g., cyber-attacks, (cyber-)piracy), especially when complemented with unmanned ships.[61]

---

56 Maria Luiza Ribeiro Viotti, 'Remarks at Security Council high-level open debate on 'Enhancing Maritime Security: A case for international cooperation'', United Nations, 9 August 2021, available https://www.un.org/sg/en/content/remarks-security-council-high-level-open-debate-%E2%80%98enhancing-maritime-security-case-for-international-cooperation%E2%80%99-delivered; accessed 10 November 2021.

57 K Willsher, 'UK takes part in huge French naval exercise to counter 'emerging threats'', *The Guardian* (5 December 2021).

58 NATO, Wales Summit Declaration: Issued by the Heads of State and Government participating in the meeting of the North Atlantic Council in Wales, 5 September 2014, para 13.

59 NATO, Brussels Summit Declaration: Issued by the Heads of State and Government participating in the meeting of the North Atlantic Council in Brussels, 11–12 July 2018, para 21. NATO, Brussels Summit Communiqué: Issued by the Heads of State and Government participating in the meeting of the North Atlantic Council, Brussels 14 June 2021, para 31.

60 NATO, Brussels Summit Communiqué 2021, *op. cit.*, para 3.

61 On the meaning of grey maritime networks, see C Callaghan, R Schroeder, W Porter, 'Mapping Gray Maritime Networks for Hybrid Warfare', Center for International Maritime Security, 1 July 2020. On the concept of chiefly non-human naval warfare based on the use of unmanned warships, see, e.g., ER Jonson, 'The Hydra and the Leviathan: Unmanned Maritime Vehicles and the Militarized Seaspace', in I Braverman, ER Jonson (eds.), *Blue Legalities: The Life and Laws of the Sea* (Duke University Press, Durham 2019), 186–191.

Since Frank Hoffman coined the term *hybrid warfare* in 2007,[62] numerous articles and books have been written on this theme from the perspective of military studies and international relations. Some research articles have approached the general concept and rather the land domain of hybrid warfare and conflict also from the legal perspective.[63] However, in the legal literature, hybrid conflicts and hybrid warfare have not been explored in sufficient depth from the perspective of maritime security law.

Although some research has been published on hybrid warfare and conflict in the maritime domain, authors have rarely adopted a legal perspective.[64] Overall, only few articles have focused on hybrid conflict from the perspective of the law of the sea and the law of naval warfare.[65] A notable exception is Steven Haines' 2017 article on the law of armed conflict at sea in which he concluded that "it is not clear that the law is well placed to regulate so-called "hybrid" warfare at sea."[66] Likewise, in their 2013 book on maritime security law, Kraska and Pedrozo embrace the notion of 'hybrid threats' and observe that:

> Today naval warfare most likely means hybrid conflict–set at the nexus of peacetime and armed conflict. … [T]he wartime laws that applied

62 Hoffman, *op. cit.*, 29.

63 See, e.g., AB Munoz Mosquera, SD Bachmann, JA Munoz Bravo, 'Hybrid Warfare and the Legal Domain' (2019) 31(1) *Terrorism and Political Violence*, 98–104. R Värk, 'Legal element of Russia's hybrid warfare' (2017) 6 ENDC *Occasional Papers*, 45–51, and Värk 2020, *op. cit.*, 27–43.

64 H Gardner, *Hybrid Warfare: Iranian and Russian Versions of „Little Green Men" and Contemporary Conflict* (NATO, Rome 2015). M Murphy, G Schaub Jr, '"Sea of Peace" or Sea of War Russian Maritime Hybrid Warfare in the Baltic Sea' (2018) 71(2) *Naval War College Review*. M Murphy, FG Hoffman, G Schaub, Jr, *Hybrid Maritime Warfare and the Baltic Sea Region* (University of Copenhagen, Copenhagen, 2016). A Radin, *Hybrid Warfare in the Baltics: Threats and Potential Responses* (RAND Corporation, Santa Monica 2017). Ş Oğuz, 'Russian Hybrid Warfare and Its Implications in The Black Sea' (2017) 1(1) *Bölgesel Araştırmalar Dergisi*.

65 For example, in few instances, the law of the sea perspective has been taken to discuss the Kerch Strait incident. See, e.g., VJ Schatz, D Koval, 'Russia's Annexation of Crimea and the Passage of Ships Through Kerch Strait: A Law of the Sea Perspective' (2019) 50(2–3) *Ocean Development & International Law*. See also D Gorenburg, *The Kerch Strait skirmish: a Law of the Sea perspective* (The European Centre of Excellence for Countering Hybrid Threats, Helsinki, 2018). Another example where the authors have addressed hybrid threats from a legal perspective is J Savolainen, T Gill *et al.*, *Handbook on Maritime Hybrid Threats – 10 Scenarios and Legal Scans* (The European Centre of Excellence for Countering Hybrid Threats, Helsinki, 2019).

66 S Haines, 'War at sea: Nineteenth-century laws for twenty-first century wars?' 2016 98(2) *International Review of the Red Cross*, 419, 443.

> during the First and Second World Wars no longer offer a complete rulebook for management of today's irregular, asymmetric or hybrid warfare at sea.[67]

The authors' assessment that hybrid warfare characterizes modern naval conflicts was particularly insightful considering that it predated the rapid rise of hybrid warfare in the next few years. Kraska and Pedrozo describe the frames of hybrid warfare and observe that:

> Addressing the panoply of threats within hybrid warfare at sea or irregular naval warfare requires application of the law of naval warfare, but done in deft combination with other rules derived from peacetime law of the sea and maritime law enforcement. … Lying at the intersection of war and peace, irregular naval warfare raises a host of legal issues … . Most importantly, what rule set (or sets) pertains to irregular naval warfare?[68]

Kraska and Pedrozo point in the right direction but abstain from presenting clear answers to the questions that they raise. Their analysis does not purport to establish how the rules of maritime enforcement and armed conflict operate in hybrid warfare or, perhaps most importantly, the limit where the peacetime rules on the use of force are replaced with the rules of naval warfare. Similarly, McLaughlin notes that:

> [T]here are a range of issues that continue to present significant interpretive challenges to identifying and defining the "dividing line" between situations where the applicable legal regime is the MLE [maritime law enforcement] regime, and often very similar situations that ought properly to be assessed in accordance with the application of IHL at sea. This is a critical vulnerability when analyzing the use of force at sea …[69]

Chang has observed that State practice shows the increasing use of military activities that occur in a grey zone of international law of the sea, somewhere between the rules of armed conflict and law enforcement, and that there is a need for studies on how international law operates in such situations.[70]

---

67 Kraska, Pedrozo, *op. cit.*, 860–862.

68 Ibid., 863.

69 R McLaughlin, 'Authorizations for maritime law enforcement operations' 2016 98(2) *International Review of the Red Cross*, 488.

70 Chang, *op. cit.*, 1–2.

Haines, who previously acted as a British naval commander, has raised a number of questions in respect of hybrid naval warfare and the applicable legal framework, all of which have not yet received a clear answer. He notes that hybrid warfare has invited lengthy debates among scholars and practitioners in relation to armed conflicts on land, whereas "they are only now emerging as serious issues in the naval context".[71] Similarly, the former Supreme Allied Commander Europe of NATO, admiral James Stavridis has advised that for States that need to counter hybrid naval warfare the most important task currently is to "build intellectual capital" by examining "how the ideas of hybrid warfare as practiced today will both translate to the maritime sphere and develop there in lethal ways."[72] Hence, as acknowledged by these commanders, the main research gap lies in the lack of understanding on how the law of the sea operates in hybrid conflict. This book aims to contribute to fulfilling this research gap.

The present study checks the validity of the postulate that State practice demonstrates the emergence of a new concept of hybrid naval conflict, which should be distinguished from the traditional phenomena of naval warfare and law enforcement. In this connection, it also seeks to verify if the concept of hybrid conflict is useful for assessing the (il)legality of a State's actions in the maritime domain and seeks to find out if the challenges of hybrid naval warfare can be addressed within the existing legal framework governing peacetime law enforcement and naval warfare.

This hypothesis is addressed mainly via case studies of the Russian Federation and Iran because these are the two States that are primarily associated with the adoption of techniques of hybrid conflict.[73] They are important law of the sea actors, whose maritime areas include or are next to strategic waterways. The Baltic Sea is the area where approximately 15% of global cargo is trafficked.[74] The Baltic Sea, the Strait of Hormuz, and the Black Sea are strategically important routes for oil shipments. The Baltic Sea, which is already heavily used for the export of Russian oil, is also destined to become the biggest route for the transportation of Russian natural gas to Europe, overshadowing the main alternative transit route in Ukraine.[75] The Black Sea, which holds itself as much natural gas reserves as the North Sea, is used by

---

71 Haines, *op. cit.*, 444.

72 Stavridis, *op. cit.*

73 See, e.g., ibid.

74 M Stankiewicz *et al.*, 'Ensuring safe shipping in the Baltic' (HELCOM, Helsinki 2009), 2.

75 G Kuczyński, 'Nord Stream 2: A Trap for Ukraine', The Warsaw Institute Review, 10 February 2019.

the Russian Federation as one of its main routes for oil shipments and is also destined to become crossed by many submarine pipelines.[76] Furthermore, the Strait of Hormuz is one of the main global chokepoints for the transportation of oil. Approximately a fifth of global oil exports are shipped via the Strait of Hormuz.[77]

In addition, this book maps the risks of hybrid threats in the straits serving as the main gateways to and from the South China Sea. It is suggested that roughly a third of global shipping crosses the South China Sea.[78] According to other accounts, the rate of crossings in the South China Sea amounts to more than half of the world's merchant fleet capacity.[79] In Chapter 9 of Part 3 and Chapter 14 of Part 4, particular emphasis is on recent developments in the maritime security of the Taiwan Strait and the impact of piracy in the Straits of Malacca and Singapore.[80]

The strategic importance of these maritime regions shows how significant it is to uphold the rule of law and safeguard passage rights therein. However, these maritime regions are also areas where the stability of navigation is currently under pressure due to the coastal states' shifting security considerations and methods of hybrid conflict. Hence, it is examined below, *inter alia*, if there are any limits set by the coastal States of these maritime areas unilaterally to the enjoyment of the passage rights and freedoms in the straits of the Baltic Sea, the Black Sea, the South China Sea, and around the Arabian Peninsula. Such developments in the maritime domain are intertwined with politics on land, particularly with the threat or use of force and armed attack as regulated under Articles 2(4) and 51 of the UN Charter.

Foreign ships that were navigating through important chokepoints of maritime commerce have recently repeatedly been subject to the use of force, coercion or other discriminatory navigational restrictions by some coastal States. Notable examples include the Kerch Strait incident and the attacks against two oil tankers at the approaches to the Strait of Hormuz in the summer of 2019. In these instances, the Russian Federation and, allegedly, Iran have strived to

---

76 M Papatulica, 'Black Sea area at the crossroad of the biggest global energy players' interests. The impact on Romania' (2015) 22 *Procedia Economics and Finance*, 475, 478.

77 P Nobakht, 'Why Does the Strait of Hormuz Matter?', *BBC News* (11 June 2019).

78 Y Nakayama, 'China's claims on the South China Sea are a warning to Europe', *Financial Times* (8 April 2019).

79 K Zou, 'Navigation in the South China Sea: Why Still an Issue?' (2017) 32(2) *The International Journal of Marine and Coastal Law*, 244.

80 On China's use of coercion at the South China Sea and East China Sea, see A Patalano, 'When strategy is 'hybrid' and not 'grey': reviewing Chinese military and constabulary coercion at sea' (2019) 31(6) *The Pacific Review*, 820–821.

operate in a so-called grey zone for complicating decision-making for other States.

The book will now take a closer look at specific incidents that have occurred in straits and that meet the characteristics of a hybrid warfare. The next part begins with a case study of the use of force and discriminatory navigational restrictions in the Kerch Strait (Chapter 4). Chapter 5 of the next part of the book approaches hybrid conflicts from the perspective of the rules governing the use of force against sovereign immune vessels under the law enforcement and humanitarian law paradigms. For this, it sets an emphasis on the 2018 Kerch Strait incident. It also discusses some recent developments in China's domestic legal framework on maritime law enforcement. Chapter 6 examines the Yemeni armed conflict and the Iran-Israel 'shadow war' in the waters around the Arabian Peninsula and discusses issues related to State responsibility and the right of self-defence against attacks carried out by non-State actors. Chapter 7 discusses unconsented-to military operations by Russian military aircraft and suspected submarines in the territories of the Viro Strait's coastal States.

PART 2

Use of Force in Maritime Hybrid Warfare

CHAPTER 4

Permit-Based Passage v. Transit Passage in an Occupied Area

The 2018 Kerch Strait Incident and the 2022 Ukraine-Russia Naval Warfare

4.1 The Kerch Strait Incident and Its Implications for the Passage Regime in the Sea of Azov

Geopolitical developments in the Black Sea region in the past decade have exerted considerable pressure on the stability of passage regimes owing to a shift in the coastal States' security considerations, particularly in the light of the occupation of Crimea in February 2014 by the Russian Federation.[1] This has triggered multiple arbitral proceedings between Ukraine and the Russian Federation, including, the *Dispute Concerning Coastal State Rights in the Black Sea, Sea of Azov, and Kerch Strait* and the *Dispute Concerning the Detention of Ukrainian Naval Vessels and Servicemen*, both before Annex VII Arbitral Tribunals.[2] They were preceded, in May 2019, by the prescription of provisional measures by the International Tribunal for the Law of the Sea (hereafter ITLOS) in response to the seizure of three Ukrainian naval vessels and detainment of their crew by the Russian Federation in the Kerch Strait on 25 November 2018.[3]

The roots of the Kerch Strait incident lie in the annexation of Crimea by the Russian Federation in 2014, as a result of which it now controls both the eastern and western coasts of the Kerch Strait. The overwhelming majority of States consider the occupation and annexation of Crimea as a manifest breach of

1 For a historical account of the legal regime of the Black Sea from the Ottoman Empire to the Soviet Union and its dissolution, see N Oral, 'Ukraine v. The Russian Federation: Navigating Conflict over Sovereignty under UNCLOS' (2021) 91 *International Law Studies*, 481–486.

2 See Annex VII Arbitral Tribunal, *Dispute Concerning Coastal State Rights in the Black Sea, Sea of Azov, and Kerch Strait* (*Ukraine v. the Russian Federation*), Case No. 2017–06, available https://pca-cpa.org/en/cases/149/; accessed 5 April 2021. Annex VII Arbitral Tribunal, *Dispute Concerning the Detention of Ukrainian Naval Vessels and Servicemen* (*Ukraine v. the Russian Federation*), Case No. 2019–28, available https://pca-cpa.org/en/cases/229/; accessed 5 April 2021.

3 International Tribunal for the Law of the Sea, *Case concerning the detention of three Ukrainian naval vessels* (*Ukraine v. Russian Federation*), *Provisional Measures*, Order of 25 May 2019, available https://www.itlos.org/en/main/cases/list-of-cases/case-concerning-the-detention-of-three-ukrainian-naval-vessels-ukraine-v-russian-federation-provisional-measures/; accessed 5 April 2021.

international law, particularly the rules governing the use of force and territorial integrity. The UN General Assembly has stressed by a vote of 100 in favour, 11 against, with 58 abstentions the importance of a policy of non-recognition towards the Russian Federation's occupation and annexation of Crimea and the need to refrain from any action or dealing that might be interpreted as recognizing any such altered status.[4]

However, in the current *Dispute Concerning Coastal State Rights* before the Annex VII Arbitral Tribunal, the determination of Crimea's status under international law is not the object of the proceedings. The Arbitral Tribunal has clearly concluded, pursuant to Article 288(1) of LOSC, that "it lacks jurisdiction over the dispute as submitted by Ukraine to the extent that a ruling of the Arbitral Tribunal on the merits of Ukraine's claims necessarily requires it to decide, expressly or implicitly, on the sovereignty of either Party over Crimea."[5] Nevertheless, this does not preclude the Arbitral Tribunal from deciding on the legality of the Russian Federation's various activities in the Sea of Azov and the Kerch Strait,[6] including on the alleged harassment of Ukrainian vessels and impediments to their navigation through the Kerch Strait.[7] Notably, the rights of third States in the Sea of Azov and the Kerch Strait are also excluded from the scope of the dispute, although the Arbitral Tribunal's determination of the applicable passage regime inevitably affects the rights of third States who may, in principle, submit another claim against Ukraine or the Russian Federation (or both) in the future.

By contrast, the Annex VII Arbitral Tribunal has not yet decided on its jurisdiction in another case brought before it by Ukraine in *the Dispute Concerning the Detention of Ukrainian Naval Vessels and Servicemen*, which addresses the legality of the Russian Federation's activities in the Kerch Strait on 25 November 2018.[8] In this case, Ukraine submitted its memorial to the Arbitral Tribunal on 22 May 2020, in response to which the Russian Federation raised preliminary

4 UN General Assembly Resolution 68/262, adopted 27 March 2014 available https://www.un.org/en/ga/search/view_doc.asp?symbol=A/RES/68/262; accessed 5 April 2021.

5 Annex VII Arbitral Tribunal, *Dispute Concerning Coastal State Rights*, Award 21 February 2020, para 197.

6 Ibid., para 297.

7 Ibid., paras. 338–339.

8 Annex VII Arbitral Tribunal, *Dispute Concerning the Detention of Ukrainian Naval Vessels and Servicemen, Procedural Order No. 1*, 22 November 2019, paras. 1–4. See also The Russian Federation's Ministry of Foreign Affairs, 'Comment by the Information and Press Department on Ukraine filing an arbitration memorandum regarding the Kerch Strait incident', 26 May 2020, available https://www.mid.ru/en/foreign_policy/news/-/asset_publisher/cKNonkJE02Bw/content/id/4138495; accessed 5 April 2021.

objections and contended that the Arbitral Tribunal does not have jurisdiction because, *inter alia,* Ukraine's claims relate to a dispute concerning military activities (the Russian Federation made the same preliminary objection earlier in the *Dispute Concerning Coastal State Rights*, as explained below). The Arbitral Tribunal decided in October 2020 that the Russian Federation's preliminary objections will be addressed in a preliminary phase and suspended proceedings on the merits.[9]

The Kerch Strait incident involved three Ukrainian naval vessels that were on their journey half-way around Crimea and intended to transit the Kerch Strait in order to enter the Sea of Azov. The *Berdyansk* and the *Nikopol* – two artillery boats – and the *Yani Kapu* (a naval tugboat) were heading from the Ukrainian Black Sea coastal city of Odesa to a Ukrainian port[10] in the Sea of Azov. The Ukrainian ships carried onboard 24 naval personnel.

The Kerch Strait (Russian: *Керченский пролив*; Ukrainian: *Керченська протока*) connects the Sea of Azov and the Black Sea. It lies between the Crimean Peninsula and the Taman Peninsula.[11] The strait is 41 km long and, at its narrowest point, only 4 km wide.[12] The Russian Federation constructed a bridge over the Kerch Strait after its annexation of Crimea. The Crimean Bridge comprises a road bridge (used since 2018) and a railway bridge (used since 2019) that run in parallel from the Russian mainland coast to Crimea. On Ukraine's request, the Annex VII Arbitral Tribunal is expected to rule in the *Case Concerning Coastal State Rights* on the legality of the Crimean Bridge over the Kerch Strait.[13] Thus, the Arbitral Tribunal's award is expected to serve

9 Annex VII Arbitral Tribunal, *Dispute Concerning the Detention of Ukrainian Naval Vessels and Servicemen, Procedural Order No.* 2, 27 October 2020, paras. 1–5.

10 The ITLOS provisional order refers to the port of Berdyansk, whereas Ukraine's diplomatic notes to the UN claim that the ships were heading to Mariupol Port. See the *Case concerning the detention of three Ukrainian naval vessels* (*Ukraine v. Russian Federation*), *ITLOS Order of 25 May 2019*, para 31. See also Annex to the letter dated 27 November 2018 from the Permanent Representative of Ukraine to the United Nations, UN Doc. A/73/605–S/2018/1053, (30 November 2018), available https://www.un.org/Depts/los/LEGISLATIONANDTREATIES/STATEFILES/UKR.htm; accessed 5 April 2021.

11 See maps 2 and 3.

12 Internet Encyclopedia of Ukraine, 'Kerch Strait', available http://www.encyclopediaofukraine.com/display.asp?linkpath=pages%5CK%5CE%5CKerchStrait.htm; accessed 5 April 2021.

13 Ukraine argues that the construction of the bridge, the laying of the submarine cables and pipelines in the Kerch Strait "are not compatible with the Convention and constitute internationally wrongful acts for which the Russian Federation bears international responsibility". *Dispute Concerning Coastal State Rights*, 2020 Award on Preliminary Objections, *op. cit.*, paras. 9, 492.

as the first judgment which addresses the compatibility of the construction of a bridge with the legal regime of straits.[14]

The Russian Federation, which claims sovereignty over Crimea and its adjacent territorial sea,[15] is required, under Articles 17 and 24(1) of LOSC and in conformity with the 1989 Jackson Hole statement,[16] to respect the innocent passage of Ukrainian ships in the Black Sea. While the Russian Federation was required to respect the Ukrainian ships' right of innocent passage off the western and southern coast of Crimea, the applicable navigation regime changed in time as the Ukrainian ships reached the maritime area leading to the Kerch Strait (south-east of Crimea). Passage through the Kerch Strait is regulated under Article 2 of the Agreement between the Russian Federation and Ukraine on Cooperation in the Use of the Sea of Azov and the Kerch Strait (*2003 Kerch Treaty*).[17] Article 2(1) of the 2003 Kerch Treaty stipulates that Ukrainian and Russian warships enjoy freedom of navigation in the Sea of Azov and the Kerch Strait. Thus, Ukraine's ships ought to have enjoyed the freedom of navigation in the entrance to the Kerch Strait since the freedom of navigation in the Kerch Strait, as stipulated in Article 2 of the 2003 Kerch Treaty, would be devoid of any practical effect if it did not apply in the waters leading to the Kerch Strait.

---

14 Notably, the construction of a bridge over a strait has served as a source of dispute between the user State and strait State in the past, as demonstrated by the proceedings initiated by Finland in 1992 before the International Court of Justice. This case concerned a Danish bridge over the Great Belt, the construction of which was prejudicial to the Finnish navigation interests. However, Finland discontinued the case after reaching a settlement with Denmark pursuant to which Denmark paid Finland monetary compensation. See *Case concerning Passage through the Great Belt* (*Finland v. Denmark*), *Order* of 29 July 1991, Provisional Measures, ICJ Reports 1992, p. 12. See also M Koskenniemi, 'Case Concerning Passage Through the Great Belt' (1996) 27 *Ocean Development & International Law*, 255–289. AG Oude Elferink, 'The Regime of Passage Through the Danish Straits' (2000) 15 *The International Journal of Marine and Coastal Law*, 555–566.

15 See *Dispute Concerning Coastal State Rights*, 2020 Award on Preliminary Objections, *op. cit.*, para 211.

16 Joint Statement by the United States of America and the Union of Soviet Socialist Republics: Uniform Interpretation of Rules of International Law Governing Innocent Passage, 23 September 1989 Jackson Hole, 4, 14 *Law of the Sea Bulletin* 12, available http://www.un.org/depts/los/doalos_publications/LOSBulletins/bulletinpdf/bulE14.pdf (accessed 5 April 2021). See also, e.g., K Hakapää, EJ Molenaar, 'Innocent Passage – past and present' (1999) 23 *Marine Policy*, 143.

17 Agreement between the Russian Federation and Ukraine on Cooperation in the Use of the Sea of Azov and the Kerch Strait, adopted 24 December 2003, entered into force 5 May 2004. Available in Ukrainian: https://zakon.rada.gov.ua/laws/show/643_205?lang=en#Text; accessed 5 April 2021. For an unofficial English version of the treaty, see: https://www.jura.uni-hamburg.de/die-fakultaet/professuren/proelss/dateien-valentin/agreement-sea-of-azov; accessed 5 April 2021.

The transit of the Ukrainian vessels in the entrance to the Kerch Strait was obstructed by Russian Coast Guard and navy vessels, which commenced a pursuit after the three Ukrainian ships had turned around and headed to the Black Sea proper.[18] The Russian Federation has submitted its description of the Kerch Strait incident to the Annex VII Arbitral Tribunal, according to which:

> [I]t is undisputed that Russian forces used force against the Ukrainian Military Vessels and the Ukrainian Military Servicemen. Specifically, the Russian forces rammed the "*Yani Kapu*", and subsequently opened fire (with first warning, then target, shots) on the "*Berdyansk*". That use of force resulted in the wounding of three Ukrainian military personnel on board and caused damage to the Military Vessel. The use of force was deployed pursuant to the Decree of the Government of the Russian Federation No. 80 of 24 February 2010 "On Approving the Rules of Use of Weapons and Military Equipment When Protecting the State Border of the Russian Federation, the Exclusive Economic Zone, and the Continental Shelf of the Russian Federation" (the Decree applies to both military personnel of the Russian Armed Forces and the FSB when defending and protecting Russia's State border).[19]

While the Russian Federation characterises the Kerch Strait incident as "a prolonged stand-off between the Ukrainian military force and the Russian combination of military and paramilitary forces",[20] Ukraine has disputed this claim before the Annex VII Arbitral Tribunal and argues that Russia did not resort to military activities, but instead used law enforcement measures.[21] Presumably, Ukraine's reasoning is influenced by the limitations to the jurisdiction of international courts and tribunals under Article 298(1)(b) of LOSC, since both Ukraine and the Russian Federation have made an optional declaration to exclude all disputes that concern military activities from compulsory dispute settlement.[22] Ukraine maintains in the arbitral proceedings that:

---

18 ITLOS 25 May 2019 Order on Provisional Measures, *op. cit.*, 31. Annex VII Arbitral Tribunal, *Dispute Concerning the Detention of Ukrainian Naval Vessels and Servicemen,* Preliminary Objections of the Russian Federation, 24 August 2020, paras. 2, 40.

19 Preliminary Objections of the Russian Federation, *op. cit.*, 24 August 2020, para 44.

20 Ibid., para 43.

21 Annex VII Arbitral Tribunal, *Dispute Concerning the Detention of Ukrainian Naval Vessels and Servicemen,* Observations of Ukraine on the Question of Bifurcation, 7 September 2020, para 13.

22 UN Treaty Collection, United Nations Convention on the Law of the Sea, status at 10 December 2021. The Russian Federation's declaration upon signing the LOSC on 10

> [T]he Ukrainian vessels communicated with and followed the instructions of Kerch Traffic Control as they waited to transit the Strait; received clearance from Kerch Traffic Control to wait at the anchorage point; were "periodically" requested by Russian coast guard vessels to "leave the Kerch Strait and go beyond the 12-mile zone"; and, upon confirmation that the Kerch Strait was closed to navigation, departed the area as they had been requested to do.[23]

Nonetheless, on the same day of the Kerch Strait incident, Ukraine alleged before the UN that: "Ships of the Russian Federation, in violation of freedom of navigation, unlawfully used force against the ships of the Ukrainian Naval Forces."[24] During the pursuit, the Russian ships fired at *Berdyansk*, wounding three members of the Ukrainian crew, after which the Ukrainian ships were seized and the crew detained by the Russian Federation.[25]

In response to Ukraine's request for provisional measures, the ITLOS Order of 25 May 2019 required the Russian Federation to release the Ukrainian vessels and servicemen and to allow them to return to Ukraine.[26] The ITLOS considered that the continuing detention of the Ukrainian servicemen and naval ships would irreparably prejudice their immunity.[27] The seized Ukrainian navy ships and their crew have since been returned to Ukraine. The ITLOS found in its Order that "at the core of the dispute was the Parties' differing

---

December 1982 and ratifying it on 12 March 1997. Ukraine's declaration upon signing the LOSC on 10 December 1982 and ratifying it on 26 July 1999.

23 Ibid.

24 Annex to the letter dated 25 November 2018 from the Permanent Representative of Ukraine to the United Nations, UN Doc A/73/601–S/2018/1052, 28 November 2018, available https://www.un.org/Depts/los/LEGISLATIONANDTREATIES/STATEFILES/UKR.htm; accessed 5 April 2021.

25 ITLOS 25 May 2019 Order on Provisional Measures, *op. cit.*, paras. 31–32. According to the memorandum submitted by the Russian Federation to ITLOS, the Ukrainian Navy servicemen were apprehended under Article 91 of the Code of Criminal Procedure of the Russian Federation as persons suspected of having committed a crime of aggravated illegal crossing of the State border and were placed in detention.

26 ITLOS 25 May 2019 Order on Provisional Measures, *op. cit.*, paras. 8, 118. The Russian Federation did not participate in the ITLOS hearing on provisional measures as it considered that the dispute concerned its military activities which are exempted from the ITLOS' jurisdiction. It also did not immediately respond to the ITLOS order. Nonetheless, the Russian Federation freed the servicemen under a prisoner exchange deal in September 2019. The seized navy ships were returned to Ukraine in November 2019.

27 Ibid., para 111. This follows from the fact that warships and other government ships operated for non-commercial purposes are entitled to sovereign immunity in a foreign territorial sea and EEZ under Articles 32 and 95–96 in combination with Article 58 of LOSC.

interpretation of the regime of passage through the Kerch Strait"[28] and concluded that "what occurred appears to be the use of force in the context of a law enforcement operation rather than a military operation".[29] The Annex VII Arbitral Tribunal will likely clarify in *the Dispute Concerning the Detention of Ukrainian Naval Vessels and Servicemen* whether the Kerch Strait incident of 25 November 2018 concerned a law enforcement (rather than a military) operation against Ukrainian sovereign immune vessels.[30] The incident also raises questions about the extent of navigational freedoms that Ukraine and the Russian Federation enjoy in the Kerch Strait and the Sea of Azov.

This case study explores the passage regime(s) applicable to the Kerch Strait and its adjacent maritime areas. It asks how the law of the sea and general international law can contribute to ensuring the rule of law and legal certainty in the shipping routes in the Black Sea, the Sea of Azov and the Kerch Strait that are affected by the conflicting sovereignty claims over Crimea. The Kerch Strait incident is used as a case study and as a basis for a critical analysis of the Ukrainian and Russian perspectives on navigational rights in the Kerch Strait while focusing on both the international legal framework as well as the domestic rules on navigation in the Kerch Strait. It also scrutinizes how Ukraine and the Russian Federation have interpreted the applicable law in their current arbitration proceedings and the implications of this for passage rights of ships and aircraft in the Kerch Strait. This chapter investigates the possibility that navigation through the Kerch Strait and its adjacent maritime areas might be subject to parallel legal regimes, pursuant to which, the regimes of transit passage and authorisation-based passage may simultaneously apply to the Kerch Strait under the law of the sea and general international law, thereby creating a fertile ground for further hybrid conflicts in this maritime area. This chapter concludes by examining the Kerch Strait incident from the perspective of the legal regime of a belligerent strait subject to the rules of *jus in bello*.

4.2 Freedom of Navigation of Ukrainian and Russian Ships in the Kerch Strait

Article 2 of the 2003 Kerch Treaty stipulates the passage rights of Ukrainian, Russian and foreign ships in the Sea of Azov and the Kerch Strait. Article 2(1)

28 Ibid., para 72.

29 Ibid., para 74.

30 The significance of this distinction for hybrid naval conflicts is discussed below, see *infra* Chapter 5 of Part 2.

of the 2003 Kerch Treaty provides that merchant ships and warships, as well as other State vessels flying the flag of the Russian Federation or Ukraine, operated for non-commercial purposes, enjoy freedom of navigation in the Sea of Azov and the Kerch Strait. By contrast, warships and other State vessels of third States operated for non-commercial purposes may enter the Sea of Azov and pass through the Kerch Strait if they are visiting a port in Ukraine or the Russian Federation with the permission of both parties (Article 2(3) of the 2003 Kerch Treaty). The right of passage of commercial ships of third States is more liberal since under Article 2(2) of the Treaty such vessels "may enter the Sea of Azov and pass through the Kerch Strait if they go to or return from a Russian or Ukrainian port." Yet the 2003 Kerch Treaty does not stipulate the conditions under which foreign commercial ships may enter the Sea of Azov. This might be explained by the fact that under the 2003 Kerch Treaty, foreign commercial ships' access to the Sea of Azov is dependent on their visiting a Ukrainian or Russian port. Thus, under the terms of the 2003 Kerch Treaty, their right of navigation through the Kerch Strait is presumably intertwined with the conditions for entering ports.

The freedom of navigation granted by Article 2(1) of the 2003 Kerch Treaty is applicable in the Kerch Strait only to the ships of coastal States of the Sea of Azov, i.e. Ukraine and the Russian Federation, and not to the ships of third States.[31] The freedom of navigation is a high seas freedom guaranteed under Article 87(1)(a) of LOSC and is also applicable to all ships in an EEZ (Article 58(1) of the Convention). It is not clear whether the entire regime of freedom of navigation as laid down in LOSC is applicable to ships registered in Ukraine and the Russian Federation in the Sea of Azov and the Kerch Strait.[32] In general, however, there seems to be no good reason why States should not enjoy a broad navigational freedom in waters under their sovereignty.

It is not unprecedented for the freedom of navigation to made applicable by an agreement among the strait States in respect of a territorial sea. Under Article 5(2) of the 1979 Peace Treaty between Egypt and Israel, the two parties agreed that they "consider the Strait of Tiran and the Gulf of Aqaba to be international waterways open to all nations for unimpeded and non-suspendable freedom of navigation and overflight."[33] If the coastal States of the Strait of

31 Notably, Article 2(1) of the 2003 Kerch Treaty grants only the freedom of navigation and does not explicitly provide for the freedom of overflight.

32 Schatz, Koval, *op. cit.*, 285.

33 Peace Treaty between Israel and Egypt, adopted 26 March 1979, entered into force 25 April 1979, 1138 UNTS 59. This is reiterated in Article 14(3) of the Treaty of Peace between the State of Israel and the Hashemite Kingdom of Jordan, adopted 26 October 1994, entered into force 10 November 1994, 2042 UNTS 351.

Tiran had not agreed on the applicability of such a liberal transit regime, then passage through the Strait of Tiran would be subject to the regime of non-suspendable innocent passage under Article 45(1)(b) of LOSC. Although navigation through the Strait of Tiran would therefore be safeguarded under international law, the passage regime would be more restrictive for flag States in comparison to freedom of navigation and would not include the freedom of overflight.[34]

By contrast, the passage regime stipulated in the 2003 Kerch Treaty is based on the premise that the Sea of Azov and the Kerch Strait comprise internal waters of Ukraine and the Russian Federation. Article 1 of the 2003 Kerch Treaty stipulates that the Sea of Azov and the Kerch Strait have historically been internal waters of the Russian Federation and Ukraine. This allowed the coastal States of the Sea of Azov to agree that only their ships enjoy the freedom of navigation, whereas the ships of third States need to request prior authorisation to enter the Sea of Azov via the Kerch Strait.[35]

Nonetheless, while the Russian Federation maintains that "it has been exercising exclusive sovereignty over the waters of the Kerch Strait since it has been exercising its sovereignty on both sides of the strait",[36] it claims that the Kerch Strait is still open for transit for Ukrainian ships and commercial ships of other States entering Russian or Ukrainian ports in the Sea of Azov. The Russian Federation argues that, pursuant to the 2003 Kerch Treaty, Ukrainian ships enjoy freedom of navigation and foreign non-military vessels sailing to and from Ukrainian ports are entitled to 'free passage' in the Kerch Strait.[37]

It is not clear what the reference to 'free passage' means. It holds connotations with legal concepts such as the freedom of navigation or transit passage. Yet, as analysed above, all ships, including Russian-flagged as well as foreign ships, need to apply for a prior permit from the Russian authorities to transit the Kerch Strait according to the terms of the Kerch Strait vessel traffic service (hereafter VTS). It is thus questionable whether, in practice, foreign commercial ships have 'free passage' to enter the Sea of Azov.

Notably, the 2003 Kerch Treaty does not refer to 'free passage'. Instead, it uses, in Article 2(2), more general terms: "Commercial vessels flying the flags

34 See further, e.g., EJ Molenaar, *Coastal State Jurisdiction over Vessel-Source Pollution* (Kluwer, The Hague/Boston/London, 1998), 319.

35 Notably, the 2003 Kerch Treaty does not grant the freedom of overflight to Ukraine or the Russian Federation, nor to any other State.

36 *Dispute Concerning Coastal State Rights*, 2020 Award on Preliminary Objections, *op. cit.*, para 211.

37 Ibid.

of third states may enter the Sea of Azov and pass through the Kerch Strait if they go to or return from a Russian or Ukrainian port." Therefore, foreign commercial ships that intend to cross the Kerch Strait, not for the purpose of visiting Ukrainian or Russian ports, are, in any case, not entitled to enter the Sea of Azov under Article 2 of the 2003 Kerch Treaty.

Article 2(2) of the 2003 Kerch Treaty does not exclude the possibility that strait States may exercise considerable control over the passage of ships of third States in the Kerch Strait. In principle, this provision appears to allow for an authorisation-based passage regime in respect of commercial vessels flying the flags of third states. Moreover, this provision explicitly makes foreign commercial ships' access to the Sea of Azov dependent on whether they are seeking access to either Ukrainian or Russian ports. Under international law, coastal States have considerable discretion to regulate a foreign ship's access to ports (see, Articles 25(2), 38(3) and 211(3) of LOSC). A general right of foreign ships to enter ports is absent from LOSC and States have retained their freedom to close ports,[38] subject to the exception relating to instances requiring humanitarian assistance, as well as to conditions of proportionality and the prohibition of discrimination. The ICJ has concluded, with regard to the contemporary State practice, that it is "*by virtue of its sovereignty that the coastal State may regulate access to its ports*".[39] Therefore, the coastal State has a wide discretion in deciding whether to allow foreign ships to enter its ports.[40] Hence, the Russian Federation may arguably exercise its permit-system in relation to foreign commercial ships that seek access to the Sea of Azov for the purpose of entering its ports under Article 2(2) of the 2003 Kerch Treaty.

In respect of ships that seek to enter the Sea of Azov not for the purpose of visiting ports, the Russian Federation's permit-based passage regime could be lawful if it meets the conditions of Article 311(2) of LOSC which provides that: "This Convention shall not alter the rights and obligations of States Parties which arise from other agreements compatible with this Convention and which do not affect the enjoyment by other States Parties of their rights or the performance of their obligations under this Convention." These conditions could be satisfied if the maritime area of the Kerch Strait and the Sea of

38 Narrowly, Article 255 of LOSC stipulates an obligation of means according to which States shall endeavour to facilitate, subject to the provisions of their laws and regulations, only research vessels' access to their harbours.

39 *Military and Paramilitary Activities in and against Nicaragua, op. cit.*, para 213.

40 Molenaar 1998, *op. cit.*, 101. RR Churchill, AV Lowe, *The Law of the Sea* (Manchester University Press, Manchester, 1999), 52.

Azov constitutes a historic bay owing to which no passage rights would apply therein, as discussed further below.

The Russian Federation's authorisation-based Kerch VTS rules clearly hinder the transit of those commercial ships that seek access to Ukrainian ports in the Sea of Azov. Therefore, the Russian Federation's claim in the judicial proceedings about the applicability of 'free passage' in the Kerch Strait to foreign non-military vessels sailing to and from Ukrainian ports appears to contradict both the Russian Federation's previous practice and its domestic rules. The Russian Federation presumably cannot apply the permit requirement in relation to commercial ships that seek access to Ukrainian ports in the Sea of Azov under Article 2(2) of the 2003 Kerch Treaty. Furthermore, Ukraine contests *in toto* the legality of the Russian Federation's permit-based passage regime on the grounds that, instead, the regime of transit passage is applicable to the Kerch Strait, as discussed below.

4.3 A Critical Analysis of Ukraine's Arguments about the Applicability of Transit Passage to Ships and Aircraft in/over the Sea of Azov and the Kerch Strait

Ukraine maintained in the *Coastal State Rights Case* that: "[T]he Sea of Azov and the Kerch Strait are not internal waters; rather, the Sea of Azov is an enclosed or semi-enclosed sea within the meaning of the Convention, containing a territorial sea and exclusive economic zone, and the Kerch Strait is a strait used for international navigation."[41] Ukraine also stated that: "[T]he Kerch Strait is an international strait [...] connecting "one part of [...] an exclusive economic zone" in the Sea of Azov to "an exclusive economic zone" in the Black Sea."[42] On this interpretation, the regime of transit passage would apply in the Kerch Strait. The regime of transit passage would grant *grosso modo* the freedom of navigation but also the freedom of overflight to all ships and aircraft of all States in the Kerch Strait, thereby rendering the 2003 Kerch Treaty incompatible with LOSC by virtue of Article 311(2) of the Convention.

Thus, the passage regime under Article 2 of the 2003 Kerch Treaty could not restrict the passage rights of ships and aircraft by virtue of the Treaty if, instead, the regime of transit passage is applicable to the Kerch Strait under LOSC. This position finds support from the legal literature.

41 *Dispute Concerning Coastal State Rights*, 2020 Award on Preliminary Objections, *op. cit.*, para 200.

42 Ibid., para 215.

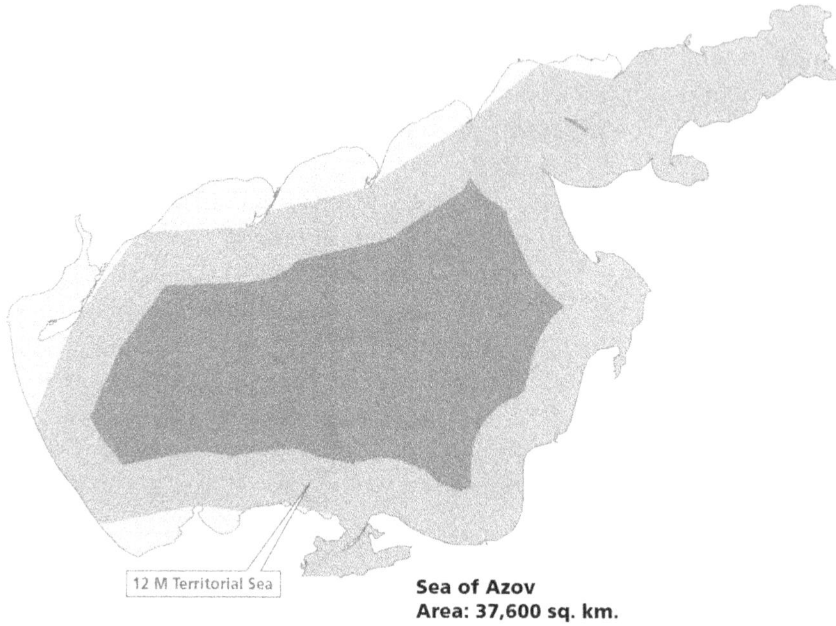

MAP 2 The maritime zones in the Sea of Azov
SOURCE: ANNEX VII ARBITRAL TRIBUNAL, *DISPUTE CONCERNING COASTAL STATE RIGHTS*, WRITTEN OBSERVATIONS AND SUBMISSIONS OF UKRAINE ON JURISDICTION, 27 NOVEMBER 2018, PARA 73. THE MAP DEPICTS THE INTERNAL WATERS, TERRITORIAL SEA AND EEZ OF UKRAINE AND THE RUSSIAN FEDERATION PURSUANT TO THE UKRAINIAN POSITION IN THE ARBITRAL PROCEEDINGS. BY CONTRAST, THE RUSSIAN FEDERATION MAINTAINS THAT THE ENTIRE SEA OF AZOV FALLS UNDER THE REGIME OF INTERNAL WATERS.

López Martín considers that the regime of internal waters as declared in the 2003 Kerch Treaty is not consistent with international law and argues that:

> [I]t does not seem that there are any of the parameters required for the proclamation of historic waters, therefore, such a declaration, subjecting the passage of foreign military vessels to the consent of the coastal States, is a clear infringement of the right of passage in transit which should be in force in the Kerch Strait in accordance with the provisions in article 37 of the Convention of 1982, which both States are parties to.[43]

43 AG López Martín, *International Straits: Concept, Classification and Rules of Passage* (Springer, Heidelberg/Dordrecht/London/New York, 2010), 71.

Alexander Skaridov shares López Martín's critique in connection with the legal implications of the reference to 'internal waters' in the 2003 Kerch Treaty and finds that this reference does not have much legal significance, but rather, has more general and historic implications.[44] Skaridov opined in 2014, that the regime of transit passage should be applicable to the Kerch Strait in order to preserve the freedom of navigation of merchant vessels.[45]

Similarly, Ukraine has downplayed the legal value of the reference to internal waters in Article 1 of the 2003 Kerch Treaty and Article 5 of the Agreement between the Russian Federation and Ukraine on the Russian-Ukrainian State Border[46] which provides: "Questions pertaining to contiguous maritime waters shall be settled by agreement between the Contracting Parties in accordance with international law. Nothing in this Treaty shall prejudice the positions of Ukraine and the Russian Federation regarding the status of the Sea of Azov or the Kerch Strait as internal waters."[47] In the *Coastal State Rights Case*, Ukraine contends that after the dissolution of the Soviet Union, the Sea of Azov and the Kerch Strait "no longer qualify as internal waters",[48] as only bays, the coasts of which belong to a single State under the terms of Article 10 of LOSC, can be potentially categorized as internal waters.[49] Yet, as pointed out by the Russian Federation, this position ignores the opposite conclusion reached by the ICJ in the *Gulf of Fonseca case* and Arbitral Tribunal in the arbitration between Slovenia and Croatia.[50]

Ukraine claims that the Sea of Azov comprises the following maritime zones as provided for in LOSC: internal waters, territorial sea, EEZ and continental shelf (see Map 2). It follows from this that Ukraine's contiguous zone,

44 A Skaridov, 'The Sea of Azov and the Kerch Straits', in Caron and Oral (eds), *op. cit.*, 234–235.

45 Ibid., 237.

46 Agreement between the Russian Federation and Ukraine on the Russian-Ukrainian State Border, adopted 28 January 2003, entered into force 23 April 2004, available https://treaties.un.org/doc/Publication/UNTS/No%20Volume/54132/Part/I-54132-08000002803fe18a.pdf; accessed 5 April 2021.

47 Ibid., Art 5.

48 *Dispute Concerning Coastal State Rights*, 2020 Award on Preliminary Objections, *op. cit*, para 212.

49 Ibid., para 214.

50 Final Award of 29 June 2017 pursuant to the Arbitration Agreement between the Government of the Republic of Croatia and the Government of the Republic of Slovenia, signed on 4 November 2009, paras. 883–885. *Land, Island and Maritime Frontier Dispute (El Salvador v. Honduras: Nicaragua intervening), Judgment,* ICJ Reports 1992, p. 351, para 399.

which was established by the Contiguous Zone of Ukraine Act in December 2018,[51] also exists in the Sea of Azov and extends up to 24 NM as measured from the baselines in conformity with Article 33(2) of LOSC. The Act does not however, explicitly include or exclude the Sea of Azov from its application. In this context, the Russian Federation has maintained that:

> With regard to the adoption of the Contiguous Zone of Ukraine Act, it is the understanding of the Russian Federation that the geographical area to which this Act applies is the part of the Black Sea that is contiguous to the coast of Ukraine. The Sea of Azov, we recall, is part of the internal waters of Russia and Ukraine. Therefore, the provisions on contiguous zones of the United Nations Convention on the Law of the Sea of 1982 do not apply to it, nor, consequently, does the Act establishing the contiguous zone of Ukraine under the Convention.[52]

If the Sea of Azov is included in Ukraine's normal maritime zones as provided in LOSC, then the Kerch Strait satisfies the criteria of Article 37 of LOSC for the regime of transit passage, as shown below.

Ukraine also asserts that, in practice, it has invoked the right of transit passage in the Sea of Azov.[53] In support of this claim, in the *Dispute Concerning Coastal State Rights*, Ukraine referred to the 2001 *note verbale* of its Ministry of Foreign Affairs that explicitly refers, in the context of the passage regime in the Kerch Strait, to the provision of LOSC which regulates the designation of sea lanes and traffic separation scheme (hereafter TSS) in international straits.[54]

---

51 Law about adjacent zone of Ukraine of December 6, 2018 No. 2641-VIII, signed by the President of Ukraine on 29 December 2018, available in Ukrainian at https://zakon.rada.gov.ua/laws/show/2641-VIII; accessed 5 April 2021. Available in English at https://cis-legislation.com/document.fwx?rgn=112881; accessed 5 April 2021.

52 Annex to the letter dated 7 March 2019 from the Permanent Representative of the Russian Federation to the United Nations, Position of the Russian Federation in connection with the adoption of the Contiguous Zone of Ukraine Act, UN Doc A/73/802, 20 March 2019, available https://www.un.org/Depts/los/LEGISLATIONANDTREATIES/STATEFILES/UKR.htm; accessed 5 April 2021.

53 *Dispute Concerning Coastal State Rights*, 2020 Award on Preliminary Objections, *op. cit.*, para 242.

54 Ukraine has alleged that the Russian Federation breached Article 41(4)-(5) of LOSC, which provides that before designating or substituting sea lanes or TSS, strait States are required to draft these proposals in close consultation with each other and the International Maritime Organization (hereafter IMO) as the competent organization, before referring them to the IMO with a view to their adoption. The strait States may designate, prescribe or substitute the sea lanes or TSS if the IMO has first approved them. Only then may such sea lanes or TSS in a strait where the regime of transit passage applies be considered as

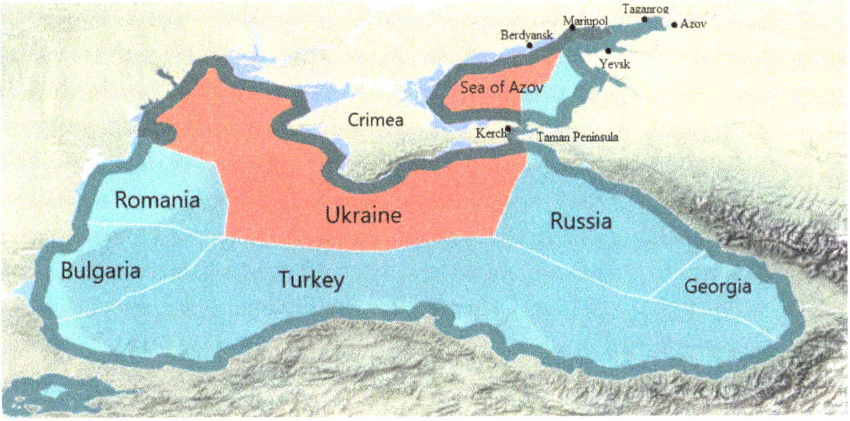

MAP 3 The maritime zones in the Black Sea
SOURCE: MARINEREGIONS.ORG, 'OVERLAPPING CLAIM UKRAINIAN EXCLUSIVE ECONOMIC ZONE', FLANDERS MARINE INSTITUTE (VLIZ) 2020, AVAILABLE HTTP://WWW.MARINEREGIONS.ORG/EEZDETAILS.PHP?MRGID=5695; ACCESSED 5 APRIL 2021. THE MAP IS MODIFIED BY THE AUTHOR TO INCLUDE THE NAMES OF, *INTER ALIA*, THE STATES, PENINSULAS AND PORTS MENTIONED IN THE CHAPTER. THE MAP DEPICTS THE INTERNAL WATERS, TERRITORIAL SEA AND EEZ OF UKRAINE AND THE RUSSIAN FEDERATION IN THE SEA OF AZOV PURSUANT TO THE UKRAINIAN POSITION IN THE ARBITRAL PROCEEDINGS. BY CONTRAST, THE RUSSIAN FEDERATION MAINTAINS THAT THE ENTIRE SEA OF AZOV FALLS UNDER THE REGIME OF INTERNAL WATERS.

"generally accepted international regulations" which ships in transit passage are required to respect (Art 39(2)(a) of LOSC). By contrast, in international straits where innocent passage applies, sea lanes and TSS can be adopted by the strait State(s) by only taking into account the recommendations of the IMO (Art 22(3)(a) of LOSC). Despite the Ukrainian petitions and claims that the new rules are dangerous for mariners, the Russian Federation established the new navigation conditions between the fairways in the allegedly Ukrainian part of the internal waters of the Kerch Strait. Soon after, on 5 September 2002, the Russian-flagged oil tanker Lidiya collided with another ship in the Kerch Strait. It was found during the investigation that the accident was partly caused by the new Russian navigation rules between fairways Nos. 50 and 52 which, the Ukrainian Ministry of Foreign Affairs believed, "could have resulted in human fatalities and an oil spill from the tanker Lidiya". Ukraine reiterated the importance of Article 41(4)-(5) of LOSC and called for the revocation of the new navigation rules that were established unilaterally by the Russian agencies in respect of the Kerch Strait's area between fairways Nos. 50 to 52. UA-516, Ministry of Foreign Affairs of Ukraine, 'For the attention of the Ministry of Foreign Affairs of the Russian Federation', No. 72/22-446-2110, 15 September 2002, 3–4, available https://files.pca-cpa.org/pcadocs/ua-ru/04.%20UA%20Rejoinder%20Memorial/01.%20Exhibits/; accessed 5 April 2021. UA-515, Ministry of Foreign Affairs of Ukraine, 'For the attention of the Ministry of Foreign Affairs of the Russian Federation', No. 21/20-410-747, 24 May 2001, 4, available https://files.pca-cpa.org/pcadocs/ua-ru/04.%20UA%20Rejoinder%20Memorial/01.%20Exhibits/; accessed 5 April 2021.

Yet the instances referred to by Ukraine, in the arbitration proceedings, in support of the claim that it previously invoked the transit passage regime in the Kerch Strait occurred in 2001 and 2002, and thus preceded the conclusion of the 2003 bilateral treaties. Ukraine also referred to a 1992 treaty with the Russian Federation on cooperation in the fisheries sector in the Black Sea and Sea of Azov, and claimed that the treaty makes no reference to the Sea of Azov having any status other than a semi-enclosed sea comprising normal maritime zones.[55] In addition, Ukraine points to its "List of geographical coordinates of points defining the baselines for measuring the breadth of the territorial sea, exclusive economic zone and the continental shelf in the Sea of Azov",[56] which it deposited with the UN in 1992.[57]

In conclusion, the State practice invoked by Ukraine in support of its claim that the regime of transit passage applies to the Kerch Strait, precedes the conclusion of the 2003 bilateral treaties, which stipulate that the Sea of Azov and the Kerch Strait are internal waters of the Russian Federation and Ukraine, and establish a restrictive passage regime in the Kerch Strait which is clearly incompatible with the right of transit passage. In a similar vein, the 2002 draft law on internal waters, the territorial sea and the contiguous zone of Ukraine, which provided for a Ukrainian territorial sea in the Sea of Azov,[58] was never adopted, and instead was followed by the conclusion of the 2003 bilateral treaties, which expressly applied the internal waters regime to the Sea of Azov. Therefore, neither treaty law nor Ukraine's State practice prior to the arbitral proceedings necessarily supports Ukraine's claim that the Kerch Strait is subject to the transit passage regime.

---

55 *Dispute Concerning Coastal State Rights*, 2020 Award on Preliminary Objections, *op. cit.*, para 237.

56 Ibid. See also Ukraine, 'Legislation', Division for Ocean Affairs and the Law of the Sea, available https://www.un.org/depts/los/LEGISLATIONANDTREATIES/STATEFILES/UKR.htm; accessed 5 April 2021.

57 See Ukraine's 'List of geographical coordinates of points defining the baselines for measuring the breadth of the territorial sea, exclusive economic zone and the continental shelf in the Sea of Azov', Division for Ocean Affairs and the Law of the Sea, *Law of the Sea Bulletin*, No. 36, (UN, 1998).

58 See ВЕРХОВНА РАДА УКРАЇНИ, Проект Закону про внутрішні води, територіальне море та прилеглу зону України (draft law on internal waters, the territorial sea and the contiguous zone of Ukraine), No. 2605, від 30.12.2002 року, available in Ukrainian at https://w1.c1.rada.gov.ua/pls/zweb2/webproc4_2?id=&pf3516=2605&skl=5; accessed 5 April 2021.

4.4 The Significance of 2003 Bilateral Treaties for the Passage Regime of the Kerch Strait

Ukraine's position that the regime of transit passage applies to the Kerch Strait is somewhat ambiguous particularly due to the fact that it explicitly agreed in Article 5 of the 2003 State Border Treaty that the Sea of Azov and the Kerch Strait constitute internal waters within Ukraine and the Russian Federation. Likewise, Article 1 of the 2003 Kerch Treaty stipulates that the Sea of Azov and the Kerch Strait "have historically been internal waters of the Russian Federation and Ukraine". Moreover, under Article 2 of the Kerch Treaty, Ukraine consented to apply a restrictive passage regime to the Kerch Strait, which is clearly incompatible with the rights of transit passage and of innocent passage. This passage regime restricts the access of foreign merchant vessels to the Sea of Azov and prohibits the entrance of foreign warships to the Sea of Azov unless both Ukraine and the Russian Federation explicitly give their prior permission. Furthermore, the 2003 Kerch Treaty does not guarantee the right of foreign aircraft to fly over the Kerch Strait, a right that would be applicable under the transit passage regime for the purpose of entering the EEZ in the Sea of Azov.

Therefore, it is doubtful that the regime of transit passage was applicable to ships and aircraft in the Kerch Strait after Ukraine became a party to the 2003 Kerch Treaty. However, Ukraine could argue that the Sea of Azov and the Kerch Strait were internal waters, as agreed in the 2003 bilateral treaties, but that legal regime changed as a result of the Russian Federation's occupation and annexation of Crimea. The Russian Federation's aggression against Ukraine would have provided, arguably, sufficient grounds for suspending or terminating the 2003 bilateral treaties to the extent that they set out the internal waters regime and regulate passage rights in the Sea of Azov and the Kerch Strait. Notably, pursuant to Article 3 of the ILC Draft Articles on the Effects of Armed Conflicts on Treaties, the 2003 bilateral treaties should not be considered as *ipso facto* terminated or suspended owing to the outbreak of hostilities between Ukraine and the Russian Federation in 2014, even assuming that this dispute constitutes an armed conflict.[59] The 2003 Kerch Treaty has not been suspended or terminated by its States Parties.

59 General Assembly Resolution 66/99, adopted 9 December 2011, 2, available https://undocs.org/en/%20A/RES/66/99; accessed 5 April 2021. Pursuant to its Article 18, the Draft Articles on the Effects of Armed Conflicts on Treaties are in any case without prejudice to the termination, withdrawal or suspension of treaties as a consequence of a fundamental change of circumstances.

Nonetheless, Ukraine could invoke the Kerch Strait incident of 25 November 2018 as a material breach of the freedom of navigation within the terms of Article 2(1) of the 2003 Kerch Treaty. The transit of Ukrainian ships through the strait was blocked by the Russian Federation by means of placing a tanker under the Crimean Bridge and using force which resulted in casualties amongst the Ukrainian crew and were subsequently charged with the crime of aggravated illegal crossing of a border and detained in breach of sovereign immunity of warships and government ships. Thus, the Kerch Strait incident potentially constitutes a material breach of the 2003 Kerch Treaty within the meaning of Article 60(1) of the Vienna Convention on the Law of Treaties[60] (VCLT), which would entitle Ukraine to terminate the treaty or suspend its operation in whole or in part. The Russian Federation's unilateral imposition of restrictions on the passage of ships in the Kerch Strait have arguably precluded the enjoyment of freedom of navigation by the Ukrainian ships. It can be argued that these freedoms are essential to the accomplishment of the object or purpose of the 2003 Kerch Treaty in terms of Article 60(3) of the VCLT.

In this context, it is also possible for Ukraine to invoke the *rebus sic stantibus* clause under Article 62 of the VCLT to terminate or suspend the operation of the 2003 Kerch Treaty on the grounds that the Russian Federation's annexation of Crimea and other actions that have hampered the freedom of navigation of Ukrainian ships for the purpose of accessing the Sea of Azov have fundamentally changed the circumstances based on which Ukraine initially consented to be bound by the treaty.[61] The 2003 Kerch Treaty does not regulate the procedure for withdrawing from it. Thus, pursuant to Articles 65(1) and 67 of the VCLT, Ukraine would have to notify the Russian Federation in writing of its claim and indicate the measure proposed to be taken with respect to the treaty and the reasons thereof.

In recent years, the possible termination of the 2003 Kerch Treaty has been extensively debated in the Ukrainian parliament and by the government. In July 2015, a draft law for the denunciation of the 2003 Kerch Treaty was submitted to the Ukrainian parliament by its future chairman (2016–2019) Andriy Parubiy, but the representatives of the Ministry of Foreign Affairs, the Ministry of Defence, the Ministry of Justice, the Ministry of Infrastructure and the Security Service decided in a special meeting that the current national interests

60 Vienna Convention on the Law of Treaties, adopted 23 May 1969, entered into force 27 January 1980, 1155 UNTS 331.

61 Notably, Art 62(2) of the VCLT does not exclude the possibility of invoking the *rebus sic stantibus* clause as the 2003 Kerch Treaty does not establish a boundary.

of Ukraine did not necessitate its denunciation.[62] Subsequently, Ukrainian parliamentarians have made petitions for the denunciation of the 2003 Kerch Treaty to the President of Ukraine and the Minister of Defence in which they argue for the establishment of an EEZ in the Sea of Azov as they claim that this would, *inter alia*, allow the entrance of NATO warships to the Sea of Azov.[63] Currently, such visits require the consent of the Russian Federation under Article 2(3) of the Kerch Treaty.

Furthermore, shortly after the Kerch Strait incident of 25 November 2018, the Ukrainian Minister of Foreign Affairs claimed on television that "with its actions, the Russian Federation has confirmed that bilateral agreements on the Kerch Strait and the Sea of Azov are null and void. We understand that Russia has never had any intention to follow them."[64] Nonetheless, this declaration has apparently not been supplemented with any actual steps for terminating or suspending, either in whole or in part, the 2003 bilateral treaties. Ukraine has not initiated the procedure set forth in section 4, Part V of the VCLT for terminating or suspending the operation of the 2003 bilateral treaties.

Owing to domestic political considerations, Ukraine might be tempted to terminate or suspend the 2003 bilateral treaties if the Annex VII Arbitral Tribunal supports the position of the Russian Federation that the Sea of Azov comprises internal waters based on the concept of historic bay and Ukraine's alleged acceptance of that regime in the light of the 2003 bilateral treaties. The Kerch Strait would then connect unambiguously a Ukrainian EEZ in the Sea of Azov with EEZs in the Black Sea. This would imply the applicability of the right of transit passage to the Kerch Strait, which would conflict with the Russian Federation's potential claim that the Kerch Strait would still constitute a strait falling under the category of Article 35(a) of LOSC, as discussed below.

Rather than terminating the 2003 bilateral treaties, Ukraine maintains, as argued in the *Coastal State Rights Case* that, notwithstanding the conclusion of the 2003 bilateral treaties, it has not reached a final agreement with the Russian Federation regarding the status of the Sea of Azov, as any final agreement would be contingent on maritime boundary delimitation.[65] Notably,

62 RB Urcosta, 'Russia's Strategic Considerations on the Sea of Azov', *Warsaw Institute* (3 December 2018), 34. See also ВЕРХОВНА РАДА УКРАЇНИ, Голова Комітету, До реєстр. No. 0051, від 16.07.2015 року, available in Ukrainian at http://w1.c1.rada.gov.ua/pls/zweb2/webproc34?id=&pf3511=56077&pf35401=364420; accessed 5 April 2021.

63 Urcosta, *op. cit.*, 34–35.

64 Anonymous, 'Ukraine-Russia sea clash: Who controls the territorial waters around Crimea?', *BBC News* (27 November 2018).

65 *Dispute Concerning Coastal State Rights*, 2020 Award on Preliminary Objections, *op. cit.*, 239–240.

Ukraine has not fixed a maritime boundary with the Russian Federation in the Sea of Azov. Yet this claim ignores the fact that a maritime boundary is not a prerequisite for the existence of an internal waters regime in a historic bay. As will be discussed below, the ICJ made it clear in the *Gulf of Fonseca case* that sovereignty over internal waters of a historic bay may be exercised jointly by its coastal States.

4.5 The Sea of Azov as a Potential Historic Bay and Its Implications for the Regime of Passage in the Kerch Strait under Article 35(a) of LOSC

As examined above, Ukraine clearly rejects the Russian Federation's argument that the Sea of Azov and the Kerch Strait comprised solely internal waters throughout the 1990s. For that reason, Ukraine has requested the Annex VII Arbitral Tribunal to declare that the Sea of Azov comprises its EEZ, as a result of which, the regime of transit passage would apply to ships and aircraft crossing the Kerch Strait (Article 37 of LOSC). Even if the Arbitral Tribunal accedes to this request, then the scope of applicability of the regime of transit passage in the Kerch Strait could still, irrespective of the Arbitral Tribunal's findings, remain unclear and subject to debate. One may expect the Russian Federation to continue to deny the applicability of the right of transit passage in the Kerch Strait, as discussed next.

For those States interested in retaining the passage regime of the Kerch Strait that is stipulated in the 2003 Kerch Treaty, it is important that the Arbitral Tribunal supports the claim that the Sea of Azov constitutes a historic bay. The Kerch Strait would then potentially fall under the exception stipulated in Article 35(a) of LOSC: "Nothing in this Part affects: (a) any areas of internal waters within a strait, except where the establishment of a straight baseline in accordance with the method set forth in article 7 has the effect of enclosing as internal waters areas which had not previously been considered as such". This implies that the legal regime of straits used for international navigation does not affect any areas of internal waters within a strait if such maritime areas had been considered as internal waters prior to the first establishment of the relevant straight baselines (hereafter referred to as *long-standing internal waters*).[66] However, in the existing case law, the question of whether a strait

66 See SN Nandan, DH Anderson, 'Straits Used for International Navigation: A Commentary on Part III of the United Nations Convention on the Law of the Sea 1982' (1989) 60 *The British Yearbook of International Law* 173. Caminos, Cogliati-Bantz, *op. cit.*, 66–67.

that meets the geographic and functional criteria of a strait can be classified as internal waters, including by reason of historic title, has not yet received a clear answer.[67] Thus, the Annex VII Arbitral Tribunal has the potential to clarify this question in the current proceedings between Ukraine and the Russian Federation.

The States that are interested in the application of the regime of transit passage to the Kerch Strait may espouse a different reading of Article 35(a) of LOSC. Pursuant to an interpretation supporting this position, Article 35(a) of LOSC merely clarifies that Part III of the Convention affects areas of internal waters within an international strait to the extent that the otherwise applicable innocent passage regime would be replaced with that of transit passage if the strait meets the conditions of Article 37 of the Convention.[68]

Clearly, the latter interpretation of Article 35(a) of the Convention would support the position of Ukraine in the determination of the passage regime applicable to the Kerch Strait. The Russian Federation could adopt the opposing reading of the same provision by claiming that the passage rights of foreign ships are not safeguarded under international law in the Article-35(a)-category of straits, where the area constitutes long-standing internal waters. For example, in the Baltic Sea, this exception has particular relevance in connection with the Sea of Straits in Estonia, Kalmarsund in Sweden and the multiple straits in the Åland region of Finland. All these areas constituted the internal waters of the relevant coastal State, probably since 1938 under the Nordic neutrality rules,[69] and well before Estonia, Finland, and Sweden first established their system of straight baselines.[70] This exception could also have significance for the passage regime of some straits in the Northern Sea Route.[71]

67 CR Symmons, *Historic Waters in the Law of the Sea: A Modern Re-Appraisal* (Martinus Nijhoff, Leiden/Boston, 2008), 33.

68 H Caminos, 'The Legal Regime of Straits in the 1982 United Nations Convention on the Law of the Sea', in *Recueil des cours de l'Académie de droit international de la Haye 1987* (Martinus Nijhoff, Dordrecht/Boston/Lancaster, 1989), 130.

69 Declaration between Denmark, Finland, Iceland, Norway and Sweden for the Purpose of Establishing Similar Rules of Neutrality, 27 May 1938 Stockholm, available http://www.histdoc.net/history/nordic1938_en.html; accessed 5 April 2021. See also: 'Denmark-Finland-Iceland-Norway-Sweden: Declaration Regarding Similar Rules of Neutrality' (1938) 32 *The American Journal of International Law*, 141–163. The northern countries Denmark, Finland, Iceland, Sweden, Norway and the Baltic States adopted analogous domestic legal acts on neutrality on the basis of the above-mentioned 1938 declaration.

70 See further Lott, *op. cit.*, 25, 213–221.

71 See further on the Russian Federation's claims in, e.g., JJ Solski, 'Russia' in RC Beckman, T Henriksen, KD Kraabel, EJ Molenaar and JA Roach (eds), *Governance of Arctic Shipping: Balancing Rights and Interests of Arctic States and User States* (Brill, Leiden/Boston, 2017), 192–197.

A restrictive interpretation of Article 35(a) of LOSC is functionally equivalent to the exception provided for in Article 8(2) of LOSC but it addresses, specifically, navigational rights in straits, whereas Article 8(2) is more generally applicable to internal waters.[72] Such a reading of Article 35(a) of LOSC serves as a potential legal basis for establishing a passage regime that may entail a permit-based system in a strait even if the strait would otherwise be subject to the regime of transit passage. This is significant, particularly if the Annex VII Arbitral Tribunal finds in support of the Russian Federation that the Sea of Azov is a historic bay and constitutes internal waters and that Ukraine has accepted that regime in light of the 2003 bilateral treaties. If such a finding were made, Ukraine might be tempted to terminate the 2003 bilateral treaties altogether, consequently triggering the applicability of the transit passage regime in the Kerch Strait, as discussed above. The scope of Article 35(a) arguably covers the Sea of Azov, which it is argued is a historic bay and for which the straight baseline segment at the entrance of the Kerch Strait was established in 1985.[73] Pursuant to a teleological interpretation of Article 35(a) in combination with customary international law, the exception is potentially also applicable in cases where the coastal State has not (yet) established a system of straight baselines, but its relevant maritime area has been recognized as constituting a historic bay.

In the case of the Sea of Azov and the Kerch Strait, the legitimacy of the Russian Federation's claim to long-standing internal waters rests on the recognition of this maritime area as a historic bay. LOSC does not directly regulate historic bays (Article 10(6) of the Convention),[74] as their status is instead governed by customary international law. Should the Annex VII Arbitral Tribunal conclude that the Sea of Azov and the Kerch Strait do not (any longer) comprise long-standing internal waters that meet the criteria of Articles 8(2) and 35(a) of LOSC, then there appears to be no other legal basis for the restrictive passage regime that currently applies in the Kerch Strait and Sea of Azov under Article 2 of the 2003 Kerch Treaty. General international law cannot provide a legal basis for other historic passage regimes that are incompatible with LOSC.

72 On the interpretation of Article 35(a), see further Lott, *op. cit.*, 21–27.

73 The Decree no. 4450 of the Council of Ministers of the Soviet Union on the Confirmation of a List of Geographic Coordinates Determining the Position of the Baseline in the Arctic Ocean, the Baltic Sea and Black Sea from which the Width of the Territorial Waters, Economic Zone and Continental Shelf of the U.S.S.R. is Measured, 15 January 1985.

74 Except for the possibility for a State to declare, pursuant to Article 298(1)(a)(i) that it does not accept compulsory procedures entailing binding decisions with respect to disputes concerning the interpretation or application of articles 15, 74 and 83 involving historic bays or titles.

This conclusion follows from the Annex VII Arbitral Tribunal's South China Sea award where it was emphasized that:

> [T]he prohibition on reservations is informative of the Convention's approach to historic rights. It is simply inconceivable that the drafters of the Convention could have gone to such lengths to forge a consensus text and to prohibit any but a few express reservations while, at the same time, anticipating that the resulting Convention would be subordinate to broad claims of historic rights.[75]

For the Sea of Azov to be recognized as a historic bay, the claim needs to be accepted by other States and based on a long and consistent assertion of dominion over the bay which includes the coastal State's right to exclude foreign vessels entering the bay without its permission.[76]

The Russian Federation asserts that the Sea of Azov and the Kerch Strait were historically internal waters of the Russian Empire, and, later, the Soviet Union, and, since 1991, the common internal waters of Ukraine and the Russian Federation, the status of which has not been protested by other States.[77] Notably, although there appears to be no explicit protests by States against the internal waters status of the Sea of Azov prior to the change in the Ukrainian Government's position on this matter after the annexation of Crimea, the United States, in its announcements and official documents has consistently refrained from using the term *juridical bay* for the waters of the Sea of Azov that were enclosed by the straight baseline pursuant to the Decree no. 4450 of the Council of Ministers of the Soviet Union in 1985.

It can possibly be argued that characterizing the Sea of Azov as a historic bay is *per se* contrary to customary international law. The Sea of Azov includes an extensive maritime area which falls outside the 12-NM-limit of territorial sea as measured from the baselines. The maritime area which spans the Sea of Azov outside the 12-NM-limit is relatively large as it has a maximum length of over 60 NM and maximum width of over 90 NM. Consequently, it may be argued that the Sea of Azov does not lie in the immediate vicinity of Ukrainian and Russian coasts and thus cannot be considered as a historic bay under customary international law. This claim, however, is somewhat weakened by the

75 South China Sea Arbitration (the Philippines v. China). Award of the LOSC Annex VII Tribunal, 12 July 2016, para 254.

76 Churchill, Lowe, *op. cit.*, 44. Caminos, Cogliati-Bantz, *op. cit.*, 60–61.

77 *Dispute Concerning Coastal State Rights*, 2020 Award on Preliminary Objections, *op. cit.*, paras. 199, 202.

fact that State practice includes examples of much larger historic bays, e.g., Hudson Bay,[78] as compared to the maritime area of the Sea of Azov. In 1934, Johnston commented that:

> In 1906, however, notwithstanding the assumptions of the world as to the status of Hudson Bay, the Government of Canada placed on its statute books a statute declaring the waters of Hudson Bay to be territorial waters of Canada. That statute is still in force in Canada, without, so far as is known, any protest having been made by any foreign government. This statute has been and presumably still is being actively enforced in Canada and in Hudson Bay as part of Canada. The Government of Canada, therefore, has appropriated and continues to appropriate Hudson Bay and presumably Hudson Strait as Canadian national waters, as much a part of Canada as Toronto or Montreal. Furthermore, Canada's predecessor in title to this whole area, the Hudson's Bay Company, maintained for a century and a half exclusive title and possession, not only to the territories surrounding the Bay and Strait, but also to the Bay and the Strait.[79]

The Russian Federation refers to the 1992 judgment of the ICJ in the *Gulf of Fonseca case*, according to which: "A State succession is one of the ways in which territorial sovereignty passes from one State to another; and there seems no reason in principle why a succession should not create a joint sovereignty where a single and undivided maritime area passes to two or more new States."[80] A similar question was recently addressed in the arbitration between Slovenia and Croatia where the Arbitral Tribunal found, referring to the *Gulf of Fonseca case*, that the Convention's framework on bays under Article 10 does not exclude "the existence of bays with the character of internal waters, the coasts of which belong to more than one State."[81] Thus, the current case law accepts the possibility that a historic bay falls under the joint sovereignty of its coastal States.

78 BB Jia, *The Regime of Straits in International Law* (Clarendon Press, Oxford, 1998), 76.

79 K Johnston, 'Canada's Title to Hudson Bay and Hudson Strait', *British Year Book of International Law* (1934) 15, 2. Notably, the United States has protested against the Canadian claims declaring its waters in the Arctic archipelago, including in the Hudson Strait, as its internal waters where the regime of international straits under Part III of the LOSC does not apply. See J Kraska, 'The Law of the Sea Convention and the Northwest Passage' (2007) 22(2) *The International Journal of Marine and Coastal Law*, 263, 268. However, Kraska still refers to the Hudson Bay as a historic bay. See Ibid., 271.

80 *Land, Island and Maritime Frontier Dispute*, Judgment, *op. cit.*, para 399.

81 *Slovenia v. Croatia Arbitration*, 2017 Award, *op. cit.*, paras. 883–885.

The Russian Federation claims that it exercises sovereignty over the Sea of Azov jointly with Ukraine. It argues that the historic bay status of the Sea of Azov dates back to the Soviet era and the Russian Empire,[82] and that "any waiver or renunciation of a State's rights must either be express or unequivocally implied by the conduct of the State".[83] According to the Russian Federation, the internal waters status of the Sea of Azov and the Kerch Strait has remained unchanged and this is confirmed in Article 1 of the 2003 Kerch Treaty and Article 5 of the 2003 State Border Treaty.[84]

In this respect, Ukraine's State practice is relevant to an assessment of the legality under customary international law of the regime of internal waters as stipulated in the 2003 bilateral treaties. Pursuant to the findings of the ICJ in the *Gulf of Fonseca case*, both Ukraine and the Russian Federation need to recognize the continuous historical status of the bay.[85] In that regard, Ukraine argues that after its restoration of independence, it "made clear its position that the Sea of Azov was subject to the normal rules of the international law of the sea".[86] Ukraine seems to imply that the historic bay regime was disrupted after Ukraine deposited its "List of geographical coordinates of points defining the baselines for measuring the breadth of the territorial sea, exclusive economic zone and the continental shelf in the Sea of Azov" with the UN in 1992. If the Annex VII Arbitral Tribunal finds that the historic bay regime of the Sea of Azov was interrupted in the 1990s, then this could undermine the legality of the legal regime of the Sea of Azov as stipulated in the 2003 bilateral treaties *in toto*. Thus, a broad interpretation of Ukraine's arguments in the *Coastal State Rights Case* is that it rejects the position that it has continuously recognized the Sea of Azov as a historic bay.

If Ukraine had unequivocally made it clear that it did not accept the joint sovereignty over the Sea of Azov as a historic bay in the 1990s, then one could argue that the exercise of the coastal States' dominion over the Sea of Azov has not been continuous as it was interrupted during the 1990s and prior to the conclusion of the 2003 treaties. If this was the case, then Ukraine would have vetoed the Russian Federation's endeavours to continue to apply the historic bay regime to the Sea of Azov. Similarly, Estonia rejected, in the 1990s, the Gulf

82 *Dispute Concerning Coastal State Rights*, 2020 Award on Preliminary Objections, *op. cit.*, para 205.
83 Ibid., para 206.
84 Ibid.
85 *Land, Island and Maritime Frontier Dispute*, Judgment, *op. cit.*, para 394.
86 *Dispute Concerning Coastal State Rights*, 2020 Award on Preliminary Objections, *op. cit.*, para 237.

of Riga as a historic bay as proposed by Latvia on the basis of the centuries-long practice of the Russian Empire and the Soviet Union.[87] Yet Ukraine's position towards the Sea of Azov as a historic bay has been ambiguous. On the one hand, Ukraine has claimed in the arbitral proceedings that the Sea of Azov includes its EEZ, on the other hand however, it has not terminated or suspended, in whole or in part, the 2003 bilateral treaties, which both declare that the Sea of Azov constitutes the internal waters of Ukraine and the Russian Federation. This reluctance may be explained by the recognition of freedom of navigation of Ukrainian ships in the Kerch Strait and the Sea of Azov under Article 2 of the 2003 Kerch Treaty.

4.6 The Importance of the Obligation of Non-recognition for the Passage Regime of the Kerch Strait

Even if the Arbitral Tribunal finds that the Sea of Azov does not (any longer) constitute entirely internal waters and, instead, comprises other maritime zones, including an EEZ, then the Russian Federation might, in response, connect Crimea with its system of straight baselines from the Taman Peninsula. This would have the effect to maintaining the maritime area in and adjacent to the Kerch Strait as internal waters from the perspective of those States that recognize the Russian Federation's sovereignty over Crimea. In support of this, the Russian Federation could cite Article 1 of the 2003 Kerch Treaty and Article 5 of the State Border Treaty, which stipulate that the status of the Kerch Strait is internal waters, and refer to the fact that these treaties have remained in force and that the passage regime stipulated therein has been so far, largely respected by other States.

Continuing this hypothetical scenario, after the potential establishment of a system of straight baselines around Crimea, the Russian Federation might potentially claim that the Kerch Strait still constitutes an Article 35(a)-category of non-international strait[88] as it comprises internal waters which were considered as such prior to the establishment of the system of straight baselines around Crimea (see Articles 7 and 8(2) of LOSC). It is not impossible that the Russian Federation would thereby strive to exclude the applicability of the regime of transit passage to the Kerch Strait. The Russian interpretation of the

87 On the comparisons with between the Gulf of Riga and the Sea of Azov in the context of the historic bay see also the *Dispute Concerning Coastal State Rights*, 2020 Award on Preliminary Objections, *op. cit.*, paras. 224, 233, 252.

88 For an explanation on the use of the term *non-international strait*, see Lott, *op. cit.*, 7–8.

applicable law would be based on its sovereignty claim over Crimea. Deciding on the legality of the Russian Federation's potential internal waters-claim in respect of the Kerch Strait is unlikely as it would require the Arbitral Tribunal to decide on the legality of the Russian Federation's alleged sovereignty over Crimea. The Arbitral Tribunal has already expressly excluded questions of sovereignty over land territories from the scope of its final award and will not address any claims of Ukraine on the premise of Ukraine being sovereign over Crimea.[89]

Hence, should the Arbitral Tribunal support the position of Ukraine that the Kerch Strait is an international strait which is subject to the regime of transit passage, then this ruling would not be able to take into account the Russian Federation's claim to sovereignty over the whole maritime area of the Kerch Strait which, from the Russian Federation's perspective, would possibly entitle it to categorize the Kerch Strait as a non-international strait under Article 35(a) of LOSC.

If, by the time the Arbitral Tribunal delivers its award, the passage regime stipulated in Article 2 of the 2003 Kerch Treaty should hypothetically be devoid of any legal effect, then the Russian Federation would likely consider Ukrainian ships as foreign ships that need to comply with its restrictive passage regime in the Kerch Strait. This would cause further tension and serve as a potential basis for the escalation of the conflict in the Sea of Azov region. In the light of this sophisticated legal and geopolitical perspective, Ukraine's restraint towards the potential termination or suspension of the 2003 bilateral treaties, as examined above, may be considered a balanced approach. One may even wonder if the passage regime as stipulated in the 2003 Kerch Treaty could, in principle, still serve as a compromise between the parties' otherwise conflicting approaches to the passage regime of the Kerch Strait. Had the Russian Federation not hampered the passage of merchant vessels to and from Ukrainian ports in the Sea of Azov and had respected the freedom of navigation of Ukrainian naval vessels navigating through the Kerch Strait, then the parties to the current dispute might still potentially regard the legal regime of the 2003 Kerch Treaty as a pragmatic solution that effectively accommodates the parties' main interests.

Nonetheless, the compatibility of the Russian Federation's potential claim with the Convention is doubtful. Pursuant to a restrictive interpretation of Article 35(a) of LOSC,[90] the legal regime of straits used for international

89 *Dispute Concerning Coastal State Rights*, 2020 Award on Preliminary Objections *op. cit.*, para 197.

90 A liberal interpretation of Art 35(a) of LOSC would not entitle the Russian Federation to restrict passage through the Kerch Strait in any case, see the discussion above.

navigation does not affect any areas of internal waters within a strait if such maritime areas were considered internal waters prior to the establishment of straight baselines. The notion of "not previously been considered as such" in Article 35(a) of the Convention does not grant the coastal State an unlimited discretionary right to restrict passage rights in straits under its domestic legal acts. The coastal State's internal waters also need to have been "considered as such" by other States. Thus, the main criterion under Article 35(a) of LOSC which the coastal State needs to satisfy if it seeks to declare a particular strait as its non-international strait, is recognition by other States of such a passage regime and the relevant domestic legal acts which, e.g., establish the relevant straight baselines or declare the area as the coastal State's historic bay. In that regard, the majority of States that follow the policy of non-recognition in respect of the annexation and occupation of Crimea do not recognize the Russian Federation's sovereignty over the internal waters in the western part of the Kerch Strait.

Therefore, the obligation of non-recognition could serve as the key factor in determining whether or not the right of transit passage applies in the Kerch Strait. The obligation of non-recognition is stipulated in Article 41 of the ILC Articles on State Responsibility,[91] according to which no State shall recognize as lawful a situation created by a serious breach, nor render aid or assistance in maintaining that situation. From Ukraine's perspective, Crimea's status as an integral part of Ukraine is 'settled' and the Russian Federation's claim to Crimea is devoid of any legal effect.[92] In the event that the Annex VII Arbitral Tribunal reaches the conclusion that the Sea of Azov does not comprise internal waters based on the historic bay concept, then flag States should presumably avoid consenting to the current restrictive passage regime in the Kerch Strait and instead claim the right of transit passage. This follows from the rationale that the Russian Federation will continue to claim sovereignty over both coasts of the Kerch Strait. If they recognize the Russian Federation's restrictive passage regime in the Kerch Strait in such circumstances, then this might, arguably, constitute an implicit recognition of the Russian Federation's sovereignty over Crimea. In practice, access of foreign merchant vessels to the Sea of Azov would likely be hampered even more as compared to the situation so far, leading to further complications for international shipping and the development of the coastal regions of the Sea of Azov.

---

91 International Law Commission, Draft Articles on Responsibility of States for Internationally Wrongful Acts, November 2001, Supplement No. 10, A/56/10, Art 41.

92 *Dispute Concerning Coastal State Rights*, 2020 Award on Preliminary Objections, *op. cit.*, paras. 99, 144.

The significance of geopolitical considerations, particularly the policy of non-recognition, to the passage regime in the Kerch Strait somewhat resembles the situation in the Sea of Straits in the Estonian Western Archipelago.[93] Under its domestic legislation, Estonia does not recognize the right of transit passage (nor fully, the right of innocent passage) to the Sea of Straits, notwithstanding that the Sea of Straits connects the EEZs between the Gulf of Finland and the Baltic Sea proper with the Latvian EEZ in the Gulf of Riga. Third States, including neighbouring States Finland and Latvia, recognize the Estonian restrictive passage regime in the Sea of Straits. Similar to the legal framework applicable to the Kerch Strait, the legal basis for such State practice can be found in Article 35(a) of LOSC, since the Sea of Straits can be considered among such internal waters recognized prior to the establishment of straight baselines by Estonia after its restoration of independence in 1991. Yet the Article 35(a)-exception is applicable to the Sea of Straits only if one recognizes Estonia as a continuous State. This is because Estonia established its internal waters in accordance with the 1938 Nordic Rules of Neutrality under Section 2(3) of its 1938 Neutrality Act pursuant to which the whole maritime area of the Sea of Straits was considered as internal waters.[94] A State which does not recognize Estonia's State continuity, could, in principle, claim that it is not bound with the exception stipulated in Article 35(a) of LOSC and thus retain its right of transit passage for crossing the Sea of Straits.[95]

Similarly, should the Arbitral Tribunal find that the current *sui generis* regime no longer applies to the Kerch Strait and it is replaced instead with the regime of transit passage, then the Russian Federation's approach to the applicable passage regime in the Kerch Strait could potentially be diametrically opposed to the approach of those States and entities that pursue a policy of non-recognition towards the occupation and annexation of Crimea, including

93 The obligation of non-recognition was used by, *inter alia*, the United States and numerous European States in response to the unlawful occupation and annexation of the Baltic States by the Soviet Union. Strict non-recognition policy was consistently used, e.g., by Belgium, Spain, Germany, Portugal, Ireland and Vatican. See S Talmon, *Recognition of Governments in International Law* (Clarendon Press, Oxford, 1998), 103.

94 See Lott, *op. cit.*, 207–223.

95 In such hypothetical case, the right of transit passage would nonetheless be inapplicable as it would be replaced, pursuant to the Messina exception, with the regime of non-suspendable innocent passage, as provided in Articles 38(1) and 45(1)(a) in combination with Article 45(2) of LOSC. This right could be considered applicable to the ships of other protesting States, including the United Kingdom and Germany, as they submitted protests against some of the sections of the Estonian Waterways Act and the Neutrality Act of 1938, just as they did with other Nordic States that adopted the uniform neutrality acts of 1938. See further Lott, *op. cit.*, 223–228.

Ukraine, the EU and the United States. The Russian Federation could consider the strait as a non-international strait subject to the exception of Article 35(a) of LOSC, whereas the policy of non-recognition implies that most States would rather consider the Kerch Strait as an international strait subject to the right of transit passage.

From the perspective of the majority of States, the maritime area in the Kerch Strait is generally not considered as comprising entirely the Russian Federation's internal waters. Instead, the policy of non-recognition entails that most States regard the western part of the Kerch Strait as comprising Ukrainian internal waters. Therefore, if the Arbitral Tribunal respects Ukraine's request and finds that the Sea of Azov and the Kerch Strait include Ukraine's normal maritime zones, then any unilateral declaration of the Kerch Strait as a non-international strait by the Russian Federation after the establishment of a system of straight baselines around the Crimean and Taman peninsulas would fail to meet the conditions of Article 35(a) of LOSC primarily owing to the lack of recognition by the international community.

Based on a systemic interpretation of LOSC, the potential for the categorization of the Kerch Strait as a non-international strait is summarized in the table below (see Table 2). The table also debates the perceived positions of the Russian Federation and Ukraine in relation to the legal categorization of the Kerch Strait as a non-international strait.

4.7 Parallel Legal Regimes vs *Sui Generis* Regime of the Kerch Strait

The legal regime of the Kerch Strait continues to be determined by such factors as the outer limits of maritime zones of the Russian Federation and Ukraine, their bilateral treaties, as well as their domestic law on internal waters and baselines. In addition, the key determinant lies in geopolitical factors, particularly the obligation of non-recognition.

These primary determinants enable States to approach the legal regime applicable to the Kerch Strait from diametrically opposing perspectives, possibly even after the final award of the Annex VII Arbitral Tribunal. In the *Coastal State Rights Case*, Ukraine has alleged that the regime of transit passage is applicable to the Kerch Strait, whereas the Russian Federation rejects this claim and, instead, finds that the passage regime is governed by the 2003 Kerch Treaty. Should the Annex VII Arbitral Tribunal decide that the Sea of Azov constitutes a historic bay, which comprises internal waters as stipulated in the 2003 bilateral treaties concluded between Ukraine and the Russian Federation, then one option for Ukraine would be to terminate the 2003 bilateral treaties

TABLE 2 Potential classification of the Kerch Strait as a non-international strait and the perceived positions of the Russian Federation and Ukraine

Kerch Strait's classification as a non-international strait	The Russian Federation's perceived position	Ukraine's perceived position
Long-standing internal waters exception (Art 35(a))	Potentially affirmative based on the restrictive reading of Art 35(a): entitled to enclose the strait with its straight baselines; stressing that the Kerch Strait has previously comprised entirely internal waters based on the 2003 bilateral treaties that have been respected also by third States.	Rejective based on the liberal reading of Art 35(a) which merely clarifies that Part III of LOSC affects areas of internal waters in an international strait to the effect that the otherwise applicable passage regime of innocent passage would be replaced with that of transit passage if the strait meets the conditions of Art 37.
Not used for international navigation	N/A: the strait is frequently used by foreign ships.	N/A: the strait is frequently used by foreign ships.

and establishing normal maritime zones in the Sea of Azov. The transit passage regime would then be applicable to the Kerch Strait as it would connect Ukrainian EEZ in the Sea of Azov with EEZs in the Black Sea.

To counter this or in a situation where the Annex VII Arbitral Tribunal favours Ukraine's claim on the applicability of the regime of transit passage to the Kerch Strait, the Russian Federation could enclose the Kerch Strait with its system of straight baselines and declare that the Kerch Strait is a non-international strait. Consequently, the maritime area of the Kerch Strait would form internal waters which had been previously considered as such, based on the historic bay concept, provided that the Russian Federation substantiates this claim with a solid legal basis pursuant to Article 35(a) of LOSC. For example, the Russian Federation could cite Article 1 of the 2003 Kerch Treaty and

Article 5 of the State Border Treaty, which stipulate that the status of the Kerch Strait is internal waters, and refer to the fact that these treaties have remained in force and the passage regime stipulated therein has been thus far, largely respected by other States. Hence, the Russian Federation would potentially be able to exclude the right of transit passage in the Kerch Strait in accordance with a restrictive interpretation of Articles 35(a) and 8(2) of LOSC.

This would certainly conflict with Ukraine's approach to the applicable law and that of States that do not recognize the Russian Federation's alleged sovereignty over Crimea. They could adopt a diametrically opposing interpretation of Article 35(a) of LOSC, arguing that it serves merely to clarify that Part III of LOSC affects areas of internal waters in the Kerch Strait to the extent that the otherwise applicable passage regime in internal waters is replaced with that of transit passage. States that follow the obligation of non-recognition in respect of the annexation and occupation of Crimea could also claim that even if one adopts the restrictive reading of Article 35(a) of LOSC, then its conditions are not met in relation to the Kerch Strait as most States do not recognize the Russian Federation's sovereignty over the internal waters of the western part of the Kerch Strait.

Therefore, the previously mentioned determinants of the legal regime of the Kerch Strait create further instability regarding the Kerch Strait's passage regime, exacerbated by the possible exercise of coastal State unilateral discretion even after the arbitral proceedings. In this context, navigation through the Kerch Strait and its adjoining maritime areas might potentially be subject to parallel passage regimes. Based on the previous analysis, the table below debates the asserted positions of the Russian Federation and Ukraine in relation to the legal categorization of the Kerch Strait as an international strait (see Table 3).

Nonetheless, the determinants of the legal regime of the Kerch Strait also provide a broad set of means for Ukraine and the Russian Federation to reach a compromise on the applicable passage regime. In particular, the 2003 Kerch Treaty establishes a passage regime which is compatible with LOSC in terms of Article 311(2) of the Convention if the Annex VII Arbitral Tribunal upholds the Russian Federation's claim that the Sea of Azov constitutes a historic bay. In this situation, the 2003 Kerch Treaty stipulates a more liberal passage regime as compared to the one which would otherwise be applicable to the Kerch Strait under LOSC. Under Articles 8(2) and 35(a) of LOSC, foreign commercial ships would not be entitled to enter the waters forming the historic bay without the coastal State's prior permission, whereas Article 2(2) of the 2003 Kerch Treaty stipulates that commercial ships flying the flags of third States may enter the Sea of Azov and pass through the Kerch Strait if they are going to or returning from a Russian or Ukrainian port (notably, for entering the port,

TABLE 3 Potential classification of the Kerch Strait as an international strait: the asserted positions of the Russian Federation and Ukraine

Kerch Strait's classification as an international strait	**The Russian Federation's perceived position**	**Ukraine's perceived position**
Strait links two parts of an EEZ or the high seas (Art 37)	Rejective: transit passage is not applicable in the Kerch Strait; the Sea of Azov forms a historic bay.	Affirmative: transit passage applies in the Kerch Strait; the Sea of Azov is no longer a historic bay.
Strait connects an EEZ or the high seas with the territorial sea of a foreign State (Art 45(1)(b))	Rejective: foreign warships cannot enjoy the right of non-suspendable innocent passage.	Rejective: the Kerch Strait connects two EEZs (Art 37); Ukraine is a strait State, not a foreign State; Ukraine rejects non-suspendable innocent passage.
Strait includes an EEZ or high seas corridor (Art 36)[a]	Rejective: freedom of navigation and overflight are not applicable in the Kerch Strait; the Sea of Azov forms a historic bay.	Potentially affirmative: freedom of navigation and overflight could be applicable in the Kerch Strait; the Sea of Azov is no longer a historic bay.
Sui generis strait (Art 311(2))	Affirmative: the Kerch Strait is regulated by the 2003 Kerch Treaty which is compatible with the LOSC.	Potentially affirmative: Ukraine has not terminated the 2003 Kerch Treaty which stipulates the passage regime.

a Technically, it is possible for the Russian Federation to stipulate under its domestic legal acts that there are no/only marginal belts of territorial sea or internal waters in the Kerch Strait (which has a minimal width of approx. 3 NM), thereby creating a narrow EEZ/high seas corridor in the strait.

ships may eventually still be required to seek a clearance). Thus, the Kerch Strait currently can be categorized as a *sui generis* strait in terms of Article 311(2) of LOSC.

This shows potential for reaching a compromise between the otherwise conflicting claims of the Sea of Azov coastal States over the legal classification of the Kerch Strait. The *sui generis* regime could allow, similarly to the passage regime under the 2003 Kerch Treaty, unimpeded passage of all commercial ships, freedom of navigation for all Ukrainian and Russian ships, but significant restrictions on the passage of foreign warships and other non-commercial ships in the Sea of Azov and the Kerch Strait. This *sui generis* regime has not raised any objections prior to the measures taken in recent years by the Russian Federation, which hampered the passage of commercial ships and Ukrainian naval vessels through the Kerch Strait. Moreover, Ukraine has not terminated nor suspended, in whole or in part, the 2003 Kerch Treaty.

Should the parties to the dispute not reach a compromise, then a final award of the Annex VII Arbitral Tribunal that upholds either Ukraine's or the Russian Federation's claims could potentially lead to the application of parallel legal regimes of transit passage and permit-based passage to the Kerch Strait, causing increased legal uncertainty for international shipping. Such instability regarding the applicable passage regime could also constitute a fertile ground for any potential future conflict between Ukraine and the Russian Federation and likely hinder the economic development of the Sea of Azov region.

Reaching a compromise solution on the applicable passage regime in the Kerch Strait would not necessarily require new treaty negotiations between the parties to the dispute. It follows, from the discussion above, that the law of the sea and general international law is already clearly able to reconcile the conflicting interests of the coastal States and to ensure the rule of law and legal certainty in the shipping routes of the Sea of Azov. Therefore, it is rather a matter of *pacta sunt servanda* that the rights and freedoms stipulated in the 2003 Kerch Treaty are guaranteed by its States parties towards each other and third States.

So far, the Kerch Strait incident was assessed from a peacetime legal perspective. However, it is also possible that the Kerch Strait incident occurred within the frames of an armed conflict between the two States.

4.8 The Kerch Strait as a Belligerent Strait

4.8.1 *Was the Kerch Strait a Belligerent Strait in 2018?*

Ukraine initially claimed that the seizure of its warships *Berdyansk* and *Nikopol* and the naval tugboat *Yani Kapu* in the approaches of the Kerch Strait and detention of the crew not only violated LOSC, which grants immunity to warships and members of their crews, but also the Third Geneva Convention relative to the Treatment of Prisoners of War (1949).[96] Ukraine explicitly referred to the crew as prisoners of war.[97] On 29 November 2018, Ukraine alerted the Annex VII Arbitral Tribunal of the Kerch Strait incident, noting that "Russia's latest actions, including firing and seizure of Ukrainian naval vessels, mark a serious escalation of a months'-long pattern, in which vessels flagged both to Ukraine and to third states have repeatedly faced obstacles to navigation".[98]

In that context, it is possible to approach the Kerch Strait incident from the perspective of *jus in bello*. James Kraska has argued that the legal framework of humanitarian law applies to the Kerch Strait incident rather than LOSC, since Ukraine and the Russian Federation are engaged in an international armed conflict.[99] Indeed, it is possible to approach the Ukraine-Russia relations in the past decade from the perspective of a prolonged international armed conflict that started with the occupation and annexation of Crimea and war in East Ukraine and that continues to date in the light of, for example, repeated clashes in East Ukraine and the Russian Federation's invasion of Ukraine in 2022.[100] Reportedly, from 2014 to 2021, over 5000 members of the armed forces and civilians died or were injured in the Donbas region.[101] It is estimated that the Russian invasion of Ukraine in 2022 has caused many thousands of fatalities among belligerent fighters and civilians.[102]

---

96 Annex to the letter dated 18 April 2019 from the Permanent Representative of Ukraine to the United Nations, UN Doc A/73/844–S/2019/334, 23 April 2019, available https://www.un.org/Depts/los/LEGISLATIONANDTREATIES/STATEFILES/UKR.htm; accessed 5 April 2021.

97 Annex to the letter dated 10 December 2018 from the Permanent Representative of Ukraine to the United Nations, UN Doc A/73/659–S/2018/1112, 14 December 2018, available https://www.un.org/Depts/los/LEGISLATIONANDTREATIES/STATEFILES/UKR.htm; accessed 5 April 2021.

98 Annex to the letter dated 29 November 2018 from the Permanent Representative of Ukraine to the United Nations, UN Doc A/73/619–S/2018/1079, 5 December 2018, available https://www.un.org/Depts/los/LEGISLATIONANDTREATIES/STATEFILES/UKR.htm; accessed 5 April 2021.

99 J Kraska, 'The Kerch Strait Incident: Law of the Sea or Law of Naval Warfare?' 3 December 2018, *EJIL: Talk!*, available https://www.ejiltalk.org/the-kerch-strait-incident-law-of-the-sea-or-law-of-naval-warfare/comment-page-1/; accessed 5 April 2021.

100 See, e.g., S Harris, P Sonne, 'Russia planning massive military offensive against Ukraine involving 175,000 troops, U.S. intelligence warns', *The Washington Post* (3 December 2021). H Cooper, E Schmitt, 'Biden Weighs Deploying Thousands of Troops to Eastern Europe and Baltics', *The New York Times* (23 January 2022).

101 Anonymous, 'Ukraine: AOAV's data on harm to civilians by explosive weapons', *Action on Armed Violence* (1 March 2022).

102 S Nebehay, 'Civilian death toll in Ukraine now 474 but more casualties reported -U.N.', *Reuters* (8 March 2022). K Korobtsova, L King, 'Putin vs. the web: Russia tries to hide casualties and searing war images', *Los Angeles Times* (4 March 2022).

Albeit at the time of the Kerch Strait incident in November 2018 there had not been any significant hostilities between the Ukrainian and Russian forces in or near the Crimean Peninsula for four years, the hostilities in the Donbas Region in eastern Ukraine had not ceased and continue to date. The ICTY has concluded that:

> International humanitarian law applies from the initiation of such armed conflicts and extends beyond the cessation of hostilities until a general conclusion of peace is reached; or, in the case of internal conflicts, a peaceful settlement is achieved. Until that moment, international humanitarian law continues to apply in the whole territory of the warring States or, in the case of internal conflicts, the whole territory under the control of a party, whether or not actual combat takes place there. ... Notwithstanding various temporary cease-fire agreements, no general conclusion of peace has brought military operations in the region to a close.[103]

By the time of the Kerch Strait incident, Ukraine and the Russian Federation had not concluded peace in relation to the international armed conflict that commenced in February 2014 with the occupation of Crimea by the Russian Federation and continued with the Russian Federation's direct support to the separatist forces in East Ukraine. Furthermore, in a letter to the UN, Ukraine claimed that the Russian Federation's actions in the Kerch Strait incident "constitute an act of armed aggression ... undermining the peaceful settlement of the Ukrainian-Russian armed conflict".[104]

Yet, notably, in the arbitration proceedings in *the Coastal State Rights Case*, neither Ukraine nor the Russian Federation have referred to the Kerch Strait incident as being governed by the rules of naval warfare. They debate whether the occupation of the Crimean Peninsula in 2014 constitutes use of force.[105]

---

103 ICTY, *Prosecutor v Tadić*, Decision of 2 October 1995, *op. cit.*, para 70.

104 Annex to the letter of 10 December 2018 from Ukraine to the UN, *op. cit.* As a reaction to the Kerch Strait incident, the United States carried out a freedom of navigation operation in the Peter the Great Gulf in the Russian maritime area of the Sea of Japan and, in support of Ukraine, sent a United States warship to the Black Sea. See J Johnson, 'U.S. warship conducts Sea of Japan operation in challenge to Russia's 'excessive maritime claims'', *The Japan Times* (6 December 2018). HL Smith, 'US sends warship into Ukraine's Black Sea crisis', *The Times* (6 December 2018).

105 *Dispute Concerning Coastal State Rights*, 2020 Award on Preliminary Objections, *op. cit.*, paras. 6, 49, 79, 305, 310, 328.

The Kerch Strait incident of 2018 has not been brought to the attention of the Arbitral Tribunal by Ukraine as a clear example of an alleged use of force, but rather, the Ukrainian claims are based on the impediments imposed by the Russian Federation on the passage of ships in the Kerch Strait and the Sea of Azov.[106] It was also the view of the Arbitral Tribunal in response to the Russian Federation's preliminary objections that "the fact that some of the Ukrainian vessels whose navigation was impeded belonged to Ukraine's navy does not cause the dispute to concern military activities."[107] However, this decision does not necessarily preclude the Arbitral Tribunal from reaching a different conclusion in *the Dispute Concerning the Detention of Ukrainian Naval Vessels and Servicemen*, the object of which is specifically the Kerch Strait incident of 25 November 2018.

With the Kerch Strait incident serving as a primary reference point, Chapter 5 of this part of the book focuses on the legal aspects of hybrid naval warfare from the perspective of *jus ad bellum*, *jus in bello*, law enforcement measures, and the laws of State responsibility.

4.8.2 *The Kerch Strait as a Belligerent Strait in 2022: Russia's Blockade of the Sea of Azov*

On 24 February 2022, the Russian Federation launched an invasion of Ukraine. The UN General Assembly adopted on 2 March 2022 the resolution "Aggression against Ukraine" (141 States voted in favor, 5 States against) condemning the Russian aggression in violation of article 2(4) of the Charter and demanding the full withdrawal of Russian forces from Ukraine.[108] Two days after the launch of the invasion, Ukraine instituted proceedings against the Russian Federation at the ICJ and requested the Court to "[a]djudge and declare that the 'special military operation' declared and carried out by the Russian Federation on and after 24 February 2022 is based on a false claim of genocide".[109] The ICJ stressed in its order of 16 March 2022 on Ukraine's request for the indication of provisional measures that:

> The Court is profoundly concerned about the use of force by the Russian Federation in Ukraine, which raises very serious issues of international

106 Ibid., paras. 250, 311.
107 Ibid., para 338.
108 General Assembly Resolution ES-11/1, adopted 2 March 2022.
109 Allegations of Genocide under the Convention on the Prevention and Punishment of the Crime of Genocide (Ukraine v. Russian Federation), Request for the indication of provisional measures, ICJ, Order of 16 March 2022, paras. 1–2.

> law. … It deems it necessary to emphasize that all States must act in conformity with their obligations under the United Nations Charter and other rules of international law, including international humanitarian law.[110]

The ICJ issued almost unanimously the following provisional measures:

> The Russian Federation shall immediately suspend the military operations that it commenced on 24 February 2022 in the territory of Ukraine; The Russian Federation shall ensure that any military or irregular armed units which may be directed or supported by it, as well as any organizations and persons which may be subject to its control or direction, take no steps in furtherance of the military operations…; Both Parties shall refrain from any action which might aggravate or extend the dispute before the Court or make it more difficult to resolve.[111]

However, the Russian Federation continued its invasion of Ukraine contrary to the ICJ's order. In two weeks after the launch of the invasion, approximately two and a half million Ukrainian refugees were forced to relocate mostly to European Union Member States.[112] At the same time, hundreds of thousands Ukrainian civilians did not have a possibility to evacuate from besieged cities of eastern Ukraine. According to media reports, the worst humanitarian situation was found in the port city of Mariupol that has a strategic location on the coast of the Sea of Azov separating the Russian-annexed Crimean Peninsula from the Russian-controlled breakaway regions of Donetsk and Luhansk.

Mariupol's population of over 400 000 was subject to constant shelling that caused a humanitarian crisis.[113] According to the International Committee of the Red Cross (hereafter ICRC) spokesperson, the situation in Mariupol in March 2022 was 'apocalyptic'.[114] Civilians of Mariupol were cut off from heat while suffering from freezing temperatures, and they were deprived from water, electricity, medical, and food supplies. In this context, this subchapter

110 Ibid, para 18.

111 Ibid, para 86.

112 The UN Refugee Agency, 'Refugees fleeing Ukraine (since 24 February 2022)', available: https://data2.unhcr.org/en/situations/ukraine; accessed 11 March 2022.

113 J Gunter, 'Mariupol under siege: 'We are being completely cut off'', *BBC News* (3 March 2022).

114 M Francis, 'Aid workers describe 'apocalyptic' scenes in Mariupol, a Ukrainian city under siege', *Yahoo News* (9 March 2022).

debates Russia's blockade of the Sea of Azov and the obligation to allow free passage of foodstuffs and other essential supplies to a blockaded port.

It is a matter of debate whether Russia's suspension of shipping in the Sea of Azov amounted to a blockade. Blockade is a legal concept which, according to Wolff Heintschel von Heinegg, has been unjustly deemed by some scholars to be obsolete.[115] During the negotiations of the San Remo Manual, there reportedly was an "extensive discussion on the issue of whether the practice of blockade was, on the one hand, entirely archaic or, on the other, remained a viable method of naval warfare".[116]

The Russian invasion of Ukraine showed that the laws of blockade are still relevant today. In the wake of its invasion of Ukraine, at 4am of 24 February 2022, the Russian Federation suspended commercial navigation in the Sea of Azov until further notice.[117] Under Article 2(3) of the 2003 Kerch Treaty, the access of neutral States' warships and other State vessels operated for non-commercial purposes to the Sea of Azov was closed during the war as it was dependent on Russia's and Ukraine's mutual prior permission. The Russian Federation also controlled the airspace above the Sea of Azov that, according to the 2003 Kerch Treaty, are the internal waters of the Russian Federation and Ukraine (Art 1(1)). Belligerents' government ships and warships, as well as merchant vessels flying their flag provided that they meet certain conditions,[118] serve as military objectives under the rules of naval warfare. Thus, they can be attacked by force.

In effect, it appears that since 24 February 2022 the Russian Federation implemented a blockade against the Ukrainian cities Berdyansk and Mariupol that are located on the coast of the Sea of Azov. Blockade is left undefined in positive law (see, e.g., Art 42 of the UN Charter, Art 3(c) of the General Assembly Resolution 3314 *Definition of Aggression*).[119] The Commander's Handbook on the Law of Naval Operations defines blockade as "a belligerent operation to prevent vessels and/or aircraft of all States, enemy as well as neutral, from entering or exiting specified ports, airfields, or coastal areas

115 W Heintschel von Heinegg, 'Naval Blockade' (2000) 75 *International Law Studies*, 213.

116 'Methods and means of warfare at sea', in L Doswald-Beck (ed.), *San Remo Manual on International Law Applicable to Armed Conflicts at Sea* (Cambridge University Press, Cambridge, 1995), 176.

117 Anonymous, 'Russia confirms suspension of movement of commercial vessels in the Azov sea – Interfax', *Reuters* (24 February 2022).

118 San Remo Manual, *op. cit.*, Rules 41, 59–60.

119 General Assembly Resolution 29/3314, adopted 14 December 1974, Annex 'Definition of Aggression'.

belonging to, occupied by, or under the control of an enemy State."[120] A blockade does not have to cover the whole coastline of a belligerent State and may cover just some part of it.[121]

A valid blockade must be declared and notified to all belligerents (Rule 93 of the San Remo Manual). It is unclear to what extent Russia's announcement of the suspension of commercial shipping in the Sea of Azov can be seen as a declaration of a blockade. Frostad comments that: "No specific form is needed for the notification of a blockade. What is important, however, is the effectiveness of the notification ... Traditionally, notification often took the form of diplomatic notes, but the issuing of Notices to Airmen or Notices to Mariners will suffice today."[122] The suspension of commercial navigation in the Sea of Azov was ordered by the Russian Ministry of Defence and announced by the Federal Agency for Maritime and River Transport.[123]

The Russian Federation did not *expressis verbis* announce a blockade of the Sea of Azov.[124] But, arguably, this formality is not decisive for the legal classification of Russia's announcement. During the negotiations of the San Remo Manual, it was held that the rules of naval blockade "were applicable to blockading actions taken by States regardless of the name given to such actions."[125]

One might even raise the question if the requirement that a State needs to declare a blockade for it to be legally binding still serves as a *conditio sine qua non* in the context of contemporary armed conflicts. The issuance of a declaration of war lost long ago its significance for the determination of the existence of an international armed conflict. If an aggressor State denies that it has waged a war against another State and brands its aggression as, e.g., "military

120 *The Commander's Handbook on the Law of Naval Operations* (US Navy, US Marine Corps, US Coast Guard, Norfolk, 2017), 7–10.

121 M Frostad, 'Naval Blockade' (2018) 9 *Arctic Review on Law and Politics*, 203.

122 Ibid, 202.

123 Anonymous, 'Rosmorrechflot confirms suspended navigation in Sea of Azov', *Interfax* (24 February 2022).

124 The question is even more complex in the general context of Russia's blockade of the Black Sea outside the Sea of Azov basin. There appear to be no announcements by which the Russian Federation had declared a general blockade of Ukraine's coast in the Black Sea. Yet as noted by, for example, the British Ministry of Defence, Russia as a matter of fact has established a distant blockade of Ukraine's whole Black Sea coast. Russia's declaration of 10 February 2022 of naval exercises in the Black Sea is likely the closest to a declaration of blockade of Ukraine's coast in the Black Sea, but it is certainly unclear if it amounts to an actual declaration of belligerent blockade in law. See Anonymous, 'Российские военные проведут учения с корабельными группами в Черном море', *Interfax* (10 February 2022).

125 Doswald-Beck, *op. cit.*, 177. See also Frostad, *op. cit.*, 200.

exercises" or a "special military operation", then such State will also likely deny the existence of naval warfare and intentionally avoids issuing a declaration of a naval blockade. Pursuant to the *bona fide* interpretation of the laws of war, such manipulations with the law by an aggressor State should not prevent the objective determination of the existence of a blockade in law. A so-called "unofficial blockade" does not serve the interests of the victim State, nor legal certainty in respect of the laws of naval warfare in general.

In the case of the Russian Federation's aggression against Ukraine, a clear declaration of blockade would have been somewhat incompatible with Russia's official position that it is not in a war with Ukraine and instead has launched a so-called "special military operation".[126] In this context, a strict interpretation of the requirements of declaration and notification for determining the existence of a naval blockade in law appears to favour the phenomenon of hybrid naval warfare. Instead, as the law has adapted to the reality of undeclared wars by determining the existence of an armed conflict based on the objective facts, the same approach should be adopted for determining the existence of a naval blockade. It would be useless to wait for the aggressor State to declare a blockade when it clearly has no intention to do so, but still harasses and attacks neutral international navigation in the relevant maritime area.

Pursuant to Rule 95 of the San Remo Manual a blockade must be effective and this is a question of fact. The blockade of the Sea of Azov was effective as the Russian Federation exerts complete control over the Kerch Strait. According to data received from ships' automatic identification system,[127] the access of commercial ships to the Sea of Azov was blocked in the Kerch Strait and a significant number of merchant ships remained anchored either in the Kerch Strait or at its approaches. In March and April 2022, the present author did not notice any crossings of the Sea of Azov by commercial ships based on the data received from ships' automatic identification system.[128]

According to Article 2 of the 1909 London Declaration[129] concerning the Laws of Naval War, the effectiveness of a blockade means that it must be maintained by a force sufficient to prevent access to the enemy coastline. The Russian Federation fulfilled that requirement in respect of the Ukrainian coastline since the start of the hostilities on 24 February 2022. Still, Martin Fink has

126 See 'Full text: Putin's declaration of war on Ukraine', *op. cit.*

127 Marine Traffic, 'Sea of Azov', available https://www.marinetraffic.com/en/ais/home/centerx:37.7/centery:45.7/zoom:8; accessed 11 March 2022, 1 April 2022, 21 April 2022, and 27 April 2022. Screenshots are on file with the author.

128 Ibid. The present manuscript was sent for production in the end of April 2022.

129 Declaration concerning the Laws of Naval War, London, adopted 26 February 1909.

concluded that: "[A]lthough different factors have effectively minimized maritime traffic into and from the Ukrainian ports in the Sea of Azov, Russia has not established a naval blockade in the Sea of Azov ... Apart from an unspecified announcement of suspension, nothing more indicates that Russia has established a blockade that might give Russian naval and air forces enforcement powers against merchant vessels."[130] In support of this argument, Fink refers to the press announcement of the Russian Federal Agency for Maritime and River Transport of 24 February 2022, according to which: "Navigation in the Kerch Strait can take place; it was not suspended; however, traffic is minimal there because vessels have nowhere to go after navigation in the Sea of Azov was temporary suspended."[131] Yet the announcement made it explicitly clear that the Russian Federation only permits the marginal cross-strait navigation between the Kerch Strait's two coasts on Crimea and the Russian mainland coast.[132] Thus, that announcement did not concern passage between the Sea of Azov and the Black Sea.

In addition, even if the Russian Federation allowed some commercial ships to leave – but not to enter – the Sea of Azov in the end of February 2022, as claimed by some reports,[133] then it did not have a real impact on the overall effectiveness of the blockade against the Ukrainian coast on the Sea of Azov that lasted for months. Moreover, it is a standard practice that upon the commencement of a blockade, the blockading force provides a period of grace for neutral ships to leave the blockaded area.[134]

Furthermore, in case the Russian Federation, hypothetically, allowed some ships to enter or leave its ports in the Sea of Azov and navigate through the Kerch Strait, then this does not render the blockade against Ukraine's coast on the Sea of Azov ineffective. It is doubtful that any ships from the Ukrainian ports of Berdyansk or Mariupol were allowed to leave the Sea of Azov as the war progressed, but even if such exceptional instances occurred, then it would not render the blockade ineffective. Article 7 of the 1909 London Declaration stipulates that: "In circumstances of distress, acknowledged by an officer of the blockading force, a neutral vessel may enter a place under blockade and

130 M Fink, 'Ukraine Symposium – The War at Sea: Is there a Naval Blockade in the Sea of Azov?', *Articles of War* of Lieber Institute, West Point (24 March 2022).

131 Anonymous, 'Navigation in Kerch Strait not suspended - Russian agency', *Interfax* (24 February 2022).

132 Ibid.

133 M Juliano, 'Bulkers Cluster Off Bosphorus And Kerch Straits Amid Russia-Ukraine Conflict', *TradeWinds* (1 March 2022). J Wallace, 'Ukraine / Russia - Port update', *Standard Club* (25 February 2022).

134 See Art 16 of the 1909 London Declaration. Heintschel von Heinegg 2000, *op. cit.*, 209.

subsequently leave it, provided that she has neither discharged nor shipped any cargo there." Furthermore, Frostad has commented that:

> In the San Remo Manual, reference is made to a reasonable risk of effectively preventing ingress and egress of the blockaded coastline, and the main issue is always whether there is a real risk of being captured, but not destroyed, if one seeks to break the blockade. As a consequence, the occasional breach of a blockade does not prove that the blockade is ineffective, although it may be hard to identify when the number of breaches is sufficient to lift the blockade.[135]

One should not avoid calling Russia's blockade of Ukraine's coast in the Sea of Azov by its name in fear of acknowledging the blockading party's rights under the laws of blockade to capture and, where necessary, ultimately attack ships that breach the blockade. When enforcing its blockade against Ukraine's coast, the Russian Navy reportedly launched numerous attacks against neutral merchant ships without issuing a prior warning, as examined below.

Therefore, pursuant to a *bona fide* interpretation of the law, Russia's practice in the Sea of Azov following its declaration of 24 February 2022 appears to meet the main requirements of naval blockade (declaration, notification, impartiality and effectiveness). Rule 100 of the San Remo Manual stipulates that a blockade must be applied impartially to the vessels of all States. At the same time, the Russian Federation as the blockading party was obliged to provide for free passage of foodstuffs and other essential supplies to the Mariupol Port, including 'medical supplies for the civilian population or for the wounded and sick members of armed forces', since sufficient help did not reach Mariupol via land (see San Remo Manual, Rules 103–104). This obligation has particular significance at a time when the fighting in Mariupol stopped humanitarian convoys to reach the city.[136] The humanitarian corridors leading to other areas of Russian-controlled parts of Ukraine were ineffective as they were targeted, even on the agreed day-long ceasefire on 9 March, by the Russian artillery and were full of land mines.[137]

---

135 Frostad, *op. cit.*, 206.

136 A Prentice, 'Aid convoy to Ukraine's Mariupol turns back due to fighting - deputy PM', *Reuters* (10 March 2022).

137 Anonymous, 'Ukraine: Safe passage for civilians from Mariupol halted for a second day; ICRC calls on parties to agree to specific terms', *ICRC* (6 March 2022). L Harding, J Borger,

It is also possible that the blockade in the whole maritime area of the Sea of Azov is in general unlawful under the laws of naval warfare. Ukraine maintains in the Dispute Concerning Coastal State Rights in the Black Sea, Sea of Azov, and Kerch Strait that the regime of transit passage applies to the Kerch Strait (see *supra* Chapter 4.3 of Part 2). If correct (this claim is disputed by the Russian Federation, see *supra* Chapters 4.5–4.7 of Part 2), then according to Rule 27 of the San Remo Manual the regime of transit passage continued to apply during the war and the Russian Federation was required to ensure safe passage through the Kerch Strait to neutral ships and aircraft not heading to the blockaded area.[138] This follows from the ICJ's judgment in the *Corfu Channel case* as well as from the San Remo Manual (Rules 27–28).[139] In this case, Russia's suspension of all commercial navigation in the Sea of Azov from 24 February 2022 was not lawful. Notably, the Annex VII Arbitral Tribunal is yet to decide whether it respects Ukraine's above-referred request to establish that the Sea of Azov and the Kerch Strait include Ukraine's normal maritime zones, which would imply that the regime of transit passage applies to the Kerch Strait (Art 37 of LOSC).

Irrespective of the outcome of Ukraine's request to the Arbitral Tribunal, the Russian Federation was required to respect the right of the civilians and armed forces in Mariupol to receive foodstuffs and other essential supplies, including medical supplies, via a sea route. After its extraordinary session on 10–11 March 2022, the IMO Council 'underscored the need to preserve the security of international shipping and the maritime community, and the supply chains that sustain other nations, as well as supply chains providing necessary food and medicines to the people of Ukraine' and 'encourage[d] the establishment, as a provisional and urgent measure, of a blue safe maritime corridor to allow the safe evacuation of seafarers and ships from the high-risk and affected areas in the Black Sea and the Sea of Azov to a safe place in order to protect the life of seafarers, ensure the mobilization and commercial navigation of vessels intending to use this corridor by avoiding military attacks and protecting and securing the maritime domain.'[140] The ICRC and neutral States could have facilitated the deployment of such relief shipments for the Mariupol Port. Such a mission could have been launched also from the Mediterranean as ships carrying humanitarian

J Henley, 'Russian bombing of maternity hospital 'genocide', says Zelenskiy', *The Guardian* (9 March 2022).

138 Heintschel von Heinegg 1998, *op. cit.*, 265–266. Frostad, *op. cit.*, 203.

139 The Corfu Channel Case, *op. cit.*, 29.

140 Decisions of the International Maritime Organization (IMO) Council, Extraordinary session 10–11 March 2022, C/ES.35, para 8, 'Blue Safe Maritime Corridor'.

aid to Mariupol were allowed to pass through the Turkish Straits which were closed under the Montreux Convention only to belligerent warships (see *infra* Chapter 4.8.3 of Part 2).

While the humanitarian corridors around the besieged coastal city of Mariupol proved ineffective, establishing one on the sea would have potentially enabled to provide humanitarian relief to its civilian population and members of the Ukrainian armed forces. Yet this would have caused direct risks to ships carrying humanitarian aid. To minimize the risks to neutral ships carrying humanitarian relief to the Port of Mariupol, it would have been possible to first seek guarantees from the Russian Federation that it grants protection to ships carrying humanitarian cargo to the Port of Mariupol. The importance of seeking such an assurance is underlined by the fact that, in February and March 2022, numerous attacks targeted neutral merchant ships in the western part of the Black Sea. According to media reports, on 1 March 2022, the Russian Navy seized in the Odesa Port a Panama-flagged 80-metres long cargo ship *Helt* that was owned by an Estonian company.[141] The Russian Navy reportedly forced the ship to enter a dangerous zone off Odesa Port and used it as a sort of human shield to cover the movement of its warships off Odesa.[142] *Helt* sunk on 3 March 2022 after an explosion had caused damage below the ship's water-line, approximately 16 NM off Odesa Port, while its six members of the crew were rescued.[143]

There were no grounds to assume that *Helt* had made an effective contribution to Ukraine's military action in terms of Rule 67 of the San Remo Manual and as a consequence of which it could have lost its status as a neutral merchant ship giving rise to the Russian Navy's right to attack and seize it on 1 March 2022 and deploy it for advancing its military objectives off Odesa. After seizing the neutral ship against the laws of neutrality and prize, the Russian Navy used *Helt* in a manner that stripped it from its status as a neutral merchant ship, since it made an effective contribution to the Russian Navy's military action by way

141 Anonymous, 'Estonian-owned cargo ship sinks off Odesa after Russian action', ERR *News* (3 March 2022). K Kivil, 'Odessa lähedal läks põhja Eesti firmale kuuluv kaubalaev', ERR *Uudised* (3 March 2022).

142 M Santora, 'What Happened on Day 6 of Russia's Invasion of Ukraine', *The New York Times* (2 March 2022). M Starr, 'Russian navy using civilian ships as human shields, Ukraine claims', *The Jerusalem Post* (3 March 2022).

143 J Saul, 'Cargo ship sinks off Odessa after explosion, crew members missing -ship manager', *Reuters* (3 March 2022). ERR *News, op. cit.*, 3 March 2022. Anonymous, 'Ukraine: Estonian cargo ship sinks after blast in Black Sea', BBC *News* (4 March 2022).

of offering cover to the Russian warships that were expected to launch their amphibious landing operation in Odesa.[144]

In addition, during the first days of the Russian invasion of Ukraine, many other neutral merchant ships sailing in the Black Sea were targeted by missile strikes. The first such attack occurred in the evening of 23 February 2022, i.e. a day before Russia's declaration of its invasion of Ukraine.[145] An explosion occurred on-board a Turkish-owned bulk carrier *Yasa Jupiter* sailing under the flag of the Marshall Islands as it was *en route* to Romanian maritime area off Odesa.[146] On 25 February 2022, a Moldova-flagged, but Ukrainian-owned chemical tanker *Millenial Spirit* was shelled off Odesa allegedly by Russian forces and the crew had to abandon the ship equipped only with life jackets.[147] On the same day, a Panama-flagged merchant ship was shelled at Odesa Port.[148] On 2 March 2022, a missile hit a Bangladeshi-flagged bulker ship *Banglar Samriddhi* at Olvia Port in Ukraine leaving one member of the crew dead.[149] According to the above-referred media reports, Ukraine claims that the Russian Federation is responsible for these attacks.[150] The Council of the IMO issued a statement on the situation in the Black Sea and Sea of Azov, according to which it, *inter alia*, 'deplored the attacks of the Russian Federation aimed at commercial vessels, their seizures, including Search-and-Rescue vessels, threatening the safety and welfare of seafarers and the marine environment'.[151]

The ships that were attacked were flying the flags of Bangladesh, the Marshall Islands, Moldova, and Panama. Whatever the ownership of a commercial ship that is attacked, the right of self-defence rests on the flag of the State with whom the attacks on the commercial ships can be equated.[152] None of those States invoked their right of self-defence under Article 51 of the UN Charter in response to the unlawful use of force that Ukraine alleges was carried out by

144 San Remo Manual, *op. cit.*, Rule 67.

145 Anonymous, 'Full text: Putin's declaration of war on Ukraine', The Spectator (24 February 2022).

146 D Bush, 'Turkish bulker hit by bomb off Odessa', *Lloyd's List* (24 February 2022).

147 J Payne, 'Ukraine says two commercial ships hit by Russian missiles near Odessa port', *Reuters* (26 February 2022).

148 Ibid.

149 Anonymous, 'Bangladeshi Ship Hit in Attack Near Mykolaiv, Killing One Engineer', *The Maritime Executive* (2 March 2022).

150 Ibid. Payne, *op. cit.*

151 IMO Council decisions of 10–11 March 2022,*op. cit.*, para 5.

152 Oil Platforms (Islamic Republic of Iran v. United States of America), Judgment, ICJ Reports 2003, p. 161, para 64.

the Russian Federation. Had Russian forces, hypothetically, launched attacks against neutral merchant ships carrying humanitarian relief to the Port of Mariupol, then the risk would have existed of a different response.

In the *Oil Platforms Case*, the ICJ did not clearly decide on whether the use of force against a single commercial ship can amount to an armed attack under Article 51 of the UN Charter on the flag State. The ICRC has also left the question somewhat open in relation to whether an armed conflict would come into existence.[153] Under Article 3(d) of the General Assembly Resolution 3314 *Definition of Aggression*, an act of aggression includes "[a]n attack by the armed forces of a State on the land, sea or air forces, or marine and air fleets of another State". How many attacks on a single flag State would suffice, however, is difficult to determine. Yet the ICJ has found that cases of low-intensity use of force against ships can amount to an armed attack when assessed cumulatively.[154]

The United States claimed in the *Oil Platforms Case* that Iran's attack in 1987 against its commercial ship during the Iran-Iraq war amounted to an armed attack,[155] but the ICJ disregarded the United States' claim based on the lack of evidence of Iran's responsibility and the conclusion that the missile was not specifically aimed at that particular commercial ship, "but simply programmed to hit some target in Kuwaiti waters."[156]

Distinct from the episodes of attacks against the commercial ships flying either Israeli or Irani flag in the recent Israel-Iran 'shadow war' (see *infra* Chapter 6 of Part 2), the attacks against neutral ships in the Black Sea in 2022 did not target systemically any particular State. Furthermore, it is unclear if there is sufficient evidence of Russia's direct involvement in these attacks and it is equally possible that these attacks were indiscriminate as the missiles were simply aimed to hit some target in the relevant area.[157] The clear exception to this is the attack against the Panama-flagged *Helt* as it was specifically selected for boarding by Russian soldiers and its crew was reportedly forced to follow the orders from the Russian Navy in its naval operations off Odesa.

153 ICRC 2016 commentary, *op. cit.*, on Common Article 2, para 227. ICRC, *Commentary on the Second Geneva Convention: Convention (II) for the Amelioration of the Condition of Wounded, Sick and Shipwrecked Members of Armed Forces at Sea*, 2nd edition, 2017, para 249.

154 *Oil Platforms Case*, Judgment, *op. cit.*, para 64.

155 ICJ, *Oil Platforms Case*, Counter-Memorial and Counter-Claim Submitted by the United States of America, 23 June 1997, para 4.10. ICJ, *Oil Platforms Case*, Rejoinder Submitted by the United States of America, 23 March 2001, para 5.22.

156 *Oil Platforms Case*, Judgment, *op. cit.*, para 64.

157 Ibid.

If the humanitarian corridor via the Sea of Azov had been created for Mariupol and the Russian forces, hypothetically, had violated the rules of naval warfare and systemically attacked neutral ships carrying humanitarian relief to the Port of Mariupol, there would likely have been increased public pressure for neutral States to intervene militarily in the conflict. This risk could have been mitigated by seeking assurances from the Russian Federation that its forces respect the right to deploy humanitarian relief to the civilians and members of the Ukrainian armed forces in Mariupol in accordance with the rules of blockade to the extent that these rules are applicable in the Sea of Azov.

4.8.3 *The Closure of the Turkish Straits to Warships during the Ukraine War*

In the context of belligerent hostilities in and around the Black Sea during the Russian invasion of Ukraine in 2022, Turkey closed the Istanbul Strait (Bosporus) and the Çanakkale Strait (Dardanelles) to warships. This calls for an examination of the legal basis of the Turkish decision from the perspective of the law of the sea.

Passage through the Turkish Straits is regulated under the 1936 Montreux Convention.[158] In addition to the Danish Straits, Åland Strait, and the Strait of Magellan, the Istanbul Strait (Bosporus) and the Çanakkale Strait (Dardanelles) are generally recognised as falling under Article 35(c) of the LOSC.[159] Article 35(c) stipulates that nothing in Part III of the LOSC on straits used for international navigation affects the legal regime in straits in which passage is regulated in whole or in part by long-standing international conventions in force specifically relating to such straits.

The Montreux Convention grants extensive rights for the passage of warships through the Turkish Straits to the coastal States of the Black Sea. The passage of warships from other States not littoral of the Black Sea through the Turkish Straits and their stay in the Black Sea is limited by the number of ships (up to 9 warships at a time), the temporal scope of their stay in the Black Sea (up to 21 days) and their tonnage (aggregate tonnage of up to 45 000 tons).[160]

158 Convention regarding the Régime of the Straits, adopted 20 July 1936, entered into force 9 November 1936, 173 LNTS 213. See further on the Montreux Convention, in E Brüel, *International Straits. A Treatise on International Law, vol. II. Straits Comprised by Positive Regulations* (Sweet & Maxwell, London, 1947), 380–424.

159 N Ünlü, *The Legal Regime of the Turkish Straits* (Martinus Nijhoff, Dordrecht, 2002), 54. Caminos, Cogliati-Bantz, *op. cit*, 77. LM Alexander, 'International Straits', in HB Robertson, Jr. (ed), *The Law of Naval Operations* (Naval War College Press, Newport, 1991), 101.

160 See Arts 14(2), 18(1)(b), 18(2) of the Montreux Convention.

In addition, States are required to give a prior notification to Turkey for their warships to enter the Turkish Straits. According to Article 15 of the Montreux Convention, the normal period of notice is eight days, while 'it is desirable that in the case of non-Black Sea Powers this period should be increased to fifteen days.'

In addition, under Article 11 in combination with Annex II to the Montreux Convention, the passage of aircraft carriers through the Turkish Straits is prohibited. This applies irrespective of whether the aircraft carrier flies the flag of the Black Sea coastal State or not. Hence, when France's aircraft carrier *Charles De Gaulle* was tasked to patrol the airspace above and around the Black Sea during the Russian invasion of Ukraine in 2022, it carried out its operations from the Mediterranean.[161]

Thus, the Montreux Convention in general grants special rights of passage through the Turkish Straits to the warships of the Black Sea coastal States. Nonetheless, their passage is prohibited if they are belligerents in a war in respect of which Turkey acts as a neutral State (Art 19 of the Montreux Convention). According to Article 19 of the Montreux Convention, the exceptions to this rule include 'cases of assistance rendered to a State victim of aggression in virtue of a treaty of mutual assistance binding Turkey' and warships of belligerent States that have become separated from their bases and that may return to their base.

The Russian Federation and Ukraine are in a prolonged international armed conflict. In essence, since February 2014, the Russian Federation has been the aggressor State in a war with Ukraine, the main elements of which are the occupation and annexation of Crimea and the ongoing hostilities in Donbas that erupted in 2014, the Kerch Strait incident in 2018, and the Russian full-scale invasion of Ukraine in 2022. In the wake of the escalation of the armed conflict on 24 February 2022, Ukraine requested Turkey to close the Turkish Straits to Russian warships.[162]

On 27 February 2022, Turkey announced that it deems that Ukraine and the Russian Federation are at 'war', thus triggering the application of Article 19 of the Montreux Convention and prohibiting the passage of Russian warships to the Black Sea.[163] This assessment of the nature of the Russian invasion

161 P Suciu, 'French Flagship to Support NATO Mission as Tensions Rise in Europe', *The National Interest* (2 March 2022).

162 R Michaelson, 'Kyiv piles pressure on Ankara to close straits to Russia's warships', *The Guardian* (26 February 2022).

163 E Erkoyun, T Gumrukcu, 'Turkey to implement pact limiting Russian warships to Black Sea', *Reuters* (27 February 2022).

of Ukraine was contrary to the claims of the Russian Federation according to which it launched a 'special military operation' against Ukraine that did not reach the threshold of a 'war'.[164] In accordance with Article 15 of the Montreux Convention, the Russian Federation had notified Turkey in advance that it intends to send on 27 and 28 February 2022 four warships to the Black Sea, of which only one was registered to Russia's Black Sea base, but following Turkey's decision, the Russian Federation cancelled their planned transit through the Turkish Straits.[165]

The Turkish Foreign Minister referred to Article 19 of the Montreux Convention when explaining the decision to close the Turkish Straits and commented that:

> When Turkey is not a belligerent in the conflict, it has the authority to restrict the passage of the warring states' warships across the straits. If the warship is returning to its base in the Black Sea, the passage is not closed. We adhere to the Montreux rules. All governments, riparian and non-riparian, were warned not to send warships across the straits.[166]

However, as stressed by many commentators,[167] Article 19 of the Montreux Convention prohibits the passage of belligerent warships and does not grant Turkey the authority to close the Turkish Straits to the warships of neutral States. Such a right is vested with Turkey under Article 21 of the Montreux Convention provided that Turkey as a neutral State considers herself being threatened with imminent danger of war in case of which the right of passage of warships through the Turkish Straits is left entirely to the discretion of the Turkish Government.

Turkey has not indicated that it considers herself threatened with imminent danger of war in the context of the 2022 Russian invasion of Ukraine. Hence, Turkey's decision of 27 February 2022 may be interpreted as resulting in the closure of the Turkish Straits to the warships of the Russian Federation and Ukraine in accordance with Article 19 of the Montreux Convention, while

164 See 'Full text: Putin's declaration of war on Ukraine', *op. cit.*

165 E Erkoyun, T Gumrukcu, 'Turkey says Russia cancelled Black Sea passage bid upon its request', *Reuters* (2 March 2022).

166 T Ozberk, 'Turkey Closes The Dardanelles And Bosphorus To Warships', *Naval News* (28 February 2022). See also Anonymous, 'Turkey warns against passing of warships from its straits', *Al Jazeera* (1 March 2022).

167 See, e.g., Ozberk, *op. cit.* C Overfield, 'Turkey Must Close the Turkish Straits Only to Russian and Ukrainian Warships', *Lawfare* (5 March 2022).

other (non-warring) States were issued a legally non-binding warning of dangers to navigation in the Black Sea due to the outbreak of hostilities in the region. Alternatively, it has been suggested that Turkey could invoke Article 21 of the Montreux Convention by claiming that it is threatened with imminent danger of war given its collective self-defense obligations under Article 5 of the Northern Atlantic Treaty[168] in the context of the danger of escalation of the Russia-Ukraine war and its impact on the territories (including the cyber domain) of NATO Member States, especially the ones bordering Ukraine.[169]

4.8.4 *The Closure of Ports to Russian Ships*

While Turkey closed its straits to Russian warships due to the war in Ukraine, other NATO Member States – all being neutral States in the Russia-Ukraine armed conflict – responded to Russia's aggression against Ukraine in 2022 by, *inter alia*, closing their ports to Russian ships. The United Kingdom decided to prohibit Russian owned, operated, controlled, chartered, registered or flagged ships from entering its ports.[170] On the same day that the United Kingdom's ban came into force, the Canadian Government announced that it 'intends to ban Russian-owned or registered ships and fishing vessels in Canadian ports and internal waters' under the Special Economic Measures (Russia) Regulations.[171] Section 3.4 was added to these Regulations which now stipulates that: "It is prohibited for any person to dock in Canada or pass through Canada any ship that is registered in Russia or used, leased or chartered, in whole or in part, by or on behalf of or for the benefit of Russia, a person in Russia or a designated person, unless such docking or passage is necessary to safeguard human life or to ensure navigational safety."[172] Likewise, in the beginning of the Russian invasion of Ukraine, the European Parliament called 'for access to all EU ports to be refused for ships whose last or next port of call is in the Russian Federation,

168 The North Atlantic Treaty, adopted 4 April 1949, entered into force 24 August 1949, 34 UNTS 243.

169 A Aliano, R Spivak, 'Ukraine Symposium – The Montreux Convention and Turkey's Impact on Black Sea Operations', *Articles of War* of Lieber Institute, West Point (25 April 2022).

170 The Russia (Sanctions) (EU Exit) (Amendment) (No. 4) Regulations 2022, Part III, adopted 1 March 2022, entered into force 1 March 2022.

171 Government of Canada, 'Government of Canada prohibits Russian ships and fishing vessels from entering Canadian ports and internal waters', *Press Release* (1 March 2022). Special Economic Measures (Russia) Regulations, SOR/2014-58, adopted 17 March 2014, last amended 6 March 2022.

172 Regulations Amending the Special Economic Measures (Russia) Regulations, adopted 6 March 2022, entered into force 6 March 2022.

except in the case of necessary justified humanitarian reasons'.[173] In April 2022, the Council of the EU decided to prohibit to provide access to ports in the territory of the EU to any vessel registered under the flag of Russia and extended the scope of this prohibition so that it also applied to vessels that changed their Russian flag or their registration, to the flag or register of any other State after 24 February 2022.[174]

Under international law, coastal States have a considerable discretionary right to regulate foreign ships' access to ports. A general right for foreign ships to enter ports is absent from LOSC as it merely stipulates in Article 255 an obligation of means according to which States shall endeavour to facilitate, subject to the provisions of their laws and regulations, only research vessels' access to their harbours. Thus, States have retained their freedom to close ports, subject to the conditions of proportionality and prohibition of discrimination. Nevertheless, in order to foster maritime commerce, many States have either unilaterally in their domestic acts or under bilateral and multilateral treaties stipulated the right of foreign ships to enter their ports on the basis of reciprocity.[175]

International case law on foreign ships' right to enter ports is inconsistent. In the *Aramco case*, the arbitral tribunal recognised such a right and found that ports may be closed to foreign ships only if the vital interests of the coastal State so require.[176] Yet this conclusion has triggered opposing views from eminent scholars.[177] Churchill and Lowe have commented that although it is generally right to assume that international ports are open to foreign merchant ships, it is nevertheless highly doubtful that such a practice has acquired the status of a right in customary law.[178] State practice was at the time of the arbitral award in the *Aramco case* controversial as most ports in numerous States, e.g. the Soviet Union, were not open to foreign ships.[179]

173 European Parliament resolution (2022/2564(RSP)), of 1 March 2022, On the Russian aggression against Ukraine, para 17.

174 Council Decision (CFSP) 2022/578 of 8 April 2022 amending Decision 2014/512/CFSP concerning restrictive measures in view of Russia's actions destabilising the situation in Ukraine, Art 1, para 18.

175 See, e.g., Convention and Statute on the International Régime of Maritime Ports, adopted 9 December 1923, entered into force 26 July 1926, 58 LNTS 285.

176 Saudi Arabia v. Arabian American Oil Co. (Aramco), Arbitration Tribunal (1958), 27 International Law Reports 117 (1963), p. 212.

177 See L Sohn, JE Noyes, E Franckx, K Juras, (eds) *Cases and Materials on the Law of the Sea* (Brill, Leiden, Boston, 2014), 353–354.

178 RR Churchill, AV Lowe, *The Law of the Sea* (Manchester University Press, Manchester, 1992), 52.

179 A Uustal, *Rahvusvaheline õigus V: rahvusvaheline mere- ja ilmaruumiõigus* (Tartu State University Press, Tartu, 1977), 43.

At the time of the *Aramco case*, uniform State practice that could confirm the existence of a customary right to the openness of ports was thus lacking. Similarly, the ICJ has concluded with regard to the contemporary State practice that it is "*by virtue of its sovereignty that the coastal State may regulate access to its ports*".[180] On the basis of international treaties and State practice, Molenaar has found that a general right for foreign ships to enter ports does not exist.[181] The coastal State thus has a wide discretion in deciding over whether to close its ports.[182]

Indeed, in the Russian Federation, for example, foreign ships may only call in such seaports that are opened for calls by foreign ships.[183] Furthermore, ports may be closed to foreign ships on grounds of, *inter alia*, maintaining public order. For example, in 2018, the Estonian Ministry of Foreign Affairs did not grant on three occasions its permission to Russian government-operated ships to stay in the Estonian territorial sea.[184] The Estonian Foreign Intelligence Service has cautioned against the activities of the Russian Federation's government-operated and civilian ships in the territorial sea, internal waters and ports of Estonia by claiming that all ships sailing under the Russian flag can be used to gather information, to pursue military objectives, or to carry out covert operations, and therefore it should be better examined under which conditions the Russian Federation's non-governmentally operated ships are allowed to enter the territorial sea and stay in foreign ports.[185] The Estonian Foreign Intelligence Service has listed the following controversial activities of the Russian-flagged non-governmentally operated ships: attempts to enter the naval training areas of other countries or to access areas closed to ship traffic (testing areas for new military technology, surroundings of naval bases, etc) and areas that are not normally used for navigation but pose an interest for strategic reasons.[186]

180 *Military and Paramilitary Activities in and against Nicaragua, op. cit.*, para 213.

181 Molenaar 1998, *op. cit.*, 101.

182 Churchill and Lowe 1992, *op. cit.*, 52.

183 See Arts 5(2) and 6 of the Federal Act on the internal maritime waters, territorial sea and contiguous zone of the Russian Federation, adopted 16 July 1998, entered into force 31 July 1998.

184 S Punamäe, 'Eestisse mittelastud purjelaev pani Vene meedia kihama', *Postimees* (11 April 2019).

185 Estonian Foreign Intelligence Service, *International Security and Estonia 2019* (Tallinn, 2019), 14.

186 Ibid, 12.

In 2019, Estonia did not allow the Russian Federation's four-masted barque and the world's biggest sailing ship STS *Sedov*, which was *en route* to the Port of Tallinn to enter the Estonian territorial sea, since her crew included cadets from the Kerch State Maritime Technological School which was seen as problematic from the perspective of the Estonian non-recognition policy towards the annexation of Crimea by the Russian Federation.[187] The Russian Ministry of Foreign Affairs and media reacted strongly to this decision.[188] Poland refused STS *Sedov*'s entry to its port two days later on the same ground.[189]

187 A Whyte, 'Estonia bars Russian vessel entering waters, on Crimea annexation issue', *ERR News* (12 April 2019).

188 See, e.g., Anonymous, 'Estonia, Poland deny entry to Russian ship over Crimea cadets', *RTL Today* (12 April 2019).

189 Anonymous, 'Ka Poola keelas Vene purjelaeval oma vetesse sisenemise', *Postimees* (12 April 2019).

CHAPTER 5

Use of Force against Sovereign Immune Vessels

Law Enforcement v. Humanitarian Law Paradigm

In the previously discussed Kerch Strait incident of 2018, the Russian Federation arguably made use of legal uncertainty by operating in a grey zone for complicating decision-making for other States. It seized three Ukrainian naval ships, including two warships, and arrested their crew as they were entering the Kerch Strait under freedom of navigation. In the context of the annexation of Crimea and armed conflict in Donbas region, this incident has raised the question of whether Russia's actions in the Kerch Strait should be considered as being undertaken in the legal framework of international humanitarian law.[1] The annexation of Crimea has been referred to as an international armed conflict not only in the relevant literature, but also by, for example, the Office of the Prosecutor of the International Criminal Court,[2] which has also pointed to the possibility that there apparently was a "direct military engagement between the respective armed forces of the Russian Federation and Ukraine, suggesting the existence of an international armed conflict in the Donbas region from 14 July 2014 at the latest, in parallel to the non-international armed conflict."[3]

If the Annex VII Arbitral Tribunal delivers its ruling based on a peacetime legal framework, then it will provide guidance for assessing the legality of similar hybrid naval conflicts also in the future. Conversely, should the Arbitral Tribunal find that the legality of the Russian Federation's actions against the Ukrainian warships need to be assessed from the perspective of international humanitarian law, then it sends an equally significant signal for any State that intends to adopt similar measures against its adversary in the future.

1 See Kraska 2018, *op. cit.*

2 The Office of the Prosecutor, *Report on Preliminary Examination Activities 2016* (International Criminal Court 2016), para 158. The Office of the Prosecutor, *Report on Preliminary Examination Activities 2017* (International Criminal Court 2017), para 88.

3 Report on Preliminary Examination Activities 2017, *op. cit.*, para 94.

5.1 In dubio pro jus in bello?

In the context of the laws of peace and war, hybrid naval conflicts are by their nature borderline cases. The Kerch Strait incident is not the first and will not remain the last of its kind. From that perspective, one may wonder if there is a need for developing a simplifying principle for addressing such borderline cases. For example, if after a proper consideration of the merits of the case one is in doubt over the nature of an inter-State conflict, should we categorize it first and foremost as an armed conflict rather than a peacetime incident? In other words – *in dubio pro jus in bello*. The development of a guideline of such sort would be reasonable if it contributes to decreasing the current uncertainty as to the legal classification of hybrid naval conflicts.

Such principle might also serve as a deterrence against those States that seek to employ means of hybrid naval warfare. After all, currently their practices are, to a significant extent, based on exploiting the ambiguous thresholds of naval warfare. If an aggressor State acknowledges from the outset of its planned grey zone operations that the measures it seeks to adopt amount to an armed attack and will trigger an armed conflict for which it has to bear international responsibility, then it might potentially decrease its willingness to actually launch such operations. Such understanding would also contribute to balancing the position of a State that falls victim of a hybrid naval offensive as it would be arguably in a more solid legal standing for invoking the right of self-defence under Article 51 of the UN Charter for countering the hybrid naval attack. For example, in this context, the Russian Federation's measures against the Ukrainian warships in the Kerch Strait incident of 2018 can potentially be categorized as an armed attack.[4]

Nonetheless, it is unclear how such principle which relies inevitably to some extent on the subjective assessment of the targeted State would reconcile with the case law of international courts and tribunals. This is discussed below (*infra* Chapter 5.3 of Part 2) with a focus on the ICJ's *Oil Platforms* judgment and the Annex VII Arbitral Tribunal's *Guyana v. Suriname* award. First, the significance of the *Oil Platforms* judgment for the contemporary naval conflicts is discussed in the context of the threshold of an armed attack under Article 51 of the UN Charter.

4 This potential categorisation is supported by the general ramifications of the Kerch Strait incident in the context of the annexation of Crimea and the Russian Federation's involvement in the conflict in the Donbas region.

5.2 Threshold of an Armed Attack in a Hybrid Naval Conflict

For unriddling the legal quagmire pertaining to grey zone conflicts, hybrid naval warfare needs to be legally assessed through the lens of an armed attack and the accompanying right of self-defence. Chapter 6 of Part 2 and Chapter 8.1 of Part 3 elaborate on the mine attacks that were carried out in 2019 against commercial ships sailing through the Strait of Hormuz as well as the attacks against ships sailing through the Bab el-Mandeb in the on-going Yemeni armed conflict. Chapter 4.8 of Part 2 examines the missile attacks against neutral merchant ships in the Black Sea in the context of the Russian invasion of Ukraine in 2022. The above-mentioned incidents bear resemblance to mine attacks against international vessel traffic in the Persian Gulf during the Iran-Iraq armed conflict (1980–1988). In this context, the Yemeni and Ukraine-Russia armed conflicts resemble the Iran-Iraq armed conflict since in both cases ships of neutral States were targeted by parties engaged in hostilities.

The mine attacks that occurred near the Strait of Hormuz against neutral ships in 1987 and 1988 were at the centre of the ICJ's proceedings in the *Oil Platforms Case*. In its judgment, the ICJ addressed the question of the threshold of an armed attack under Article 51 of the UN Charter in the context of what one may characterize in modern terminology as a hybrid naval warfare. Hence, that judgment serves as one of the primary sources for the subsequent legal assessment of the implications of modern hybrid naval warfare to international security law and State responsibility.

In the 2003 *Oil Platforms Case*, the United States claimed that Iran attacked its vessels and lay mines in the Persian Gulf, thereby hampering international navigation.[5] In particular, the United States alleged that Iran was responsible for a missile attack in 1987 against the United States-flagged tanker *Sea Isle City*, mining of two tankers (the United States-flagged *Bridgeton* and Panamanian-flagged *Texaco Caribbean* in 1987), mining of the USS *Samuel Roberts* in 1988 and firing on United States Navy helicopters from gunboats and the Reshadat oil platform, while Iran denied responsibility for these acts.[6] The United States, claiming the right of self-defence under Article 51 of the UN Charter, responded to these incidents by destroying first the Iranian Reshadat and Resalat oil platforms as well as later the Salman and Nasr platforms after it had issued a prior warning for allowing the evacuation of the platforms.[7]

5 *Oil Platforms Case*, Judgment, *op. cit.*, paras. 19, 120.
6 Ibid., paras. 50, 63, 69, 70.
7 Ibid., paras. 48–49, 64–66.

The ICJ's judgment in the *Oil Platforms Case* bears great significance for the legal regime governing contemporary hybrid naval warfare, particularly to the extent where the Court found that:

> On the hypothesis that all the incidents complained of are to be attributed to Iran, and thus setting aside the question, examined above, of attribution to Iran of the specific attack on the Sea Isle City, the question is whether that attack, either in itself or in combination with the rest of the "series of … attacks" cited by the United States can be categorized as an "armed attack" on the United States justifying self-defence. The Court notes first that the Sea Isle City was in Kuwaiti waters at the time of the attack on it, and that a Silkworm missile fired from (it is alleged) more than 100 km away could not have been aimed at the specific vessel, but simply programmed to hit some target in Kuwaiti waters. Secondly, the Texaco Caribbean, whatever its ownership, was not flying a United States flag, so that an attack on the vessel is not in itself to be equated with an attack on that State. As regards the alleged firing on United States helicopters from Iranian gunboats and from the Reshadat oil platform, no persuasive evidence has been supplied to support this allegation. There is no evidence that the minelaying alleged to have been carried out by the Iran Air, at a time when Iran was at war with Iraq, was aimed specifically at the United States; and similarly it has not been established that the mine struck by the Bridgeton was laid with the specific intention of harming that ship, or other United States vessels. Even taken cumulatively, and reserving, as already noted, the question of Iranian responsibility, these incidents do not seem to the Court to constitute an armed attack on the United States, of the kind that the Court, in the case concerning Military and Paramilitary Activities in and against Nicaragua, qualified as a "most grave" form of the use of force.[8]

This part of the Court's reasoning in the *Oil Platforms Case* highlights the underlying legal premises because of which hybrid warfare has gained increasing momentum in international affairs. It demonstrates that the root causes that enable States to effectively employ methods of hybrid warfare lie in the laws defining State responsibility and an armed attack.

The United States Department of State legal adviser William Taft has reflected upon the ICJ's judgment in the *Oil Platforms Case* and found that,

8 Ibid., para 64.

there is language in the opinion that might be read to suggest:

- that an attack involving the use of deadly force by a State's regular armed forces on civilian or military targets is not an "armed attack" triggering the right of self-defense unless the attack reaches some unspecified level of gravity;
- that an attack must have been carried out with the intention of harming a specific State before that State can respond in self-defense;
- that self-defense may be directed only against targets of the attacking State that have been the subject of specific prior complaints by the defending State; and
- that measures taken in self-defense must be proportional to the particular attack immediately preceding the defensive measures rather than proportional to the overall threat being addressed.[9]

Taft came to the conclusion that if this interpretation of the judgment corresponds to the ICJ's real intentions, then it would "undermine the ability of States to deter aggression and would therefore have the unfortunate effect of encouraging, rather than discouraging, the use of force."[10] Indeed, recent State practice shows that low-intensity armed conflicts between the armed forces of States have gained an increased momentum, e.g., the annexation of Crimea in 2014 or the alleged hybrid naval warfare between Iran and Israel in the waters around the Arabian Peninsula.

When occupying the Crimean Peninsula, the Russian Federation was cautious in avoiding any intensive fighting with the Ukrainian forces stationed in Crimea. Moreover, as in the conflict in the Donbas region, the Russian Federation ordered its troops in Crimea to remove their fixed distinctive emblems in order to conceal the direct control over its troops.[11] Only months later the Russian Federation admitted that Crimea was annexed by the Russian Federation's forces,[12] but has still denied any direct control over the armed

9 WH IV Taft, 'Self-Defense and the Oil Platforms Decision' (2004) 29(2) *Yale Journal of International Law*, 299.

10 Ibid. Such disappointment on the judgment is shared by other scholars, see, e.g., A Garwood-Gowers, 'Case concerning Oil Platforms (Islamic Republic of Iran v. United States of America) - Did the ICJ Miss the Boat on the Law on the Use of Force' (2004) 5(1) *Melbourne Journal of International Law*, 254–255.

11 See E MacAskill, 'Russian troops removing ID markings 'gross violation'', *The Guardian* (6 March 2014).

12 A Anischchuk, 'Putin admits Russian forces were deployed to Crimea', *Reuters* (17 April 2014).

troops in the eastern Ukrainian conflict. Allen, Hodges and Lindley-French have explained that the threat to the international legal order that accompanies such low-intensity warfare with the minimal war-fighting cost is that:

> Over time adversaries become de-sensitized to low-level coercion and see it as 'white' noise, part of the new 'normal' in an engineered unstable relationship between Russia and its neighbours, affording Moscow the ability to apply pressure where and when it wishes across a whole swath of Europe. ... Russian developments in artificial intelligence (AI), super-computing, and machine learning, as well as nano-technologies, drones, and other semi or fully autonomous delivery systems, are all designed to intimidate Europeans short of war, in what some rather unhelpfully call the 'grey zone'. They are also effectively exploiting the emergence of new weapons systems for political effect. The result is the kind of imbalance upon which complex strategic coercion feeds. ... Russia's overall aim is to re-draw the political map of eastern and south-eastern Europe to re-establish a new/old sphere of influence therein, by applying a model of warfare across a mosaic of conflict that incorporates hybrid war, cyber war, and, in the worst case, high-end hyperwar.[13]

In this context, it becomes increasingly important to acknowledge the limits of an armed conflict, as provided in, e.g., the *Tadić test* (see *supra* Chapter 3.2 of Part 1). The *Tadić test* does not mention the gravity threshold which had a significant role in the ICJ's judgment in the *Oil Platforms Case*. The *Tadić test* uses the broad expression 'whenever there is a resort to armed force'. Another authoritative definition of an armed conflict is developed by the International Law Association that concluded that:

> [A]s a matter of customary international law a situation of armed conflict depends on the satisfaction of two essential minimum criteria, namely:
> a. the existence of organized armed groups
> b. engaged in fighting of some intensity.[14]

The International Law Association's report refers to a 'fighting of some intensity'. It does not appear to imply a strict gravity threshold that would serve as a criterion for qualifying an aggression against another State to reach the level of

13 Allen, Hodges, Lindley-French, *op. cit.*, 94, 110, 112.

14 ME O'Connell *et al.*, *Final Report on the Meaning of Armed Conflict in International Law* (International Law Association, The Hague Conference, 2010) 32.

an armed conflict. The ICRC has explained in its commentaries on Common Article 2 of the Geneva Conventions that:

> For international armed conflict, there is no requirement that the use of armed force between the Parties reach a certain level of intensity before it can be said that an armed conflict exists. Article 2(1) itself contains no mention of any threshold for the intensity or duration of hostilities. ... Even minor skirmishes between the armed forces, be they land, air or naval forces, would spark an international armed conflict and lead to the applicability of humanitarian law. In the decades since the adoption of the Conventions, there has been practice and doctrine in support of this interpretation. Some States, for example, have considered that an international armed conflict triggering the application of the Geneva Conventions had come into existence after the capture of just one member of their armed forces. The lack of a requirement of a certain level of intensity has also been endorsed by international tribunals, with, for example, the ICTY holding that 'the existence of armed force between States is sufficient of itself to trigger the application of international humanitarian law'. This view is also shared by a significant number of academic experts. There are compelling protection reasons for not linking the existence of an international armed conflict to a specific level of violence. This approach corresponds with the overriding purpose of the Geneva Conventions, which is to ensure the maximum protection of those whom these instruments aim to protect.[15]

The ICRC's above-cited commentary found support in the case law of the ICTY in downplaying the 'gravity threshold'. Nonetheless, it should be mentioned that although the ICTY's *Tadić test* affirms the existence of an armed conflict "whenever there is a resort to armed force between States", the same decision still embraces the criterion of intensity of fighting. After defining the threshold of an armed conflict, the ICTY found in relation to the disputed events in the former Yugoslavia that:

> These hostilities exceed the intensity requirements applicable to both international and internal armed conflicts. There has been protracted, large-scale violence between the armed forces of different States and between governmental forces and organized insurgent groups.[16]

15 ICRC 2016 commentary, *op. cit.*, on Common Article 2, paras. 236–239.

16 ICTY, *Prosecutor v Tadić*, Decision of 2 October 1995, *op. cit.*, para 70.

However, three years later, the ICTY unequivocally distanced itself from the 'gravity threshold' when it found in relation to the threshold of an international armed conflict that:

> [T]he existence of armed force between States is sufficient of itself to trigger the application of international humanitarian law ... In its adjudication of the nature of the armed conflict with which it is concerned, the Trial Chamber is guided by the Commentary to the Fourth Geneva Convention, which considers that "[a]ny difference arising between two States and leading to the intervention of members of the armed forces" is an international armed conflict and "[i]t makes no difference how long the conflict lasts, or how much slaughter takes place.[17]

In 2007, that position was adopted by the International Criminal Court that also referred to the same quote of the ICRC's Commentary to the Fourth Geneva Convention.[18]

By contrast, Greenwood observes that both case law (the ICJ's judgment in the *Nicaragua Case*) and State practice often do not treat isolated incidents between States - especially if they occur in the maritime domain - as an armed conflict.[19] On the other hand, Dinstein notes that an international armed conflict may be a minor episode, which is commonly understood as a 'short of war' situation, e.g. attacks by naval units against ships of another State.[20] Ruys concludes that "the idea of a general de minimis threshold, in the sense of a minimum gravity that must be attained before forcible acts can qualify as a use of force, is not supported by state practice and must be dismissed."[21] In the context of the divergence of views on that matter, it is significant that the ICJ has not ruled out that the use of force against "a single military vessel might be sufficient to bring into play the 'inherent right of self-defence'".[22] This statement somewhat balances the otherwise restrictive approach of the ICJ to the

17 ICTY, *Prosecutor v. Zejnil Delalić, Zdravko Mucić also known as "Pavo", Hazim Delić Esad Landžo also known as "Zenga"*, Judgment of 16 November 1998, paras. 184, 208.

18 International Criminal Court, *Prosecutor v. Thomas Lubanga Dyilo*, Decision on the confirmation of charges, 29 January 2007, para 207.

19 C Greenwood, 'Scope of Application of Humanitarian Law', in D Fleck (ed.), *The Handbook of International Humanitarian Law* (2nd Ed, Oxford University Press, Oxford, 2009), 48.

20 Y Dinstein, *War, Aggression and Self-Defence* (6th Ed, Cambridge University Press, Cambridge, 2017), 3.

21 Ruys, *op. cit.*, 209.

22 *Oil Platforms Case*, Judgment, *op. cit.*, para 72.

limits of an armed attack under international law, as illustrated by the judgment in the *Oil Platforms Case*.

In the relevant legal literature, it has been even argued that "forcible action by a coastal State against a foreign fishing vessel may be considered an armed attack should the action result in casualties or major property damage and consequently, lead to the exercise of the right of self-defence."[23] By drawing an analogy from the ICJ's judgment in the *Oil Platforms Case*, it is questionable whether the use of force against a single fishing vessel can amount to an armed attack. After all, a fishing vessel is a commercial vessel, whereas, as recognised by the ITLOS, "a warship is an expression of the sovereignty of the State whose flag it flies."[24] This does not exclude the possibility that a systemic use of force against fishing vessels of a concrete flag State can amount to an armed attack. Heintschel von Heinegg has concluded that:

> [D]isproportionate or otherwise illegal measures, including disabling fire (i.e., shots into the rudder or bridge) or the sinking of a foreign merchant vessel, cannot be considered a use of force by a State against the flag State. This may, however, be different if the measures are taken not against individual ships only but against the entire merchant fleet of another State.[25]

The legal classification of such situations should be assessed on a case-by-case basis considering the context of each incident. For example, where a flag State's campaign of hybrid warfare includes its fleet of fishing vessels systemically harassing the ships of another State, then the classification of the use of coercive measures against the fishing vessels as an armed attack against the relevant flag State would potentially result in unreasonably favouring the actual aggressor State in its campaign of hybrid warfare. After all, the systemic aggressive harassment by a fleet of fishing vessels of a particular flag State against the ships of another State can result in achieving the geopolitical aims of such hybrid campaign with a minimal risk for the aggressor State of its fishing vessels' activities being categorised as an armed attack or the use of force.

The criterion of 'sufficient gravity' is found in the UN General Assembly Resolution 3314 *Definition of Aggression*. Its Article 2 stipulates that the first use of armed force by a State in contravention of the UN Charter constitutes *prima facie* evidence of an act of aggression although the Security Council

23 Chang, *op. cit.*, 3.

24 "ARA Libertad" 2012 Provisional Measures Order, *op. cit.*, para 94.

25 W Heintschel von Heinegg, 'Methods and Means of Naval Warfare in Non-International Armed Conflicts' (2012) 88 *International Law Studies*, 461–462.

may, in conformity with the UN Charter, conclude that a determination that an act of aggression has been committed would not be justified in the light of other relevant circumstances, including the fact that the acts concerned or their consequences are not of sufficient gravity. In essence, the ICJ has used the same standard in deciding over the limits of an armed attack as that reserved for the UN Security Council in determining whether an aggression has occurred.

As examined below, the gravity of an aggression is one of the key elements that has created a 'room of manoeuvre' for States involved in hybrid naval warfare. This phenomenon is next debated on a general theoretical level by drawing comparisons between the law enforcement and humanitarian law paradigms. In this context, special emphasis lies on discussing the borderline case of the 2018 Kerch Strait incident. In addition, recent developments in China's domestic legal framework are debated from the perspective of whether they may give rise to similar conflicts to the one in the Kerch Strait also in the South China Sea or East China Sea.

5.3 Distinction between Law Enforcement and Humanitarian Law Paradigms

5.3.1 *Lessons from the Kerch Strait*

The recent hybrid naval conflicts in and around the Kerch Strait, the Bab el-Mandeb, and the Strait of Hormuz demonstrate that States have got accustomed to reaching their strategic and tactical aims via means of low-intensity clashes at sea that do not necessarily constitute an armed attack under the current case law of international courts and tribunals. On this basis, an aggressor can promote its strategic aims in the conflict and cause confusion about the legality of its measures.

In this context, one may wonder, for example, if the Annex VII Arbitral Tribunal should approach in its on-going proceedings the Russian Federation's 2018 aggression against Ukrainian warships in the Kerch Strait as a *most grave form of the use of force* that reaches the threshold of an armed attack under Article 51 of the UN Charter, as interpreted by the ICJ in the Nicaragua and *Oil Platforms Cases*. Klein has distilled from the *Oil Platforms Case* the following two key points:

> First, there is an emphasis that the armed attack must clearly be targeted against the state that acts in individual self-defence. Second, the particular acts in question, namely mining of vessels and firing on helicopters,

> were not grave enough to be viewed as 'armed attacks' triggering the right of self-defence, even when considered cumulatively.[26]

Distinct from the 1988 mine attack against the United States warships in the Persian Gulf, it was clear in the Kerch Strait incident that the use of force was specifically targeted against the Ukrainian warships. The ITLOS observed that the context of the use of force was the following:

> After being held for about eight hours, the Ukrainian naval vessels apparently gave up their mission to pass through the strait and turned around and sailed away from it. The Russian Coast Guard then ordered them to stop and, when the vessels ignored the order and continued their navigation, started chasing them. It was at this moment and in this context that the Russian Coast Guard used force, first firing warning shots and then targeted shots. One vessel was damaged, servicemen were injured and the vessels were stopped and arrested.[27]

However, it is unclear whether this constituted a *most grave* form of the use of force. In the on-going proceedings on the Kerch Strait incident, the Arbitral Tribunal can provide its understanding of what constitutes a *most grave* form of the use of force.

Notably, the suitability of the gravity threshold *per se* in assessing whether the use of force has triggered the right of self-defence has been questioned. Ruys, while noting that the legal concept of the gravity threshold is gaining ground,[28] notes that:

> [E]ven small-scale incursions may, under certain circumstances—in particular, when the intruder displays an obvious hostile intent—justify a (similarly small-scale) recourse to lethal force. Moreover, … the legality of such (small-scale) recourses to force cannot be explained by claiming that they remain below the alleged gravity threshold of Article 2(4) and fall, instead, within the "law enforcement" paradigm. It follows that the

26 Klein, *op. cit.*, 265.

27 ITLOS 25 May 2019 Order on Provisional Measures, *op. cit.*, para 73. Aside the context of the use of force, the ITLOS considered that the previous conduct leading to the conflict between the parties and the cause of the incident are particularly relevant for deciding on whether an incident takes place in the context of a military operation or a law enforcement operation. See Ibid., paras. 67–72.

28 Ruys, *op. cit.*, 159.

> application of Article 2(4) is not subject to a general gravity threshold. The better view seems to be that whenever state A deliberately uses lethal force—even within its own territory—against the military or police units of state B, such actions come within the scope of Article 2(4).[29]

Furthermore, Taft has cautioned that the gravity threshold "would encourage States to engage in a series of small-scale military attacks, in the hope that they could do so without being subject to defensive responses."[30] Notably, still, the ICJ has made it clear that such low intensity use of arms at sea can amount to an armed attack when assessed cumulatively.[31]

In the Kerch Strait incident, it likely was difficult for the Ukraine Navy to determine whether the Russian Federation's use of force against its warships was of sufficient gravity for entitling it to the right of self-defence. The ITLOS found in its provisional order on the Kerch Strait incident that "what occurred appears to be the use of force in the context of a law enforcement operation rather than a military operation".[32] Notably, Article 301 of LOSC prohibits "any threat or use of force" that is inconsistent with the UN Charter. The ITLOS' classification of the Kerch Strait incident as falling within the ambit of the use of arms in the law enforcement paradigm does not necessarily mean that according to the ITLOS' provisional assessment the measures taken by the Russian Federation were in conformity with the threshold of the prohibition of the threat or use of force under Article 2(4) of the UN Charter.

Use of arms in the law enforcement framework can amount to a breach of the prohibition of the threat or use of force just like use of arms in the military activities paradigm can fall short of the threshold of Article 2(4) of the UN Charter. In other words, a violation of the prohibition of the threat or use of force is not dependent on whether the relevant measures are classified under the law enforcement or military activities paradigm. Under both frameworks, the assessment of the legality of the relevant measures is subject to the same standard under Article 2(4) of the UN Charter.

It has been argued that the primary criteria for the differentiation between the law enforcement and armed conflict paradigms are 'the status, function or conduct of the person against whom force may be used'.[33] In this context, the use of force by a State against the warships of another State, as in the case

29 Ibid., 171.

30 Taft, *op. cit.*, 300–301.

31 *Oil Platforms Case*, Judgment, *op. cit.*, para 64.

32 ITLOS 25 May 2019 Order on Provisional Measures, *op. cit.*, para 74.

33 Gaggioli, *op. cit.*, 59. See also Gill and Fleck, *op. cit.*, 79.

of the Kerch Strait incident, falls *prima facie* within the framework of military operations paradigm.

The *Guyana v. Suriname case* is particularly relevant for assessing the potential outcome of a dispute over the Kerch Strait incident as brought before the Annex VII Arbitral Tribunal in the *Dispute Concerning the Detention of Ukrainian Naval Vessels and Servicemen*. In their dispute before the Tribunal, both Ukraine and the Russian Federation made surprisingly scarce references to the *Guyana v. Suriname arbitration* in their submissions to the Annex VII Arbitral Tribunal.

Yet the two disputes have considerable overlap as they concern incidents that occurred in a disputed maritime area and that one of the parties to the dispute characterises as a law enforcement measure, whereas the other party claims that the relevant incident concerned military activities. In the Kerch Strait incident, force was *actually* used by one State against the warships of another State: targeted shots caused casualties among the servicemen and the shots as well as ramming resulted in material damages to the Ukrainian warships. The table below provides a short comparison between the two incidents from the perspective of the categorisation of the maritime incidents as falling either under the law enforcement or military activities paradigm (see Table 4).

Based on the comparison between the two incidents, it is fair to say that the Russian Federation's measures against the Ukrainian warships in the Kerch Strait incident exceeded the limits of a mere law enforcement operation. If the warnings issued from the Surinamese warships to a private person constituted a military activity partly due to the disagreements between Guyana and Suriname over the title to the relevant maritime area, then actual use of force against warships in a disputed maritime area in the wider framework of a prolonged armed conflict between the relevant two States should presumably also be deemed as falling under the *jus ad bellum* and *jus in bello* framework.

Furthermore, the test applied by the Annex VII Arbitral Tribunal in the *Guyana v. Suriname case* for determining whether the measures used by Suriname fell under the law enforcement paradigm or amounted to a military activity involved to a significant level the subjective element which was combined with the *ex post* objective assessment by the Tribunal. The Tribunal explicitly put emphasis in its categorisation of the incident as falling outside the scope of law enforcement measures on the victim State's and private persons' subjective perspective according to which they felt themselves as being threatened by the use of force, although the other Party to the conflict strongly denied in the judicial proceedings that it had any intention to resort to the use of force.

TABLE 4 A comparison between *Guyana v. Suriname* and *Ukraine v. Russia* cases before the annex VII Arbitral Tribunal

	Guyana v. Suriname	*Ukraine v. Russia*
Parties' categorisation of the incident: Law enforcement v. military activities	Conflicting	Conflicting
The location of the incident	Disputed maritime area	Disputed maritime area
Ships involved	Suriname: two warships vs. Guyana: a commercial ship and an oil rig	Russia: a combination of ten Russian warships and Coast Guard vessels, a combat helicopter vs. Ukraine: two warships & a navy support vessel
Threat of force	Explicit	Explicit
Use of force	No	Yes: ramming, targeted shots, detention.
Casualties & material damages	No	Yes
Result	Military activities, not merely a law enforcement operation	To be decided

In such border-line cases that even international judicial bodies are unable to definitely classify in their *ex post* (final or preliminary) assessments as either falling to the law enforcement or military operations category, the Annex VII Arbitral Tribunal's approach in the *Guyana v. Suriname case* to favour the 'stronger' categorisation, i.e. military activity over a law enforcement one, and relying on the subjective assessment of the situation by the targeted persons or State is a reasonable one. The different approach adopted by the ICJ in the *Oil Platforms Case* entails that a victim State in a low-intensity hybrid naval warfare risks the possibility of being eventually dubbed as an aggressor State if it has subjectively deemed itself entitled to the right of self-defence, whereas the objective *ex post* assessment reaches the opposite conclusion that the initial aggression did not meet the threshold of *most grave form of the use of force*.

The present author considers that if members of the crew of a government ship or warship are not entitled in a certain naval incident to the right of self-defence under Article 51 of the UN Charter and thus do not have the right to use force under the framework of international humanitarian law, then the legality of their measures to counter an aggression would be presumably assessed based on the criminal law concept of self-defence, even though it is meant to govern offences between private persons. The law enforcement paradigm does not usually apply on such occasions, since the attacked government ship or warship is not on a mission to enforce its laws against the sovereign immune vessel or private ship, but instead, as the Kerch Strait incident illustrates, force is unexpectedly used against it. In addition, the law of countermeasures, as recognised by international courts and tribunals, does not apply when confronting unlawful use of force. The Annex VII Arbitral Tribunal has unequivocally found that: "It is a well established principle of international law that countermeasures may not involve the use of force."[34] These issues are discussed further in Chapter 6.7 of Part 2 below.

In such circumstances of confronting use of force under criminal law framework of self-defence that sets stricter criteria on proportionality and necessity as compared to *jus in bello*, the actual victim State can somewhat paradoxically turn out to have violated the prohibition on the use of force under Article 2(4) of the UN Charter and Article 301 of LOSC. Consequently, it could be perceived as an aggressor by the public and international courts and tribunals in the potential proceedings in the aftermath of the conflict. This would cause, among other things, reputational harm to the actual victim State. In effect, such potential outcome can shift the general ramifications of a hybrid naval conflict in favour of the initial aggressor State as the victim State needs to exercise self-restraint in grey zone conflicts when responding to an actual use of force that possibly does not meet the strict threshold of Article 51 of the UN Charter.

In this context, it is possible that, for example, the Kerch Strait incident reached the threshold of an armed attack given that it (different from the circumstances of the *M/V Saiga Case* and the *Guyana v. Suriname Case*) involved the existence of two conflicting organized armed groups who were engaged in fighting of some intensity as illustrated by the exchange of fire and casualties

34 Annex VII Arbitral Tribunal, *Guyana v. Suriname Award*, *op. cit.*, para 446.

among the crew of the Ukrainian Navy. Notably, Ukraine has pointed out in the arbitral proceedings that its ships "never engaged with the Russian coast guard (or military)" and that they "took overt measures to demonstrate their arms were not being used or deployed"[35] as they were "peacefully leaving an area" after abandoning the plan to transit the Kerch Strait and "not arrayed in opposition" to the Russian Federation's ships that were at the same time using force against the Ukrainian warships.[36] Ukraine's description of the events in the Kerch Strait incident as presented to the Annex VII Arbitral Tribunal are in contrast with Ukraine's earlier claims to the UN according to which the Russian Federation's actions in the Kerch Strait incident "constitute an act of armed aggression… undermining the peaceful settlement of the Ukrainian-Russian armed conflict".[37]

In other words, the Ukrainian Navy did not fight back when the Russian Federation used force against its ships. This has relevance for assessing the intensity of fighting. Yet reciprocity in fighting is not a precondition for the aggressor State's use of force to be qualified as an armed attack triggering the right of self-defence of the targeted State. For example, should a tactical nuclear weapon, such as the Russian Poseidon or Burevestnik,[38] be used in a surprise attack against a foreign warship, then it would clearly meet the criteria of an armed attack and trigger an international armed conflict between the two States even if the Russian 'deterrence' has such an effect on the targeted State that it does not respond militarily to the Russian use of force. In recent State practice, the 2010 torpedo attack against the South Korean warship *Cheonan* has been qualified as an armed conflict even though South Korea did not respond to the attack that was predominantly associated with North Korea.[39]

The ITLOS concluded on the basis of the facts presented by Ukraine and the Russian Federation that:

35 At the same time, the Russian Federation argues that certain weapons on board of the Ukrainian warships were operational. Preliminary Objections of the Russian Federation, *op. cit.*, 24 August 2020, para 42.

36 Annex VII Arbitral Tribunal, *Dispute Concerning the Detention of Ukrainian Naval Vessels and Servicemen,* Written Observations and Submissions of Ukraine on the Preliminary Objections of the Russian Federation, 27 January 2021, paras. 39–41.

37 Annex to the letter of 10 December 2018 from Ukraine to the UN, *op. cit.*

38 See T Nilsen, 'Norway intelligence warns about new nuclear weapons technology developed by Russia', *The Barents Observer* (8 February 2021).

39 Heintschel von Heinegg 2016, *op. cit.*, 452.

> After being held for about eight hours, the Ukrainian naval vessels apparently gave up their mission to pass through the strait and turned around and sailed away from it. The Russian Coast Guard then ordered them to stop and, when the vessels ignored the order and continued their navigation, started chasing them. It was at this moment and in this context that the Russian Coast Guard used force, first firing warning shots and then targeted shots. One vessel was damaged, servicemen were injured and the vessels were stopped and arrested.[40]

The armed groups included on the Ukrainian side two warships and a naval tugboat that were targeted and detained in a Russian operation that involved in total ten naval warships and coast guard ships and a Russian combat helicopter.[41] At the same time, the Russian fighter jets patrolled the Kerch Strait.

It remains to be seen what weight, if any at all, the Annex VII Arbitral Tribunal puts on the fact that the Russian Coast Guard (instead of its warships, including a corvette, that were also involved in the operation) detained the Ukrainian warships in the Kerch Strait incident.[42] According to Article 3(d) of the UN General Assembly Resolution 3314 *Definition of Aggression*, an act of aggression includes, *inter alia*, an attack by the armed forces of a State on the land, sea or air forces, or marine and air fleets of another State. The reference to the 'armed forces of a State' in the said provision of the *Definition of Aggression* may potentially also include a State's Coast Guard. Notably, the Russian Federation's Coast Guard, similarly to that of China's,[43] and many other major maritime powers, is closely intertwined with its Navy.[44]

The line between the activities of warships and law enforcement vessels has become blurred. Under the domestic legal frameworks of various coastal States, warships are used for various law enforcement functions, including search and rescue, disaster relief, prevention and elimination of ship-based marine pollution, peacetime countermine operations, etc. The Kerch Strait incident demonstrates that Coast Guard vessels can be equally effectively employed to use force against foreign warships.

40 ITLOS Order of 25 May 2019, *op. cit.*, para 73.
41 Preliminary Objections of the Russian Federation, *op. cit.*, 24 August 2020, paras. 2, 43. See also *supra* Map 1, Ibid., 37.
42 In this context, see South China Sea arbitral award, *op. cit.*, para 1161.
43 China's Coast Guard is under the Central Military Commission's command, and it functions as a division of China's armed forces. Liu, Xu, Chang, *op. cit.*, 493.
44 Preliminary Objections of the Russian Federation, *op. cit.*, 24 August 2020, para 40.

Against this background, the ITLOS has observed that "the traditional distinction between naval vessels and law enforcement vessels in terms of their roles has become considerably blurred … and it is not uncommon today for States to employ the two types of vessels collaboratively for diverse maritime tasks."[45] The Annex VII Arbitral Tribunal has reached a similar conclusion: "Forces that some governments treat as civilian or law enforcement forces may be designated as military by others, even though they may undertake comparable tasks."[46] The ITLOS has explained further that:

> Nor can the distinction between military and law enforcement activities be based solely on the characterization of the activities in question by the parties to a dispute. This may be a relevant factor, especially in case of the party invoking the military activities exception. However, such characterization may be subjective and at variance with the actual conduct. In the view of the Tribunal, the distinction between military and law enforcement activities must be based primarily on an objective evaluation of the nature of the activities in question, taking into account the relevant circumstances in each case.[47]

It is widely understood that the distinction between the law enforcement and humanitarian law paradigms does not depend on whether the activities were carried out by the military (armed forces in a strict sense) or law enforcement officials (police, coast guard, etc).[48] This is particularly important in the context of hybrid warfare as it demonstrates that the classification of an aggression is based on the actual merits of the incident, not its form. By comparison, as Gill and Fleck note, law enforcement operations can equally be conducted by the military or civilian State agents:

> The concept of law enforcement could thus be said to comprise all measures taken by civilian or military State agents to maintain, restore, or impose public security, law, and order or to otherwise exercise its authority or power over individuals, objects, or territory.[49]

45 ITLOS Order of 25 May 2019, *op. cit.*, para 64.
46 *Dispute Concerning Coastal State Rights*, 2020 Award on Preliminary Objections, *op. cit.*, para 335.
47 ITLOS Order of 25 May 2019, *op. cit.*, paras. 65–66.
48 Gaggioli, *op. cit.*, 12.
49 Gill and Fleck, *op. cit.*, 64.

Gill and Fleck conclude that: "As a matter of generic concept, therefore, law enforcement and military hostilities are not mutually exclusive, but may overlap considerably."[50] For example, what initially was planned as a law enforcement operation may in practice gradually develop to a situation of naval warfare.[51] In practice, such gradual escalation of a maritime incident was evident in the conflict between the Russian Federation's Coast Guard and Ukrainian warships in the Kerch Strait. The enforcement of the Russian Federation's domestic rules on passage through the Kerch Strait eventually resulted in the use of arms against the Ukrainian warships and their detention along with crew.

5.3.2 *Lessons for the South China Sea*

The Kerch Strait incident indicates that the risk for the escalation of maritime enforcement operations is highest in areas where there are conflicting claims to title over relevant land and adjacent maritime areas. Such regions include, most notably, China's so-called nine-dash-line that disregards other coastal States' claims over the contested areas of the South China Sea. For example, the Annex VII Arbitral Tribunal has categorized a prolonged stand-off between Chinese and the Philippines' armed groups over Second Thomas Shoal as a situation not falling under the law enforcement paradigm, but as one amounting to military activities. The Tribunal found that:

> [T]he essential facts at Second Thomas Shoal concern the deployment of a detachment of the Philippines' armed forces that is engaged in a stand-off with a combination of ships from China's Navy and from China's Coast Guard and other government agencies. In connection with this stand-off, Chinese Government vessels have attempted to prevent the resupply and rotation of the Philippine troops on at least two occasions. Although, as far as the Tribunal is aware, these vessels were not military vessels, China's military vessels have been reported to have been in the vicinity. In the Tribunal's view, this represents a quintessentially military situation, involving the military forces of one side and a combination of military and paramilitary forces on the other, arrayed in opposition to one another.[52]

50 Ibid., 65.
51 Fink, *op. cit.*, 194.
52 *South China Sea Arbitration*, Award of 12 July 2016, *op. cit.*, para 1161.

Conflict-prone regions also include Senkaku Islands in the East China Sea that are administered by Japan but claimed also by China and Taiwan. The use of arms against sovereign immune vessels in these areas would have a significant risk of escalation into an armed conflict between the conflicting States and their allies.

Such risk has recently somewhat increased by the adoption in 2021 of China's Coast Guard Law[53] that enables China's Coast Guard to use force against foreign ships if they do not comply with China's domestic laws. Under Article 46 of the Coast Guard Law, law enforcement measures need to meet the proportionality criteria when used gradually to counter violations of China's domestic laws in the waters falling under its jurisdiction. Liu, Xu, and Chang refer to it as an 'incremental scheme' included in Article 46 of the Coast Guard Law that explicitly requires the following:

> First, coast guard officers may use non-firearm weapons (1) to forcibly bring vessels to a halt in the course of boarding, inspection, interception, or pursuit; (2) to forcibly expel or tow away vessels; (3) to respond to obstruction faced in performing their duties; or (4) to stop other unlawful activities.[54]

The extent of the Coast Guard's jurisdiction under the Act covers also disputed islands in the South China Sea and East China Sea, including Senkaku Islands.[55] Yet it is unlikely that this development in China's maritime security policy and legal framework would lead to a recurrence on behalf of China's Coast Guard (CCG) of a Kerch Strait incident-like conflict in the disputed areas of the South China Sea, Taiwan Strait, or East China Sea.

On the one hand, Article 22 of the Coast Guard Law stipulates that: "When the sovereignty, sovereign rights and jurisdiction of a State are confronted with an imminent danger of unlawful infringement or unlawful violation by foreign organizations and individuals at sea, the CCG Organization shall, in accordance with this Law and other laws or regulations, take all necessary measures, including the use of weapons." On the other hand, such use of force is only

53 Coast Guard Law of the People's Republic of China, adopted 22 January 2021, entered into force 1 February 2021, available https://npcobserver.com/legislation/coast-guard-law/; accessed 2 September 2021.

54 The incremental scheme under Article 46 of China's Coast Guard Law as translated from Chinese by Liu, Xu, Chang, *op. cit.*, 500.

55 Liu, Xu, Chang, *op. cit.*, 495.

allowed against foreign ships that are not subject to sovereign immunity under Article 32 of LOSC (e.g., foreign warships or coast guard vessels). China's Coast Guard Law does not appear to allow the use of weapons against foreign warships and other government ships operated for non-commercial purposes. However, if they refuse to leave and cause serious harm or threat, then China's Coast Guard "has the right to take measures such as forced eviction and forced towing" (Article 21). Nonetheless, the measures that China's Coast Guard is allowed to adopt in respect of sovereign immune vessels appear to fall short of the level of aggression used by the Russian Federation's Coast Guard against Ukrainian warships in the Kerch Strait, including the use of force.

In this context, Liu, Xu, and Chang comment that:

> The CCG's power to use force under the new law is the issue of most concern to other States who are concerned about China's growing maritime power. For example, the United States plans to include its coast guard in their integrated naval force, which highlights the expanded role for non-military 'grey zone' maritime activities. Zhou argues that this US strategy formalises ways of countering China's enhanced coast guard mandate, which is utilised heavily to project power and assert claims in disputed waters. Despite some concerns by other States, the present authors take the view that China will refrain from the unilateral use of force in order to avoid provoking the conflicts, especially in disputed maritime areas. This reflects China's sensitivity to the complicated international situation in the Asian-Pacific region.[56]

The distinction in Articles 21 and 22 of China's Coast Guard Law between foreign sovereign immune vessels and other foreign ships appears to mandate the use of force against the latter, but not against the former category of ships. Notably, this does not exclude the use of force against government ships operated for commercial purposes.[57]

56 Ibid., 501.

57 Cf. Sakamoto, *op. cit.* who argues that "the CCG has authorization to use weapons without warning against both government vessels and civilian vessels as a matter of its domestic law." On the distinction between the categories of government ships operated for commercial or non-commercial purposes, see e.g., TD McDorman, 'Sovereign Immune Vessels: Immunities, Responsibilities and Exemptions', in H Ringbom (ed), *Jurisdiction over Ships: Post-UNCLOS Developments in the Law of the Sea* (Brill, Leiden/Boston, 2015), 89–90.

Notably, the limits and scope of sovereign immunity of warships in territorial sea and EEZ is at the centre of current arbitral proceedings between Ukraine and the Russian Federation in the dispute concerning the detention of Ukrainian naval vessels and servicemen.[58] Ukraine maintains that "Article 32 prescribes a rule that warships and non-commercial government ships are immune within the territorial sea" and that provision in combination with Article 30 of LOSC implies, "as the sole recourse of the coastal State, that it may require a warship or non-commercial government vessel to exit the territorial sea."[59] Ukraine also refers to a previous example from State practice involving a Soviet submarine that got stranded in Swedish internal waters in 1981: "Sweden requested Soviet permission to board the vessel and inspect it, which the Soviet Union refused on the basis of the immunity of its warship; Sweden made no attempt to exercise jurisdiction over the vessel or its crew, and the Soviet submarine departed Swedish waters as soon as it was able to do so."[60] The Russian Federation argues that such sovereign immunity in the territorial sea is not granted under Article 32 of LOSC nor anywhere else in the Convention,[61] but it acknowledges that the immunity of warships is guaranteed under customary international law.[62] If successful, the Russian Federation's claim would mean that the Annex VII Arbitral Tribunal would lack jurisdiction in the *Dispute Concerning the Detention of Ukrainian Naval Vessels and Servicemen* as the dispute would not concern the interpretation of LOSC to the extent that Ukraine alleges that the sovereign immunity of its warships had been violated in the Kerch Strait incident (the Russian Federation also challenges the Tribunal's jurisdiction based on the military activities exception).

However, while the Russian Federation argues that the Ukrainian ships were seized in its territorial sea,[63] Ukraine maintains that the detainment of its naval ships occurred in an EEZ.[64] In an EEZ and the high seas, the

58 Preliminary Objections of the Russian Federation, 24 August 2020, *op. cit.*, paras. 75–89. Observations of Ukraine on the Question of Bifurcation, 7 September 2020, *op. cit.*, paras. 16–20. Written Observations and Submissions of Ukraine on the Preliminary Objections of the Russian Federation, *op. cit.*, paras. 18–25, 68–79, 85–100.

59 Written Observations and Submissions of Ukraine on the Preliminary Objections of the Russian Federation, *op. cit.*, 27 January 2021, para 88.

60 Ibid., para 69.

61 Preliminary Objections of the Russian Federation, *op. cit.*, 24 August 2020, paras. 75, 82.

62 Ibid., paras. 81ff.

63 See Preliminary Objections of the Russian Federation, 24 August 2020, *op. cit.*, para 85.

64 Written Observations and Submissions of Ukraine on the Preliminary Objections of the Russian Federation, *op. cit.*, 27 January 2021, paras. 8, 72, 78.

sovereign immunity of warships and ships used only on government non-commercial service is explicitly granted under Articles 58(2), 95, and 96 of LOSC. Thus, the dispute over the violation of Ukraine's warships' sovereign immunity in the Kerch Strait incident would clearly fall within the Annex VII Arbitral Tribunal's jurisdiction. Both Ukraine and the Russian Federation have provided evidence to the Tribunal that show the exact coordinates of the location of the Ukrainian and Russian ships during the Kerch Strait incident and the boarding and detainment of the Ukrainian ships. However, the Tribunal needs to assess if the relevant evidence submitted by the Russian Federation is reliable. Notably, reports have emerged about the practices that are associated with the Russian Federation in repeatedly manipulating Russian and foreign warships' Automatic Identification System data that allows the tracking and identification of vessels based on their coordinates.[65]

Ships other than those entitled to sovereign immunity are subject to the flag State's exclusive jurisdiction in an EEZ and the high seas, except for ships engaged in certain illegal activities such as piracy, the slave trade or unauthorized broadcasting. In this connection, the Annex VII Arbitral Tribunal has explained that "[a]s a result of the exclusive jurisdiction of the flag State over ships in the EEZ, a coastal State may only exercise jurisdiction, including law enforcement measures, over a ship, with the prior consent of the flag State."[66] Notably, the protection against coastal State's law enforcement measures is even greater for ships that are entitled to sovereign immunity.

In this context, the legality of forced eviction and towing measures that China's Coast Guard can use in respect of sovereign immune vessels in its maritime areas, including China's territorial sea, is highly controversial even though they fall short of the use of force. Liu, Xu, and Chang maintain that while Articles 32, 95, 96 of LOSC grant sovereign immunity to military vessels, military support vessels and government ships, they are at the same time expected to comply with the laws and regulations of the coastal State concerning passage through the territorial sea.[67] Yet in case such measures as forced eviction and towing are used against e.g., the coast guard vessels in disputed areas in the South China or East China Sea, the situation may easily escalate

65 M Harris, 'Phantom Warships Are Courting Chaos in Conflict Zones', *Wired* (27 July 2021). M Lysberg, HC Ekroll, 'Russisk forskningsskip arrestert i dansk havn - danske myndigheter avviser meldinger om russisk krigsskip i området', *Aftenposten* (4 November 2021). H Lied, M Gundersen, 'Norske marineskip ble manipulert inn i russisk farvann', *NRKbeta* (25 September 2021).

66 Arctic Sunrise Award, *op. cit.*, para 231.

67 Liu, Xu, Chang, *op. cit.*, 496.

and evolve from a law enforcement operation into a military one. For example, both Ukraine and the Russian Federation agree that "enforcement of domestic law was the stated reason for the arrest [of the Ukrainian naval vessels near the Kerch Strait] on the evening of 25 November 2018."[68] Yet according to Ukrainian repeated diplomatic statements the Russian law enforcement operation gradually evolved into "an act of military aggression" and "unlawful use of force", triggering Ukraine's "right to self-defence, as provided for in Article 51 of the Charter" and rendering the detained Ukrainian servicemen "prisoners of war".[69] The Russian Federation, on its own part, admits that in the Kerch Strait incident its "military has used force against another State's warship",[70] but denies that this incident constitutes an armed conflict.[71]

The delicate distinction between the law enforcement and humanitarian law paradigms is also exemplified by the so-called shadow war between Iran and Israel in the waters around the Arabian Peninsula, as discussed next. This conflict also highlights the legal complexities that arise in relation to regulation of State responsibility and the right of self-defence against attacks carried out by non-State actors in a hybrid naval warfare.

68 Written Observations and Submissions of Ukraine on the Preliminary Objections of the Russian Federation, *op. cit.*, 27 January 2021, para 24. Annex VII Arbitral Tribunal, *Dispute Concerning the Detention of Ukrainian Naval Vessels and Servicemen,* Response of the Russian Federation to the Observations of Ukraine on the Question of Bifurcation, 21 September 2020, para 19.

69 For a collection of Ukraine's official statements on the Kerch Strait incident with detailed references, see Preliminary Objections of the Russian Federation, *op. cit.*, 24 August 2020, para 49. Notably, for reasons of the admissibility of judicial proceedings initiated by Ukraine before the Annex VII Arbitral Tribunal, Ukraine denies that the Kerch Strait incident concerned military activities and instead "everything about Russia's arrest, detention, and prosecutions indicate law enforcement — after all, Russia expressly said it was *enforcing its laws*." Written Observations and Submissions of Ukraine on the Preliminary Objections of the Russian Federation, *op. cit.*, 27 January 2021, para 37.

70 Preliminary Objections of the Russian Federation, *op. cit.*, 24 August 2020, para 50. The Russian Federation considers that the dispute concerns its military activities which are exempted from the Annex VII Arbitral Tribunal's jurisdiction under Article 298(1)(b) of LOSC.

71 Ibid., para 52.

CHAPTER 6

Iran-Israel 'Shadow War' in Waters around the Arabian Peninsula and Incidents near the Bab el-Mandeb

6.1 Legal Regime of the Bab el-Mandeb

The Bab el-Mandeb connects Djibouti's, Yemen's and Somalia's EEZs in the Gulf of Aden on the one hand, and the EEZs of Eritrea, Yemen, Sudan, Saudi Arabia, and Egypt in the Red Sea on the other hand. These States, except Eritrea, are States party to the LOSC.[1] Hence, similar to the legal regime of the Strait of Hormuz, the regime of transit passage applies in the Bab el-Mandeb (Art 37 of LOSC).

The Bab el-Mandeb strait is long (over 70 NM) and deep (mostly over 200 metres), but narrow. In two sections, between Yemeni Perim Island and Djibouti as well as between Eritrea's fringe of islands/rocks and the Yemeni Hanish Islands, the strait is less than 10 NM wide as measured from the relevant baselines (for a more detailed explanation, see below). This implies that ships that exercise their right of transit passage in the Bab el-Mandeb can relatively easily be targeted by missiles, mines, remotely controlled explosive-laden boats and other means of arms that have been frequently employed by terrorists, pirates, rebels and other armed forces for disrupting international trade and shipping in the region.

Since it is unclear whether the right of transit passage forms part of customary international law,[2] it is possible that Eritrea as a non-State-Party to the Convention might reject this liberal passage regime and instead respects the right of non-suspendable innocent passage in its waters leading to and from the Bab el-Mandeb. This might cause problems near the Eritrean Haycock Islands and South West Rocks where Eritrea's territorial sea is crossed by the international TSS.[3]

1 UNDOALAS, 'The United Nations Convention on the Law of the Sea of 10 December 1982: Chronological lists of ratifications of, accessions and successions to the Convention and the related Agreements', 28 May 2021.

2 See *infra* Chapter 8 of Part 3.

3 The TSS in the Strait of Bab el-Mandeb was adopted in 1973 by a resolution of the Inter-Governmental Maritime Consultative Organization (nowadays IMO) and initially consisted of two lanes and a 1-NM-wide separation zone. The TSS in the Strait of Bab el-Mandeb is

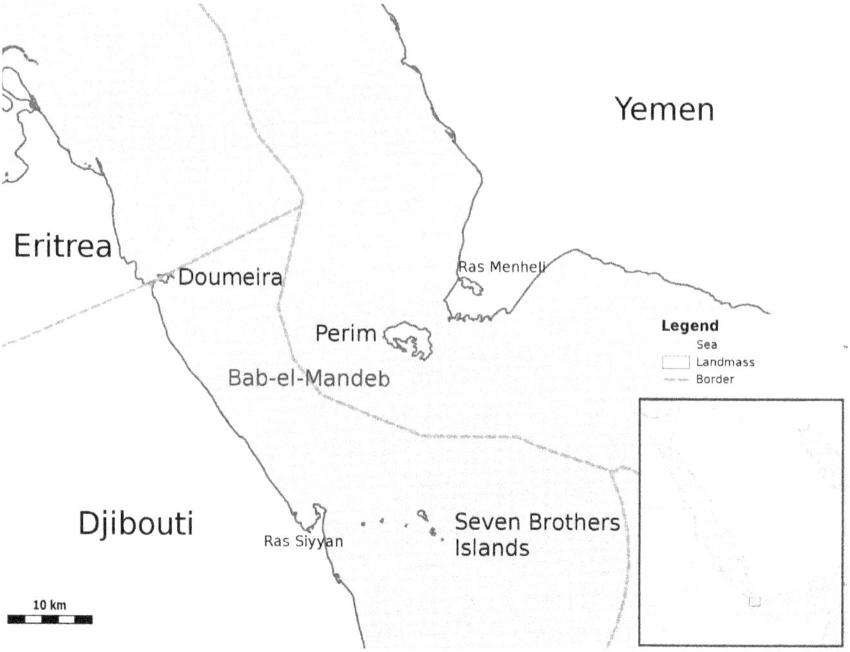

MAP 4 The Bab el-Mandeb proper
SOURCE: WIKIMEDIA COMMONS. THE MAP SERVES AN ILLUSTRATIVE PURPOSE ONLY AND IS NOT NECESSARILY COMPLETELY ACCURATE IN RELATION TO THE DELIMITATION OF MARITIME BOUNDARIES IN THE AREA. THE MAP IS TURNED INTO BLACK AND WHITE COLOUR BY THE AUTHOR.

The sea passage between the Red Sea and the Gulf of Aden is less than 24 NM wide not only in the area near Perim Island where the territorial sea of Djibouti and Yemen overlap (the Strait of Bab el-Mandeb proper, see Map 4), but also between the Yemeni Hanish Islands and the Eritrean mainland coast in the southern part of the Red Sea. Therefore, in this part of the sea passage, the territorial sea of strait states Yemen and Eritrea overlap, thus satisfying

one of the oldest TSS globally as the 1973 resolution was adopted only a year after the adoption of the International Regulations for Preventing Collisions at Sea, including its rule 10 on TSS. The 1973 Resolution established TSS also in numerous other international straits of the world, including the Strait of Hormuz, Øresund, the Strait of Dover, and the Strait of Gibraltar. Inter-Governmental Maritime Consultative Organization, Resolution A.284(VIII), "Routeing Systems", adopted on 20 November 1973, "In the Strait of Bab El Mandeb", 41 available https://wwwcdn.imo.org/localresources/en/KnowledgeCentre/IndexofIMOResolutions/AssemblyDocuments/A.284(8).pdf; accessed 5 April 2021. Convention on the International Regulations for Preventing Collisions at Sea, adopted 20 October 1972, entered into force 15 July 1977, 1050 UNTS 16.

the criteria of an international strait where the regime of transit passage applies.[4] It can be considered as the northern limit of the strait of Bab el-Mandeb. It is located some 72 NM north of the southern limit of the Bab el-Mandeb near Perim Island.

Both Eritrea and Yemen claimed title over Hanish Islands in the arbitration proceedings between the two states. Eritrea maintained that after gaining its independence from Ethiopia in 1991, it acquired sovereign title to Hanish Islands and exercised authority over them.[5] After examining all relevant historical, factual and legal considerations, the Arbitral Tribunal decided in 1998 that Hanish Islands belong to Yemen.[6] In support of this, the Tribunal found that "these islands fell under the jurisdiction of the Arabian coast during the Ottoman Empire; and that there was later a persistent expectation reflected in the British Foreign Office papers submitted in evidence by the Parties that these islands would ultimately return to Arab rule".[7]

There is a fringe of Eritrean small islands/rocks located between the Yemeni Hanish Islands and Eritrean mainland coast. These islands/rocks include Harbi Island, Sayal Island, Flat Island, High Island, North East Haycock, South West Haycock, and South West Rocks.[8] In the arbitration proceedings between Eritrea and Yemen, the Arbitral Tribunal decided that Eritrea has sovereign title over that fringe of islands/rocks.[9] The distance from the closest of the Yemeni Hanish Islands to the Eritrean North East Haycock is only about 6.5 NM. In addition, the title over South West Rocks, situated only about 4 NM west of the Yemeni Hanish Islands, was awarded to Eritrea.[10] South West Rocks and Haycock Islands are situated in the middle of the 7.5-km-wide buffer zone between the two traffic lanes of the TSS that has been established in this international waterway that is situated between the Eritrean fringe of islands/rocks and Yemeni Hanish Islands.[11]

Thus, for the sake of clarity and simplicity, it may be concluded that the regime of transit passage applies in the strait of Bab el-Mandeb in an area

4 See *supra* Chapter 2 of Part 1.
5 Award of the Arbitral Tribunal in the first stage of the proceedings between Eritrea and Yemen (territorial sovereignty and scope of the dispute), Decision of 9 October 1998, para 29.
6 Ibid., para 527.
7 Ibid., para 508.
8 Award of the Arbitral Tribunal in the second stage of the proceedings between Eritrea and Yemen (Maritime Delimitation), *op. cit.*, p 334.
9 Award of the Arbitral Tribunal in the first stage of the proceedings between Eritrea and Yemen (territorial sovereignty and scope of the dispute), *op. cit.*, para 527.
10 Ibid.
11 Navionics, *op.cit.*, 'Hanish Islands'.

which is about 72 NM long. It is less than 10-NM-wide in two sections. First, between Yemeni Perim Island and Djibouti, the strait is 9.5 NM wide. Second, between Eritrea's South West Rocks and the Yemeni Hanish Islands, the strait is only approximately 4 NM wide. In the latter part of the strait, there exists a roundabout route via the Abu' Ali Channel between Hanish Islands and the Yemeni mainland coast that is at least 15.5-NM-wide.

Therefore, in the maritime area around Hanish Islands, the TSS in the Bab el-Mandeb is divided into two alternative sections before reaching the EEZs in the Red Sea. This is significant because in case Eritrea would start impeding international navigation along the international shipping route in its territorial sea near the Haycock Islands and South West Rocks, then foreign ships and aircraft can use the alternative route to and from the Bab el-Mandeb via the Abu' Ali Channel. This maritime area comprises Yemen's territorial sea. Yemen appears not to have connected Hanish Islands by straight baseline segments with its mainland coast, as discussed below. In the Abu' Ali Channel, the Yemeni territorial sea is crossed by international sea lanes (including a TSS).[12]

At one of its narrowest points between the Red Sea and the Gulf of Aden, the Bab el-Mandeb is separated into two channels by the Yemeni Perim Island (13 km^2). The narrowest channel is only about 1.5 NM wide and formed by Perim Island and the Yemeni mainland coast. Despite its narrowness, this channel is relatively deep (depths range from 10 to 31 metres). It is mainly used for local navigation, while the international sea lanes traverse the strait of Bab el-Mandeb proper.

The geographic features of the Bab el-Mandeb are generally favourable to international navigation: it is a wide, deep and straight strait which does not have many islets or rocks that would significantly decrease the safety of navigation.[13] Between the Yemeni Perim Island and Djibouti's Kadda Dabali Island (part of Djibouti's Seven Brothers Islands),[14] the strait is about 9.5 NM wide.

12 Ibid.

13 For a detailed account of the geographical and physical features of the Red Sea and the Bab el-Mandeb, see R Lapidoth-Eschelbacher, *The Red Sea and the Gulf of Aden* (Martinus Nijhoff, The Hague/Boston/London, 1982) 1–12.

14 Djibouti has connected its Seven Brothers Islands (also referred to as Sawabi or Seba Islands) with its system of straight baselines. The longest straight baseline segments, respectively about 6.5 NM and 10 NM long, connect the islands of Ounda Komaytou and Kadda Dabali with Djibouti's mainland coast. The internal waters regime applies within the limits of the straight baselines around the Seven Brothers Islands (Art 8 of LOSC), but this does not have much significance for the passage regime in the Bab el-Mandeb. The international vessel traffic that follows the TSS in the Bab el-Mandeb runs northwards of the Seven Brothers Islands through the territorial sea of Djibouti and Yemen. Decree No. 85-048 PR/PM, Defining Maritime Limits and Frontiers of Djibouti, adopted and entered

Measured from Yemeni Perim Island to the mainland coast of Djibouti, the Bab el-Mandeb is 11.5 NM wide. Even in this narrow section of the Bab el-Mandeb, the depth of the strait mostly stays close to 200 metres or above.[15]

Pursuant to the 1977 Act on its maritime zones, Yemen has applied the method of straight baselines for measuring the breadth of its territorial sea.[16] The 1977 Act was repealed and replaced with a new Act on Yemen's maritime zones in 1991 following the unification of Yemen in 1990.[17] In 2014, Yemen established the coordinates of 743 points that serve as the basis for measuring the breadth of its up to 12-NM-wide territorial sea in the Red Sea, the Gulf of Aden, the Arabian Sea, and the Indian Ocean.[18] However, the 2014 law does not specify in which points around its coastline the method of straight baselines is used. In 2015, Yemen deposited a list of illustrative maps that depict its baselines in four maritime areas: Masamirit to Bab el Mandeb, Gulf of Aden, Ra's al Kalb to Ra's Marbāţ, and Socotra Island.[19] According to these maps, Yemen has drawn straight baselines around its coast in each of the afore-mentioned four maritime areas. Notably, however, Yemen appears not to have connected the islands located in the Bab el-Mandeb (Perim Island and Hanish Islands) by straight baseline segments with its mainland coast.

In effect, the 1.5-NM-wide maritime area in the Bab el-Mandeb between Perim Island and Yemen's mainland coast does not comprise Yemen's internal waters, but instead falls under the regime of territorial sea. In this narrow channel, foreign ships and aircraft enjoy the right of transit passage similarly to the Strait of the Bab el-Mandeb proper on the other side of the Perim Island.

---

into force on 5 May 1985. See Marineregions.org, 'Djibouti', available www.marineregions.org; accessed 18 March 2021.

15 See Navionics ChartViewer, 'The Bab el-Mandeb', Garmin 2021, available https://webapp.navionics.com/?lang=en; accessed 15 April 2021.

16 See Section 5(f) of the Act No. 45 Concerning the Territorial Sea, Exclusive Economic Zone, Continental Shelf and other Marine Areas, adopted on 17 December 1977, entered into force on 15 January 1978.

17 Republican Resolution on Law No. 37 of 1991 on the Territorial Sea, Contiguous Zone, Exclusive Economic Zone and Continental Shelf, adopted on 13 April 1991, entered into force on 13 April 1991 (published in the Official Gazette No. 7, 15 April 1991), accessible in Arabic: http://extwprlegs1.fao.org/docs/pdf/yem39356.pdf; accessed 18 March 2021.

18 Law establishing the maritime baseline of the Republic of Yemen, adopted and entered into force on 23 November 2014, available https://www.un.org/Depts/los/LEGISLATIONANDTREATIES/PDFFILES/law_26_2014_e.pdf; accessed 18 March 2021.

19 See M.Z.N.112.2015.LOS of 7 January 2015, "Deposit of a list of geographical coordinates of points concerning the baselines for measuring the breadth of the territorial sea of the Republic of Yemen", List of illustrative maps, available https://www.un.org/Depts/los/LEGISLATIONANDTREATIES/STATEFILES/YEM_Deposit_MZN112.html; accessed 18 March 2021.

The so-called Messina exception of non-suspendable innocent passage (Arts 38(1) and 45(1)(a) of LOSC) does not apply to passage through this channel, since it provides for an exception to the regime of transit passage only in such straits that are formed by an island of a strait State and its mainland coast, if there exists seaward of the island a route through the high seas or through an EEZ of similar convenience with respect to navigational and hydrographical characteristics. The Strait of Bab el-Mandeb proper does not include a high seas or EEZ corridor between Djibouti and Perim Island.

The area north of Perim Island is located in the unsettled trijunction point of the maritime zones of Djibouti, Yemen, and Eritrea.[20] Eritrea and Yemen agreed to an international arbitration on the disputed title over Red Sea islands and the delimitation of their maritime boundary line. The Arbitral Tribunal did not decide on the delimitation of the maritime boundary line near the Bab el-Mandeb in the trijunction point. The Arbitral Tribunal concluded in its 1999 award that the "line should stop short of the place where any influence upon it of Perim Island would begin to take effect."[21] The Tribunal made it clear that it did not have the competence and the authority to decide on the maritime boundary line between Yemen and Eritrea to the extent that it also needs to decide on the delimitation of the maritime boundary of a neighbouring state (Djibouti).[22]

6.2 Geopolitical Characteristics of the Bab el-Mandeb

The strait of Bab el-Mandeb separates Africa from the Arabian Peninsula and is an important element in the connection of the Mediterranean Sea and the Red Sea with the Indian Ocean. While the Suez Canal interlinks the Mediterranean with the Red Sea, the Bab el-Mandeb connects the Red Sea with the Indian Ocean. In Arabic, *Bāb al-Mandab* stands for *the gate of tears*,[23] which in the present-day context is a fitting name for a sea passage in a region that has borne tragic sufferings: a protracted humanitarian crisis and armed conflicts in Yemen, Somalia, and the Ethiopian province of Tigray, a brutal dictatorship

20 For the location of the overlapping claim, see 'Yemen', Marineregions.org, available www.marineregions.org; accessed 18 March 2021.

21 Award of the Arbitral Tribunal in the second stage of the proceedings between Eritrea and Yemen (Maritime Delimitation), Decision of 17 December 1999, para 46.

22 Ibid., para 136.

23 Encyclopaedia Britannica, 'Bab el-Mandeb Strait'.

in Eritrea, and genocide in Sudan. Geopolitically, the Bab el-Mandeb is the most sensitive chokepoint of international navigation in the long waterway that comprises the Strait of Gibraltar, the Mediterranean, the Suez Canal, the Red Sea, and the Gulf of Aden (see Map 5).

At the same time, the Bab el-Mandeb is the world's third-largest maritime oil chokepoint after the Strait of Hormuz and the Strait of Malacca. The oil flow through the Bab el-Mandeb increased from 5.1 million barrels a day in 2014 to 6.2 million in 2018 which accounts for roughly a tenth of total seaborne-traded oil.[24] The Bab el-Mandeb bears particular strategic importance for Europe as most of its maritime commerce with Asia crosses this narrow sea passage.

The significance of the Bab el-Mandeb for the global economy was illustrated by a shipping accident in the Suez Canal in March 2021. This incident involved one of the world's largest container ships, a Suezmax-class *Ever Given* that beached the bank of the Suez Canal and caused a six-days-long blockage of the Suez Canal. The cost of this blockage for the global commerce was estimated at roughly six to ten billion dollars.[25]

The free flow of maritime commerce via canals remains vulnerable to such incidents also in the future, particularly as the industry constructs ever bigger ships. It does not necessarily take a Suezmax-class of ship to block passage through the Suez Canal. Passage of ships through a canal can be blocked not only by means of grounding a vessel, but also due to scuttling a ship in the narrow fairway of a canal (the minimal width of the Suez Canal is about 200 metres). For example, in occupying Crimea in 2014, the Russian Federation blocked the passage of Ukraine's Navy ships from their naval base in Crimea to the Black Sea by means of scuttling a decommissioned cruiser *Ochakov* in the narrow channel that formed the port's fairway.[26]

The route via the Bab el-Mandeb and the Suez Canal is about 8 to 9 days shorter than the alternative route around the Cape of Good Hope as calculated on the basis of a ship's average speed of 16.43 knots.[27] The *Ever Given* incident shows that it takes just one ship to significantly disrupt global commerce, particularly between Europe and Asia, reroute global commercial and military

24 'The Bab el-Mandeb Strait is a strategic route for oil and natural gas shipments', The United States Energy Information Administration, 27 August 2019.

25 MA Russon, 'The cost of the Suez Canal blockage', *BBC News* (29 March 2021).

26 SI Loiko, 'Russians sink a boat off Ukraine coast - their own', *Los Angeles Times* (5 March 2014).

27 Russon, *op. cit.*

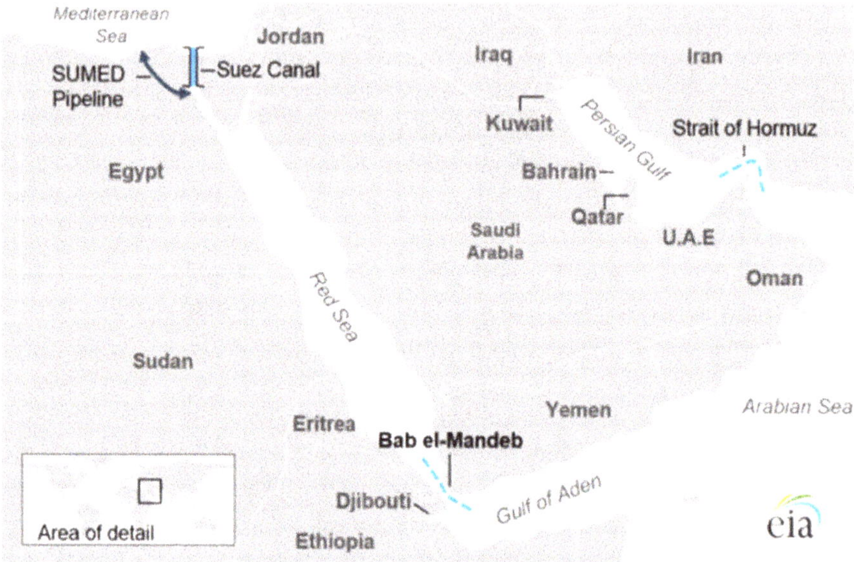

MAP 5 The Bab el-Mandeb

SOURCE: MAP OF THE BAB EL-MANDEB STRAIT AND MARITIME AREAS AROUND THE ARABIAN PENINSULA, IN THE UNITED STATES ENERGY INFORMATION ADMINISTRATION 27 AUGUST 2019 RELEASE, *OP. CIT.*

shipping to alternative trajectories (e.g., the Cape of Good Hope and, in the future, increasingly the Northern Sea Route) and cause a rise in the global oil price. In the context of hybrid conflicts, this constitutes a potential threat. For example, should a State deem that such outcomes advance its strategic aims, it might be tempted carry out a clandestine operation, e.g., by blocking the canal using a commercial ship, to reach its aims without necessarily having to bear State responsibility for such actions.[28]

28 In the case of the *Ever Given*, the Suez Canal Authority initially made a claim of 916.5 million dollars against the owner of the ship. Eventually, the two parties significantly reduced the amount of compensation in their agreement after which the *Ever Given* was released in July 2021. Such consequences will likely deter threats that emanate from potential clandestine operations aiming at blocking a canal. See Anonymous, 'Ship owner says Suez Canal was at fault over Ever Given grounding- lawyer', *Reuters* (22 May 2021). R Michaelson, 'Ever Given released from Suez canal after compensation agreed', *The Guardian* (7 July 2021).

6.3 Terrorism and Piracy in and Near the Bab el-Mandeb

Prior to the intensification of the Yemeni armed conflict in 2016, navigation through the Bab el-Mandeb was mainly under threat from terrorism and a widescale campaign of pirate attacks against international shipping in the Gulf of Aden and around Somalia's coast in the Horn of Africa. In October 2000, the naval destroyer *USS Cole* was attacked in the Yemeni port Aden, some 80 NM east of the Bab el-Mandeb, by militants who were associated with the terrorist organisation Al-Qaeda.[29] 17 members of the crew of *USS Cole* died and 39 more were wounded in the attack.[30] The suicide attack was carried out by two Yemeni nationals who were trained in terrorist training bases in Sudan and used a rubber boat carrying over 200 kg of explosives.[31] Two years later, in October 2002, al-Qaeda launched a similar suicide attack against the French oil tanker *Limburg*; collision with the explosive-laden boat left the tanker's one crew member dead, 12 injured and the marine environment of the Gulf of Aden polluted with more than 90.000 barrels of oil.[32]

Since 2005, pirate attacks against commercial shipping in the Gulf of Aden (the Bab el-Mandeb's eastern approach) surged and the attacks doubled each year from 2007 to 2009 and continued to increase until 2011, leading Clive Schofield to conclude that: "… in the 2009–2011 period Somali pirates were responsible for over half of global piracy attacks, making these waters the most dangerous in the world in terms of the threat of attacks against shipping."[33] In 2008, the EU established its anti-piracy operation Atalanta (ongoing) in the Gulf of Aden and off the coast of Somalia based on a series of UN Security Council resolutions.[34] This was followed by the establishment of the multinational Combined Task Force 151 (ongoing). In addition, NATO ran three

29 Encyclopaedia Britannica, 'USS Cole attack'.
30 Ibid.
31 Anonymous, 'USS Cole bombing: Sudan agrees to compensate families', *BBC News* (13 February 2020).
32 Anonymous, 'Yemen says tanker blast was terrorism', *BBC News* (16 October 2002). Anonymous, 'Guantanamo prisoner al-Darbi admits MV Limburg attack', *BBC News* (20 February 2014). J Saul, 'Boat that attacked gas tanker off Yemen carried explosives: shipowner', *Reuters* (3 November 2016).
33 C Schofield, 'Securing the World's Most Dangerous Strait? The Bab-Al Mandeb and Gulf of Aden', in DD Caron and N Oral (eds), *Navigating Straits: Challenges for International Law* (Martinus Nijhoff, Leiden/Boston, 2014) 280.
34 UN Security Council Resolution 1816, adopted 2 June 2008 and Resolution 2316, adopted 9 November 2016.

anti-piracy operations in the Gulf of Aden: The Allied Provider (in 2008), the Allied Protector (in 2009), and the Ocean Shield (2009–2016).

The intervention of navies of international coalition forces (among others the United States, the EU, China, Japan, the Russian Federation, India) was successful. The rate of pirate attacks off the Somalian coast were reduced to 7 in 2013, while the number of total attacks was 24 in 2008, 163 in 2009, 174 in 2010, 176 in 2011, and 34 in 2012.[35] From 2014 to 2020, the number of total attacks ranged between 0 to 2 (with the exception of 7 attacks in 2017).[36] Thus, the threat of pirate attacks in the Gulf of Aden was minimized in 2014, only to be replaced with a new menace to the stability of international shipping through the Bab el-Mandeb – the intensification of the Yemeni armed conflict in 2015.

6.4 Armed Conflict in Yemen

The armed conflict between Yemen's Government and the Houthi forces has lasted nearly twenty years. It gained a new momentum when protests against Yemen's Government resulted in the ousting in 2012 of President Saleh. In 2012, Saleh's deputy Hadi was elected Yemen's new president. Yemen's domestic political situation entered turmoil when Houthi forces overtook Yemen's capital Sana'a in the end of 2014. Soon, the Houthi movement consolidated its control over much of the north-western part of Yemen bordering Saudi Arabia and the Red Sea. This region *grosso modo* overlaps with the area that formed the territory of the Arab Republic of Yemen, also known as North Yemen, between 1962–1990.

In March 2015, Yemen's internationally recognised President Hadi moved his offices to the port town Aden and declared it the new capital of Yemen. He soon became a president in exile in Saudi Arabia and invited an international coalition to intervene in the Yemeni armed conflict.[37] In 2017, with the backing of the United Arab Emirates, a new secessionist movement emerged in Yemen – the Southern Transitional Council. In 2018, with the military support of the United Arab Emirates, the Southern Transitional Council gained control

35 EU Naval Force – Somalia, Operation ATALANTA, 'Key Facts and Figures', available https://eunavfor.eu/key-facts-and-figures/; accessed 15 March 2021.

36 Ibid.

37 The coalition forces are led by Saudi Arabia and its other members include Egypt, the United Arab Emirates, Bahrain, Jordan, Kuwait, Morocco, Qatar, and Sudan. On the background of the conflict, see further WA Qureshi, 'The Crisis in Yemen: Armed Conflict and International Law' (2020) 45 *North Carolina Journal of International Law*, 230–231.

over the strategic port town Aden.[38] In 2021, the Southern Transitional Council actively campaigned for international support for holding a UN-mandated referendum on declaring the independence of South Yemen.

According to the United States' position, the Houthi forces are supported by Iran that provides Houthis with financial and material assistance, including small arms, missiles, explosives, and drones, complemented with military guidance and training.[39] In this context, the president of the Southern Transitional Council commented in 2021 that: "Without Iran's support the Houthis would have been defeated very early on."[40] Notably, Iran's support falls short of direct control over the Houthi forces.[41] Nonetheless, it illustrates the extent of the influence that Iran has over some of the world's most important trade routes that pass through not only the Strait of Hormuz, but also the Bab el-Mandeb.

Soon after the intensification of hostilities in Yemen in the beginning of 2015, the UN Security Council adopted a resolution under which it imposed an arms embargo by calling on States to adopt measures for the prevention of any supply, sale or transfer to Yemen, "from or through their territories or by their nationals, or using their flag vessels or aircraft, of arms and related materiel of all types."[42] The UN Security Council also called upon States "to inspect, in accordance with their national authorities and legislation and consistent with international law, in particular the law of the sea and relevant international civil aviation agreements, all cargo to Yemen, in their territory, including seaports and airports" subject to reasonable doubt that such cargo breaches the arms embargo.[43]

The UN Security Council resolution was implemented, *inter alia*, by the establishment of the UN Verification and Inspection Mechanism for Yemen, situated in Djibouti. Under this mechanism, commercial ships carrying cargo to the Houthi-controlled ports located on Yemen's Red Sea coast, e.g., Hodeidah and Saleef, are required to apply for a clearance and are subject to inspection.[44]

---

38 See 'Yemen war: Who is the Southern Transitional Council?', Middle East Eye, 30 August 2019.

39 The United States Department of the Treasury, 'Treasury Sanctions Key Military Leaders of the Ansarallah Militia in Yemen', Press Release, 2 March 2021. See also J Drennan, 'The Gate of Tears: Interests, Options, and Strategy in the Bab-el-Mandeb Strait', Center for International Maritime Security, 30 January 2018.

40 P Wintour, 'Biden can help end Yemen civil war by backing referendum, say secessionists', *The Guardian* (1 March 2021).

41 Qureshi, *op. cit*, 248.

42 UN Security Council Resolution 2216, adopted 14 April 2015, para 14.

43 Ibid., para 15.

44 UN, 'About UNVIM', The United Nations Verification and Inspection Mechanism for Yemen webpage, available https://www.vimye.org/about; accessed 23 March 2021.

Nonetheless, reportedly most ships heading to the ports of Hodeidah or Saleef have been held for weeks by the warships of the Saudi Arabia-led international coalition irrespective of whether they have received the UN clearance.[45] The arms embargo is particularly relevant in the light of claims that Iran supplies the Houthi movement with anti-ship cruise missiles.[46] Such alleged supplies enable to effectively destabilize navigation in and around the Bab el-Mandeb.

From 2015 to 2020, the main threat to international navigation in the Red Sea, the Bab el-Mandeb and the Gulf of Aden stemmed from the Houthi movement. There have been numerous naval attacks from Houthi forces against the Saudi Arabian-led coalition forces in the Bab el-Mandeb and its approaches during the Yemeni armed conflict.[47] For example, in May and July 2018, two Saudi Arabian oil tankers, respectively, the *Abqaiq* and *Arsan*, were attacked near the Yemeni port Hodeidah and resulted in Saudi Arabia suspending its tankers from crossing the Bab el-Mandeb.[48]

In addition, both warships and commercial ships under the flag of a neutral State have been repeatedly attacked near Yemen's coastline. In October 2016, attacks from the Yemeni mainland coast targeted the United States warships navigating in the Bab el-Mandeb. In the beginning of October 2016, the former United States Navy test ship *HSV-2 Swift*, operated by the National Marine Dredging Company of the United Arab Emirates under the control of the Saudi Arabia-led international coalition, was destroyed in the vicinity of the Bab el-Mandeb by a rocket attack from Yemen's mainland coast for which the Houthi rebels claimed responsibility.[49] In response, the United States sent three warships (*USS Mason* and *USS Nitze* accompanied with the amphibious

45 P Wintour, 'Saudi Arabia proposes ceasefire plan to Yemen's Houthi rebels', *The Guardian* (22 March 2021).

46 B Bowman, K Zimmerman, 'Biden Can't Bring Peace to Yemen While Iran Keeps Sending Weapons', *Foreign Policy* (4 March 2021). Y Bayoumy, P Stewart, 'Exclusive: Iran steps up weapons supply to Yemen's Houthis via Oman – officials', *Reuters* (20 October 2016).

47 See further C Weiss, 'Analysis: Houthi naval attacks in the Red Sea', *FDD's Long War Journal* (17 August 2019). For example, in 2017, three small explosive-filled and remote-controlled boats attacked a Saudi Arabian frigate *Al Madinah* west of the strategic Hodeidah Port and caused an explosion which killed two and wounded three crew members of the frigate. M Ghobari, A Abdelaty *et al.*, 'Yemen's Houthis attack Saudi ship, launch ballistic missile', *Reuters* (30 January 2017). CP Cavas, 'New Houthi weapon emerges: a drone boat', *Defense News* (19 February 2017).

48 M Knights, F Nadimi, 'Curbing Houthi Attacks on Civilian Ships in the Bab al-Mandab', The Washington Institute for Near East Policy, 27 July 2018.

49 Anonymous, 'Missile Attack Destroys Ex-Navy Ship off Yemen', *The Maritime Executive* (3 October 2016).

staging base *USS Ponce*) to secure the area near the Bab el-Mandeb.[50] Upon their arrival in the middle of October 2016, the United States warships were targeted by a round of attacks: first against the destroyer *USS Mason* and *USS Ponce*, followed by a cruise missile attack three days later against *USS Mason* and the amphibious transport dock ship *USS San Antonio*.[51] The United States warships adopted defensive measures and did not suffer any major damage. The United States asserted that the attacks were launched from the Houthi-controlled regions in Yemen and responded with Tomahawk missile strikes against three radar sites on the Yemeni coast.[52]

About two weeks later, in the end of October 2016, the Spanish-flagged LNG-tanker *Galicia Spirit* was approached in the Bab el-Mandeb, near the Yemeni Perim Island, by an apparent suicide boat carrying explosives that detonated approximately 20 metres away from the tanker, destroying the suicide boat, but causing no major harm to the tanker.[53] In the same week, the Tuvalu-flagged LNG-tanker *Melati Satu*, while on her voyage from the Black Sea to the Indian Ocean, was attacked by a rocket-propelled grenade near the Bab el-Mandeb, but was saved upon its distress call by a Saudi Arabian warship and later escorted through the Bab el-Mandeb.[54]

Attacks against international navigation in or near the Bab el-Mandeb continued in the subsequent years. In addition to missile attacks and attacks carried out by small boats,[55] including remote-controlled and suicide boats, the international navigation through the Bab el-Mandeb is threatened by naval mines that are placed by Houthi forces in the Red Sea. From 2015 to 2018, the international coalition forces disarmed close to 90 naval mines in the Red

---

50 Anonymous, 'U.S. Navy Sends Warships to Secure Bab el-Mandeb', *The Maritime Executive* (4 October 2016).

51 E Slavin, 'Navy strikes radar sites in Yemen in response to missile attacks on ships', *Stars and Stripes* (13 October 2016). S LaGrone, 'CNO Richardson: USS Mason 'Appears to Have Come Under Attack'', *USNI News* (15 October 2016).

52 Ibid.

53 Saul, *op. cit.*

54 Anonymous, 'Pirates attack oil tanker near Bab al-Mandab', *Al Arabiya News* (27 October 2016).

55 For example, in May 2018, an explosion struck the Turkish-flagged vessel *Ince Inebolu* as she was transporting wheat to Yemen. Anonymous, 'Explosion damages vessel carrying wheat to Yemen', *Reuters* (11 May 2018). In February 2020, an unmanned boat laden with explosives was discovered and destroyed in the Red Sea by the Saudi Arabia-led international coalition. The boat was launched from the rebel-held Hodeidah province in Yemen. N Abdallah, D Nehme *et al.*, 'Saudi-led coalition says it foiled Red Sea attack by Yemen's Houthis', *Reuters* (23 February 2020).

Sea.[56] Some cargo ships have struck these mines in the Red Sea and they have also caused casualties among local fishermen.[57] In addition, some of the hundreds of floating mines that have been released by Houthi forces north of the Bab el-Mandeb have drifted southwards through the strait into the Gulf of Aden, causing explosions in commercial vessels.[58]

As the Houthi forces advanced in their offensive in northern Yemen against the internationally recognised Hadi's government in 2021,[59] Saudi Arabia and the United States made ceasefire proposals to the Houthi rebels that involve the lifting of the blockade on the Houthi-controlled capital Sana'a and the Red Sea ports that they control.[60] In 2021, approximately 5 million Yemenis were on the brink of famine and there is no clear end in sight for the armed conflict; there is not much progress in the Yemeni peace process.[61]

Therefore, while the legal regime of the Bab el-Mandeb has not attracted much controversy and contributes to the stability of international navigation through the strait, the main threat to international commerce and navigation in the area stems from geopolitical factors. Currently, the prospects of the geopolitically turbulent waters of the Bab el-Mandeb for returning to times of tranquillity look distant.

As discussed next, in 2019 a new conflict between Iran and Israel has escalated in the region threatening international shipping in and near the Bab el-Mandeb. The Israeli-Iranian hybrid naval warfare has been marked by a series of missile and mine attacks mostly against commercial ships in the waters leading to the Bab el-Mandeb. The 3-years-long maritime hybrid warfare between Israel and Iran in the maritime areas around the Arabian Peninsula had a significant impact on international shipping in the straits of Bab el-Mandeb and Hormuz. Geopolitically, the maritime security in the Persian Gulf, the Arabian Sea and the Red Sea is interlinked. For example, attacks against foreign ships in the Strait of Hormuz can have repercussions in the

---

56 Anonymous, 'Arab coalition destroys 86 Houthi-planted naval mines in Red Sea', *Arab News* (25 November 2018).

57 Ibid.

58 Knights and Nadimi, *op. cit.* See also the US Department of the Treasury 2 March 2021 Press Release, *op. cit.* A Egozi, 'Houthis Lay Sea Mines In Red Sea; Coalition Boasts Few Minesweepers', *Breaking Defense* (14 June 2021).

59 Wintour, 1 March 2021, *op. cit.* P Wintour, 'Hopes for Yemen peace deal fade as 'obscene' Marib death toll rises', *The Guardian* (7 May 2021).

60 Wintour, 22 March 2021, *op. cit.*

61 Anonymous, 'No end to Yemen civil war on the horizon, senior UN official briefs Security Council', UN News (23 August 2021). P Wintour, 'New UN envoy to Yemen urged to broaden talks to end civil war', *The Guardian* (7 October 2021).

maritime security of the other parts of the region, e.g., the Red Sea and the Bab el-Mandeb. The field of operations of the armed forces of Israel and Iran spread throughout the long waterway from the Persian Gulf to the Arabian Sea, Red Sea, and the Mediterranean.

6.5 Background of the Iran-Israel Conflict

In the shadow of the armed conflict in Yemen, a hybrid naval conflict emerged between Iran and Israel in 2019. Reportedly, since 2019, Israel has carried out at least a dozen clandestine attacks in the Red Sea and other maritime areas around the Arabian Peninsula against Iranian-flagged oil tankers heading to Syria.[62] In the summer of 2019, a series of attacks and intrusions against commercial ships were conducted in or near the Strait of Hormuz, for which Iran was widely held responsible.[63] The first Israeli attack against Iranian-flagged tankers occurred only a few months later, in October 2019, when the *Sabiti* tanker was subject to an apparent missile or limpet mine attack in the Red Sea near the mainland coast of Saudi Arabia, leaving two holes above the ship's waterline.[64]

Iran has allegedly also carried out attacks against Israeli commercial ships in the waters around the Arabian Peninsula. For example, in late February 2021, an Israeli cargo ship *Helios Ray* sustained damage from explosions that hit her from both sides in the Gulf of Oman.[65] Israel's Prime Minister attributed this attack to Iran. Only a month later, an Iranian missile hit Israeli-flagged container ship in the Arabian Sea.[66]

April 2021 marked the escalation of the hybrid naval warfare between Israel and Iran as an alleged Israeli clandestine operation targeted for the first time an Iranian military ship.[67] A United States' official confirmed to the media that Israel had notified the United States about the attack.[68] The limpet mine attack

62 G Lubold, B Faucon, F Schwartz, 'Israeli Strikes Target Iranian Oil Bound for Syria', *The Wall Street Journal* (11 March 2021).

63 See, e.g., Blair, *op. cit.* Graham-Harrison, *op. cit.*

64 Anonymous, 'Gulf tanker attacks: Iran releases photos of 'attacked' ship', BBC *News* (14 October 2019).

65 Anonymous, 'Netanyahu accuses Iran of attacking Israeli-owned ship in Gulf', *The Guardian* (1 March 2021).

66 F Fassihi, E Schmitt, R Bergman, 'Israel-Iran Sea Skirmishes Escalate as Mine Damages Iranian Military Ship', *The New York Times* (7 April 2021).

67 Ibid.

68 Ibid.

left two holes below the water line of an Iranian freighter *Saviz* that, according to media reports, was used in the Red Sea at least since 2016 for military purposes, including purportedly for the support of the Houthi rebels.[69] According to Iran's Islamic Revolutionary Guards Corps, she was deployed in the Red Sea to combat pirates in and near the Bab el-Mandeb.[70] At the time of the attack, the *Saviz* was situated near the Eritrean Dahlak archipelago in the Red Sea.

In defiance of the United States and European Union-sanctioned oil embargo,[71] Iran has continued to ship oil to Syria. This leaves Iran dependent on the safe passage of its ships through the Strait of Bab el-Mandeb and the Suez Canal. Iran could use the alternative route around the Cape of Good Hope for transporting oil to Syria, but this is not necessarily a safer trajectory for reaching the eastern Mediterranean. In July 2019, the tanker *Grace 1* that carried approximately 2 million barrels of Iranian oil to Syria in breach of the sanctions was seized by the United Kingdom's marines in the Strait of Gibraltar.[72] *Grace 1* was released over a month later, in August 2019, on the condition that she will not travel to Syria which both the captain of the ship and the flag State (Iran) confirmed.[73] The April 2021 attack against the Iranian oil tanker near the Syrian province Tartus shows that Iranian oil tankers encounter also in the Mediterranean significant impediments to their passage to Syrian ports even if they have successfully transited the straits of Bab el-Mandeb or Gibraltar.[74]

6.6 Problems with Attributing State Responsibility

In the Irani-Israeli 'shadow war', numerous mine attacks have been carried out mostly against commercial ships in or near the Strait of Hormuz and the Bab el-Mandeb Strait. These attacks demonstrate that it is possible for States to hamper international navigation in a busy waterway without necessarily having to

69 Ibid. See also Anonymous, 'Iranian ship thought to be used as military base attacked, says Tehran', *The Guardian* (7 April 2021).

70 Ibid.

71 Council of the EU, 'Syria: EU renews sanctions against the regime by one year', Press Release (17 May 2019). S Al-Khalidi, 'Syria says U.S. sanctions behind acute fuel crisis', *Reuters* (17 September 2020).

72 V Ratcliffe, J Lee, A Shahla, 'British Marines Seize Supertanker Carrying Iranian Oil to Syria, Causing Diplomatic Row', *Time* (4 July 2019).

73 J Marcus, 'Iran tanker row: US requests detention of Grace 1 in Gibraltar', *BBC News* (15 August 2019).

74 Anonymous, 'Three killed in attack on Iran fuel tanker off Syria after suspected drone attack', *Al Arabiya* (24 April 2021).

bear State responsibility for such measures. The flag State of a targeted ship may initiate legal proceedings against the State suspected of carrying out the mine attacks but will have to bear the burden of proof in demonstrating that the suspected State was in fact responsible for the relevant mining operation.

In the *Oil Platforms Case*, the United States was not able to sufficiently substantiate its claim that the damage to its warship USS *Samuel B. Roberts* was caused by an Iranian mine even though it provided evidence that these mines were manufactured in Iran and laid in a sea-lane that was usually navigated by the United States-flagged ships.[75] The ICJ found that, in principle, a mine attack against a single warship can constitute an armed attack in response to which a State may claim the right of self-defence under Article 51 of the UN Charter, but that there has to exist conclusive evidence that the suspected State was responsible for the mine attack.[76] In other words, as noted by Klein, whether a State is entitled to act in self-defence under Article 51 of the UN Charter, is an 'objective assessment' that does not necessarily call for the victim State's (subjective) perspective.[77]

This illustrates that one of the legally most challenging aspects of hybrid naval warfare is the attribution of State responsibility for missile and mine attacks similar to those that were carried out in the Persian Gulf against the United States in 1987 and 1988, but which the ICJ was unable to categorize as an armed attack. When international navigation passes through an international strait that is made a theatre of war, such as in the cases of the Bab el-Mandeb and the Strait of Hormuz in the context of the current Yemeni armed conflict or the Iran-Iraq war (1980–1988), it is very difficult for a neutral flag State to provide conclusive evidence that the mines that its ship struck were deployed by a belligerent with the intention of specifically targeting that specific ship or ships of any other neutral State. It is rather easier for a belligerent to counter such claims by asserting that the relevant mines were laid against legitimate targets in an armed conflict and that it was an unfortunate accident that a ship of a neutral State struck a mine.

In the context of hybrid naval warfare, it is important that an aggressor State cannot evade responsibility for its mine and missile attacks against a neutral State. As examined above, as of 2019, commercial ships sailing in or near the Strait of Hormuz and the Bab el-Mandeb Strait have been repeatedly subject to limpet mine attacks allegedly carried out by Iran and Israel. Such mines can be deployed by professional military divers (so-called frogmen) since they are

75 *Oil Platforms Case*, Judgment, *op. cit.*, para 67.
76 Ibid., para 72.
77 Klein, *op. cit.*, 299.

of relatively small size and attach to a ship by magnets. In hybrid naval warfare where States seek to evade international responsibility for their attacks, limpet mines have been often used, since apparently such attacks are easier to conceal as compared to mining by conventional naval mines.

On the other hand, should a limpet mine attack be discovered prior to the mine explosion, it is easier for the flag State of a ship that was targeted to satisfy the criteria set by the ICJ in the *Oil Platforms Case*. According to these criteria, it needs to be proved that the mine attack was aimed specifically at a particular State or that the mine struck by the ship was laid with the specific intention of harming that ship.[78] These criteria apply at least in the context where a State suspected of carrying out the mine attack is engaged in an armed conflict with another State in the region, but where mines have struck a ship of a neutral State, as in the case of the Iran-Iraq war. Taft has criticized the above-referred criteria which, arguably, can result in legally bolstering intentionally indiscriminate attacks against which the victim State would not be entitled to exercise its right of self-defence.[79] Likewise, Dominic Raab has questioned the suitability of the 'mental element' in the ICJ's understanding of the definition of armed attack. Raab argues that:

> Any such requirement of a mental element might be found in the primary rules of international law, namely the substantive rules covering the subject matter in question, in this case the rules on self-defence. However, it is reasonably clear from the relevant primary rules, governing the exercise of the right of self-defence, that there is nothing in the customary law definition of 'armed attack' requiring intention or any other mental condition on the part of a state in order for an unlawful use of force by that state to constitute an 'armed attack'. Nor did the Court seek to demonstrate otherwise. The Court did not draw any support from state practice (or elsewhere) for such a view.[80]

The on-going Yemeni armed conflict and its impact on international navigation through the Bab el-Mandeb has stressed the risk that accompanies so-called proxy wars in strait States where rebel groups may be supplied with naval mines that are deployed by non-State actors over whom the State that supplied the weapons does not have an effective control. The Houthis are not

78 *Oil Platforms Case*, Judgment, *op. cit.*, para 64.
79 For the United States critique on this position, see, e.g., Taft, *op. cit.*, 299–300, 303.
80 D Raab, 'Armed Attack after the *Oil Platforms Case*' (2004) 17(4) *Leiden Journal of International Law*, 728.

completely dependent on Iran to the extent that they would be considered as an 'agent' of the Iranian Government under the ICJ's standard in the *Nicaragua Case*,[81] nor does Iran's support to the Houthis amount to an 'effective control'[82] that could trigger Iran's responsibility for their activities.[83] Klein has observed that "[a]t most, the shipment of weapons to support a terrorist attack against another state is a threat of force."[84] This creates problems as the mine attacks that are carried out by such armed groups may significantly advance the strategic aims of a State that supplied irregulars with mines, but that State need not necessarily bear international responsibility for the irregulars' actions.[85] In hybrid naval warfare, aggressor States can effectively exploit such loopholes in the current laws regulating State responsibility.

Scholars have proposed to consider the prospect of lowering the threshold of State responsibility or introducing the concept of complicity into the law of State responsibility in view of circumstances "when the territorial States provide terrorists with support such as financial and military support, arms supplies and (military) training, although the requirement of the effective control is not satisfied."[86] Kanehara notes that "[j]udging from the ICJ jurisprudence in the *Nicaragua* case and the *Genocide Convention* case, various types of support, namely, financial and military support, training, and provision of personnel, etc., may not bring as a result the attribution of terrorist attacks to the supporting State."[87] Kanehara proposes to consider such instances as violations of the due diligence obligation that would entail a separate ground for State responsibility, particularly where it is not possible to directly attribute the acts of non-State actors to a particular State under the effective control test.[88]

Thus, the lowering of the currently rather strict threshold of State responsibility for direct support to non-State actors that conduct attacks against other States, including their warships and commercial ships, is one possibility

81 *Military and Paramilitary Activities in and against Nicaragua, op. cit.*, paras. 109–112.
82 Ibid, para 115.
83 L Alghoozi, 'The Houthi Attacks Against the UAE: Rules of Conflict and International Law of State Responsibility', *EJIL: Talk!*, 12 March 2022.
84 Klein, *op. cit.*, 270.
85 See also Armed Activities on the Territory of the Congo (Democratic Republic of the Congo v. Uganda), Judgment, ICJ Reports 2005, p. 168, paras. 146–147.
86 A Kanehara, 'Reassessment of the Acts of the State in the Law of State Responsibility – A Proposal of an Integrative Theoretical Framework of the Law of State Responsibility to Effectively Cope with the Internationally Harmful Acts of Non-state Actors' (2019) 399 *Collected Courses of the Hague Academy of International Law*, 159.
87 Ibid., 160.
88 Ibid., 161–162.

to tackle the phenomenon of hybrid naval warfare within the existing legal framework. It would potentially allow holding States responsible for supplying irregulars with naval mines and other arms that are used by non-State actors for targeting neutral ships and disrupting vessel traffic through international waterways.

In the alleged Iran-Israel hybrid naval warfare it is not clear if the attacks against ships sailing around the Arabian Peninsula are carried out by States, non-State actors or a combination of both. In this context, it is relevant to assess the measures available for the State whose ship has been targeted by non-State actors to defend itself from such attacks.

6.7 Non-state Actors and Article 51 of the UN Charter

The concept of self-defence, as traditionally understood, applies to an armed response to an attack by a State.[89] It is notable that, despite the fact that the UN General Assembly Resolution 3314 *Definition of Aggression* did not intend to provide the definition of an 'armed attack',[90] its references to different acts of aggression in Article 3 are limited to inter-State attacks. According to the ICJ, this includes a State's 'substantial involvement' in "the sending by or on behalf of a state of armed bands, groups, irregulars or mercenaries, which carry out acts of armed force against another state",[91] in the event that "such an operation, because of its scale and effects, would have been classified as an armed attack rather than as a mere frontier incident had it been carried out by regular armed forces."[92]

In the *Palestinian Wall*, the ICJ established that an 'armed attack' under Article 51 is confined to States, either in direct or indirect terms,[93] and does

89 EPJ Myjer, ND White, 'The Twin Towers Attack: An Unlimited Right to Self-Defence?' (2002) 7 *Journal of Conflict & Security Law*, 7. See also A Cassese, 'Terrorism is Also Disrupting Some Crucial Legal Categories in International Law' (2001) 12 *European Journal of International Law*, 993.

90 T Ruys, S Verhoeven, 'Attacks by Private Actors and the Right of Self-defence' (2005) 10 *Journal of Conflict & Security Law*, 302–303.

91 Definition of Aggression, *op. cit.*, Art 3(g).

92 *Military and Paramilitary Activities in and against Nicaragua, op. cit.*, para 195.

93 See for the difference between the two concepts in TD Gill, 'The Law of Armed Attack in the Context of the Nicaragua Case' (1988) 1 *Hague Yearbook of International Law*, 49. See also General Assembly, *Report of the Secretary-General: Implementing the Responsibility to Protect* (2009, UN Doc. A/2211), 56. See also SM Schwebel, *Justice in International Law* (Cambridge University Press, Cambridge, 1994), 561.

not encompass actions by non-State actors which are not attributable to States.[94] This is problematic in the context of hybrid naval warfare because often attacks against commercial vessels or warships cannot be attributed to any State. For example, the Houthi rebels control much of Yemen's coastline in the Red Sea and have allegedly conducted attacks against neutral commercial vessels and warships in and around the Bab el-Mandeb Strait with the support of Iran.[95] In this context, the ICJ's judgment in the *Palestinian Wall* entails that under the restrictive approach to Article 51 of the UN Charter, the victim State cannot invoke the right of self-defence.[96] Previous research on this matter has concluded that "State practice has consistently upheld the need for a certain link with a state."[97] Furthermore, with reference to the principles of non-intervention and State sovereignty, it has been pointed out that a different conclusion would undermine the fundamental principles of State sovereignty and non-intervention.[98]

However, in the immediate aftermath of the 11 September 2001 terrorist attacks, the conditions for invoking the right of self-defence were subject to extensive debate. It was argued that due to the scale and effects of the operations, an armed attack in terms of Article 51 of the UN Charter encompasses non-State actors.[99] In this context, the ICJ's opinion in the *Palestinian Wall* that Article 51 covers only States but not non-State actors, has been subject to criticism. It has been noted that "[t]his finding is inconsistent with the Court's own judgment in *Nicaragua* and state practice before and after 9/11."[100] It has also been underlined that Article 51, due to the inherent character of the right of self-defence, "must reflect the realities of the international system and the

94 *Legal Consequences of the Construction of a Wall in the Occupied Palestinian Territory* (Advisory Opinion), ICJ Reports 2004, p. 136, para 139. See also A Orakhelashvili, 'Legal Consequences of the Construction of a Wall in the Occupied Palestinian Territory: Opinion and Reaction' (2006) 11 *Journal of Conflict & Security Law*, 125. See also NA Shah, 'Self-defence, Anticipatory Self-defence and Pre-emption: International Law's Response to Terrorism' (2007) 12 *Journal of Conflict & Security Law*, 97. See also K Oellers-Frahm, 'The International Court of Justice and Article 51 of the UN Charter', in K Dicke *et al.* (eds), *Weltinnenrecht: Liber amicorum Jost Delbrück* (Duncker & Humblot, Berlin, 2005) 510.

95 See *supra* Chapter 6.4 of Part 2.

96 *Military and Paramilitary Activities in and against Nicaragua, op. cit.*, para 211.

97 Ruys and Verhoeven, *op. cit.*, 312.

98 Ibid.

99 R Müllerson, '*Jus Ad Bellum*: Plus Ca Change (Le Monde) Plus C'est La Même Chose (Le Droit)?' (2002) 7 *Journal of Conflict & Security Law*, 176–178. See also T Gazzini, 'A Response to Amos Guiora: Pre-Emptive Self-Defence Against Non-State Actors?' (2008) 13 *Journal of Conflict & Security Law*, 27.

100 Ruys and Verhoeven, *op. cit.*, 305.

aspirations of the international community."[101] Indeed, among the UN Member States, only Iran and Iraq challenged the legality of the 7 October 2001 military operation against Afghanistan.[102]

Notably, Article 51 does not explicitly limit the scope of perpetrators of an 'armed attack' to States.[103] Hence, it is widely argued, contrary to the ICJ in the *Palestinian Wall* opinion, that Article 51 also includes attacks of sufficient scale and effects that have been committed by non-State actors.[104]

The *Nicaragua*, *Palestinian Wall*, and *Oil Platforms* cases set a high threshold for an armed attack that triggers the right of self-defence under Article 51 of the UN Charter. This raises the question of the range of available measures for a conflicting side that has nevertheless been a victim of an unlawful use of force. This matter is important to address because the State that has been targeted by militias, in the case that the use of force has not reached the strict conditions of an armed attack in terms of Article 51 of the UN Charter, could not invoke the right of self-defence.

In this regard, it is relevant to recall that the prohibition on the use of force under Article 2(4) of the UN Charter, widely considered as a *jus cogens* rule, is subject to another exception under the UN Charter: the authorisation for the use of force by the UN Security Council under Chapter VII.[105] Due to a political impasse in the Security Council, its potential power to authorise measures under Article 2(4) often cannot provide any remedy to the counterparties. Hybrid naval warfare thus provides an illustrative example of the gap between Articles 2(4) and 51 of the UN Charter.

However, in regard to this gap in the UN Charter-based security regime, it is notable that the ICJ has introduced an innovative concept of countermeasures under its case law. The applicability of this "very controversial and contested concept"[106] to hybrid naval warfare thus merits further discussion. In particular, it needs to be examined whether States that are targeted in hybrid naval warfare are entitled to undertake proportional countermeasures in accordance

101 T Gill, 'The Temporal Dimension of Self-Defence: Anticipation, Pre-emption, Prevention and Immediacy' (2006) *Journal of Conflict & Security Law*, 369.

102 Ruys and Verhoeven, *op. cit.*, 297.

103 See on *travaux préparatoires*, ibid., 291.

104 See Shah, *op. cit.*, 104–105.

105 N Schrijver, 'Challenges to the Prohibition to Use Force: Does the Straitjacket of Artice 2(4) UN Charter Begin to Gall Too Much?', in N Blokker, N Schrijver (eds), *The Security Council and the Use of Force: Theory and Reality – a Need for Change?* (Martinus Nijhoff, Leiden/Boston, 2005) 36.

106 Ruys and Verhoeven, *op. cit.*, 309. Despite referring to its controversiality, the authors adopted the concept in their substantive analysis. Ibid., 318.

with Article 22 of the ILC Articles on State Responsibility as a means for redress when confronting unlawful use of force.[107]

When employing countermeasures, States are still bound with the rules of attribution of State responsibility. This means that when a State is using countermeasures it will have to attribute that act to which the countermeasures are directed to a specific State and will have to bear the burden of proof. In some hybrid conflicts, this criterion can be relatively easily met, e.g., in relation to the Kerch Strait incident of 2018. Mostly, however, hybrid naval warfare involves clandestine operations. For example, the hybrid naval warfare between Iran and Israel, according to media reports, allegedly involves mine and missile attacks against Irani and Israeli ships sailing in the long waterway that stretches from the Strait of Hormuz to the Bab el-Mandeb Strait and onwards to the Red Sea and the Mediterranean.[108] In such clandestine maritime operations, the responsible State cannot be easily identified.

As generally understood, countermeasures exclude the responsibility of the actor and preclude the wrongfulness of the act *per se*.[109] This is further evidenced in the ICJ's judgments in *United States Diplomatic and Consular Staff in Tehran*,[110] *Military and Paramilitary Activities in and Against Nicaragua*,[111] and in *Gabčikovo-Nagymaros Project*.[112] The ILC Articles on State Responsibility under Articles 51 and 52 as well as the ICJ in its case law have limited the use of countermeasures to the preconditions of proportionality and necessity.[113] Notably, the condition of proportionality is determined and evaluated on the basis of the aim of the countermeasures, which entails that, if necessary, the measures undertaken may exceed the limits of the unlawful action that is being repelled.[114] For example, when British warships were denied the right of innocent passage through the Corfu Channel, then the United Kingdom's

107 H Lesaffre, 'Circumstances Precluding Wrongfulness in the ILC Articles on State Responsibility: Countermeasures', in J Crawford, A Pellet, S Olleson (eds), *The Law of International Responsibility* (Oxford University Press, Oxford, 2010) 471.

108 See *supra* Chapter 6.5 of Part 2.

109 Lesaffre, *op. cit.*, 473.

110 *United States Diplomatic and Consular Staff in Tehran* (*United States of America v. Iran*), ICJ Reports 1980, p. 3, para 53.

111 *Military and Paramilitary Activities in and against Nicaragua*, *op. cit.*, para 248.

112 *Gabčikovo-Nagymaros Project* (*Hungary v Slovakia*) ICJ Reports 1997, p. 7, para 82.

113 Shah, *op. cit.*, 108. Oellers-Frahm, *op. cit.*, 508. See also *Gabčikovo-Nagymaros Project*, *op. cit.*, para 85. See also R O'Keefe, 'Proportionality', in Crawford, Pellet, Olleson, *op. cit.*, 1160, 1165–1166.

114 A Tanca, *Foreign Armed Intervention in Internal Conflict* (Martinus Nijhoff, Dordrecht/Boston/London, 1993) 57. See also E Cannizaro, 'The Role of Proportionality in the Law of International Countermeasures' (2001) 12 *European Journal of International Law*, 910–912.

show of force by sending its warships with their servicemen on action stations through the Corfu Channel was considered as a legal measure by the ICJ.[115]

The ICJ has not addressed the question if States are allowed to use firearms under the concept of countermeasures for deterring unlawful use of force. Klein has argued that States may also employ proportionate countermeasures involving force.[116] Van Logchem has discussed the substantive rules applicable to the use of countermeasures but did not elaborate on the permissibility of the use of force under the framework of countermeasures.[117]

As a rule, force cannot be used as a countermeasure against another (flag) State. Employing countermeasures that involve use of force outside the UN Charter system is superseded by Article 50(1)(a) of the ILC Articles on State Responsibility according to which: "Countermeasures shall not affect the obligation to refrain from the threat or use of force as embodied in the Charter of the United Nations." Furthermore, the Annex VII Arbitral Tribunal has unequivocally found that:

> It is a well established principle of international law that countermeasures may not involve the use of force. This is reflected in the ILC Draft Articles on State Responsibility at Article 50(1)(a), which states that countermeasures shall not affect "the obligation to refrain from the threat or use of force as embodied in the Charter of the United Nations". As the Commentary to the ILC Draft Articles mentions, this principle is consistent with the jurisprudence emanating from international judicial bodies. It is also contained in the Declaration on Principles of International Law concerning Friendly Relations and Cooperation among States in accordance with the Charter of the United Nations, the adoption of which, according to the ICJ, is an indication of State's *opinio juris* as to customary international law on the question.[118]

This is not without prejudice to the right of the crew of a ship that has been attacked by non-State actors to adopt protective measures under the law enforcement and criminal law paradigms. As discussed above (see *supra* Chapters 5.2–5.3 of Part 2), recourse to administrative law-based framework of law enforcement measures and criminal law-based concept of self-defence is available for the targeted crew on-board a government ship or warship. This

115 Corfu Channel Case, *op. cit.*, 30. See Klein, *op. cit.*, 267.

116 Klein, *op. cit.*, 267, 270.

117 Van Logchem, *op. cit.*, 46–47, 315–316.

118 Annex VII Arbitral Tribunal, *Guyana v. Suriname Award*, *op. cit.*, para 446.

right also applies in cases where the crew needs to deter the use of force against a ship flying its flag even if such aggression does not meet the gravity threshold for triggering the right of self-defence under Article 51 of the UN Charter as interpreted by the ICJ.

When countering an unlawful act under the law enforcement or criminal law framework, the person must not exceed the limits of self-defence that are mostly set by the principles of proportionality and necessity (see *supra* Chapters.5.2–5.3 of Part 2). Thus, for example, it is prohibited to cause intentionally clearly excessive damage to the attacker. The main problem in relation to the use of law enforcement or criminal law-based measures against such aggression is that the State vessel needs to comply with Article 2(4) of the UN Charter in its response to such unlawful use of force in hybrid naval conflicts. Consequently, its use of arms needs to strictly stay within the confines of the limits of proportionality that are much narrower in the law enforcement and criminal law paradigms as compared to the right of self-defence under Article 51 of the UN Charter and *jus in bello* (see *supra* Chapters 5.2–5.3 of Part 2). This is another factor that shows the disadvantages of the interpretation of the threshold of an armed conflict that relies on the 'gravity threshold' in situations of hybrid warfare.

The next chapter focuses on examples of incidents that can be qualified as an international armed conflict from a legal perspective, even though they have not been perceived as such by the public nor the States concerned. In particular, the focus of the study is next shifted to the illegal incursions of foreign submarines and military aircraft into the territory of the Viro Strait's coastal States.

CHAPTER 7

Russia's Military Operations in the Territories of the Viro Strait's Coastal States

7.1 Geographical and Geopolitical Characteristics of the Viro Strait

The passage through the Gulf of Finland—the Viro Strait—spans the maritime area between Finland and Estonia.[1] It leads to the Russian Federation's maritime area in the Gulf of Finland proper, located east of the trijunction point of the Estonian, Finnish, and the Russian Federation's maritime boundaries. The Viro Strait is less than 24 NM wide (at its narrowest point 17 NM) as measured from the Estonian and Finnish straight baselines in an area that is about 100-NM-long and located between Osmussaar Island in the west and Vaindloo Island in the east.

Therefore, legally speaking, the Gulf of Finland spans only the maritime area which is located east of the Viro Strait. The Gulf of Finland proper lies between the port towns of Loviisa (NW), Kunda (SW), Narva-Jõesuu (SE), St Petersburg (E), Vyborg (NE). Its coastal States are Finland, the Russian Federation, and Estonia.

The Viro Strait is crossed by the busy shipping lanes that connect the Russian Federation's maritime area with the Baltic Sea proper. Ship traffic heading to and from these Russian ports via the Viro Strait is one of the busiest in the world, exceeding that of any other strait in the Baltic Sea.[2] This is largely due to the fact that the Gulf of Finland is the main export route for Russian oil and gas. The Russian Federation's major ports on the coasts of the Gulf of Finland include

- Ust-Luga (2nd largest Russian port, about 104 million tons of cargo handled in 2019),
- Primorsk (5th largest Russian port, approximately 61 million tons of cargo handled in 2019),
- Big Port St Petersburg (6th largest Russian port, approximately 60 million tons of cargo handled in 2019),

1 See Map 6.
2 See HELCOM Map and Data Service, *op. cit.*

 | DOI:10.1163/9789004509368_008

- Vysotsk (13th largest Russian port, 19.4 million tons of cargo handled in 2019), and
- naval port Kronstadt.[3]

In addition, St Petersburg has been one of the most popular destinations in Europe among cruise ship passengers.[4]

The Estonian and Finnish economies are strongly connected to maritime commerce, particularly in the light of heavy passenger flows across the strait between Helsinki and Tallinn. The ports of Helsinki and Tallinn rank, respectively, as the European biggest and third-biggest passenger port (alongside the ports of Dover and Messina) and popular cruise ship destinations.[5] The main factor contributing to the growth of the two passenger ports is the frequent commuting across the strait by the residents of Helsinki and Tallinn.

This implies that if political tensions in the Gulf of Finland increase and its strait States were to be subject to widescale cyber-attacks, as Estonia was in 2007,[6] then ships' electronic systems as well as port facilities could be selected as potential targets, thereby causing significant disruptions to the economy of the targeted coastal State. In June 2019, the first large-scale training exercise of the Joint Expeditionary Force, which includes the forces of the Baltic States, the Netherlands, Norway, Denmark, Sweden, Finland and the United Kingdom, was located in the Viro Strait and constituted a landing operation which was aimed at countering threats emanating from a hypothetical hybrid warfare in Estonia.[7]

Yet as Finland, Estonia, and the Russian Federation are equally dependent on maritime commerce, it is unlikely that any of these States would be interested in destabilizing the current balance of international shipping in this maritime area. This does not exclude the possibility that the Russian Federation imposes unilaterally impediments to navigation between Finnish and Estonian ports

3 See D Elagina, 'Volume of cargo handled in Russia in 2019, by largest port', *Statista* (16 January 2020).
4 Anonymous, 'Passenger Port of St. Petersburg summed up 2019 navigation results', *PortNews* (2 December 2019).
5 Port of Helsinki, 'The world's busiest passenger port', Press Announcement, 29 May 2018, available https://www.portofhelsinki.fi/en/emagazine/worlds-busiest-passenger-port; accessed 19 April 2021; See also Eurostat, 'Maritime ports freight and passenger statistics', 18 March 2020, 11–12, available https://ec.europa.eu/eurostat/statisticsexplained/index.php?title=File:Top_20_ports_embarking_and_disembarking_passengers,_2018_(thousand).png; accessed 19 April 2021.
6 See D McGuinness, 'How a cyber attack transformed Estonia', BBC *News* (27 April 2017).
7 See V Lauri, 'Salmistul toimub brittide meredessant', ERR *Uudised* (29 June 2019). See also D Cavegn, 'UK planning landing operations exercise in Estonia in summer 2019', ERR *News* (9 December 2018).

via the Russian Federation's territorial sea in the eastern part of the Gulf of Finland. The Russian Federation has unlawfully restricted navigation in that maritime area in response to political developments in the region before, for example by prohibiting the innocent passage of the commercial ferry *Vironia* in 2007 in response to the relocation of a Soviet Union's war memorial and the following unrest among the Russian-speaking minority in Tallinn, as a result of which the ferry line had to be closed and has not been relaunched ever since.[8]

7.2 The Legal Regime of the Viro Strait

The Viro Strait meets the geographic and functional criteria of an international strait as it leads to the territorial sea and EEZ of a third State (see Maps 9 and 10), that is, the Russian Federation, and is heavily used for international navigation.

The Viro Strait bears strategic importance as it allows the Russian Federation's military aircraft and ships to navigate freely between the Russian mainland and the Kaliningrad exclave without crossing any neighbouring State's territory. Finland and Estonia have ensured the freedom of navigation and freedom of overflight (Articles 87(1) and 58(1) of LOSC) through and over the Viro Strait by the establishment in 1994 of an EEZ corridor. Both States agreed to limit the width of their territorial sea in the Viro Strait, so that it extends no closer than 3 NM to the median line (see Map 6).[9] Thus, the EEZ corridor is at least 6 NM wide as the territorial sea of Estonia and Finland reaches no closer than 3 NM to the maritime boundary line in an approximately 100-NM-long maritime area where the width of the strait is less than 24 NM, as measured from the straight baselines. Hence, the Viro Strait meets the characteristics of an Article 36-category of strait under the LOSC.

If the EEZ corridor in the Viro Strait would be non-existent, then one would assume that the regime of non-suspendable innocent passage (which applies only to ships, not to aircraft) would be applicable to the Viro Strait, since it leads to the Russian Federation's territorial sea (Art 45(1)(b) of LOSC). However, this is not the case. If the outer limits of the Estonian and Finnish territorial sea in the Viro Strait were extended, thereby abolishing the EEZ corridor, then the regime of transit passage would be applicable instead. This is due to the existence of the Russian Federation's tiny EEZ north of Gogland Island (Art

8 *Infra* Chapter 11 of Part 3.

9 1994 Exchange of Notes Constituting an Agreement on the Procedure to be followed in the Modification of the Limits of the Territorial Waters in the Gulf of Finland, *op. cit.*

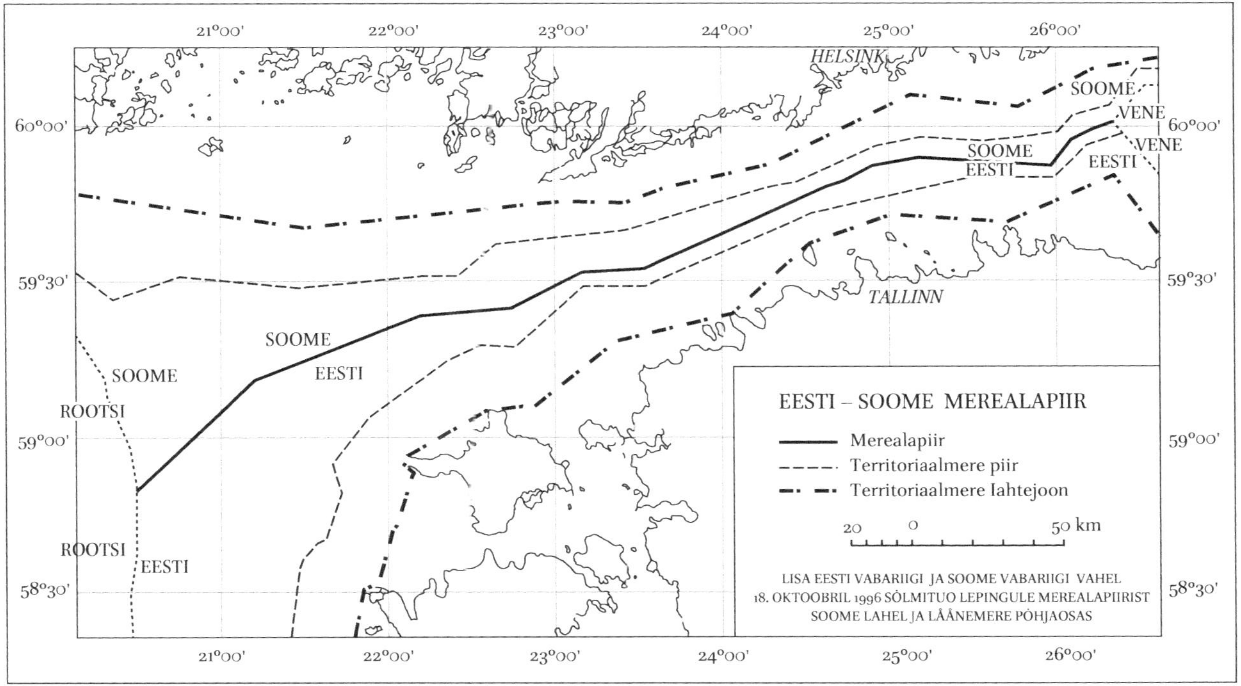

MAP 6 The EEZ Corridor in the Viro Strait

SOURCE: MAP ADDED TO THE AGREEMENT BETWEEN THE REPUBLIC OF FINLAND AND THE REPUBLIC OF ESTONIA ON THE BOUNDARY OF THE MARITIME ZONES IN THE GULF OF FINLAND AND THE NORTHERN BALTIC SEA, ADOPTED 18 OCTOBER 1996, ENTERED INTO FORCE 7 JANUARY 1997. THE MAP DEPICTS THE MEDIAN LINE, THE LIMIT OF THE TERRITORIAL SEA AND STRAIGHT BASELINES OF ESTONIA (SOUTH) AND FINLAND (NORTH) IN THE GULF OF FINLAND AND IN THE NORTHERN BALTIC SEA.

38 of LOSC).[10] Under the 1940 Peace Treaty between Finland and the Soviet Union,[11] Finland ceded Gogland and other islands in the centre of the Gulf of Finland proper to the Soviet Union. They are now under the sovereignty of the Russian Federation.

The regime of transit passage would allow all ships and aircraft to sail through or fly over the entire maritime area of the Gulf of Finland, including areas reaching close to Tallinn Bay and Helsinki. This would cause increased threats to, *inter alia*, the Viro Strait's coastal States' security and passenger traffic, particularly in the light of repeated incursions of the Russian military aircraft into the Estonian and Finnish territory so far. The Russian military aircraft could fly close to Tallinn and Helsinki under the right of transit passage, which would raise risks of an air-collision in the busy air traffic areas near Tallinn Bay and Helsinki, as discussed next in the context of the breaches of the Viro Strait's overflight regime.

In conclusion, the existence of the EEZ corridor in the Viro Strait allows its coastal States to exercise effectively control over their territorial sea and ensure maritime and air safety in the Gulf of Finland. At the same time, it also enables unhampered international navigation to and from the Russian Federation's maritime area in the Gulf of Finland. Thus, the establishment of the EEZ corridor in the Viro Strait has served as an efficient tool for properly addressing the primary concerns and aims of the main interested parties in the region. As examined above, for similar reasons, EEZ corridors have been established in other straits of the world, including in the Danish and Japanese Straits.

7.3 Foreign Military Activities in the Viro Strait: Incursions of Foreign Submarines and Military Aircraft

The Viro Strait has been at the centre of geopolitical tensions in the northern Baltic Sea region, largely due to its role as a military transport route for the deployment of Russian warships and aircraft to the Baltic Sea and beyond. This

---

10 On the Russian federation's EEZ in the Gulf of Finland, see further in, e.g., AG Oude Elferink, *The Law of Maritime Boundary Delimitation: A Case Study of the Russian Federation* (Martinus Nijhoff, Dordrecht, 1994), 183–186, 189.

11 Peace Treaty between the Soviet Union and Finland, adopted 12 March 1940, entered into force 13 March 1940, (1940) 34(3) *American Journal of International Law* (Supplement: Official Documents) 127–131; see also Treaty of Peace with Finland, adopted 10 February 1947, entered into force 16 September 1947, (1948) 42(3) *American Journal of International Law* (Supplement: Official Documents) 203–223, Article 1.

has resulted in numerous illegal crossings of Russian military aircraft and vessels to the territory of neighbouring States.

Finland has spotted and chased, most recently in 2015, suspected foreign submarines close to Helsinki in its territorial waters in the Viro Strait, in response to which it fired depth charges.[12] Under Section 25(1) of the Territorial Surveillance Act of Finland, the Finnish authorities are authorized to issue a reprimand and, if necessary, a warning to anyone who violates or is in danger of violating the provisions or regulations issued under that Act.[13] Such violations include, first and foremost, illegal intrusions into the Finnish territory of foreign military units. According to Section 25(2) of the Government Decree on Territorial Surveillance, a warning to a submarine on dive is given with a warning charge or a depth bomb so that the target is unlikely to be damaged.[14] This serves as the legal basis for the Finnish practice of firing depth charges when deterring the illegal intrusions of foreign submarines into its territory.

Finland's response to illegal incursions of foreign submarines into its territory follows the previous practice of Sweden. In 2014 and 2015, Sweden spotted and chased foreign submarines in its territorial sea in the Stockholm archipelago.[15] Similar intrusions have occurred in the Swedish internal waters and territorial sea also in the previous decades. Mahmoudi has observed that:

> In almost all reported cases, the Swedish Navy has responded by chasing and attacking suspected submarines with depth charge bombs, by increasing patrols, and by mining and electronically monitoring passages. However, no hits or casualties have ever been recorded.[16]

The legal basis for these measures is Section 15 of the Regulation on the Intervention of the Swedish Armed Forces in Case of the Violation of the

12 J Rosendahl, 'Finnish military fires depth charges at suspected submarine', *Reuters* (28 April 2015). Anonymous, 'Finland drops depth charges in 'submarine' alert', BBC *News* (28 April 2015). Anonymous, 'New submarine search off Porvoo', *Helsingin Sanomat* (15 August 2001).

13 Territorial Surveillance Act (Aluevalvontalaki), adopted 18 August 2000, entered into force 1 January 2001, Section 25(1).

14 Government Decree on Territorial Surveillance (Valtioneuvoston asetus aluevalvonnasta), adopted 16 November 2000, entered into force 1 January 2001, Section 25(2).

15 S Mahmoudi, 'Use of Armed Force against Suspected Foreign Submarines in the Swedish Internal Waters and Territorial Sea' (2018) 33(3) *The International Journal of Marine and Coastal Law*, 587. J Ahlander, 'Foreign submarine sighted in Sweden last year: Dagens Nyheter', *Reuters* (26 February 2016).

16 Mahmoudi 2018, *op. cit.*, 587.

Swedish Territory in Time of Peace and Neutrality,[17] according to which force may be used without prior warning against a foreign submarine in the Swedish internal waters or territorial sea, including by means of such weapons that pose a risk of the submarine being sunk or rendered unmanageable in any other way. In Sweden, the use of force against the suspected submarine situated in the territorial sea must be made by the commander-in-chief, while any commander is authorized to employ use of arms on the spot within the limits of Sweden's internal waters.[18]

Sweden's and Finland's use of potentially lethal force by employing depth charges and mines to counter illegal intrusions of foreign submarines to their territory should be considered as a proportionate measure. According to the ICRC, a military operation in the course of which the flag State's submarine intentionally intrudes into the territory of the coastal State should *prima facie* be considered as triggering an armed conflict within the meaning of Common Article 2 of the Geneva Conventions.[19] Likewise, Heintschel von Heinegg has concluded that such intrusions by foreign submarines can amount to "a use of force bringing into existence an international armed conflict."[20]

In a similar vein, Ruys "dismisses the view that incursions that do not result in direct confrontations with the territorial state automatically remain outside the scope of Article 2(4). Instead, logic dictates that any incursion *that would have warranted* deliberate recourse to lethal force (primarily because it demonstrates a manifest hostile intent) itself constitutes a use of force in the sense of Article 2(4), irrespective of the actual response of the territorial state."[21] He concludes that "whenever a state deliberately uses (potentially) lethal force within its own territory—including its territorial sea and its airspace—against military or police units of another state acting in their official capacity, such action amounts to the interstate use of force in the sense of Article 2(4)."[22] On

17 Förordning (1982:756) om Försvarsmaktens ingripanden vid kränkningar av Sveriges territorium under fred och neutralitet (Regulation on the Intervention of the Swedish Armed Forces in Case of the Violation of the Swedish Territory in Time of Peace and Neutrality), adopted 17 June 1982, as amended SFS 2019: 776, available https://www.riksdagen.se/sv/dokument-lagar/dokument/svensk-forfattningssamling/forordning-1982756-om-forsvars maktens_sfs-1982-756; accessed 23 December 2021.

18 Mahmoudi 2018, *op. cit.*, 592.

19 ICRC 2017 commentary, *op. cit.*, on Common Article 2, Art. 2, para 259. "Any unconsented-to military operations by one State in the territory of another State, including its national airspace and territorial sea, should be interpreted as an armed interference in the latter's sphere of sovereignty and thus may be an international armed conflict under Article 2(1)."

20 Heintschel von Heinegg 2016, *op. cit.*, 455.

21 Ruys, *op. cit.*, 171.

22 Ibid., 209.

the other hand, Ruys notes that incursions by foreign submarines "pose specific problems in that it may be difficult, if not impossible, to verify objectively whether the intrusion is caused by a navigation error or distress, or is undertaken deliberately".[23] Yet Ruys refers to Dinstein's argument that one cannot identify the 'state of readiness' of a foreign submarine which is why such non-accidental intrusions can be considered as an 'incipient armed attack' against which potentially lethal force may be used.[24]

The classification of a foreign submarine's incursion into a foreign territorial sea as an incident that triggers automatically an international armed conflict can create significant problems. For example, at the height of the Ukraine crisis in February 2022, a United States submarine was spotted and chased away by the Russian Federation allegedly in its territorial sea near the Kuril Islands north of Japan.[25] The precise location of the incident is unknown, and it is possible that it occurred in the part of the Kuril Islands archipelago that is a disputed maritime area and claimed by both the Russian Federation and Japan. It is also possible that the submarine was lawfully exercising its right of transit passage for crossing any one of the numerous Kuril Straits. In any case, the categorisation of the incident as an international armed conflict would have been presumably diametrically opposite to the interests of the United States that was anticipating the Russian invasion of Ukraine and was cautious in avoiding any direct military confrontation with the Russian Federation.[26] In the wake of the incident, a representative of the Russian Army commented that the Russian Federation is ready to respond to unlawful incursions into its territorial sea by opening fire on the spotted foreign submarine.[27]

As acknowledged by Ruys and examined above, many legal scholars support the view that such intrusions into the sovereign territory by foreign military submarines would likely fall outside the framework of an armed conflict and the use of force within the meaning of Article 2(4) of the UN Charter. In such a scenario, the coastal State's measures adopted in response to such intrusions,

23 Ibid., 174.

24 Ibid., 175. Dinstein, *op. cit.*, 214–215.

25 T Balmforth, 'U.S denies it carried out operations in Russian territorial waters', *Reuters* (15 February 2022).

26 President Joe Biden had commented a couple of days prior to the incident that "That's a world war when Americans and Russia start shooting at one another". A Kavi, 'Biden Warns U.S. Won't Send Troops to Rescue Americans in Ukraine', *The New York Times* (10 February 2022).

27 A Marrow, M Trevelyan, 'Russia ready to fire if foreign subs and ships intrude, military official says', *Reuters* (14 February 2022).

e.g., the use of depth charges, would form part of the law enforcement domain in the broader framework of administrative law.[28]

Notably, in other regions of the world, the use of weapons, e.g., depth charges, in response to intrusions into the sovereign territory by a foreign military submarine might not necessarily be as common as, perhaps, in the northern Baltic Sea. The use of nuclear-powered submarines is very limited in the shallow and semi-enclosed Baltic Sea, while they are more common in the vast ocean space. The use of weapons by a coastal State against a foreign nuclear-powered submarine carries an increased risk, including for the marine environment. For example, when Japan identified the unlawful entry of a Chinese nuclear-powered submarine into its territorial sea in 2004, it only traced the submarine's voyage and did not use any coercive measures against the ship.[29] Instead, the incident was solved mainly by diplomatic means and China ordered its ship to leave Japan's territorial sea.[30] It is unclear what measures Japan would have otherwise used against the Chinese submarine.

In contrast to its neighbouring northern Baltic States, intrusions by foreign military submarines have not been reported in the Estonian territorial sea in the Gulf of Finland or in the Gulf of Riga. This might be explained by Estonia's poor capabilities to properly detect and chase any such illegal intrusions.[31] There is reason to suspect that foreign submarines have carried out unconsented-to military operations in the Estonian territorial sea without the knowing of the coastal State. The Estonian maritime area in the Gulf of Finland was extensively charted by the Soviet Union's submarines that were at the time stationed in Estonian ports, e.g., in Paldiski and Hara bays.[32]

The Russian Federation has repeatedly violated the Estonian and Finnish sovereign airspace in the Viro Strait, including close to their capitals. Russian fighter jets reportedly violated Finnish border close to Helsinki in 2016 and 2020.[33] On average, incursions of foreign aircraft into Finnish airspace or

28 See further, Mahmoudi 2018, *op. cit.*, 594–598.

29 Y Ishii, *Japanese Maritime Security and Law of the Sea* (Brill, Leiden/Boston, 2022), 35.

30 Ibid.

31 See M Männi, 'Mereväelane: Eestil ei ole täielikku ülevaadet, mis meie vetes toimub', *Postimees* (19 October 2014).

32 Paldiski served as the Soviet nuclear submarine training centre.

33 M Salomaa, 'Ulkoministeriö kutsui Venäjän suurlähettilään puhutteluun – "Suomi ottaa alueloukkaukset aina vakavasti"', *Helsingin Sanomat* (7 October 2016). Anonymous, '2 Russian aircraft suspected of violating Finland's airspace', *The Washington Post* (28 July 2020).

territorial sea occur between one and six times a year.[34] Ruys explains that if a coastal State's airspace is violated, then the following rules apply:

> It is generally accepted that the "victim" state may lawfully take measures, short of the use of armed force, to intercept a foreign military aircraft that makes an unauthorized passage through its territorial airspace and to force it to land. Intruding aircraft must obey all reasonable orders of the territorial sovereign, including orders to land, turn back, or fly on a certain course. If a military aircraft ignores orders to land, forcible measures may be undertaken. Intruding aircraft whose intentions are known to be harmless must not be attacked even if they disobey orders to land. In principle, no aircraft may be shot down unless prior warning has been given or warning shots have been fired. The foregoing requirement does not apply, however, when the aerial intruder is the first to open fire or when the available evidence suggests that the intruder is on the verge of attacking one or more targets. Finally, at least in the context of aerial incursions, the permissibility of a forcible response arguably extends to intrusions for intelligence-gathering purposes.[35]

In some States, the intrusion of foreign military aircraft[36] into the coastal State's airspace is criminalised. For example, Finland stipulated under its Criminal Code shortly after the adoption of its Territorial Surveillance Act in 2000 that territorial violation is subject to criminal investigation, *inter alia*, in respect of foreign military servicemen on-board military aircraft. The Finnish legislator acknowledged that its effect is largely symbolic in the light of the immunities of State aircraft and that such territorial violations are usually addressed via diplomatic channels.[37]

Each year, some of the Russian military aircraft *en route* to Kaliningrad/St Petersburg cross into the Estonian airspace, mostly near the Estonian northernmost Vaindloo Island in the eastern end of the EEZ corridor (e.g., in 2014, six of

34 Anonymous, 'Russian fighter jets suspected of violating Finnish airspace', *Yle Uutiset* (28 July 2020).

35 Ruys, *op. cit.*, 173–174.

36 For a definition of 'military aircraft', see Art 31 of the Convention Relating to the Regulation of Aerial Navigation, adopted 13 October 1919, entered into force 1 June 1922, 11 LNTS 173.

37 S Spiliopoulou Åkermark, T Hyttinen, P Kleemola-Juntunen, 'Life on the Border: Dealing with Territorial Violations of the Demilitarised and Neutralised Zone of the Åland Islands' (2019) 88(2) *Nordic Journal of International Law*, 150–153.

ten NATO airspace violations occurred in that area).[38] In the first seven months of 2018, the Russian government-owned aircraft violated Estonia's airspace six times, including by IL-96–300 which was carrying on board the Russian Federation's president.[39] In the previous year, the same plane violated Estonia's airspace while it was transporting the Russian Federation's foreign minister.[40] Usually, incursions into the Estonian airspace of foreign government-owned or military aircraft require NATO to scramble its air defence Quick Reaction Alert's fighter jets that are stationed near Tallinn to respond to such incidents. Prior to joining NATO in 2004, Estonia was practically unable to respond to incursions of Russian military aircraft into its airspace. For example, in 2003, two Russian fighter jets flew approximately 200 km in Estonia's airspace along its northern coastline, including over Tallinn.[41]

The Estonian EEZ in the Viro Strait is crossed annually by approximately 400 Russian military aircraft, of which only 50–70 aircraft used activated transponders in 2016.[42] The tendency of the Russian Federation's military aircraft to fly over the strait with deactivated transponders has continued to date.[43] In contrast to civil aircraft, military aircraft are not required to use activated transponders. This poses a risk to the safety of international civil aviation. In 2014, two Russian aircraft that flew with deactivated transponders almost collided with passenger planes over the Swedish maritime area.[44] Apparently, States are not interested in reaching an agreement on requiring military aircraft to fly with activated transponders. But an agreement concluded between a selected number of interested States, e.g., hypothetically, Finland, the Russian Federation, and Estonia, in respect of peacetime use of transponders on military aircraft flying over the Viro Strait's EEZ corridor would presumably be compatible with LOSC as long as the States Party to such a hypothetical treaty

38 A Nardelli, G Arnett, 'NATO reports surge in jet interceptions as Russia tensions increase', *The Guardian* (3 August 2015). H Wright, 'Russian ambassador summoned after aircraft breaches Estonian airspace', *ERR News* (24 September 2019). H Wright, 'Russian plane flies in Estonian airspace without permission', *ERR News* (10 June 2020).

39 F Püss, 'Lennuamet: sagedased õhupiiri rikkumised on tingitud asjaolust, et Vaindloo saare kohal osutab lennuliiklusteenuseid Venemaa', *Delfi* (21 July 2018).

40 L Halminen, 'Viron yleisradio: Venäjän ulkoministeri Sergei Lavrovin kone loukkasi Viron ilmatilaa matkallaan Suomeen', *Helsingin Sanomat* (5 May 2017).

41 T Sildam, K Kaas, 'Vene hävituslennukid tungisid Eesti taevasse', *Postimees* (5 March 2004).

42 A Krjukov, 'Lennuliiklusteeninduse AS: Vene õhuvägi teeb Eesti neutraalvete kohal umbes 400 lendu aastas', *ERR Uudised* (12 February 2017).

43 Anonymous, 'EDF: No improvement in Russian military flight practices, despite claims', *ERR News* (27 December 2019).

44 Anonymous, 'Russian plane has near-miss with passenger aircraft over Sweden', *The Guardian* (13 December 2014).

do not require the use of activated transponders from military aircraft belonging to non-States party (see Art 311(2) of LOSC). A coastal State's unilateral requirement in respect of foreign military aircraft to activate their transponders when flying over the coastal State's EEZ would contravene the freedom of overflight (Arts 87(1)(b) and 58(1) of LOSC).

In the context of the repeated incursions of Russian military aircraft and suspected submarines into the territory of the Viro Strait's coastal States Estonia and Finland, it is notable that, due the existence of the Russian Federation's tiny EEZ north of Gogland Island, the Russian Federation is also – at least from a legal perspective – vulnerable to foreign military activities close to its security facilities. In principle, military activities in a foreign State's EEZ are permitted under the high seas freedoms (Art 58 of LOSC) as long as they do not constitute a threat or use of force against coastal States (Arts 88 and 301 of LOSC). In practice, it is questionable if a foreign State's military activities in the Russian Federation's EEZ in the Gulf of Finland proper would meet this requirement in case such activities are not coordinated with the Russian Federation.

The Russian Federation has recently invested in its military facilities on Gogland Island by, *inter alia*, constructing a new heliport.[45] Foreign military activities in the Russian Federation's EEZ just a few NM north of Gogland Island would likely cause tensions in the region. It would constitute a provocative action, particularly in the light of the alternative option of carrying out such military activities in areas that are deemed less sensitive from the coastal State's security perspective and are located in the EEZs of the Baltic Sea proper, outside the Gulf of Finland.

Estonia and Latvia, the two coastal States of the Gulf of Riga, should be wary of a potential hybrid conflict scenario involving the Latvian EEZ in the Gulf of Riga as a foreign State's military exercises area. The surface area of the Gulf of Riga (18.000 km^2) is comparable to that of Europe's largest lake, near-by Ladoga (17.700 km^2). The Gulf of Riga includes, similarly to the Gulf of Finland proper, an EEZ that has great significance to the legal regime of the Irbe Strait.

The approximately 40-NM-long and 25-NM-wide EEZ spans most of the Latvian maritime area to the east and south of Estonia's Ruhnu Island.[46] The existence of the Latvian EEZ in the Gulf of Riga implies that under the law of the sea, the regime of transit passage is applicable to the Irbe Strait as it connects EEZs in the Baltic Sea proper with an EEZ in the Gulf of Riga (Art 38 of

45 D Cavegn, 'Defense minister: No reason to worry about Russian heliport on Gogland', *ERR News* (10 August 2019).

46 Navionics, *op. cit.*, 'Gulf of Riga'.

LOSC). In practice, there have not been any reports about foreign aircraft or ships using the right of transit passage in the Gulf of Riga.

However, legally speaking, foreign warships or military aircraft could sail or fly to the Latvian EEZ under the right of transit passage, carry out activities in the EEZ under the high seas freedoms, and then sail or fly back to the Baltic Sea proper under the right of transit passage. Such activities might be objected to by Estonia and Latvia. In case a foreign State would conduct military activities in Latvia's EEZ in the Gulf of Riga or in the Russian EEZ north of Gogland Island, then it may be expected that the relevant coastal State would argue that such activities amount to a threat of force in terms of Article 2(4) of the UN Charter. Notably, at the height of the Ukraine crisis in January 2022, the Russian Federation was about to carry out military exercises in Ireland's EEZ west of the Strait of Dover, but in the wake of the Irish Government's displease and the intention of the Irish fishermen to conduct peaceful protests in the area of the military exercises during the naval drills, the Russian Federation's Defence Minister moved the military exercises outside the Irish EEZ, referring to its decision as "a gesture of goodwill" with "the aim not to hinder fishing activities by the Irish vessels in the traditional fishing areas".[47]

Security threats emanating from military activities in the EEZs of the Gulf of Finland and the Gulf of Riga would likely have a negative impact on shipping and adversely affect also other industrial activities, including fishing and, potentially, the energy security of the coastal States. While the Gulf of Finland is one of the main export routes for the Russian oil and gas, the importance of the Gulf of Riga from the perspective of energy security is due to the fact that this maritime area is destined to become the location of some of the biggest windfarms in the north-eastern part of the Baltic Sea.[48]

Nonetheless, one may expect that, just like the NATO Member States Estonia and Latvia in respect of the Gulf of Riga, the Russian Federation would likely consider military activities in its EEZ in the Gulf of Finland contradicting its security interests. This presumably creates balance, since it deters both parties from carrying out such operations in the small EEZs of each other.

47 S Burns, S Carswell, 'Russia moves naval exercises outside Ireland's Exclusive Economic Zone', *The Irish Times* (29 January 2022).

48 *Eesti Mereala Planeering. Seletuskiri* (Rahandusministeerium/Hendrikson&Ko, Tallinn, 2020), 43, 52.

PART 3

Discriminatory Navigational Restrictions in Hybrid Conflicts

The previous part examined the use of force in straits in the context of hybrid warfare. The book now continues by taking a closer look at instances of hybrid conflict that, as explained in Chapter 3.1 of Part 1, do not involve the use of force by any of the parties. Instead, in the examples studied below, States have made use of discriminatory navigational restrictions and imposed limits to the use of high seas freedoms as part of the package of measures of political and economic intimidation to advance their geopolitical interests. This chapter begins with case studies of discriminatory navigational restrictions in the Strait of Hormuz, the Kerch Strait, and the Gulf of Finland. It also focuses on the tensions in and over the Taiwan Strait in 2021.

 | DOI:10.1163/9789004509368_009

CHAPTER 8

Discriminatory Prohibition of the Right of Transit Passage of a Commercial Ship

The Arrest of Stena Impero *by Iran*

8.1 Geographical and Geopolitical Characteristics of the Strait of Hormuz

The Strait of Hormuz is the gateway between, on the one hand, the Persian Gulf and, on the other hand, the Gulf of Oman, the Arabian Sea, and the Indian Ocean (see Map 7). It is a relatively large strait as its narrowest point is approximately 27 NM wide both at its western and eastern entrance. The territorial seas of the coastal States of the Strait of Hormuz overlap only at the centre of the strait, located north of the Omani Musandam Peninsula and between the Omani island of Great Quoin and Iran's island of Larak, where the strait is approximately 21 NM wide.[1] Thus, by comparison, the Strait of Hormuz is wider than the Strait of Bab el-Mandeb (about 4 NM and 9.5 NM at two of its narrowest points) and the Strait of Dover (approx. 18 NM).

The coastal States of the Strait of Hormuz are Iran (north) and Oman (south). At the approaches to the Strait of Hormuz, both in the Persian Gulf and the Arabian Sea, are also located the maritime zones of the United Arab Emirates. The United Arab Emirates has the second-longest coastline in the Persian Gulf, behind only Iran that controls the whole eastern coast of the Persian Gulf and the Gulf of Oman. In addition, the Strait of Hormuz leads to the maritime areas of Bahrain, Iraq, Kuwait, Saudi Arabia, and Qatar.

The depth of the Strait of Hormuz is largely more than 100 metres in the areas that are crossed by the main shipping lanes. In its eastern and centre areas, the strait is deeper on the side of the Arabian Peninsula where it is navigable by even the world's largest crude oil tankers.[2] By contrast, in the Persian Gulf, the Strait of Hormuz is deeper on the Iranian side. A few islands are present in the area used for international shipping in the central and western parts

1 For a description of the geographical limits of the Strait of Hormuz, see RK Ramazani, *The Persian Gulf and the Strait of Hormuz* (Sijthoff & Noordhoff, Alphen aan den Rijn 1979) 1; see also map in ibid., 3.

2 Anonymous, 'Hormuz and Malacca Remain Top Oil Chokepoints', *Maritime Executive* (8 April 2017).

MAP 7 The Strait of Hormuz
SOURCE: A FRAGMENT OF THE MAP 'THE STRAIT OF HORMUZ' (THE UNITED STATES CENTRAL INTELLIGENCE AGENCY, WASHINGTON DC, 2004), AVAILABLE HTTPS://LEGACY.LIB.UTEXAS.EDU/MAPS/MIDDLE_EAST_AND_ASIA/IRAN_STRAIT_OF_HORMUZ_2004.JPG; ACCESSED 5 APRIL 2021. THE MAP IS TURNED INTO BLACK AND WHITE COLOUR BY THE AUTHOR.

of the Strait of Hormuz. These islands include Great Quoin and Little Quoin, Abu Musa, Bani Forur, Sirri, Greater and Lesser Tunb.

The Strait of Hormuz has great significance for the world economy as an important chokepoint for the export of oil and liquefied natural gas (hereafter LNG), accounting for more than one-quarter of global LNG trade.[3] Oil shipments through the Strait of Hormuz amounted to nearly 18.5 million barrels a day in 1973.[4] In 2014, that amount had slightly decreased (to 17.2 million) but reached 20.7 million barrels a day in 2018.[5] Thus, the rate of oil shipments through the strait has remained relatively stable throughout the past half a century.

The flow of oil through the Strait of Hormuz accounted for 21% of the consumption of global petroleum liquids in 2018.[6] Over three quarters of that oil

3 J Barden, 'The Strait of Hormuz is the world's most important oil transit chokepoint', *US Energy Information Administration* (20 June 2019).
4 Ramazani, *op. cit.*, 12.
5 Barden, *op. cit.*
6 Ibid.

is shipped to Asian countries, mostly to China, India, Japan, and South Korea.[7] Hence, most of the oil that is shipped through the Strait of Hormuz also passes through the Straits of Malacca and Singapore located between the Indian Ocean and the Pacific Ocean. Unlike the Strait of Hormuz, there are numerous round-about routes in respect of ship traffic through the straits of Malacca and Singapore, e.g., via the straits of Lombok and Makassar. The absence of round-about routes in respect of the Strait of Hormuz further underlines its strategic significance as a chokepoint for the current oil-based world economy.

In the past decades, international navigation through the Strait of Hormuz has been repeatedly hampered and subject to attacks that have been mostly aimed at oil tankers. In June 2019, two oil tankers struck mines at the approaches to the Strait of Hormuz.[8] The United States claimed that the attacks against the oil tankers were carried out by the armed forces of Iran.[9] A few days later, Iran shot down a United States' drone over the Strait of Hormuz.[10] Iran has confirmed the downing of the drone, but denied any involvement in the attacks against the oil tankers.[11] In July 2019, the Iranian armed forces arrested *Stena Impero*, a United Kingdom-flagged oil tanker, in the Strait of Hormuz for an alleged violation of, *inter alia*, the TSS. The arrest of the tanker was considered as a hostile step by the United Kingdom's government and an infringement of the applicable passage regime.[12] A similar attempt had been made by the Iranian armed forces a few days earlier, but it was abandoned as the Royal Navy's frigate intervened.[13] In January 2021, a South Korean-flagged tanker was arrested by Iran, in response to which, South Korea deployed a destroyer close to the Strait of Hormuz.[14]

These incidents all occurred in or over the Strait of Hormuz. Surprisingly, there is relatively scarce literature on the legal regime of the Strait of Hormuz. For example, Kraska has observed that "there is virtually no contemporary analysis of the far-reaching disagreement between Iran and the United States on the international law of the sea, and in particular, the appropriate legal

7 Ibid.
8 E Blair, 'Latest on tanker attacks south of the Strait of Hormuz', *Reuters* (14 June 2019).
9 Anonymous, 'Strait of Hormuz: US confirms drone shot down by Iran', *BBC News* (20 June 2019).
10 Ibid.
11 Ibid.
12 E Graham-Harrison, 'Iran's top diplomat in UK summoned over seizure of Stena Impero tanker', *The Guardian* (20 July 2019).
13 Ibid.
14 Anonymous, 'South Korea to send delegation after Iran seizes tanker', *BBC News* (5 January 2021).

regime in the Strait of Hormuz."[15] In the light of this, this study debates the legal regime of the Strait of Hormuz and adopts a law of the sea and security law perspective for examining recent maritime incidents in the Strait of Hormuz. Maritime incidents in or near the Strait of Hormuz are often rooted in disagreements between Iran and other States over the applicable passage regime, as examined next.

8.2 Legal Regime of the Strait of Hormuz

The Strait of Hormuz connects the EEZs of Iran, Iraq, Kuwait, Saudi Arabia, Bahrain, Qatar, and United Arab Emirates in the Persian Gulf with the EEZs of Iran, Oman and the United Arab Emirates in the Gulf of Oman. Thus, the Strait of Hormuz meets the criteria of Article 37 of LOSC for the regime of transit passage. Thus, for example the Royal Navy ships routinely use the right of transit passage for sailing through the strait.[16]

The right of transit passage was an innovative legal concept that was introduced in the drafting of LOSC for balancing the extension of the maximum width of the territorial sea under Article 3 of the Convention to 12 NM with rights of navigation. It provides a similar passage regime to the freedom of navigation and overflight, subject to some restrictions as stipulated in Articles 39–42 of LOSC, solely for the purpose of continuous and expeditious transit of ships and aircraft through the strait (Art 38(2) of LOSC). The right of transit passage applies in the areas of the Strait of Hormuz where the territorial sea of the strait States overlaps, i.e. where the width of the strait is 24 NM or less as measured from the baselines.

Foreign ships and aircraft are entitled to the right of transit passage also in the approaches to the Strait of Hormuz in the Persian Gulf to the extent that the relevant maritime area is subject to the sovereignty of strait States. Even though there exists an EEZ corridor of a couple of nautical miles wide in the eastern end of the Persian Gulf between, on the one hand, the islands of Abu Musa, Bani Forur, Sirri, Greater and Lesser Tunb (all under Iran's control) and, on the other hand, the United Arab Emirates' coast on the Arabian Peninsula. However,

---

15 J Kraska, 'Legal Vortex in the Strait of Hormuz' (2013) 54(2) *Virginia Journal of International Law*, 326.

16 United Kingdom Foreign, Commonwealth and Development Office, 'Written evidence (UNC0028). UNCLOS: fit for purpose in the 21st century?', UK Parliament, 26 November 2021, 26, available https://committees.parliament.uk/work/1557/unclos-fit-for-purpose-in-the-21st-century/publications/written-evidence/?page=2; accessed 1 December 2021.

that narrow EEZ corridor in the eastern part of the Persian Gulf does not render the straits regime inapplicable in the maritime area between the Iranian and the United Arab Emirates' mainland coast where the above-mentioned islands are located at.[17] The eastern end of the Persian Gulf is wholly subject to the transit passage regime due to the reason that the narrow EEZ corridor south of the Iranian-controlled islands is not "of similar convenience with respect to navigational and hydrographical characteristics" as the rest of the strait in terms of Article 36 of LOSC. Very Large and Ultra Large Crude Carriers cannot safely cross the EEZ corridor as it is located closer to the United Arab Emirates' coastline where the sea is relatively shallow. For smaller ships heading in or out of the central or western part of the Persian Gulf, the round-about route via the EEZ corridor would significantly increase the length and cost of the voyage in comparison with the main route that crosses the territorial sea between the Iranian-controlled islands of Abu Musa, Bani Forur, Sirri, Greater and Lesser Tunb. The TSS in the Strait of Hormuz also crosses the waters located between the above-mentioned Iranian-controlled islands.[18] In addition, the narrowness of the EEZ corridor means that if international vessel and air traffic is directed to the confines of this only a couple of NM-wide maritime area, ships and aircraft transiting this area would bear a much greater risk of collisions.

The determination of the legal regime applicable to the Strait of Hormuz is complicated by the fact that Iran has not ratified LOSC. Iran considers that parts of LOSC "are merely product of *quid pro quo* which do not necessarily purport to codify the existing customs or established usage (practice) regarded as having an obligatory character".[19] According to the Iranian position, the regime of transit passage, an innovative concept first introduced in LOSC to balance the extension of the territorial sea to 12 NM with the rights of navigation, is not part of customary international law and only States party to LOSC are entitled to benefit from the right of transit passage.[20] This claim and the passage regime applicable to the Strait of Hormuz is discussed below (see *infra* Chapter 8.4).

17 See 'Iran', MarineRegions.org, available https://www.marineregions.org/eezdetails.php?mrgid=8469&zone=eez; accessed 10 February 2021.

18 See Map 7.

19 Division for Ocean Affairs and the Law of the Sea, 'United Nations Convention on the Law of the Sea: Declarations made upon signature, ratification, accession or succession or anytime thereafter', Iran's declaration upon signing LOSC on 10 December 1982. Oman's declarations made upon ratification of LOSC on 17 August 1989, available https://treaties.un.org/Pages/ViewDetailsIII.aspx?src=TREATY&mtdsg_no=XXI-6&chapter=21&Temp=mtdsg3&clang=_en#EndDec; accessed 26 March 2021.

20 Ibid.

8.3 The 2019 *Stena Impero* Incident and the Traffic Separation Scheme in the Strait of Hormuz

Maritime security in the waters around the Arabian Peninsula is instable not only due to numerous conflicting parties' use of arms, explosives, and mines in their attacks against ships transiting the long waterway that stretches from the Persian Gulf to the Mediterranean via the Red Sea. Ships navigating in that area have recently also been subject to various discriminatory navigational restrictions, as discussed next based on a case study of the arrest of a foreign tanker by Iran in the Strait of Hormuz in 2019.

Similar to the Bab el-Mandeb, the TSS in the Strait of Hormuz was adopted under the 1973 Resolution.[21] The TSS in the Strait of Hormuz was modified in 1979.[22] It consists of a separation zone and two traffic lanes for, respectively, eastbound and westbound traffic in addition to an inshore traffic zone that lies in the area between the Musandam Peninsula's coast and the landward boundary of the TSS.[23]

Iran has adopted controversial measures in reacting to alleged breaches of the TSS in the Strait of Hormuz. In July 2019, the United Kingdom-flagged and Swedish-owned tanker *Stena Impero* was approached by four Iranian vessels and a helicopter and boarded by Iranian maritime forces.[24] The ship was arrested and taken to the Iranian Bandar Abbas port.[25] Iran claimed that the *Stena Impero* collided with an Iranian fishing vessel:

21 Inter-Governmental Maritime Consultative Organization, Resolution 'Routeing Systems', *op. cit.*, 'In the Strait of Hormuz', 41.

22 Inter-Governmental Maritime Consultative Organization, COLREG.2/CIRC.11, 'Amended Traffic Separation Scheme in the Strait of Hormuz', adopted on 7 June 1979, available https://www.transportstyrelsen.se/globalassets/global/sjofart/dokument/sjotrafik_dok/imo_colreg.2_cirkular.pdf; accessed 5 April 2021.

23 See Map 7. For a description of the coordinates of the TSS in the Strait of Hormuz, see IMO, COLREG.2/Circ. 33, Annex to the 'Traffic Separation Scheme "In the Strait of Hormuz" Change of Reference Chart and Chart Datum', adopted on 25 February 1994, available https://www.transportstyrelsen.se/globalassets/global/sjofart/dokument/sjotrafik_dok/imo_colreg.2_cirkular.pdf; accessed 5 April 2021.

24 Letter dated 20 July 2019 from the Chargé d'affaires a.i. of the Permanent Mission of the United Kingdom of Great Britain and Northern Ireland to the United Nations addressed to the President of the Security Council, UN Doc. S/2019/589, 22 July 2019, 1.

25 Letter dated 23 July 2019 from the Chargé d' affaires a.i. of the Permanent Mission of the Islamic Republic of Iran to the United Nations addressed to the Secretary-General and the President of the Security Council, UN Doc. S/2019/593, 23 July 2019, 1.

> As a result of that collision, the Iranian vessel suffered serious physical damage and some of the injured crew and fishermen are still in critical condition. Subsequently, the tanker disregarded the warnings by the Iranian coastal authorities, switched off its Automatic Identification System at 2059 local time and, in a dangerous operation, entered the Strait of Hormuz from the exit lane.[26]

This narrative contradicts the position of the United Kingdom, according to which the tanker was "in full compliance with all navigation and international regulations, with her Automatic Identification System (AIS) switched on and publicly available and verifiable."[27] The United Kingdom further maintained that there is no evidence of an alleged collision with an Iranian fishing boat and that "[e]ven if it had occurred, the ship's location within Omani territorial waters means that Iran would not have been permitted to intercept the Stena Impero."[28]

Iran deemed the arrest of the *Stena Impero* necessary for the investigation of alleged damages to the Iranian individuals and the fishing vessel as well as pollution of and damage to the marine environment, in addition to alleged dangerous navigation by the tanker.[29] In this context, environmental law may fall the subject of securitization, particularly where the main stakeholders engage in so-called lawfare.[30] Arguments from the field of environmental law can be used, *inter alia*, as a tool that serve broader security and related geopolitical aims for prohibiting or advocating against activities that are perceived as having a detrimental effect on the security of the coastal States.

The *Stena Impero* and its crew were released by the Iranian authorities two months later, at the end of September 2019.[31] The incident raises questions about the limits of a coastal State's right to hamper international navigation though straits for alleged violations of TSS safety rules.

Under Articles 39(3) and 41 of LOSC, the TSS does not apply to aircraft that exercise the right of transit passage. Neither are sovereign immune vessels under the regime of transit passage strictly obliged to follow a TSS, although

26 Ibid.

27 UN Security Council Doc. S/2019/589, *op. cit.*, 1.

28 Ibid.

29 UN Security Council Doc. S/2019/593, *op. cit.*, 1.

30 *Lawfare* is a term coined by Charles J. Dunlap, Jr. in 2001 for characterising "the use of law as a weapon of war". CJ Dunlap, Jr, *Law and Military Interventions: Preserving Humanitarian Values in 21st Conflicts* (Harvard University, Washington DC, 2001), 2.

31 J Marcus, 'Stena Impero: Seized British tanker leaves Iran's waters', *BBC News* (27 September 2019).

it is generally recommended to do so.[32] By contrast, non-State-owned foreign ships, such as *Stena Impero*, are obliged to follow the TSS during transit passage (Articles 39(2)(a) and 41(7) of LOSC).

Yet it is not entirely clear whether and to what extent a coastal State is entitled to take measures against a commercial ship sailing through a strait under the right of transit passage in response to violations of the TSS. Article 233 of LOSC stipulates that if a non-State-owned foreign ship has committed a violation of the laws and regulations referred to in Article 42(1)(a)-(b) of LOSC, causing or threatening major damage to the marine environment of a strait, the States bordering the relevant strait may take appropriate enforcement measures. The scope of Article 42 covers, *inter alia*, violations of the safety of navigation and the regulation of maritime traffic, including TSS, through its reference to Article 41 of LOSC. It is widely understood that these rights fall short of arresting the ship that has breached the relevant TSS. With a reference to the drafting history of Article 42(2) of LOSC, Nandan and Anderson argue that "[t]o give a right of arrest in a strait would undermine the right of transit passage (arrest in port, in an appropriate case, in respect of something done in a strait, was a different matter)".[33] Arresting a ship for a breach of the TSS and the relevant compulsory routing measures in a strait would result in hampering and suspending the right of transit passage against the terms of Article 44 of LOSC.[34] Although a ship that has breached the relevant TSS would have the right to continue its transit passage, the State bordering the strait can issue a warning to the ship and may take other relevant steps, such as seeking a compensation for any damage inflicted or issuing a fine.

However, such a liberal transit regime does not apply in a strait if it is, instead, governed by the regime of innocent passage. Notably, according to Iran's position, the legal regime of innocent passage applies in the Strait of Hormuz.[35] The question of which regime applies and the implications of this to navigation in the Strait of Hormuz is examined below.

32 See Section 8.2 of the IMO Resolution A.572(14), as amended, 'General Provisions on Ships' Routeing', adopted on 20 November 1985, entered into force (as amended) 1 January 1997. See also *The Commander's Handbook on the Law of Naval Operations*, *op. cit.*, 2–8.

33 Nandan, Anderson, *op. cit.*, 192.

34 See, e.g., SB Kempton, 'Ship Routing Measures in International Straits' (2000) 14 *Ocean Yearbook*, 241 (with further references to State practice and opinions expressed in the relevant legal literature).

35 UN Security Council Doc. S/2019/593, *op. cit.*, 2.

8.4 Parallel Passage Regimes in the Strait of Hormuz?

It has been argued that since Iran has not ratified the LOSC and rejects the right of transit passage as part of customary international law, it is entitled only to a 3-NM-wide territorial sea which was commonly adopted by coastal States for measuring the breadth of their territorial sea prior to the agreement on the 12-NM-limit under LOSC.[36] However, the 12 NM maximum breadth of a territorial is supported by consistent State practice and has been deemed, *inter alia*, by the ICJ as forming a rule of customary international law.[37] The 12-NM-limit of a territorial sea was widely considered a customary rule before the entry into force of LOSC.[38] The same cannot necessarily be said about the classification of the right of transit passage as part of customary international law.[39]

James Kraska summarizes Iran's approach, which is critical of the existence of a customary right of transit passage and has found that "[t]he regime of transit passage is reserved only for parties to [LOSC]."[40] Notably, Iran or, for example, the United States as one of the main user States of the Strait of Hormuz are not States party to LOSC. On the other hand, the position of the United States is that the right of transit passage is part of customary international law and in a diplomatic note to Iran has made it clear that "[t]he regimes of … transit passage, as reflected in the Convention, are clearly based on customary practice of long standing and reflect the balance of rights and interests among all States, regardless of whether they have signed or ratified the Convention".[41]

Distinct from the right of transit passage, the regime of innocent passage clearly enables the coastal State to take action in its territorial sea to prevent passage which is not innocent (Art 25(1) of LOSC). A ship that does not comply with rules adopted for the safety of navigation and the regulation of maritime traffic, including relevant rules relating to sea lanes and TSS, would be in a non-innocent passage (Arts 21(1) and 22(1) of LOSC).

36 Kraska 2013, *op. cit.*, 326, 328–329, 365.

37 Territorial and Maritime Dispute (Nicaragua v. Colombia), Judgment, I.C.J. Reports 2012, 624, para 177. JE Noyes, 'The Territorial Sea and Contiguous Zone', in DR Rothwell, AG Oude Elferink, KN Scott, T Stephens (eds), *The Oxford Handbook of the Law of the Sea* (Oxford University Press, Oxford, 2015), 94–95.

38 S Mahmoudi, 'Passage of warships through the Strait of Hormuz' (1991) *Marine Policy*, 339.

39 Ibid., 339, 347.

40 Kraska 2013, *op. cit.*, 360.

41 J Ashley Roach, RW Smith, *Excessive Maritime Claims* (Martinus Nijhoff, Leiden/Boston 2012, 3rd Edition), 294–295.

Nonetheless, even if ships sail through the Strait of Hormuz under the right of innocent passage, they are granted under the law of the sea additional safeguards that are aimed at protecting the stability of navigation in international straits. The ICJ has found that the right of non-suspendable innocent passage through straits forms a rule of customary international law:

> It is, in the opinion of the Court, generally recognized and in accordance with international custom that States in time of peace have a right to send their warships through straits used for international navigation between two parts of the high seas without the previous authorization of a coastal State, provided that the passage is innocent. Unless otherwise prescribed in an international convention, there is no right for a coastal State to prohibit such passage through straits in time of peace.[42]

The regime of non-suspendable innocent passage is also recognised in the 1958 Convention on the Territorial Sea and the Contiguous Zone.[43] Iran signed the 1958 Convention but has not ratified it (as is the case for UNCLOS).[44] By contrast, Oman has not signed the 1958 Convention, but it ratified LOSC in 1989.[45]

Under Article 16(4) of the 1958 Convention, it is stipulated that there shall be no suspension of the innocent passage of foreign ships through straits which are used for international navigation between one part of the high seas and another part of the high seas or the territorial sea of a foreign State. Non-suspendable innocent passage is also safeguarded under Article 45 of LOSC. The legal regime of non-suspendable innocent passage prevents the suspension of passage due to, *inter alia*, the coastal State's military exercises in a strait.

Both Iran and Oman might require foreign warships to apply for a permit if warships intend to exercise the right of innocent passage through Iran's or Oman's territorial sea.[46] This requirement is based on Iran's and Oman's interpretation of Articles 19, 21 and 25 of LOSC. Under Article 9 of the Act on the Marine Areas of Iran in the Persian Gulf and the Oman Sea, passage through

42 Ibid.

43 Convention on the Territorial Sea and the Contiguous Zone, adopted 29 April 1958, entered into force 10 September 1964, 516 UNTS 205.

44 UN Treaty Collection, Convention on the Territorial Sea and the Contiguous Zone, status at 10 February 2021.

45 UN Treaty Collection, United Nations Convention on the Law of the Sea, status at 10 December 2021.

46 Iran's declaration upon signing LOSC on 10 December 1982, *op. cit.*

the territorial sea is subject to the prior authorisation of Iran's relevant authorities in respect of the following types of ships: warships and submarines, nuclear-powered ships and vessels or any other floating objects or vessels carrying nuclear or other dangerous or noxious substances harmful to the environment.[47] However, under customary international law, as stated in the ICJ's judgment in the *Corfu Channel Case* (cited above), the permit-based passage regime cannot be applicable in respect of ships that cross the Iranian territorial sea in the Strait of Hormuz solely for transiting the strait.

Based on the previous discussion, the passage regimes of the Strait of Hormuz depend on the flag State's status as either a party or a non-party to LOSC. In this context, Said Mahmoudi has concluded that:

> In a hypothetical situation where Iran and a third State – both non-parties to the LOS Convention – have a dispute concerning the passage of a certain warship through the Strait of Hormuz, the legal implication of Iran's declaration seems to be that the status of transit passage as customary law has to be decided *proprio motu* by the court, or at any rate the onus of proof as to the existence of such status is placed on the party which invokes it. In both cases, the present position of Iran seems to be in order.[48]

It is not clear if the right of transit passage forms part of customary international law. If it does not, then non-parties to LOSC can at least invoke the customary right of non-suspendable innocent passage for transiting the Strait of Hormuz. By contrast, such prominent user States of the Strait of Hormuz as China, Japan, South Korea, the EU Member States, the United Kingdom, Norway, and other States party to LOSC can invoke the applicability of the right of transit passage in the Strait of Hormuz. Both Iran (as a signatory State to LOSC) and Oman (as a State Party to LOSC) need to respect the right of transit passage of States party to LOSC in the Strait of Hormuz.

As discussed previously in the example of the Kerch Strait,[49] the strait State's system of straight baselines might have a significant impact on the passage regime of a strait. Hence, it is examined next whether the legal regime of

---

47 Act on the Marine Areas of the Islamic Republic of Iran in the Persian Gulf and the Oman Sea, adopted on 20 April 1993, entered into force 2 May 1993, available https://www.un.org/Depts/los/LEGISLATIONANDTREATIES/PDFFILES/IRN_1993_Act.pdf; accessed 5 April 2021.

48 Mahmoudi 1991, *op. cit.*, 348.

49 See *supra* Chapters 4.6–4.7 of Part 2.

internal waters can potentially adversely affect international navigation in the Strait of Hormuz and in its approaches.

8.5 Significance of Iranian Internal Waters for the Passage Regime in the Strait of Hormuz

Iran's current system of straight baselines that connects islands in the Persian Gulf appears not have great significance for the passage regime in the Strait of Hormuz. When selecting base points for its system of straight baselines, Iran respected the rule that a base point that is located on land over which there are contested sovereignty claims cannot constitute an "appropriate point" in terms of Article 7(1) of LOSC. The title over the islands of Greater and Lesser Tunbs and Abu Musa, located in the eastern end of the Persian Gulf, is contested between Iran and the United Arab Emirates since 1971 when Iran occupied the islands.[50]

Iran has not connected Greater and Lesser Tunbs and Abu Musa by a straight baseline with its mainland coast and neighbouring islands.[51] The islands of Forur, Bani Forur and Sirri are also not part of Iran's system of straight baselines, albeit Iran's title over these islands is not disputed.[52] It is doubtful if these islands can be considered as a fringe of islands along the coast in the immediate vicinity of Iran's mainland (see Art 7(1) of LOSC). These islands are distant from the mainland coast as they are located in the centre of the eastern part of the Persian Gulf and west of Tunbs and Abu Musa islands.[53]

However, Section 3(2) of the Iranian Marine Areas Act stipulates that waters on the landward side of the baseline of the territorial sea, and waters between islands belonging to Iran, where the distance of such islands does not exceed 24 NM, form part of the internal waters and are under Iran's sovereignty. The islands of Tunbs, Abu Musa, Forur, Bani Forur and Sirri are all located within

50 Letter dated 3 December 1971 from the Permanent Representatives of Algeria, Iraq, Libyan Arab Republic and People's Democratic Republic of Yemen to the United Nations Addressed to the President of the Security Council, UN Doc. S/10409, 3 December 1971, 1. Letter dated 5 January 2017 from the Chargé d'affaires a.i. of the Permanent Mission of the United Arab Emirates to the United Nations addressed to the President of the Security Council, UN Doc. S/2017/17, 6 January 2017, 1.

51 J Ashley Roach, JT Oliver, RW Smith, *Limits in the Seas, No. 114: Iran's Maritime Claims* (United States Department of State, Washington DC, 1994), 9. Marineregions.org, 'Iran', *op. cit.*

52 Ibid.

53 See Map 7.

24-NM-limit as measured from each other.[54] Thus, they generate a continuous stretch of territorial sea that extends from the Iranian mainland coast deep into the Persian Gulf. It also extends relatively close to the coast of the United Arab Emirates on the southern coast of the Strait of Hormuz (Musandam Peninsula).

The TSS in the Strait of Hormuz crosses this maritime area. Westbound traffic is directed to waters between, on the one hand, the Iranian mainland coast and, on the other hand, the islands of Greater and Lesser Tunbs and Forur. These three islands separate eastbound traffic from westbound traffic, while Bani Forur, Sirri and Abu Musa islands are further away and bolster Iran's influence and potential control over international traffic in the Strait of Hormuz.

In case Iran would connect the afore-mentioned islands by straight baseline segments with its mainland coast, then this would result in the designation of internal waters that span a large maritime area in the centre of the eastern end of the Persian Gulf. The outer limit of Iranian internal waters would be located approximately 40 NM away from the closest point on its mainland coast. Notably, this scenario is not dependent on whether Iran extends a hypothetical straight baseline system to the contested Tunbs and Abu Musa islands. Iran's title over Sirri Island is not contested. The distance from Sirri Island to the mainland coast of Iran is comparable to that of the furthest lying Abu Musa Island.[55]

The potential for the extension of the Iranian system of straight baselines in the Persian Gulf has led Hugh Lynch to conclude that:

> The practical significance of such an Iranian "internal sea" is that Iran might attempt to divert non-Iranian shipping, especially tankers, to southern Gulf waters which would be impassable for some Very Large Crude Carriers (VLCCs) and most, if not all Ultra Large Crude Carriers (ULCCs).... If Iran held tenaciously to the concept of such *internal* waters, it might also claim that merchant ships, including tankers, might not proceed under the provisions of *innocent* passage; and warships might be challenged while exercising the right of *transit* passage.[56]

54 Abu Musa, the most distant island as measured from the Iranian coast, is located some 24 NM away from its closest neighbouring island of Sirri.

55 See Map 7.

56 HF Lynch, 'Freedom of Navigation in the Persian Gulf and Strait of Hormuz', in MH Nordquist, JN Moore (eds), *Security Flashpoints: Oil, Islands, Sea Access and Military Confrontation* (Martinus Nijhoff, The Hague/Boston/London, 1998), 327–328.

It might be tempting for Iran to unilaterally encircle, under Section 3(2) of its Marine Areas Act, the western part of the TSS in the Strait of Hormuz with its straight baseline segments. However, under the law of the sea, the establishment of such internal waters in the centre of the eastern end of the Persian Gulf would not have a significant adverse impact on international shipping. As stipulated in Articles 8(2) and 35(a) of LOSC, the rights of innocent passage and transit passage still apply in internal waters if the establishment of a straight baseline in accordance with the method set forth in Article 7 of LOSC has the effect of enclosing as internal waters areas that had not previously been considered as such.

On the basis of this legal analysis the rights of innocent and transit passage could still be used by ships transiting the western part of the TSS in the Strait of Hormuz even if Iran declares this maritime area as its internal waters. Since the maritime area between the Iranian islands of Tunbs, Abu Musa, Forur, Bani Forur and Sirri has not been previously classified as internal waters, the creation of internal waters (mis)using the method stipulated in Article 7 of UNCLOS for the drawing of straight baselines would not preclude the continued enjoyment of the rights of innocent and transit passage by foreign vessels.

However, hypothetical new straight baseline segments cannot in any case be drawn in accordance with Article 7 of LOSC as the Iranian islands of Tunbs, Abu Musa, Forur, Bani Forur and Sirri are not situated along the Iranian mainland coast in its immediate vicinity. Furthermore, even if Iran would, hypothetically, claim that these waters had been historically considered by Iran as internal waters, then this claim would, in all likelihood, not be recognised by most States. In conclusion, Iran's hypothetical establishment of new straight baseline segments around the afore-mentioned islands would not meet the criteria of Articles 7, 8(2) and 35(a) of LOSC, as a result of which such a unilateral measure by Iran would not have, from a legal perspective, an impact on international shipping in the Strait of Hormuz.

CHAPTER 9

Tensions in and over the Taiwan Strait in 2021

The previous chapter debated discriminatory navigational restrictions in the Strait of Hormuz which is characterised by a long rivalry between great maritime powers. Such geopolitical tensions are also commonplace in the Taiwan Strait which is crossed by heavy ship traffic. This includes most of the oil tankers that embark on their voyage from the Persian Gulf via the Strait of Hormuz to the Asian markets. Breaches of the applicable navigational regime and coastal State's restrictions to the passage of foreign ships in the Taiwan Strait are discussed next.

9.1 Legal and Geographical Characteristics of the Taiwan Strait

The Taiwan Strait connects the South China Sea with the East China Sea and the ports located in China's southern coast (e.g., Hong Kong) with ports in China's eastern coast (e.g., Shanghai). Thus, much of international navigation heading to or from Central and Northern China, Japan, South Korea, North Korea, and Eastern Russia crosses the Taiwan Strait. Reportedly, on average, 483 ships of over 300 GT passed through the Taiwan Strait each day in 2015–2017.[1]

The number of ships of over 300 GT crossing the Taiwan Strait daily is more than double that of the Strait of Malacca (in 2017, respectively close to 500 in the Taiwan Strait and 230 in the Strait of Malacca) and approximately ten times more than that of the Suez Canal (see Figure 2).[2] In total numbers, more than 1000 ships cross the Taiwan Strait each day; this includes the busy ferry traffic between Taiwan and mainland China (over 2 million passengers cross the strait annually).[3]

The approximately 170-NM-long Taiwan Strait is located between mainland China and Taiwan Island. At its narrowest, the Taiwan Strait is approximately 72 NM wide in its southern part (between Taiwanese Bird Island and

1 T Chai, H Xue, 'A study on ship collision conflict prediction in the Taiwan Strait using the EMD-based LSSVM method' (2021) 16(5) *PLoS ONE*, 2.

2 See the respective figures for the Strait of Singapore in M Hand, 'Malacca Straits VLCC traffic doubles in a decade as shipping traffic hits all time high in 2017', *SeaTrade Maritime News* (19 February 2018). For the Suez Canal, see Suez Canal Traffic Statistics: Annual Report 2017, Suez Canal Authority 2018, 2. See also Anonymous, 'Egypt's Suez Canal blocked by huge container ship', *BBC News* (24 March 2021).

3 台湾海峡首艘千吨级海事巡航救助船开工建造 ('Construction of the first 1,000-ton maritime cruise rescue ship in the Taiwan Strait starts'), *Xinhua* (24 May 2019).

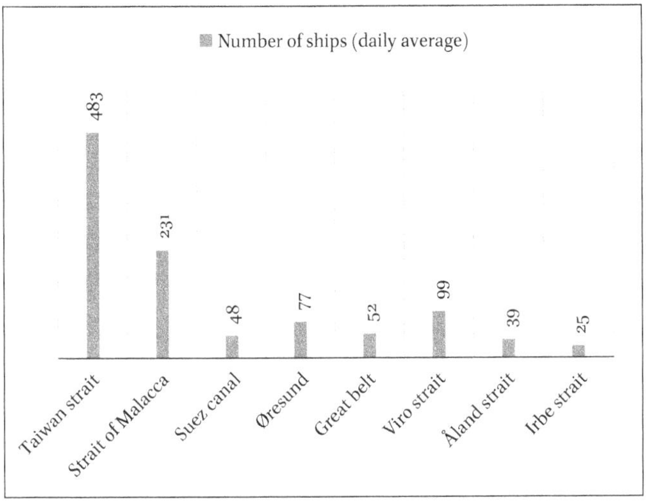

FIGURE 2 Traffic density in the straits of Taiwan and Malacca, the Suez Canal, and the Baltic Straits in 2017
Note: The number for the Taiwan Strait is an educated guess based on the fact that according to the Chinese data, on average, 483 ships of over 300 GT passed through the Taiwan Strait each day in 2015–2017, and in total numbers, more than 1000 ships cross the Taiwan Strait each day. Chai, Xue, *op. cit.*, 2. 台湾海峡首艘千吨级海事巡航救助船开工建造, *op. cit.* Calculations in respect of the Malacca Strait and the Suez Canal are based on the following sources: SUEZ CANAL TRAFFIC STATISTICS: ANNUAL REPORT 2017, *OP. CIT.*, 2. THE DATA IN RELATION TO THE BALTIC STRAITS IS COLLECTED FROM THE HELCOM MAP AND DATA SERVICE, AVAILABLE HTTP://MAPS.HELCOM.FI/WEBSITE/MAPSERVICE/, *OP. CIT.*

China's Jinmen Dao Island) and approximately 64 NM wide in its northern part (between Taiwan Island and the Chinese Niushan Dao Island). Thus, the Taiwan Strait is not a strait subject to Part III of LOSC as it falls outside the maximum outer limits of a territorial sea. This conclusion follows Article 35(b) of LOSC, according to which Part III of LOSC does not affect the legal status of the waters beyond the territorial seas of States bordering straits as EEZs or high seas. The Taiwan Strait includes a tens of NMs wide EEZ,[4] wherein the freedom

4 See Exclusive Economic Zone and Continental Shelf Act, adopted 26 June 1998, entered into force 26 June 1998; Order by the Chairman of the People's Republic of China No. 6 (on the same act) of 26 June 1998. Both accessible at China, 'Legislation', Division for Ocean Affairs and the Law of the Sea, available https://www.un.org/depts/los/LEGISLATIONANDTREATIES/STATEFILES/CHN.htm; accessed 30 August 2021. For Taiwan, see Law of the People's

of navigation and overflight is guaranteed under Article 58(1) in combination with Article 87(1)(a)-(b) of LOSC.[5]

The Luzon Strait is in respect of the Taiwan Strait an alternative sea route for ships heading to or from East China Sea or the Philippine Sea. The Luzon Strait is located between Taiwan and the Philippines and is at its narrowest point approximately 100 km (or 54 NM) wide. Hence, it includes an approximately 30-NM-wide EEZ in and over which ships and aircraft are entitled to the freedom of navigation and overflight. Consequently, Article 35(b) of LOSC also applies to the Luzon Strait.

9.2 Navigation in the Taiwan Strait in the Light of Recent Developments in China's Legislation

Against the backdrop of increased military tensions between China and Taiwan, the United States and the United Kingdom have increased their naval presence in and near the Taiwan Strait.[6] The United States has frequently conducted Freedom of Navigation operations in the Taiwan Strait. In addition, warships of many other States have recently transited that waterway. For example, the United Kingdom's and Canada's warships transited the Taiwan Strait in autumn 2021.[7] Such transits by foreign warships are usually considered by China as constituting a threat to regional peace and security.

Presumably partly as a reaction to the above-listed recent transits by the warships of the United States, UK, and Canada, China and Russia conducted a joint naval exercise in November 2021, in the course of which their flotilla of ten warships transited the Japanese Straits of Tsugaru and Osumi Strait that border Japan's main island.[8] Both the Tsugaru Strait and Osumi Strait fall under the

Republic of China on the Exclusive Economic Zone and the Continental Shelf, adopted 26 June 1998, entered into force 26 June 1998, available http://www.asianlii.org/cn/legis/cen/laws/eezatcs443/; accessed 30 August 2021.

5 The same conclusion is reached in K Zou, 'Redefining the Legal Status of the Taiwan Strait' (2000) 15(2) *The International Journal of Marine and Coastal Law*, 252. See also Kraska and Pedrozo, *op. cit.*, 224–225.

6 M Martina, I Ali, 'U.S. warship transits Taiwan Strait after Chinese assault drills', *Reuters* (28 August 2021). F Gardner, 'China warns UK as carrier strike group approaches', *BBC News* (30 July 2021). L Xuanzun, 'US warships' Taiwan Straits transit, S.China Sea drill futile to contain China: observers', *Global Times* (29 July 2021).

7 R Woo, B Blanchard, I Ali, 'China condemns U.S., Canada for sending warships through Taiwan Strait', *Reuters* (17 October 2021).

8 B Lendon, 'Why Russian and Chinese warships teaming up to circle Japan is a big deal', *CNN News* (25 October 2021).

Article 36-category of straits in which the high seas freedoms of navigation and overflight apply within the limits of the EEZ corridor. The EEZ corridors were established in the Tsugaru, Osumi, Soya, and Tsushima straits under Japan's Cabinet Order of 1993, pursuant to which the outer limit of Japan's 12-NM-wide territorial sea was limited to 3-NM-wide territorial sea in these straits.[9] A similar method has been applied in many Baltic straits (Bornholmsgat, Femer Belt, Viro Strait),[10] since it prevents the application of the transit passage regime to the relevant strait (from coast to coast).

Foreign ships are entitled under international law to the normal navigation regimes of innocent passage and freedom of navigation when navigating through the territorial sea or EEZ in the Taiwan Strait. However, China has imposed under its domestic legal acts certain limitations to the passage of foreign warships through its maritime area. Article 6(2) of China's Law on the Territorial Sea and the Contiguous Zone stipulates that for entering China's territorial sea, foreign warships are required to obtain a permission from China's Government.[11] China's permit-based right of innocent passage in respect of foreign warships is not compatible with Article 17 of LOSC.[12] On the opposite coast of the Taiwan Strait, Taiwan restricts the right of innocent passage by requiring foreign warships to submit a prior notification when navigating through its territorial sea.[13]

By revising its Maritime Traffic Safety Law in 2021, China has now also enacted a prior notification requirement in respect of the following types of foreign ships entering or leaving China's territorial sea: submersibles; nuclear-powered ships; ships carrying radioactive materials or other toxic and hazardous materials; other vessels that may endanger China's maritime traffic safety.[14] The imposition of the prior notification requirement in respect of a broad range of foreign ships is complemented with other navigational restrictions

9 Enforcement Order of the Law on the Territorial Sea and the Contiguous Zone (Cabinet Order No. 210 of 1977, as amended by Cabinet Order No. 383 of 1993, and Cabinet Order No. 206 of 1996), Annexed Schedule 2 (with reference to articles 3 and 4). RW Smith *et al.*, *Limits in the Seas, No. 120. Straight Baseline and Territorial Sea Claims: Japan* (US Department of State, Washington D.C., 1998), 13–15. Kraska and Pedrozo, *op. cit.*, 227.

10 See *supra* Chapter 2.1 of Part 1.

11 Law on the Territorial Sea and the Contiguous Zone, adopted 25 February 1992, entered into force 25 February 1992.

12 See further, e.g., Zou 2000, *op. cit.*, 254.

13 Law on the Territorial Sea and the Contiguous Zone of the Republic of China, adopted 21 January 1998, entered into force 21 January 1998, Art 7(5).

14 Maritime Traffic Safety Law of the People's Republic of China, adopted 2 September 1983 (revised 29 April 2021, entered into force 1 September 2021), Art 54.

that China can potentially impose "in the sea areas under the jurisdiction of the People's Republic of China."[15] Pedrozo has observed that such delimitation of the spatial scope of the application of the Maritime Traffic Safety Law "is not defined in the law and is purposely vague".[16]

Article 30 of China's revised Maritime Traffic Safety Law enables to establish compulsory pilotage in respect of foreign ships also in maritime areas that fall outside the limits of China's sovereign territory, but are subject to its jurisdiction, e.g., China's EEZ wherein compulsory pilotage would be incompatible with the freedom of navigation.[17] The same controversy characterises Article 44 that, in combination with Article 2 of the revised Maritime Traffic Safety Law, potentially allows for the suspension of the passage of foreign ships also in maritime areas outside China's territorial sea.

In addition, China limits the use of high seas freedoms in its EEZ by subjecting military surveying to the requirement of a prior permission. China's imposition of this requirement is due to its considerations of national security interests. China considers that military surveying falls under the scope of marine scientific research and thus requires the coastal State's prior permission.[18] The legal regime of marine scientific research and its relation to seabed surveying in an EEZ by foreign vessels is examined below in the example of an Estonian-Russian 2005 incident in the Viro Strait.[19]

In January 2021, China adopted its new Coast Guard Law, which was discussed in greater detail above (see Chapter 5.3 of Part 2). Similar to the above-discussed China's Maritime Traffic Safety Law, Article 3 of the 2021 Coast Guard Law mandates the Chinese Coast Guard to operate in the waters under China's jurisdiction, while leaving its spatial extent undefined. Thus, Liu, Xu, and Chang maintain that 'the determination of China's jurisdictional waters should be based on China's 1998 Exclusive Economic Zone and Continental Shelf Act and 1992 Territorial Sea and Contiguous Zone Act, which specifically

15 Ibid., Art 2.

16 R Pedrozo, 'China's Revised Maritime Traffic Safety Law' (2021) 97 *International Law Studies*, 957.

17 Ibid., 960.

18 See Pedrozo 2009, *op. cit.*, 101–110. See also C Rahman, M Tsamenyi, 'A Strategic Perspective on Security and Naval Issues in the South China Sea', in NA Hu, TL McDorman (eds), *Maritime Issues in the South China Sea: Troubled Waters or A Sea of Opportunity* (Routledge, New York, 2013), 47–48. See also Article 9 of China's Exclusive Economic Zone and Continental Shelf Act.

19 See *infra* Chapter 12 of Part 4.

set out the scope of China's jurisdictional waters.'[20] The adoption of the 2021 Coast Guard Law has increased concerns over China's Coast Guard's use of force against foreign sovereign immune vessels.[21] Shortly after the promulgation of China's Coast Guard Law, Taiwan and the United States established a Coast Guard Working Group that is aimed at improving communications, building cooperation, and sharing information between the two parties.[22]

9.3 Geopolitical Tensions in the Taiwan Strait and Intrusions of Taiwan's Air Defence Identification Zone

China and most other States, including the United States, do not recognise Taiwan as an independent State. Under the "one China" policy, Beijing strives to establish control over the self-ruling Taiwan. At the same time, the United States has committed itself to defend Taiwan against a Chinese invasion.[23]

In addition to Taiwan Island, Taipei governs some distant groups of islands/rocks (Mazu Islands and Kinmen Islands), some of which are located at a sight distance from mainland China (e.g., Gaodeng Island is located 9 km from mainland China and Kinmen Islands are situated a couple of km east of China's Xiamen city).[24] Taiwan also controls Taiping Dao (a.k.a. Itu Aba) that is the largest feature among the Spratly Islands located in the middle of the South China Sea and that both China and Taiwan consider as an island under Article 121(1) of LOSC.[25] In the *South China Sea arbitration*, the Annex VII Arbitral Tribunal did not agree with this position and decided that Taiping Dao (Itu Aba) nor any other feature in the Spratly Islands, including Zhongzhou Reef that is also controlled by Taiwan, is capable of sustaining an economic life of its own.[26] Thus, the features in the Spratly Islands constitute rocks that do

20 C-H Liu, Z Xu, Y-C Chang, 'Coast Guard Law of the People's Republic of China and Its Implications in International Law' (2021) 36(3) *The International Journal of Marine and Coastal Law*, 494.

21 S Sakamoto, 'China's New Coast Guard Law and Implications for Maritime Security in the East and South China Seas', *Lawfare* (16 February 2021).

22 American Institute in Taiwan, 'U.S.-Taiwan Coast Guard Working Group Advances Joint Maritime Cooperation Goals', Press Release, 11 August 2021.

23 K Liptak, 'Biden vows to protect Taiwan in event of Chinese attack', CNN *News* (22 October 2021).

24 Navionics ChartViewer, *op. cit.*

25 Ibid. *South China Sea Arbitration,* Award of 12 July 2016, *op. cit.*, paras. 467–468. For its geographical characteristics, see Ibid., para 401. See the map of the island, in Ibid., p. 125.

26 South China Sea arbitral award, *op. cit.*, paras. 626, 632.

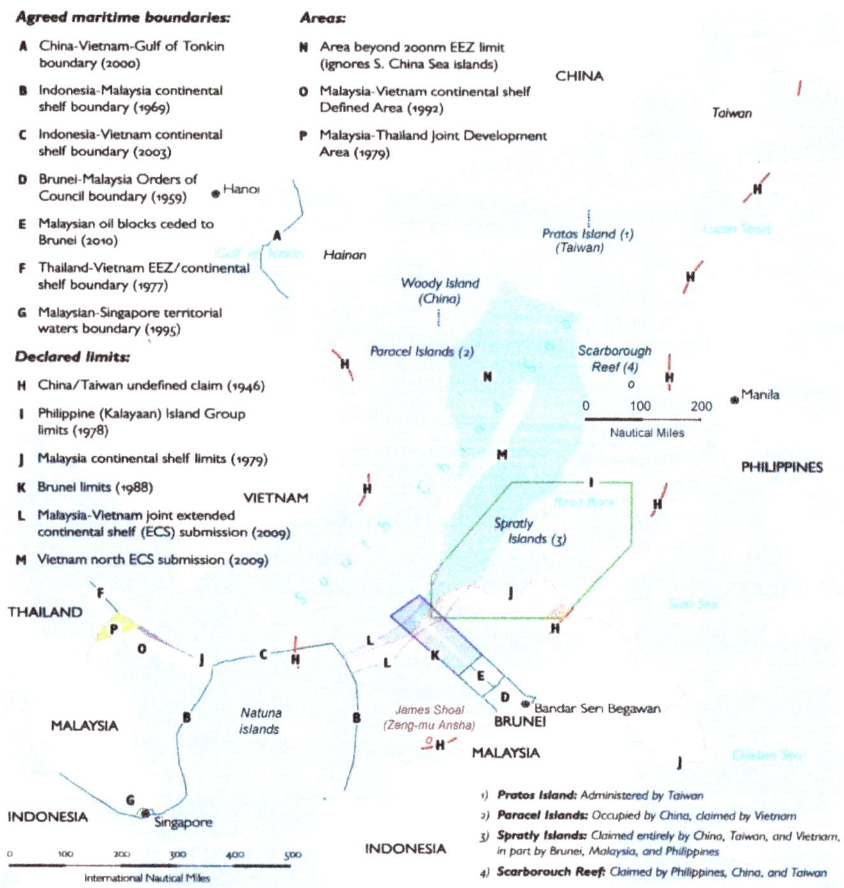

MAP 8 The Taiwan Strait and the South China Sea.
SOURCE: WIKIMEDIA COMMONS, 'SOUTH CHINA SEA CLAIMS AND BOUNDARY AGREEMENTS 2012'.

not generate an EEZ or continental shelf (Art 121(3) of LOSC). It is reasonable to expect that the same conclusion applies to the Taiwan-controlled Pratas atoll, which is a much smaller geographic feature as compared with Taiping Dao (Itu Aba); the atoll is located in the northern part of the South China Sea (approximately 435 km west as measured from Taiwan Island).[27] Most of the intrusions of Taiwan's air defence identification zone (hereafter ADIZ) in 2021 by China's aircraft occurred near the Pratas atoll and the Luzon Strait (see Map 8).

27 Navionics ChartViewer, *op. cit.*

In the beginning of 2021, the possibility of China launching an armed attack against Taiwan was considered low.[28] Notably still, as of 2020, China has increased the number of its warplanes flying near Taiwan's airspace. The number of incursions of China's warplanes into Taiwan's ADIZ peaked in September and early October 2021.[29] In addition, Taiwan is concerned about Chinese military exercises near Taiwan and alleged cyber-attacks against Taiwan's institutions.[30]

An ADIZ is defined as a "[s]pecial designated airspace of defined dimensions within which aircraft are required to comply with special identification and/or reporting procedures additional to those related to the provision of air traffic services".[31] It is used for facilitating the use of measures against the violations of sovereign airspace.[32] Numerous States have established ADIZs without much controversy, even though they lack a clear legal framework under international law.[33] Legally speaking, the identification and reporting requirements in an ADIZ outside the sovereign airspace of the relevant State are not mandatory. Hence, the operations of Chinese military aircraft in Taiwan's ADIZ might be considered as provocative, but they are not violating international law as long as they do not amount to a breach of sovereign airspace and a threat or use of force under Article 2(4) of the UN Charter.

Often an ADIZ does not overlap with the outer limits of the relevant State's own airspace. For example, Taiwan's ADIZ was created in the 1950s with the assistance of the United States military and covers not only the airspace above Taiwan Island, but extends north-westward to cover the Taiwan Strait and also significant parts of foreign airspace above mainland China mostly in Fujian province near Taiwan-controlled Mazu Islands and Kinmen Islands.[34] There

28 MJ Mazarr, N Beauchamp-Mustafaga, TR Heath, D Eaton, 'What Deters and Why? The State of Deterrence in Korea and the Taiwan Strait', *RAND*, 2021, 47.

29 B Blanchard, 'Taiwan reports largest incursion yet by Chinese air force', *Reuters* (15 June 2021). Anonymous, 'Taiwan says 19 Chinese warplanes entered air defence zone', *BBC News* (6 September 2021). S McDonell, 'China-Taiwan military tensions 'worst in 40 years'', *BBC News* (6 October 2021). C Buckley, SL Myers, "Starting a Fire': U.S. and China Enter Dangerous Territory Over Taiwan', *The New York Times* (9 October 2021).

30 Y Lee, D Lague, B Blanchard, 'China launches 'gray-zone' warfare to subdue Taiwan', *Reuters* (10 December 2020). YL Tian, Y Lee, 'China holds assault drills near Taiwan after 'provocations', *Reuters* (17 August 2021).

31 Annex 15 to the Convention on International Civil Aviation (16th ed.), International Civil Aviation Organization, Montréal 2018, Chapter 1, 1–2.

32 Ishii, *op. cit.*, 169.

33 J Su, 'The Practice of States on Air Defense Identification Zones: Geographical Scope, Object of Identification, and Identification Measures' (2020) 18(4) *Chinese Journal of International Law*, 812–813. On the various ADIZs, see Ibid., 814–825.

34 Ibid., 816.

is a significant overlap between the ADIZs of Taiwan, China, and Japan in the East China Sea region, including over Senkaku Islands.[35]

The voluntary identification and reporting requirements within an ADIZ provide additional safeguards against such intrusions of civil or military aircraft into the coastal State's airspace that might jeopardise its national security. Foreign military aircraft rarely comply with the voluntary identification and reporting requirements when crossing an ADIZ.[36] By contrast, civil aircraft normally comply with the voluntary identification and reporting requirements that apply when crossing an ADIZ.[37]

35 Ishii, *op. cit.*, 169–170.
36 Su, *op. cit.*, 826–827.
37 Ibid., 830–832.

CHAPTER 10

Discriminatory Navigational Restrictions in the Kerch Strait in Respect of Foreign Commercial Ships

Similar to the situation in the Strait of Hormuz and the Taiwan Strait, navigation through the Kerch Strait has been significantly impacted by geopolitical tensions. As discussed above,[1] prior to Russia's invasion of Ukraine in 2022, tensions over the passage rights in the Kerch Strait peaked already in November 2018 when the Russian Federation blocked the passage of three Ukrainian naval vessels, seized them and detained the crew. This incident was discussed in the context of the on-going arbitration proceedings between Ukraine and the Russian Federation. However, the Russian Federation restricts access from the Black Sea to the Sea of Azov not only in respect of foreign warships. Prior to its blockade of the Sea of Azov in 2022,[2] the Russian Federation imposed years-long navigational restrictions on foreign commercial ships seeking to navigate through the Kerch Strait for heading to or returning from Ukrainian ports in the Sea of Azov.

10.1 The Significance of the Kerch Strait for Commerce

The Kerch Strait falls entirely within the limits of territorial sea and/or internal waters. It gives access to the Ukrainian ports of Berdyansk, Mariupol and Henichesk, and to the Russian ports of Rostov-on-Don, Taganrog, Temryuk and Yeysk on the coast of the Sea of Azov. The Sea of Azov, in turn, is connected with the Caspian Sea via the Don River, Volga-Don Canal and Volga River. The Kerch Strait is the only maritime route from the major ports on the coast of the Sea of Azov to the Black Sea and beyond.

The Kerch Strait has relatively heavy traffic, reaching 15.229 crossings in 2010 and 19.451 in 2017.[3] As shown in Figure 3 below, these rates of crossings are comparable to those of, respectively, the Åland Strait (connecting the Gulf of Bothnia and the Baltic Sea) and the Great Belt (largest, but not busiest, among

1 *Supra* Chapters 4–5 of Part 2.
2 *Supra* Chapter 4.8.2 of Part 2.
3 See *infra* Figure 3.

DOI:10.1163/9789004509368_012

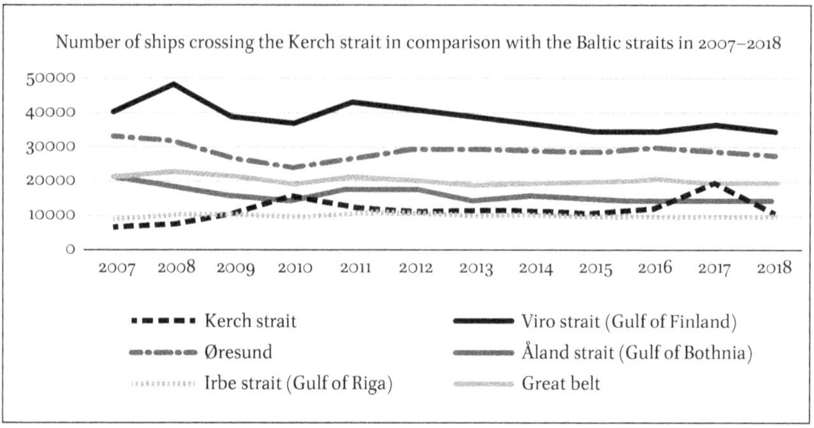

FIGURE 3 Number of annual ship crossings in the Kerch Strait and the Baltic straits
Note: Figure is based on data collected via the maps and figures of HELCOM annual reports on shipping accidents in the Baltic Sea area from 2007 to 2014, available https://helcom.fi/baltic-sea-trends/maritime/accidents/; accessed 5 April 2021. The data in relation to period 2014 to 2017 is collected from the HELCOM Map and Data Service, available http://maps.helcom.fi/website/map service/; accessed 5 April 2021. The data in relation to 2018 is collected from the Shipping accidents in the Baltic Sea 2018, HELCOM 2019, 5–6, available https://helcom.fi/baltic-sea-trends/maritime/accidents/; accessed 5 April 2021. HELCOM data does not cover 2019. The number of ships crossing the Kerch Strait decreased in 2019 to 9.361. The data on the Kerch Strait is collected from Rosmorport website, see Azovo-Chernomorsky Basin Branch, VTS Services, 'Statistics', Rosmorport 2020, available http://www.rosmorport.com/filials/nvr_serv_nav/; accessed 5 April 2021.

the Danish Straits) in the same years.[4] Nonetheless, the rate of crossings through the Kerch Strait mostly remains much lower – on average, close to 10.000 per year. For example, the strait had 10.978 crossings in 2012, 9969 crossings in 2015 and 9361 crossings in 2019.[5] This is comparable to the relatively stable rate of crossings through the Irbe Strait (leading to, e.g., the Port of Riga in the Baltic Sea), ranging from 9078 crossings in 2017 to 10.272 crossings in 2011.[6] By comparison, the traffic intensity in the Kerch Strait is many times smaller as compared with the busiest straits of the Baltic Sea, including the Viro Strait in the Gulf of Finland and Øresund between Sweden and Denmark.[7]

4 Ibid.
5 Ibid.
6 Ibid.
7 Ibid.

10.2 Restrictions on Foreign Commercial Ships' Navigation through the Kerch Strait

The Kerch Strait meets the primary geographic and functional criteria of an international strait.[8] Passage through the Kerch Strait is guaranteed under LOSC and the strait is used for international shipping, including often by ships registered in the EU,[9] between two larger maritime areas and its width is less than 24 NM.

However, passage of non-Russian ships through the Kerch Strait has been impeded, particularly as of 2014 when the Russian Federation gained control over both coasts of the strait. In 2018, the Russian Federation repeatedly obstructed the passage of ships operated for commercial as well as non-commercial purposes. The United States condemned, in August 2018, the Russian Federation's alleged harassment of international shipping, referring to Russia's practice in delaying hundreds of commercial vessels in the course of the previous five months.[10] Similarly, the European Parliament condemned, in its resolution of 25 October 2018, "the excessive stopping and inspection of commercial vessels, including both Ukrainian ships and those with flags of third-party states, including ships under flags of various EU Member States".[11] The European Parliament further condemned the infringement of navigational rights in Ukraine's territorial waters and pointed out that "Russia is bound by international maritime law and the bilateral cooperation agreement with Ukraine not to hamper or impede transit passage through the Kerch Strait and the Sea of Azov".[12]

The Russian Federation restricts navigation through the Kerch Strait via strict administrative practices as part of its VTS. In practice, these measures result in delays for foreign ships, particularly those that are passing through

8 See *supra* Chapter 2 of Part 1.

9 European Parliament resolution (EU) No 2018/2870(RSP), of 25 October 2018, *On the situation in the Sea of Azov*, point D.

10 State Department's Press Statement, 'Russia's Harassment of International Shipping Transiting the Kerch Strait and Sea of Azov', Washington DC, 30 August 2018, available https://www.state.gov/russias-harassment-of-international-shipping-transiting-the-kerch-strait-and-sea-of-azov/; accessed 5 April 2021.

11 European Parliament's 2018 resolution on the situation in the Sea of Azov, *op. cit.*, 1.

12 Ibid., 3. Although the European Parliament made a reference to transit passage, the EU has not otherwise claimed that the regime of transit passage is applicable to the Kerch Strait. Similarly, the United States has not submitted a protest for the applicability of the right of transit passage in the Kerch Strait.

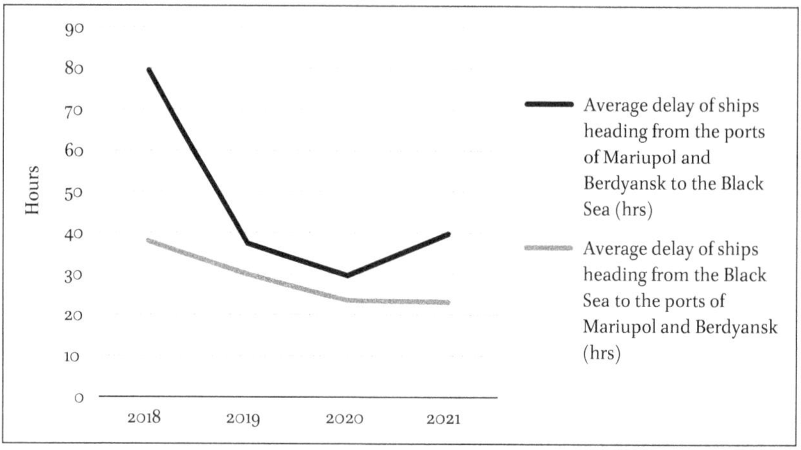

FIGURE 4 Waiting times for passing through the Kerch Strait for ships visiting the Ukrainian ports in the Sea of Azov
Note: Figure is based on data collected from the monitoring reports of the Black Sea News on the duration of artificial delays of vessels in the Kerch Strait from 2018 to 2021, available https://www.blackseanews.net/en/read/183401; accessed 12 January 2022.

the Kerch Strait for visiting the Ukrainian ports Mariupol and Berdyansk, as shown in figure 4 above.

The Russian Federation's requirements for passing through the Kerch Strait include prior notification for and authorisation of passage. It is stated in the Russian federal port authority's Rosmorport instructions "Terms and conditions of navigation services in the VTS of the Kerch Strait" that:

> A regulatory approval system of vessel movement is effective in the VTS of the Kerch Strait coverage area. Vessels enter the VTS of the Kerch Strait coverage area and leave it, approach toward to a pilot's reception position or start moving in the zone upon receipt of a VTS of the Kerch Strait operator's permit.[13]

13 VTS services, 'General Information', 'Terms and conditions of navigation services in the VTS of the Kerch Strait', Rosmorport 2020, available http://www.rosmorport.com/filials/nvr_serv_nav/#procedure_kerch; accessed 5 April 2021. The current Kerch Strait VTS system has been certified by the Russian Federation's Ministry of Transport on August 23, 2017 and the certification is valid until August 23, 2022. See 'VTS certificate of the Kerch Strait, highest category', Rosmorport 2017, available https://www.rosmorport.com/about/sertificates/certification/#lic15; accessed 5 April 2021.

According to the instructions, the use of a permit-based system in the context of a 24-hour schedule is necessary for planning the movement of vessels, in particular, using a one-way movement of vessels in the fairway (the navigable part of the shallow Kerch Strait) and priority direction of vessel movement, in addition to establishing the speed and the interval of vessel movement.[14] In practice, the Kerch Strait VTS regulates vessel movement by "conveying [to] them binding instructions as follows: movement priority and the movement start time; the route, the interval and the speed of the movement; the procedure for passing fairways and crossing them; the ban on further movement; anchoring grounds and sheltered locations."[15]

These restrictions on the navigation of foreign ships in the Sea of Azov appear not to be founded on any relevant decisions of the IMO. The Russian Federation appears to refer to IMO Resolution A.857(20)[16] as the legal basis of the VTS in the relevant maritime area, but that resolution only serves to describe the principles and general operational provisions for the operation of a VTS.[17] Notably, the resolution does refer to the possibility that a coastal State may exercise its discretionary right to establish and operate under a VTS a system of traffic clearances or VTS sailing plans or both in relation to priority of movements, allocation of space, mandatory reporting of movements in the VTS area, routes to be followed, speed limits to be observed or other appropriate measures.[18] However, the resolution does not refer to such possibility in relation to straits used for international navigation. Such requirements hamper international navigation in a strait and could only be lawful in an international strait if the measure was previously approved and adopted by the IMO (see, *inter alia*, Article 41(4) of LOSC).

The IALA's VTS Manual provides the coastal State's right to require traffic clearances explicitly only in respect of Port VTS, while distinguishing it from a Coastal VTS.[19] Clearance of ship movements is defined in the manual exclusively in relation to access to ports.[20] Clearances may also be required if

14 Rosmorport, *op. cit.*, 'Terms and conditions of navigation services in the VTS of the Kerch Strait'.

15 Ibid.

16 IMO Assembly, Resolution A.857(20), Annex 1, 'Guidelines and Criteria for VTS', adopted on 27 November 1997, entered into force 3 December 1997.

17 Rosmorport, *op. cit.*, 'Terms and conditions of navigation services in the VTS of the Kerch Strait'.

18 IMO Resolution A.857(20), Annex 1, *op. cit.*, 2.3.3.

19 International Association of Marine Aids to Navigation and Lighthouse Authorities, *IALA VTS Manual*, (Ed. 6, IALA, Saint Germain en Laye, 2016), 27.

20 Ibid., 43.

ships seek to depart from a port. Port States often make use of this possibility, especially in ports with a heavy traffic, e.g., in Europe's busiest passenger port Helsinki.[21] In respect of coastal VTS, the IALA's VTS manual explains that the types of service provided depend on the legal basis of the VTS and refers to its Guideline 1071 on the establishment of VTS in international straits.[22] The guideline does not mention the possibility of subjecting ships transiting an international strait to any unilateral prior authorisation requirement.[23]

Generally, a VTS is established where a particular maritime area exhibits high traffic density.[24] Notably, such a VTS or authorisation-based system has not been used in respect of Baltic straits that have a similar rate of annual crossings to that of the Kerch Strait, i.e. the Irbe Strait between Estonia and Latvia leading to the Gulf of Riga and the Åland Strait between Finland and Sweden.[25] There appears to be no IMO resolution which would permit the establishment of a VTS specifically in the Kerch Strait and, therefore, the above-referred VTS requirements would be unlawful if the Kerch Strait constitutes an international strait.[26] Even though a port State can, by virtue of the principle of sovereignty, regulate access to its ports located on the coasts of the Sea of Azov, this would not entitle it to restrict access to the Ukrainian EEZ in the Sea of Azov (the existence of which is, however, contested by the Russian Federation), against the terms of the right of transit passage or to the ports of the other coastal State of the Sea of Azov against bilateral agreements between the coastal States on this matter, as argued above (see Chapter 4 of Part 2).

From the perspective of commerce and international relations, it is important to have legal certainty regarding the rules regulating maritime navigation. The interrelationship of a coastal State's potential claim to internal waters in a densely navigated maritime area on the one hand and, on the other hand, the imposition of discriminatory navigational restrictions is illustrated by the *Vironia* incident in the Russian Federation's maritime area in the Gulf of Finland, as discussed next.

21 Traffic Management Finland, *Helsinki VTS Master's Guide*, 2020, 4–5, available at: https://tmfg.fi/sites/default/files/2020-02/Helsinki%20VTS%20Sector%201%20EN.pdf (accessed July 4, 2020).

22 IALA VTS Manual, *op. cit.*, 27.

23 International Association of Marine Aids to Navigation and Lighthouse Authorities, *IALA Guideline 1071 – Establishment of a Vessel Traffic Service beyond Territorial Seas*, (Ed. 1, 2009), 4ff.

24 IMO Resolution A.857(20), Annex 1, *op. cit.*, 2.3.3.

25 See also *supra* Figure 3.

26 See Regulation 12 of Chapter V, International Convention for the Safety of Life at Sea (SOLAS), adopted 1 November 1974, entered into force 25.05.1980, 1184 UNTS 278.

CHAPTER 11

Discriminatory Prohibition of the Right of Innocent Passage of a Commercial Ship

The Vironia *Incident in the Gulf of Finland*

Previously, it was examined how the passage rights of foreign commercial ships in and around the Strait of Hormuz and the Kerch Strait might be subject to discriminatory navigational restrictions by the strait State. This chapter seeks to establish whether the Russian Federation has imposed any unlawful limitations to the enjoyment of the right of innocent passage by examining the international legal framework applicable to navigation in the Russian maritime area in the Gulf of Finland. For this purpose, it raises the question of whether the Russian Federation's maritime area in the centre of the Gulf of Finland proper comprises its internal waters.

This chapter focuses specifically on the Russian Federation's approach to navigation rights and freedoms in the Gulf of Finland. It first adopts a historical method to briefly explain the Soviet Union's and the Russian Federation's approaches to the passage regime of foreign ships in the Gulf of Finland until 2000. The baselines and maritime zones of the Russian Federation in the Gulf of Finland are examined next in order to discuss the legality of the Russian Federation's permit-based passage regime in that maritime area.

To the extent of the present author's knowledge, the permit-based passage regime has not caused unlawful restrictions to navigation in that maritime area except for one instance. This concerns the Estonian-Finnish *Vironia* commercial ferry line, which soon after its opening was declined the right of innocent passage in the Russian Federation's maritime area and consequently had to be closed in 2007. As explained further in Chapter 16, the *Vironia* incident should be seen in the context of a hybrid conflict between the Russian Federation and Estonia that was triggered by the relocation of a Soviet war memorial in Tallinn in 2007. This decision triggered massive civil unrest in the Russian-speaking community in Estonia and Russian cyber-attacks against the Estonian institutions. Chapter 16 also sets the impediments to international navigation in the Gulf of Finland in a broader context and compares them with developments in the Russian Arctic and the Sea of Azov as the basis for a discussion of how the Russian Federation has balanced the application of the concepts of *mare liberum* and *mare clausum* in its maritime areas.

 | DOI:10.1163/9789004509368_013

11.1 Right of Innocent Passage in the Eastern Gulf of Finland from 1920s to 2000

The permit-based passage regime of the Soviet Union/Russian Federation has been applicable in the territorial sea in the Gulf of Finland at least since the middle of the twentieth century, albeit in multiple variations. Erik Franckx notes that the Soviet Union has required such permission from foreign warships since the late 1950s.[1] It is less known that a permit-based passage regime was applicable in some small maritime pockets (e.g., near Kotlin Island) in the eastern part of the Gulf of Finland under the 1924 instructions for the navigation of ships in coastal waters within artillery range of coastal batteries in peacetime. Article 2 provided that both Soviet and foreign commercial vessels have the right to unhindered passage, except in special zones, within the limits of territorial waters.[2] In the Baltic Sea, these restrictions could have been used only for the defence of Petrograd since the Soviet Union's maritime area was limited to a small stretch of sea west of Petrograd (the coast to the northwest of Petrograd as well as the islands in the middle of the Gulf of Finland proper were at that time still part of the Finnish territory).

Gene Glenn has referred to an incident which points to the potential applicability of a broader permit-based passage regime to commercial vessels sailing in the Gulf of Finland in the second half of 1940s.[3] The incident involved a Swedish fishing vessel, *Hamnfjord*, that sailed in 1948 into the Gulf of Finland where she was taken into custody by the Soviet Union. The ship and her crew were released after being interrogated by the Soviet Union's Coast Guard.

The Soviet Union claimed that *Hamnfjord* had unlawfully entered its coastal defence zone (also known as maritime frontier zone) and disregarded orders to stop.[4] Pursuant to the Soviet Union's 1927 instructions,[5] the Soviet Union's

1 E Franckx, 'The U.S.S.R. position on the innocent passage of warships through foreign territorial waters' (1987) 18(1) *Journal of Maritime Law and Commerce*, 56–58, 63.

2 Instructions for the navigation of ships in coastal waters within artillery range of coastal batteries in peacetime ('Инструкции для плавания судов в береговых водах в пределах зоны обстрела береговых батарей в мирное время'), Order no 897 from the Revolutionary Military Council of 5 July 1924, Article 2. This provision is quoted in A Uustal, *Международно-правовой режим территориальных вод* (Tartu State University Press, Tartu, 1958), 61. For the translation, see WE Butler, *The Soviet Union and the Law of the Sea* (The Johns Hopkins Press, Baltimore/London, 1971) 50–51.

3 G Glenn, 'Notes and comments: The Swedish-Soviet territorial sea controversy in the Baltic' (1956) 50(4) *American Journal of International Law*, 942–947.

4 Ibid., 942.

5 Butler, *op. cit.*, 52.

Coast Guard proceeded from the understanding that they are allowed to board, inspect, and detain, where necessary (particularly if the ship is suspected of having engaged in fishing), all non-military vessels that enter the coastal defence zone.

The Soviet Union alleged in its diplomatic note to Sweden that the crew of *Hamnfjord* had been interrogated since they violated its laws on territorial sea.[6] This created legal uncertainty since *Hamnfjord* was sailing outside the 4-NM-limit as measured from the Soviet Union's coast. The Soviet Union's coastal defence zone extended to 12 NM since 1927,[7] whereas its territorial sea was 4 NM wide, as first fixed in the 1920 Tartu Peace Treaty between Finland and the Soviet Russia pursuant to Nordic regional customary law.[8]

Thus, Sweden requested in its diplomatic note information on whether the Soviet Union had established a 12-NM-wide territorial sea, and referred to the right of innocent passage that ought to apply in the territorial sea.[9] The Soviet Union did not respond to this enquiry immediately, but acknowledged two years later, in a 1950 diplomatic note to Sweden, that it had extended the width of its previously 4-NM-wide territorial sea in the Baltic Sea to 12 NM.[10]

The *Hamnfjord* incident appears to indicate that already by the 1940s, the Soviet Union was denying innocent passage in its territorial sea to foreign ships, including commercial ships, if they had failed to request prior permission. On the other hand, the Soviet Union's later diplomatic statements and the views of Soviet scholars, as expressed in the relevant legal literature, were less unequivocal on this matter. In his review of Soviet textbooks of the 1950s and 1960s, Butler shows that the views of numerous Soviet jurists favoured a narrow interpretation of the scope of innocent passage that only applies strict requirements to commercial ships in the territorial sea.[11] Yet even in the 1950s other Soviet writers disagreed with such statements and claimed that a coastal State cannot hamper the innocent passage of foreign commercial ships.[12] A liberal understanding of the right of innocent passage took root in the Soviet publications in the 1970s and 1980s. Franckx has pointed out that many

6 Glenn, *op. cit.*, 942.

7 LB Schapiro, 'The limits of Russian territorial waters in the Baltic' (1950) 27 *The British Yearbook of International Law*, 447.

8 Treaty of Peace between Finland and Soviet Government of Russia, adopted 14 October 1920, entered into force 31 December 1920, 3 LNTS 65, Article 3.

9 Glenn, *op. cit.*, 943.

10 Ibid., 944.

11 Butler, *op. cit.*, 54–57.

12 Ibid., 56–57.

Soviet authors claimed years before the 1989 Jackson Hole statement[13] that foreign ships, including warships, enjoy the right of innocent passage, even if they have not requested the coastal State's prior permission.[14] Yet the views of Soviet professors were far from unanimous on this question. For example, Abner Uustal, professor of international law at the University of Tartu, found in 1984 that due to the Soviet Union's security considerations, it is in any case necessary to require from foreign warships a prior authorisation for exercising the right of innocent passage.[15]

The Soviet Union had guaranteed under its 1960 statute on the protection of its boundary the right of innocent passage to foreign non-military vessels in its territorial sea (excluding internal waters), while subjecting foreign warships to the permit-based passage regime.[16] By contrast, as of the 1989 Jackson Hole statement, the Soviet Union and its successor State, the Russian Federation, have been expected to guarantee the right of innocent passage to all foreign ships absent prior notification or a request for authorisation.[17] According to the 1989 statement, all ships, including warships, regardless of cargo, armament or means of propulsion, enjoy the right of innocent passage through the territorial sea, for which neither prior notification nor authorisation is required.[18] The Russian Federation has clearly stipulated this also in its domestic law (the 1989 statement itself is legally non-binding). The 1998 Federal Act on the internal maritime waters, territorial sea and contiguous zone provides that foreign ships, foreign warships and other government ships enjoy the right of innocent passage through the territorial sea for which a prior notification or request for authorisation is not required.[19] Such a regulation conforms with the rules on innocent passage as stipulated under Article 24(1) of LOSC.[20] However, the Russian Federation's recent State practice, as discussed below, calls into

13 1989 Joint Statement by the United States of America and the Union of Soviet Socialist Republics, *op. cit.*

14 Franckx, *op. cit.*, 37–40.

15 A Uustal, *Rahvusvaheline õigus* (Eesti Raamat, Tallinn, 1984), 260, 263.

16 Butler, *op. cit.*, 52–53.

17 See, e.g., Hakapää, Molenaar, *op. cit.*, 143.

18 Ibid.

19 See Federal Act on the internal maritime waters, territorial sea and contiguous zone of the Russian Federation, Articles 12–13.

20 The coastal State cannot deny innocent passage through its territorial waters, *inter alia*, to tankers, nuclear-powered ships and ships carrying nuclear or other inherently dangerous or noxious substances or materials (LOSC Article 23). However, in conformity with Article 25(1) of LOSC, the coastal State may take the necessary steps in its territorial sea to prevent passage which is not innocent. This provision grants coastal States necessary discretion in applying proportional measures.

question the conformity of its permit-based regime in the Gulf of Finland with the right of innocent passage under its domestic legal acts and the LOSC.

11.2 The Russian Federation's Maritime Zones in the Gulf of Finland

The Russian Federation's system of straight baselines in the Gulf of Finland is based on the Soviet Union's 1985 decree on a list of geographic coordinates determining the position of its baselines in the Baltic Sea.[21] The Russian Federation does not appear to have revised the coordinates, or notified the UN about any modifications to said decree. Thus, one may expect that this decree is still in force.

According to the 1985 decree, the starting point of the Soviet Union's straight baselines was on the north-eastern coast of the Gulf of Finland from where the straight baselines proceeded to Vaindloo Island and onwards along the Estonian coast, connecting the outermost islands.[22] The last segment of the Soviet Union's straight baselines in the Baltic Sea connected the Sõrve Peninsula on Saaremaa Island in Estonia with the Ovisi Cape in the Latvian Courland Peninsula. The Soviet Union used normal baselines south of the Ovisi Cape in the remaining parts of its eastern coast of the Baltic Sea.[23]

If the Russian Federation still measures the breadth of its territorial sea based on the system of straight baselines as established under the 1985 decree, then its extent is by now considerably reduced. Due to the restoration of Estonia's independence in 1991, the Soviet Union's/Russian Federation's system of straight baselines was interrupted and broke off in the middle of the baseline segment that connected Rodsher Island with Vaindloo Island, which is part of the Estonian territory.

For this reason, the Estonian official nautical charts depict the Russian Federation's last straight baseline segment in the Gulf of Finland as a broken line heading from Rodsher Island to Vaindloo Island. The baseline is abruptly cut at the point where it reaches the Estonian maritime boundary.[24] In effect, the Russian Federation's system of straight baselines, as established under the 1985 decree, are now relevant only to the extent that it connects the Russian

21 Council of Ministers of the Soviet Union, 1985 Decree no. 4450, *op. cit.*

22 Ibid., points 1–32.

23 Ibid., points 31–32.

24 See Chart no. 300, 'Soome laht: Paldiskist Narvani' (Estonian Maritime Administration, Tallinn, 2010); see also Charts of Estonia, vol 1, 'Gulf of Finland: Suurupi Peninsula to Narva' (Estonian Maritime Administration, Tallinn, 2015), 2.

islands of Sommers, Gogland, and Rodsher with the Russian mainland on the northern coast of the Gulf of Finland. Hence, it does not form an integral whole. Instead, it constitutes an extraordinary incomplete system of straight baselines. Presumably, such an incomplete system of straight baselines would not meet the requirement according to which straight baselines need to join 'appropriate points' (Article 7(1) of LOSC).

An incomplete system of straight baselines does not allow a State to clearly establish the outer limit of internal waters in a relevant maritime area. In the case of the Gulf of Finland, the internal waters regime ought to apply to the maritime area that falls landward side of the straight baselines that connect Sommers, Gogland, and Rodsher islands. If applicable, such a system of baselines would blur the lines between the Russian Federation's territorial sea and internal waters, rendering the relevant domestic legislation incompatible with Article 7 of LOSC. Hence, the 1985 decree no longer can be considered effective in the Gulf of Finland in whole, or in part. The maritime area falling to the landward side of the Russian Federation's islands in the middle of the Gulf of Finland proper should be considered as its territorial sea, not internal waters.

Notably, the Russian Federation's practice does not indicate whether or not the incomplete system of straight baselines is effective in the Gulf of Finland. According to the Federal Port Authority Rosmorport, the operational area of its VTS system in the Gulf of Finland is limited to the Russian Federation's territorial sea and ports. Rosmorport does not make any other explicit reference to internal waters in the Gulf of Finland proper.[25] According to Navionics charts, which are usually accurate in depicting maritime zones and straight baselines in the northern Baltic Sea, the Russian Federation's maritime area in the middle of the Gulf of Finland does not include any straight baselines.[26]

If the Russian Federation drew a new system of straight baselines in the Gulf of Finland, then it could potentially use Tyuters Islands, Vigrund island/rock, and Kurgalsky Peninsula, arguably, as appropriate points for creating new baseline segments and closing the currently incomplete system of straight baselines in the Gulf of Finland.[27] Many maps neglect the existence of Vigrund

25 See Rosmorport, North-Western Basin Branch, 'VTS coverage areas', available http://www.rosmorport.com/spb_serv_nav.html; accessed 5 April 2021; see also the Russian Federation's nautical chart 'Восточная часть Финского залива', scale 1:250 000, 19 July 1997, available http://balticborder.com/wp-content/uploads/2013/05/fin_zaliv-vostok-restriction -area2.jpg; accessed 5 April 2021.

26 Navionics, *op. cit.*, 'The Gulf of Finland'.

27 See Map 9. The map depicts the potential updated system of straight baselines in the Russian Federation's maritime area.

island/rock; as a result, Vigrund's territorial sea is mistakenly replaced with an EEZ north of Narva Bay.[28] However, Vigrund has great significance for the establishment of a new system of straight baselines. It is located approximately 8.5 NM west of the Kurgalsky Peninsula and 16.5 NM east of Bolshoy Tyuters. Vigrund is above water at high tide and a lighthouse has been stationed there for at least a hundred years.[29] Russian geographers do not hold an unanimous view on whether Vigrund constitutes an island or a rock,[30] but in either case it could serve as an appropriate point for the establishment of a new system of straight baselines.

On the other hand, it is doubtful if such a new system of straight baselines would meet the requirements of Article 7(1) and 7(3) of LOSC. According to these provisions, the method of straight baselines may be employed if it connects appropriate points on a fringe of islands along the coast in its immediate vicinity and the sea areas lying within the lines is sufficiently closely linked to the land domain to be subject to the regime of internal waters. The Russian Federation's islands in the middle of the Gulf of Finland proper depart considerably from the general direction of its mainland coast. The westernmost Rodsher Island is located approximately 43 NM away from the nearest points on the southern and northern coasts of the Russian mainland.

In addition, the Gulf of Finland proper includes the Russian Federation's EEZ that was established initially as a high seas corridor pursuant to the maritime boundary treaties concluded between Finland and the Soviet Union in 1940, 1965, and 1985.[31] The existence of this tiny Russian EEZ in the Gulf of Finland is not widely acknowledged in Estonia and Finland. For example, the Estonian Maritime Administration has had no information about the existence of the Russian Federation's EEZ in the Gulf of Finland.[32] Similarly, Estonia and Finland presumed when establishing their EEZ corridor in the Viro Strait that the right of innocent passage would apply (instead of transit passage) in the Viro Strait that leads to the Russian Federation's maritime area (see Articles 17 and 45(1)(b) of LOSC).[33]

28 See, e.g., Marineregions.org, *op. cit.*, 'Russia'.

29 Vigrund lighthouse was mentioned already in the 1920 Finnish-Soviet Peace Treaty, *op. cit.*, Article 3(4).

30 See Russian Geographical Society, 'Complex Expedition "Hogland", Islands', available https://www.rgo.ru/en/projects/expeditions/complex-expedition-hogland/islands; accessed 5 April 2021.

31 See further in Oude Elferink 1994, *op. cit.*, 189; see also Lott, *op. cit.*, 74–75.

32 Lott, *op. cit.*, 76.

33 Ibid., 75.

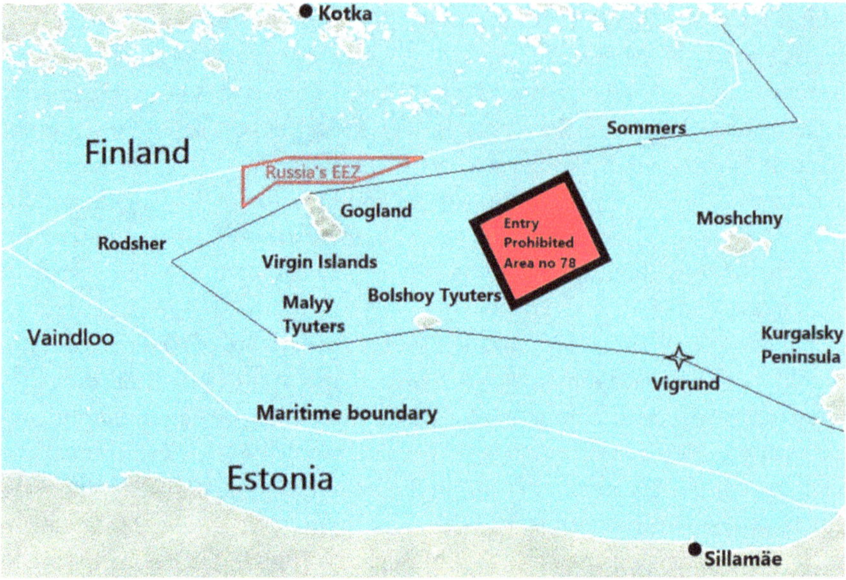

MAP 9 Map of the Russian federation's potential updated system of straight baselines in the Gulf of Finland

SOURCE: MARINEREGIONS.ORG, 'RUSSIA', FLANDERS MARINE INSTITUTE (VLIZ) 2021, AVAILABLE HTTPS://WWW.MARINEREGIONS.ORG/EEZDETAILS.PHP?MRGID=5690&ZONE=EEZ_12NM; ACCESSED 5 APRIL 2021. THE MAP IS MODIFIED BY THE AUTHOR SO AS TO DEPICT THE POTENTIAL UPDATED SYSTEM OF STRAIGHT BASELINES IN THE RUSSIAN FEDERATION'S MARITIME AREA AND INDICATIVE REFERENCES TO THE NAMES OF, *INTER ALIA*, THE STATES, PORTS, ISLANDS, PENINSULAS, MARITIME ZONES, AND RESTRICTED AREAS MENTIONED IN THE CHAPTER; SEE ALSO OFFICE FOR OCEAN AFFAIRS AND THE LAW OF THE SEA, *THE LAW OF THE SEA BASELINES: NATIONAL LEGISLATION WITH ILLUSTRATIVE MAPS* (UNITED NATIONS, NEW YORK, 1989), 352; SEE ALSO NAVIONICS, *OP. CIT.*, 'THE GULF OF FINLAND'.

The Russian Federation's EEZ in the Gulf of Finland is approximately 9 NM long and mostly about 2 NM wide (at its widest point close to 4 NM).[34] This tiny EEZ borders Gogland Island, reaching as close to it as 2 NM.[35] It has great significance for navigation, since its existence implies that if Estonia and Finland decided to extend the outer limit of their territorial sea to the maximum extent in the Viro Strait, thus abolishing the current 6-NM-wide EEZ corridor, then ships and aircraft would be entitled to the right of transit passage for

34 Ibid., 74.

35 See Navionics, *op. cit.*, 'The Gulf of Finland'.

navigating to and from the Russian Federation's maritime area in the eastern Gulf of Finland (Article 38 of LOSC). The tiny Russian EEZ is also crossed by the most direct navigation route between the Sillamäe Port in eastern Estonia and the Kotka Port in eastern Finland. During their voyage, within the limits of the Russian Federation's EEZ next to Gogland Island, under Articles 58(1) and 87(1)(a) of LOSC, ships are entitled to freedom of navigation, including the right to stop and anchor.

Therefore, ships crossing the Russian Federation's territorial sea and EEZ in the Gulf of Finland are entitled to the right of innocent passage and freedom of navigation. It is relevant to assess next if the Russian Federation has in practice respected the right of innocent passage through its territorial sea, particularly in the light of the closure in 2007 of the *Vironia* ferry line that had to cross the Russian Federation's maritime area while navigating between the Estonian and Finnish ports.

11.3 The *Vironia* Incident in the Gulf of Finland and Its Aftermath

The significance of the right of innocent passage for global maritime transport was illustrated by an incident involving the Estonian-flagged ship *Vironia*, which transported goods and passengers between Sillamäe and Kotka ports in the eastern Gulf of Finland.[36] This ferry line was launched by the Saaremaa Shipping Company in February 2006.[37] The roll-on/roll-off ferry *Vironia* had a capacity to transport 370 passengers and 940 lane meters of trucks and cars, many of which were heading to the Russian Federation.[38] *Vironia* made 10 weekly departures and its schedule was increased to 12 weekly departures during the summer season.[39]

After the ferry line was launched, its operator still had consultations with the Russian Federation authorities about receiving permission to use the shortest route through its territorial sea for navigation.[40] These negotiations were cancelled by the Russian Federation after Estonia relocated the Soviet

36 See, e.g., Anonymous, 'Päivittäinen laivaliikenne Kotkan ja Sillamäen välillä päättyy', *Yle Uutiset* (17 October 2007); J Niemeläinen, 'Kotkan ja Sillamäen välinen laivalinja lopettaa', *Helsingin Sanomat* (18 October 2007).

37 Anonymous, 'Sillamäe-Kotka laevaliin teeb avareisi 17. veebruaril', *Postimees* (12 January 2006).

38 Ibid.

39 Anonymous, 'Sillamäe-Kotka laevaliin on Ida-Viru tänavune turismitegu', *Logistikauudised* (8 December 2006).

40 *Yle Uutiset* 2007, *op. cit.*; see also Map 10.

World War II Bronze Soldier memorial from the city centre in Tallinn to the near-by military cemetery in April 2007.[41] The relocation of the monument triggered mass protests among the Russian-speaking minority, civil unrest in Tallinn and widescale cyber-attacks against Estonia's public and private websites from the Russian Federation. In the aftermath of this incident, the Russian Federation was not willing to resume negotiations over the right of passage of the passenger ferry through its maritime area in the Gulf of Finland proper. This led to the closure of the *Vironia* ferry line between the Estonian and Finnish ports since the navigation route around the Russian Federation's maritime area was not economically feasible.[42] The distance between the two ports across the Russian Federation's maritime area is 70 NM, whereas the round-about route is 90-NM-long.[43] The direct route between the two ports via the Russian Federation's maritime area would have been 2 hours shorter, which would have reduced fuel costs and increased competitiveness in comparison with the Tallinn-Helsinki ferry lines.[44]

Over the next years, attempts were made to relaunch the ferry line between the ports of eastern Estonia and eastern Finland.[45] In a 2015 maritime assembly of the Gulf of Finland's coastal States in Sillamäe, a member of St Petersburg's maritime council, Mr Andrei Berezkin, found that the ferry line's use of the Russian Federation's maritime area in the eastern Gulf of Finland had so far not been subject to proper consideration at a sufficiently high level by Russian authorities.[46] In 2016, representatives of the port town Loviisa in eastern Finland visited Kunda and Sillamäe ports in eastern Estonia. This was followed by the eastern Estonian local government's officials' visit to the Finnish port towns Kotka and Loviisa in order to agree on the timeframe for relaunching the ferry line between eastern Finland and eastern Estonia.[47] For this purpose, they still considered it necessary to first acquire permission from the Russian Federation authorities to navigate through its territorial sea in the Gulf of Finland.[48]

41 H Ellam, 'Pronksiöö tulemus: Sillamäe-Kotka laevaliin suletakse', *Äripäev* (17 October 2007).
42 Ibid. See also Niemeläinen, *op.cit.*
43 G Romanovitš, 'Soome ja Eesti otsisid mereühenduse võimalusi', *Põhjarannik* (30 June 2016); see maps 9 and 10.
44 J Eelmets, 'Sillamäe-Kotka laevaliini taastamine sõltub kokkuleppest Venemaaga', *ERR Uudised* (20 November 2015).
45 See, e.g., Anonymous, 'Kotkan ja Viron välistä laivaliikennettä viritellään taas', *Yle Uutiset* (1 February 2011).
46 Eelmets, *op. cit.*
47 G Romanovitš, 'Laevaliin vajab tasuvusanalüüsi', *Põhjarannik* (3 November 2016).
48 Ibid.

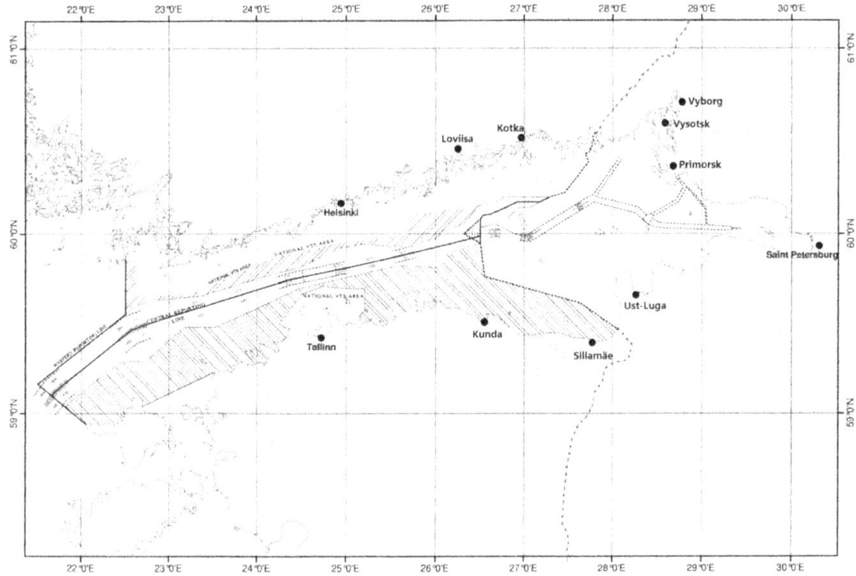

MAP 10 Ports and Coastal States of the Gulf of Finland
SOURCE: ROSMORPORT, 'GENERAL INFORMATION/VTS COVERAGE AREAS', 'VTS SERVICES', AVAILABLE HTTP://WWW.ROSMORPORT.COM/SPB_SERV_NAV.HTML; ACCESSED 12 OCTOBER 2020. THE MAP SERVES AN ILLUSTRATIVE PURPOSE AND IS MODIFIED BY THE AUTHOR TO INCLUDE THE NAMES OF THE PORTS MENTIONED IN THIS CHAPTER.

In 2018, a member of the council of the Finnish Kotka Port commented that the Finnish business sector was interested in relaunching the ferry line, but that it preferred to use for this purpose the Estonian Kunda Port, which is located west of Sillamäe Port.[49] This was due to the perceived likelihood that the Russian Federation would not grant its permission for the ferry line to navigate through its territorial sea. In this context, the alternative route between Kunda and Kotka ports has a significant advantage as it would not necessarily cross the Russian Federation's territorial sea. In order to relaunch the ferry line, the Estonian and Finnish port authorities are currently considering another alternative route that would run between Kunda and Loviisa ports.[50]

49 A Reimer, 'Vähi ja Vallbaum ristasid laevaliini nimel mõõgad', *Virumaa Teataja* (17 January 2018).
50 I Kuus, 'Kunda sadam kaalub laevaliini Loviisasse', ERR *Uudised* (11 May 2019).

11.4 Potential Legal Basis of the Russian Federation's Permit-Based Passage Regime in the Gulf of Finland

It follows from the foregoing discussion that the Russian Federation's permit-based regime for sailing through its territorial sea in the Gulf of Finland still hinders the re-establishment of a ferry line between the ports of eastern Finland and eastern Estonia. The potential legal basis of the permit-based passage regime is, however, subject to debate.

The *Vironia* incident exemplifies how the Russian Federation can make use of a permit-based passage regime in its maritime area to the detriment of international commerce. Pursuant to its national regulations, all ships entering the Russian Federation's maritime area in the Gulf Finland from the west, including by crossing the Estonian-Russian maritime boundary, are required to gain prior authorisation from its VTS centre.[51] Its broader implications to international navigation are illustrated by the fact that a group of merchant ships are constantly waiting at the eastern end of the Estonian and Finnish EEZ corridor in the Gulf of Finland to receive permission to enter the Russian Federation's territorial sea and enter a port.[52] This practice is permitted under international law based on the absence of a right of access to ports and a State's territorial sovereignty over its ports.[53] However, it is doubtful if the permit-based regime is lawful in respect of commercial ships that simply seek to navigate under the right of innocent passage through the Russian Federation's territorial sea without calling on any Russian ports, as illustrated by the *Vironia* incident.

The Russian Federation could potentially subject the passage of foreign ships to the permit-based regime in the middle of the Gulf of Finland proper if this maritime area constitutes so-called long-standing internal waters, i.e. internal waters that also were considered internal waters prior to the establishment of straight baselines. This follows from Article 8(2) of LOSC, which stipulates that where the establishment of a straight baseline in accordance with the method set forth in Article 7 of LOSC has the effect of enclosing as internal waters areas which had not previously been considered as such, a right of innocent passage exists in those waters.

51 Rosmorport, North-Western Basin Branch, 'Terms and conditions of navigation VTS services with the use of Saint Petersburg VTS', available http://www.rosmorport.com/filials/spb_serv_nav/; accessed 5 April 2021.

52 See Marine Traffic, 'Gulf of Finland', available https://www.marinetraffic.com/en/ais/home/centerx:24.3/centery:59.3/zoom:8; accessed 5 April 2021.

53 See *Military and Paramilitary Activities in and against Nicaragua*, *op. cit.*, para 213.

The maritime area in the middle of the Gulf of Finland proper hypothetically could constitute such internal waters where the right of innocent passage does not apply if the Soviet Union considered that maritime area as its internal waters prior to the adoption of the 1985 decree that established the Soviet Union's system of straight baselines, as examined above. Often such a claim may rest on the coastal State's historic title over a particular maritime area, for example, based on the historic bay concept.[54] The Russian Federation does not claim to have such historic title over the maritime area in the middle of the Gulf of Finland, and there appears to be no actual basis for such a potential claim. The islands in the middle of the Gulf of Finland proper (Tyuters Islands, Rodsher, Gogland, Virgin Islands, Sommers) were Finnish territory prior to the 1940 Peace Treaty with the Soviet Union.[55] Thus, the relevant maritime area belonged to Finland, not to the Soviet Union.

The 1985 decree lists the following maritime areas, the waters of which historically belong to the Soviet Union: the White Sea south of the line connecting Cape Svyatoy Nos with Cape Kanin Nos, the waters of Cheshskaya Bay south of the line connecting Cape Mikulkin with Cape Svyatoy Nos (Timansky), and the waters of Baidaratskaya Bay south-east of the line connecting Cape Yuribeisalya with Cape Belushy Nos.[56] This list does not include any references to maritime areas of the Gulf of Finland. This, however, does not exclude the possibility that some bays in the eastern Gulf of Finland could be considered as long-standing internal waters where the right of innocent passage does not apply, for example, Vyborg Bay, Luga Bay, and the narrow maritime area near Kronstadt and St Petersburg.

Most Baltic Sea coastal States extended the breadth of their internal waters under the definition and scope of internal waters as established under the 1912 and 1938 Nordic Rules of Neutrality. Under these rules, the Scandinavian and Baltic States delimited the scope of their internal waters so that they included ports, entrances to ports, gulfs and bays, and the waters between those islands, islets and reefs which are not constantly submerged, and between the said islands, islets and reefs and the mainland.[57] The Soviet Union as a non-neutral

54 See further, e.g., Churchill, Lowe, *op. cit.*, 44; Symmons, *op. cit.*, 33.

55 See 1940 Peace Treaty, *op. cit.*, Article 2.

56 Council of Ministers of the Soviet Union, 1985 Decree no. 4450, *op. cit.*, 1.

57 'Declaration by Norway, Denmark and Sweden relative to the Establishment of Uniform Rules of Neutrality. Stockholm, 21.12.1912' (1913) 7(3) *American Journal of International Law*, 187–191; see also Nordic 1938 Declaration, *op. cit.*; see also, e.g., Neutrality Act of Sweden ('Innefattande vissa neutralitetsbestämmelser'), No. 187, 27 May 1938, Section 2(2).

State did not contribute to the development of this regional customary international law in the Nordic region.

The Russian Federation may potentially exclude the right of innocent passage in its territorial sea under Article 21(1)(a) of LOSC, which stipulates that the coastal State may adopt laws and regulations relating to innocent passage through the territorial sea in respect of the safety of navigation and the regulation of maritime traffic. The Russian Federation's permit-based passage regime in the Gulf of Finland can potentially serve a legitimate aim of ensuring safety of navigation in a particularly sensitive sea area that exhibits a high shipping traffic density around numerous islands and shoals that pose hazards for maritime transport.

It is possible that the permit-based passage regime is also aimed at safeguarding the Russian Federation's security interests. Gogland Island in the centre of the Gulf of Finland proper bears strategic importance, which is illustrated by the Russian Federation's recent investments into its military facilities on the island, including the construction of a helipad. However, it is not entirely clear if Article 21(1)(a) of LOSC permits the coastal State to regulate the right of innocent passage based on general security considerations. One could argue that coastal States are allowed to prohibit innocent passage by foreign vessels in parts of the territorial sea that are near to features with security relevance. Clearly, the Russian Federation's fortifications on Gogland Island fall into this category. While under the above-mentioned 1924 Revolutionary Military Council's instructions on innocent passage such special areas concerned *prima facie* Kotlin Island next to St Petersburg, the extension of the Russian Federation's territory as a result of its title over the islands in the middle of the Gulf of Finland proper now potentially allow it to establish such special areas also near its military facilities around Gogland Island.

Although the permit-based passage regime may serve legitimate aims of safeguarding navigation safety, coastal State security and protection of marine environment, this does not mean that such a measure is lawful. Pursuant to Article 21(1) of LOSC, such a measure needs to be in conformity with the provisions of LOSC and other rules of international law. The permit-based passage regime in respect of ships that seek to continuously and expeditiously traverse the Russian Federation's territorial sea contradicts the LOSC rules on innocent passage, as discussed above. Thus, the Russian Federation's requirement of prior authorisation for the passage of foreign ships through its territorial sea fails to meet the criteria of Article 21(1)(a) of LOSC. In the example of the *Vironia* incident and its aftermath, the said measure has amounted to completely extinguishing regular north-south traffic of foreign commercial vessels in the area.

Notably, under Article 15(1) of the 1998 Federal Act on the internal maritime waters, territorial sea and contiguous zone, the Russian Federation has reserved itself the right to establish areas in which navigation is prohibited and which are temporarily dangerous for navigation. The aim of such measures is to ensure the safety of navigation, safeguard 'State interests', and protect the environment. In this context, the Russian Federation has established 'Entry Prohibited Area No 78', which is located between Gogland Island and Moshchny Island (see Map 9).[58] This prohibited entry area is located east of the shortest navigation route of the Kotka-Sillamäe ferry line and thus would not affect it.[59] The Russian Federation evidently cannot close its whole maritime area in the Gulf of Finland proper to navigation of foreign ships between Finland and Estonia.

The Russian Federation's prior permission requirement to the extent that it is applied in respect of ships that are not calling at the Russian Federation's port is not in conformity with the IMO Resolution A.857(20),[60] which the Russian Federation refers to as the legal basis for the VTS in the relevant maritime area.[61] The Russian Federation's maritime area in the Gulf of Finland proper is almost entirely covered by the St Petersburg VTS, which complements the smaller VTS systems of the ports of Ust-Luga, Vysotsk, Vyborg, and Primorsk.[62] Pursuant to the IMO resolution, a coastal State may exercise its discretionary right to establish and operate under its VTS a system of traffic clearances or VTS sailing plans, or both, in relation to priority of movements, allocation of space, mandatory reporting of movements in the VTS area, routes to be followed, speed limits to be observed, and adopt other appropriate measures.[63] Yet such measures cannot, by the very nature of a VTS, exclude *in toto* the expeditious navigation of a particular ship through the territorial sea that is distant from the ports of a coastal State. This is especially the case if the ship poses a marginal threat to the marine environment, for example, a commercial ferry line. Pursuant to Annex 1 of Resolution A.857(20), the aim of a VTS is to improve the safety and efficiency of vessel traffic and to protect the environment. Thus, it cannot amount to extinguishing foreign vessel traffic completely.

58 Navionics, *op. cit.*, 'Gulf of Finland'.

59 See Map 9.

60 IMO Resolution A.857(20), *op. cit.*

61 Rosmorport, North-Western Basin Branch, 'Terms and conditions of navigation VTS services', available http://www.rosmorport.com/spb_serv_nav.html; accessed 5 April 2021.

62 Rosmorport, *op. cit.*, 'VTS coverage areas'.

63 IMO Resolution A.857(20), *op. cit.*, Annex 1, para 2.3.3.

The *Vironia* incident appears to be a sort of a reprisal that the Russian Federation used against Estonia in the aftermath of the 2007 relocation of a Soviet Union's war memorial and the following civil unrest among the Russian-speaking minority in Tallinn. It indicates that the Russian Federation hampers the right of innocent passage in relation to foreign ships that need to make regular north-south crossing of the Gulf of Finland proper via its territorial sea in the Gulf of Finland. The permit-based passage regime is still the main obstacle for relaunching the ferry line between the Estonian and Finnish ports in the Gulf of Finland proper.

PART 4

Major Maritime Industrial Projects, Piracy, and Unidentified Soldiers

CHAPTER 12

The Nord Stream Project and Estonian-Russian Incidents in the Viro Strait

This chapter debates the relationship between maritime industrial projects and hybrid threats. It examines an incident between Russian research vessels and the Estonian Coast Guard in the Estonian EEZ. The chapter also debates the restrictions that were imposed by Estonia to the laying of the Nord Stream submarine pipelines in the Viro Strait.

12.1 Link between Industrial Projects and Maritime Security

The previously discussed 2007 *Vironia* incident concerned the Russian Federation's discriminatory navigational restrictions against an Estonian-flagged commercial ship sailing between the Estonian and Finnish ports. The operator of the ferry line failed to receive a permission for its ship to navigate through the Russian Federation's territorial sea. The Russian Federation refused to consider the request any further in the aftermath of the so-called Bronze Soldier incident in April 2007 that led to civil unrest among the Russian-speaking minority in Tallinn and widespread cyber-attacks against the Estonian civil and State institutions that were launched from the Russian Federation. Consequently, the ferry line was closed in autumn 2007, at least partly because of the hybrid conflict between the two States in 2007.

At the same time, the Russian Federation was seeking the Estonian government's positive reply to a request submitted by the Nord Stream consortium to conduct a seabed survey in the Estonian EEZ in the Viro Strait for the laying of submarine pipelines that by now connect the Russian and German mainland coasts and enable the transportation of Russian natural gas to the EU market. The Estonian government rejected the application in September 2007, because of which the seabed surveys were conducted and the pipelines were laid instead in the Finnish EEZ in the Viro Strait.[1]

By April 2012, two 1224-km-long submarine gas transmission pipelines had been laid on the seabed of the Baltic Sea between Vyborg in the Russian

1 A Raun, 'Paet tõi uuringust keeldumiseks kolm põhjendust', *Postimees* (20 September 2007).

© ALEXANDER LOTT, 2022 | DOI:10.1163/9789004509368_014

Federation and Greifswald in Germany. The pipelines enable the export of 55 bcm of natural gas from the Russian Arctic to satisfy the energy needs of more than 26 million European households per year. Consequently, in 2014 more Russian natural gas was exported to Europe via the offshore Nord Stream than the alternative onshore route through Ukraine and Slovakia.[2]

The Nord Stream extension project's shareholder Gazprom (the Russian Federation) and its financial investors that include Uniper and Wintershall DEA (Germany), Shell (the Netherlands/UK), OMV (Austria) and the French Engie supported the extension of the Nord Stream project in 2012.[3] In June 2021, President Putin announced that the installation of the first pipeline of the Nord Stream 2 had been successfully completed and that it was ready to be used for gas shipments.[4] The laying of the second set of pipelines of Nord Stream 2 was completed in September 2021.[5]

The Nord Stream project has a transboundary impact on the coastal States of the Baltic Sea: Denmark, Germany, Poland, Russia, Lithuania, Latvia, Estonia, Finland, and Sweden. Distinct from the landfall of the initial set of Nord Stream pipelines that is located close to Finland's land boundary near Vyborg, the extension project's landfall on the Russian coast is in the western side of the Kurgalsky Peninsula in the southern coast of the Gulf of Finland and borders Estonia. This raises numerous environmental issues, since the Kurgalsky Peninsula is a Ramsar wetland site of international importance as well as a coastal and marine Baltic Sea protected area. However, the Ramsar Convention's Secretariat established in its 2020 report that the effects of the laying of the Nord Stream pipelines in the Kurgalsky nature reserve does not amount to a significant adverse impact on its environment.[6]

Based on the example of the Nord Stream project, major energy infrastructure undertakings may also pose a direct security risk for the coastal States

2 European Parliament, 'At a glance: The Nord Stream 2 pipeline project', 2016, available http://www.europarl.europa.eu/RegData/etudes/ATAG/2016/580875/EPRS_ATA(2016)580875_EN.pdf; 25 March 2021.

3 Nord Stream 2, 'Shareholder & Financial Investors', available https://www.nord-stream2.com/company/shareholder-and-financial-investors/; accessed 5 April 2021. Nord Stream AG, 'Nord Stream to Assess Options to Further Increase Gas Import Capacities Through the Baltic Sea', Press Release (11 May 2012).

4 A Rettman, 'Russia threatens to cut Ukraine gas over Donbas war', EUobserver (7 June 2021).

5 Nord Stream, 'Last Nord Stream 2 Pipe Has Been Welded in the Baltic Sea', Press Release (6 September 2021).

6 HELCOM, '166, Kurgalsky Peninsula', available http://mpas.helcom.fi/apex/f?p =103:12:::NO::P12_ID:166; accessed 5 April 2021. G Randy Milton, T Salathe, *Report: Ramsar Advisory Mission N°93 Kurgalsky Peninsula, Russian Federation Wetland of International Importance N°690* (Ramsar Secretariat, Gland, 2020), 1–3.

whose maritime areas are used or impacted by the laying of submarine pipelines. For example, Finland's defence minister has referred to concerns that are largely shared with the neighbouring Baltic States that the Russian Federation could use its armed forces during a conflict situation to control the Nord Stream pipelines that cross Finnish, Swedish, and Danish maritime zones.[7] Ukraine has similar concerns in respect of the Kerch Strait Bridge and such concerns are widespread in relation to the artificial islands in the South China Sea.

Due to the Russian invasion of Ukraine in 2022, the second set of Nord Stream pipelines have not become operational, and their use is pending the completion of the certification process in Germany. The EU and NATO member States prepared a list of sanctions to deter the Russian invasion of Ukraine and the reintroduction of sanctions against the Nord Stream extension project has a significant role in countering Russian threats to Ukraine.[8] After the United States agreed to lifting its sanctions against the Nord Stream in May 2021, it issued a joint statement with Germany, which provides that:

> Should Russia attempt to use energy as a weapon or commit further aggressive acts against Ukraine, Germany will take action at the national level and press for effective measures at the European level, including sanctions, to limit Russian export capabilities to Europe in the energy sector, including gas, and/or in other economically relevant sectors. This commitment is designed to ensure that Russia will not misuse any pipeline, including Nord Stream 2, to achieve aggressive political ends by using energy as a weapon.[9]

Against this background, members of the German Government cautioned the Russian Federation in December 2021 that its invasion of Ukraine would mean that the second set of Nord Stream pipelines would not become operational.[10] In the wake of the Russian invasion of Ukraine in February 2022, the German

7 J Niinistö, 'Itämeren geostrateginen merkitys kasvussa', *Centrum Balticum* (2 March 2017).

8 H Foy, N Astrasheuskaya, 'Why Nord Stream 2 is at heart of US warnings to Putin over Ukraine', *Financial Times* (9 December 2021).

9 Joint Statement of the United States and Germany on Support for Ukraine, European Energy Security, and our Climate Goals, 21 July 2021, 2, available https://www.auswaertiges-amt.de/en/newsroom/news/joint-statement-usa-and-germany/2472084; accessed 20 December 2021.

10 Anonymous, 'Nord Stream 2: German minister warns Russia over Ukraine', *Deutsche Welle* (18 December 2021).

Government decided to halt its domestic certification process for the approval and operationalization of the Nord Stream 2 pipeline.[11]

The laying of the four Nord Stream pipelines in the Baltic Sea enables the Russian Federation to cut off Ukraine from the transit of Russian natural gas to Europe and, consequently, facilitates economic intimidation in potential future conflicts. Chancellor Angela Merkel had announced in 2018 that Germany supports the Nord Stream 2 project on the condition that Ukraine will not be side-lined as a transit country for the transportation of Russian natural gas to Europe.[12] Despite this, President Putin issued threats of cutting off Ukrainian transit when he was celebrating the completion of the first pipeline of Nord Stream 2 at the St Petersburg International Economic Forum together with the Austrian chancellor Sebastian Kurz and former chancellor of Germany Gerhard Schröder, now acting as the chairman of the board of Nord Stream AG and the Russian energy company Rosneft.[13]

The laying of transboundary submarine pipelines raises potential threats also for the Baltic Sea coastal States.[14] The Nord Stream extension project's two additional trans-Baltic pipelines cross the maritime areas of Finland, Sweden, and Denmark and eventually land on the German coast near Greifswald. The course of the Nord Stream pipeline runs along the territorial seas of the Russian Federation, Germany and Denmark[15] and the EEZ-s of Sweden and Finland in addition to the EEZ-s of the three aforementioned States (see Map 11). Under Article 58(1) of LOSC, the freedom to lay submarine pipelines in the coastal State's EEZ, subject to certain limitations, is granted along with other internationally lawful uses of the sea related to this freedom, e.g., actions associated with the operation of the pipeline. Additionally, the freedom to lay submarine pipelines on a continental shelf is granted under Article 79(1) of LOSC. As all the Baltic Sea

11 G Traufetter, 'Bundesregierung stoppt umstrittene Gaspipeline Nord Stream 2', *Der Spiegel* (22 February 2022).

12 T Buck, R Olearchyk, 'Merkel warns Nord Stream 2 must protect Ukraine role', *Financial Times* (10 April 2018).

13 Rettman, *op. cit.*

14 See, e.g., Savolainen, Gill *et al.*, *op. cit.*, 17–18.

15 Nord Stream had to by-pass the disputed area close to Polish border. Thus, Denmark offered the use of its territorial sea. See S Vinogradov, 'Challenges of Nord Stream: Streamlining International Legal Frameworks and Regimes for Submarine Pipelines' (2009) 52 *German Yearbook of International Law*, 286. The Nord Stream 2 pipelines do not cross the Danish territorial sea. In 2019, Denmark allowed the Nord Stream consortium to use a 147-km-long route in its EEZ south-east of Bornholm Island. See Nord Stream 2, 'Approved Danish Route Stretches South-East of Bornholm', Press Release (2019).

MAP 11 The route of the Nord Stream 2 pipelines
SOURCE: 'MAP: THE NORD STREAM 2 ROUTE', NORD STREAM 2 AG, 2019, AVAILABLE HTTPS://WWW.NORD-STREAM2.COM; ACCESSED 5 APRIL 2021.

lies within 200 NM from the coast,[16] Nord Stream is subject to the legal regimes of EEZ (Part V of LOSC) and continental shelf (Part VI of LOSC).

12.2 The Significance of the Viro Strait's EEZ Corridor for the Nord Stream Project

It was in advantage of the Nord Stream project that due to the narrowness of the Viro Strait, the outer limit of the territorial sea of Finland and Estonia had been established with the aim to never reach closer than 3 NM to the maritime boundary between the two States.[17] Thereby the territorial sovereignty of either of the States in that area was excluded and instead a six-mile wide EEZ corridor was created to maintain free passage. This has a particular importance to the Nord Stream project as otherwise its construction would have been subject to the explicit consent of either of the coastal States and the respective domestic regulations.[18] Therefore, free passage in the Gulf of Finland remains

16 Oude Elferink 1994, *op. cit.*, 169.
17 See *supra* Chapter 4 of Part 2.
18 Vinogradov, *op. cit.*, 276.

intact making it possible to lay submarine pipelines in the passageway of the 6-NM-wide EEZ corridor subject to Part V and VI of LOSC.

The Viro Strait serves as the primary channel for the export of Russian oil and gas. While oil is shipped mostly by tankers, the flow of Russian gas to the EU is dependent on submarine pipelines that run through the Viro Strait and head via the Finnish, Swedish, and Danish EEZs to Germany. In the past two decades, the Russian Federation has invested heavily into its gas and oil export facilities in the Gulf of Finland. The inauguration of the currently second-biggest Russian commercial port Ust-Luga in 2001 and its on-going development complemented with the construction of the Nord Stream pipelines ten years ago and the current laying of the second set of Nord Stream's twin-pipeline system demonstrate the importance for the Russian Federation's economy of maintaining stability in the Baltic Sea region.

In 2007 and 2012, Estonia rejected Nord Stream's application to conduct marine scientific research in its EEZ in the Viro Strait for the laying of the submarine pipelines.[19] This calls for an examination of whether coastal States have the right to decline issuing such authorisations. In the context of marine scientific research, this chapter takes next a closer look at an incident between Estonian and Russian vessels concerning unauthorized seabed surveys in the Estonian maritime area of the Viro Strait.

12.3 Marine Scientific Research in the Context of Seabed Studies on the Pipeline Route

The Nord Stream project was carried out in the context of surveying and assessing the marine environment in the Baltic Sea. That was a precondition for, *inter alia*, conducting an environmental impact assessment and surveying the suitability of the seabed for the laying of pipelines. Firstly, the question whether such investigations may be classified as a marine scientific research under Part XIII of LOSC has to be addressed. The LOSC does not provide a definition for marine scientific research. Thus, its scope has been subject to different interpretations. For example, it has been argued that:

> [Seabed studies] must be viewed as an "internationally lawful use" of the sea related to the exercise of high-seas freedoms in the EEZ, such as

19 The Estonian Government Office, 'Valitsus otsustas kabinetinõupidamisel mitte rahuldada Nord Stream AG taotlust mereuuringuteks Eesti majandusvööndis', Press Release (6 December 2012).

> those "associated with submarine cables and pipelines," as provided for in Article 58(2) LOSC.[20]

Accordingly, it is suggested that research in the context of a right to lay pipelines should be distinguished from the general concept of marine scientific research as without the right to conduct seabed studies the freedom to lay pipelines cannot be carried out.

However, traditionally marine scientific research is understood as including all forms of scientific investigations.[21] Moreover, it may be subdivided into four categories: physical oceanography, chemical oceanography, marine biology, and, finally, marine geology and geophysics.[22] The marine environment studies in relation to the Nord Stream project may be classified as falling mostly under the latter category as they are primarily concerned with sediments and topography of the seabed, including its physical properties.

Of particular importance in addressing the scope of marine scientific research is its distinction between 'fundamental' and 'applied' scientific research. In that regard:

> The former refers to scientific research intended to add to the sum of human knowledge about the world, regardless of its application, whereas the latter refers to research undertaken primarily for specific practical purposes. Marine scientific research in principle covers both kinds of scientific research.[23]

Thus, applied scientific research includes physical seabed investigations carried out for, *inter alia*, military or commercial purposes,[24] e.g., the laying of submarine pipelines, even when it is conducted without the intent of publishing the results.[25] Hence, with due respect to differing views, one may argue

20 Vinogradov, *op. cit.*, 284.

21 AHA Soons, *Marine Scietific Research and the Law of the Sea* (Kluwer, Deventer, 1982), 121–124. The *travaux préparatoires* of the 1982 LOSC indicate that States either did not include in its proposals for the definition of 'marine scientific research' any indication of the nature of the research or excluded merely activities aimed directly at the exploitation of marine resources which are not designed to increase man's knowledge and not conducted for peaceful purposes.

22 Ibid., 6.

23 Ibid.

24 Except resource exploration as it is governed by a different legal regime.

25 Soons, *op. cit.*, 7. In that context it is noteworthy that the Nord Stream consortium published the results of the research activities which were included in the project's transboundary environmental impact assessment.

that scientific investigations carried out in the marine environment in the context of the freedom to lay pipelines should be regarded as applied scientific research which fall under the scope of Part XIII of LOSC.

The question whether a coastal State has the right to deny a permit to foreign vessels to conduct marine scientific research in its EEZ is addressed next. In addition, the matter of a coastal State's right to refuse to grant permit for conducting marine scientific research in its EEZ is taken under scrutiny. For this purpose, focus is subsequently shifted to two incidents that occurred, respectively in 2005 and 2007, in the Estonian EEZ in relation with the Nord Stream project.

12.4 The Incident between the Estonian Coast Guard and Russian Research Vessels in the Viro Strait's EEZ Corridor

In 2005, the Russian 65-metre-long research ship *Pjotr Kotsov*, commonly used for seabed mapping (currently owned by the State corporation for nuclear energy ROSATOM),[26] was found by the Estonian Coast Guard conducting marine scientific research in a maritime area north of Tallinn without Estonia's prior authorisation.[27] The ship neglected the orders given to it by the Coast Guard.[28] The crew of the *Pjotr Kotsov* responded to the Estonian Coast Guard that they are conducting marine scientific research. This was confirmed on site by the Estonian Coast Guard ship and plane.[29] The Estonian Coast Guard ordered the *Pjotr Kotsov* to sail to a near-by anchorage area and wait for the orders following the Estonian procedure in cases of non-compliance with the regulations on marine scientific research. After initially setting the course to the anchorage area, the *Pjotr Kotsov* soon afterwards changed its course for leaving the Estonian maritime area. The ship's crew did not comply with the orders issued by the Estonian Coast Guard.[30] The Estonian Coast Guard decided not to use coercion for detaining the *Pjotr Kotsov* and the ship sailed out of the Estonian maritime area.[31]

26 A Staalesen, 'A major oil exploration is going on in Russia's East Arctic waters', *The Barents Observer* (24 August 2021).

27 P Paleri, *Coast Guards of the World and Emerging Maritime Threats* (Ocean Policy Studies, Tokyo, 2009), 165.

28 R Kagge, T Sildam, 'Vene laev tabati Eesti vetest uurimistöölt', *Postimees* (11 November 2005).

29 Anonymous, 'Vene uurimislaev Pjotr Kotsov eiras Eesti piirivalve korraldusi', *Eesti Päevaleht* (10 November 2005).

30 Ibid.

31 Ibid.

The Estonian authorities exercised self-restraint in responding to that incident. This might be explained by the fact that the laying of the Nord Stream pipelines, with which the incident was directly intertwined, involved significant regional political and economic interests. Hence, Estonia used diplomatic measures instead of coercive on-site measures for responding to the breach of the international and domestic legal regime of marine scientific research. One may wonder how the incident could have evolved if the Estonian authorities would have been more assertive in their orders issued to the Russian State-owned ship to stop conducting unauthorized marine scientific research in the Estonian EEZ.

In particular, would the legal classification of the incident have been any different if the law enforcement operation against the State-owned ship would have been carried out instead by an Estonian warship (analogously to the practice of numerous other coastal States) that, hypothetically, had required the ship to comply with the orders or face the consequences of non-compliance? The use of coercive maritime enforcement measures or a mere threat of using such coercive measures in a geopolitically sensitive context risks the possibility of an initially planned law enforcement operation to spiral into military activities. That risk is greater where the coastal State's Navy is exercising maritime law enforcement tasks. This is illustrated by the facts of the *Guyana v. Suriname arbitration*.

The *Guyana v. Suriname arbitration* concerned an incident in a disputed maritime area where Guyana had issued concessions for oil exploration to a Canadian company. The company's oil rig and drill ship *C.E. Thornton* were in the disputed maritime area on 3 June 2000 when they were approached by two Surinamese Navy patrol boats that ordered them to leave the area.[32] The legality of that measure was disputed by Guyana before the Annex VII Arbitral Tribunal. Guyana claimed that the expulsion from the disputed area of the oil rig and drill ship *C.E. Thornton* by Suriname constituted a threat of the use of force in breach of the LOSC, the UN Charter, and general international law. By its award of 2007 the Annex VII Arbitral Tribunal satisfied that claim.[33] The Tribunal provided little explanation on why it reached such conclusion:

> The Tribunal accepts the argument that in international law force may be used in law enforcement activities provided that such force is unavoidable, reasonable and necessary. However in the circumstances of

32 Annex VII Arbitral Tribunal, *Guyana v. Suriname Award, op. cit.*, paras. 150–151.
33 Ibid., para 488.

> the present case, this Tribunal is of the view that the action mounted by Suriname on 3 June 2000 seemed more akin to a threat of military action rather than a mere law enforcement activity. This Tribunal has based this finding primarily on the testimony of witnesses to the incident, in particular the testimony of Messrs Netterville and Barber. Suriname's action therefore constituted a threat of the use of force in contravention of the Convention, the UN Charter and general international law.[34]

Thus, the Tribunal based its conclusion to a significant extent on the subjective assessment of the situation by the persons directly involved in the incident. Their accounts of the incident, as relied on by the Tribunal, included the following:

> Mr Edward Netterville, the Rig Supervisor on the *C.E. Thornton*, described the incident in these terms in his witness statement:
>
> Shortly after midnight on 4 June 2000, while this coring process (drilling for core samples) was underway, gunboats from the Surinamese Navy arrived at our location. The gunboats established radio contact with the C.E. Thornton and its service vessels, and ordered us to "leave the area in 12 hours," warning that if we did not comply "the consequences will be yours." The Surinamese Navy repeated this order several times. I understood this to mean that if the C.E. Thornton and its support vessels did not leave the area within twelve hours, the gunboats would be unconstrained to use armed force against the rig and its service vessels.
>
> Mr. Netterville made the following observations on this incident:
>
> In my experience, Suriname's threat to use force against the C.E. Thornton is unprecedented. I have been employed for over forty years in the marine and oil industry during which time I have served aboard oil rigs throughout the world. I have never experienced, nor heard of, any similar instance in which a rig has been evicted from its worksite by the threat of armed force. Nor, in discussions with others in the industry after June 2000, has anyone told me of a similar incident.
>
> Mr. Graham Barber, who served as Reading & Bates Area Manager for the project and had overall responsibility for its rig and shore-based operations, gave similar testimony. He stated that:
>
> After midnight on 3 June 2000, during the jacking-up process, two gunboats from the Surinamese Navy approached us and shined their

34 Ibid., para 445.

search lights on the rig. A Surinamese naval officer informed us by radio that we "were in Surinamese waters" and that we had 12 hours to leave the area or "face the consequences." He repeated this phrase, or variations of it, several times. … Faced with these threats from the Surinamese Navy, in the early morning hours of 4 June 2003, I convened a meeting with other persons in authority aboard the C.E. Thornton. We decided that we had no alternative other than to evacuate the rig from the Eagle location.

Major J.P. Jones, Commander Staff Support of the LUMAR (the Suriname Air Force and Navy), recorded this exchange between himself and the drilling platform:

This is the Suriname navy. You are in Suriname waters without authority of the Suriname Government to conduct economic activities here. I order you to stop immediately with these activities and leave the Suriname waters. The answer to this from the platform was: "we are unaware of being in Suriname waters". I persisted saying that they were in Suriname waters and that they had to leave these waters within 12 hours. And if they would not do so, the consequences would be theirs. They then asked where they should move to. I said that they should retreat to Guyanese waters. He reacted by saying that they needed time to start up their departure. I then allowed them 24 hours to leave the Suriname waters. We then hung around for some time and after about one hour we left for New Nickerie.

Major Jones added:

If the platform had not left our waters voluntarily, I would definitely not have used force. I had no instructions to that effect and anyhow I did not have the suitable weapons to do so. I even had no instructions to board the drilling platform and also I did not consider that.[35]

The *Guyana v. Suriname arbitration* shows how important it is for the crew on board the vessel enforcing the coastal State's laws to be careful in issuing their orders to the ship that is suspected of violating the coastal State's laws and regulations. Such orders and the consequences that the unlawful activities bring about need to be clearly understandable to the persons against whom the law enforcement operation is directed.

In the case of the Estonian-Russian incident, the Russian officials afterwards confirmed its vessels' (*Pjotr Kotsov* and *Jakov Smirnitski*) research activities on

35 Ibid., paras. 433–437.

the planned route of the Nord Stream pipeline.[36] However, they argued that as the research was conducted outside the territorial waters of Estonia it did not call for any authorisation.[37]

Under Part XIII of LOSC, the general right to conduct marine scientific research is provided in Article 238. This right is further confirmed in Article 242(1) of LOSC which calls in this field for international co-operation for peaceful purposes. Additionally, Article 242(2) of LOSC provides that States shall offer to other States a reasonable opportunity to obtain information which is necessary to prevent and control damage to the health and safety of persons and marine environment.

However, coastal States have under Article 56(1)(b)(ii) of LOSC exclusive jurisdiction with regard to marine scientific research in their EEZ which is subject to specific rules set forth in Article 246 of LOSC. Thus, Article 246(2) of LOSC provides the 'overriding rule'[38] according to which marine scientific research in the EEZ and on the continental shelf is always subject to the consent of the coastal State. Hence, under Part XIII of LOSC the Russian Federation's vessels' marine scientific research activities in 2005, conducted in the Estonian EEZ, were in breach of the law of the sea as no prior consent from the Estonian authorities was sought. The Russian Federation's authorities' contention that the research activities in the Estonian EEZ were lawful as the vessels were situated outside the territorial sea of Estonia is in that regard not grounded.

12.5 Permit-Based Marine Scientific Research in an EEZ: Estonia's Decision to Deny Seabed Surveys

In 2007, the Finnish authorities requested the Nord Stream consortium to conduct surveys on the Estonian side of the Viro Strait for the possible rerouting of the pipeline due to geological and environmental considerations.[39] The course of the Nord Stream pipeline in the Finnish EEZ follows its outermost sections, thus closely bordering Estonia's EEZ in the strait. Hence the

36 T Sildam, 'Venemaa tunnistas Eesti majandusvetes uurimist', *Postimees* (28 November 2005).

37 Paleri, *op. cit.*, 185.

38 T Stephens, DR Rothwell, 'Marine Scientific Research', in Rothwell, Oude Elferink, Scott, Stephens (eds.), *op. cit.*, 567.

39 T Koivurova, I Pölönen, *Transboundary Environmental Impact Assessment in the Case of the Baltic Sea Gas Pipeline* (2009) 52 *German Yearbook of International Law*, 313.

consortium requested permission from the Estonian authorities to conduct a seabed survey in the Estonian EEZ.

The government of Estonia rejected the application in 2007 and made the same decision in 2012 (in respect of the Nord Stream extension project). These decisions were not challenged by the States most interested in the project, i.e. the Russian Federation and Germany. Instead, they received the consent from the government of Finland to use its EEZ for the pipeline route.[40] Nevertheless, the lawfulness of the Estonian government's decision should be analysed further in light of LOSC.

Estonia's rejection of the Nord Stream consortium's application to conduct seabed surveys in its EEZ raises the question whether its position was in conformity with Article 246(3) of LOSC. It stipulates that coastal States shall, in normal circumstances, grant their consent for marine scientific research projects performed by other States in their EEZ or on their continental shelf and such consent shall not be delayed or denied unreasonably.[41] In considering whether normal circumstances apply it has to be determined, *inter alia*, that the research activities do not relate to the seismic or other explorations, they are in accordance with the LOSC, for the benefit of mankind and for peaceful purposes, carried out with appropriate scientific methods and means, have due regard for the protection and preservation of the marine environment and do not interfere unjustifiably with other legitimate uses of the sea.[42]

However, under Article 246(5) of LOSC coastal States may in their discretion withhold their consent to the conduct of such research projects if the project is related to one of the following actions which are relevant to consider in connection with the Nord Stream project. Notably, the subparagraphs of Article 246(5) of LOSC have to be interpreted restrictively as they constitute exceptions from the general rule.

Firstly, Article 246(5)(a) of LOSC provides legal basis for Estonia's refusal on condition that the Nord Stream project is of direct significance for the exploration and exploitation of natural resources under Estonia's jurisdiction. According to the official statement of the government of Estonia, "[b]ecause the results of drilling work on the continental shelf will give information about Estonia's natural resources and their possible use, the Estonian government has the right to reject the research application."[43] The distinction between

40 Vinogradov, *op. cit.*, 261.

41 See also Eritrea v Yemen (Phase I), *op. cit.*, para 407.

42 See M Gorina-Ysern, *An International Regime for Marine Scientific Research* (Transnational Publishers, Ardsley, 2004), 315.

43 Vinogradov, *op. cit.*, 261.

exploration activities,[44] for which a different legal regime applies, and marine scientific research for data collecting activities of natural phenomena, is based on the motivations for undertaking the activities.[45] It is possible to consider the investigation activities conducted in relation to the Nord Stream project as marine scientific research as they were not necessarily carried out for the purpose of economic utilization of the natural phenomena, although their results can be relevant for the exploration or exploitation of natural resources.

Hence the question whether the submarine surveys were of direct significance for the exploration and exploitation of natural resources (either living or non-living) is at the core of the dispute in terms of Article 246(5)(a) of LOSC. Particularly due to the imprecise formulation of subparagraph (a) arguments in favour of both parties to the dispute may be found. However, the burden of proof lies with the coastal State.[46] At first glance the authorities of the coastal State have the discretionary right in interpreting the term *direct significance*.[47] Yet, on the contrary, the coastal State does not possess the right to determine whether a particular scientific research activity falls under the scope of the subparagraphs of 246(5): this determination has to be based on objective facts in accordance with Article 248 and 251 of LOSC.[48] Hence in occasions when the discretion may be exercised it might fall short of legitimacy and thus constitute an abuse of rights in terms of Article 300 of LOSC.

The formulation 'direct significance' under Article 246(5)(a) of LOSC has been generally understood to imply that:

> [T]he results of the research in question must have their own, intrinsic value from the point of view of exploration or exploitation and that it is not enough that the research results are only remotely significant (e.g., research results which can *become* useful from this point of view when they are combined with other data to be collected).[49]

Thus, scientific studies which can "reasonably be expected to produce results permitting to locate resources, to assess them, or to monitor their status and

44 Soons, *op. cit.*, 171. The term *exploration* is undefined in the LOSC but generally it is understood as including "data collecting activities concerning natural resources conducted specifically in view of the exploitation (i.e., economic utilization) of those natural resources."

45 Ibid.

46 Soons, *op. cit.*, 170.

47 Art. 246(5) of LOSC: "Coastal States may however *in their discretion* withhold their consent ..." (emphasis added).

48 Soons, *op. cit.*, 170.

49 Ibid., 171.

availability for commercial exploitation"[50] and the significance of which is at least of some importance falls under the scope of Article 246(5)(a) of LOSC. The decision whether a particular activity meets this threshold is often bound up with technical details and means of the investigation activity.

Significantly, under Article 264 and 297(2)(a) of LOSC disputes concerning the exercise by the coastal State of a right or discretion, including by withholding its consent to the conduct of a marine scientific research project, are not subject to compulsory dispute settlement. However, it has been voiced that the Russian Federation could have used under Article 297(2)(b) of LOSC its right to challenge the Estonian authorities' refusal in 2007 to grant the permit to conduct hydrographic surveys in its EEZ.[51] Yet although in essence State parties to the LOSC are permitted under Annex V, Section 2 to the LOSC to refer such disputes to compulsory conciliation, the authoritative award of the conciliation is legally non-binding.

Secondly, Article 246(5)(b) of LOSC provides, *inter alia*, the right of refusal if the project involves the introduction of harmful substances into the marine environment. However, unlike the environmental impact of the laying of the pipeline in the Baltic Sea and its operational mode, the seabed survey does not involve introducing harmful substances into the marine environment.

Thirdly, under Article 246(5)(c) of LOSC coastal States may withhold their consent if the project involves the construction of artificial installations and structures. However, no *ad hoc* artificial installations or structures were involved in the Nord Stream's research activities.

Finally, a State's refusal to grant permit for conducting subsea surveys in its EEZ would be grounded under Article 246(5)(d) of LOSC if the project would have been inaccurately documented in the information dossier presented. Yet, purportedly the documents provided to the Estonian government were accurate.

To conclude, whereas in 2005 the Russian Federation's vessels conducted marine scientific research in the Estonian EEZ in clear violation of Article 246(2) of LOSC, the lawfulness of the Estonian authorities' rejection of the Nord Stream consortium's application to conduct scientific research in its EEZ in 2007 and 2012 is subject to different interpretations in light of part XIII of LOSC. The latter may be regarded as a consequence of the imprecise formulation of Article 246(5)(a) of LOSC.

50 Ibid.

51 Vinogradov, *op. cit.*, 283–285.

CHAPTER 13

Countering the Threat of 'Little Green Men' in the Åland Strait

Close to the Viro Strait (western part of the Gulf of Finland) is located the Åland Strait that is subject to a special legal regime under the law of the sea and international security law. This chapter discusses the legal and geopolitical characteristics of the Åland Strait in the context of fears that the Åland Islands are turned into a theatre of (hybrid) war in case a foreign State is willing to breach the special legal regime of the Åland Islands which the Russian Federation has in recent years demonstrated by the occupation and annexation of Crimea in 2014 and the invasion of Ukraine in 2022.

13.1 Geopolitical Characteristics of the Åland Strait and Preparations to Counter Unidentified Soldiers on the Åland Islands

The Åland Strait is located between the Finnish and Swedish mainland coasts, some 100 NM west of the Viro Strait in the Gulf of Finland. The area that spans between the Åland Strait and the Viro Strait is the southern edge of the Archipelago Sea, which itself comprises multiple small straits that are used mostly by small craft for navigating from the Baltic Sea proper through the Åland region to the Gulf of Bothnia. The Åland Strait is in the vicinity of Stockholm and the Finnish city Turku and serves as the gateway to the Gulf of Bothnia that comprises almost one third of the overall surface area of the Baltic Sea. The Åland Strait thus exerts considerable geostrategic importance as it enables to control international shipping and air traffic between the Gulf of Bothnia and the Baltic Sea proper.

Due to the location of the Åland Islands, they are analogously to Gotland Island widely considered as a key strategic area from the perspective of the Baltic Sea region's security. Since the occupation of Crimea in 2014, Finland has set its focus on improving its capabilities in defending the Åland region, particularly in the context of a potential hybrid warfare. Sweden decided in 2016, after decades of demilitarization policy, to send its armed forces back

DOI:10.1163/9789004509368_015

to Gotland Island,[1] to reinstate conscription in 2017,[2] and, in the next year, to establish its first new military unit since the end of the Second World War that was tasked with defending Gotland Island,[3] while complementing it in 2019 with new air-defence missile system on the island.[4] Sweden reinforced the Gotland regiment at the height of the Ukraine crisis in January 2022 after the Russian Federation had sent three of its landing ships from its Arctic base to the Baltic Sea; against this background, soldiers of the Gotland regiment were patrolling the Gotland airport, main port, and military facilities.[5] By contrast, Finland has been modest in bolstering its defences on the Åland Islands. This is due to the Convention Relating to the Non-fortification and Neutralisation of the Åland Islands,[6] which prohibits the fortification and militarisation of the Åland Islands (Art 3).

Recent studies have shown that the legally binding nature of the demilitarisation regime in the Åland Islands has not been challenged by the parties to the 1921 Convention or third States and that Finland has adopted measures to ensure that the passage regime of the Åland Strait is respected both by ships as well as aircraft navigating in that area.[7] Finland is committed to protecting the regime stipulated by the 1921 Convention, irrespective of whether the demilitarisation of the Åland Islands favours its security interests. The Finnish defence minister Jussi Niinistö opined in 2017 that, in the changed security environment of the Baltic Sea, the demilitarisation of the Åland region does not contribute to Finland's interests of protecting the Åland Islands.[8] He also pointed out that the line between peacetime and war has been blurred and Finland cannot rule out the possibility that the use of force is used against it.[9]

1 K Dickerman, L d'Aki, 'Inside the Swedish military presence on Gotland, the most strategic island for defense against Russian aggression', *The Washington Post* (30 August 2018).
2 MS Sorensen, 'Sweden Reinstates Conscription, With an Eye on Russia', *The New York Times* (2 March 2017).
3 Anonymous, 'Sweden to re-establish military unit on Baltic Sea island', *The Associated Press* (13 December 2017).
4 S Johnson, 'Sweden to boost Gotland air defense amid Russia tensions', *Reuters* (1 July 2019).
5 J Granlund, 'Ökad beredskap på Gotland – försvaret kallar in reservofficerare', *Aftonbladet* (13 January 2022).
6 Convention Relating to the Non-fortification and Neutralisation of the Aaland Islands, adopted 20 October 1921, entered into force 6 April 1922, 9 LNTS 211.
7 Spiliopoulou Åkermark, Hyttinen and Kleemola-Juntunen, *op. cit.*, 177–178.
8 K Räisänen, 'Jussi Niinistön mukaan Ahvenanmaalla on "herätty todellisuuteen", kun turvallisuusuhat ovat muuttuneet: "Ei se demilitarisointi ainakaan helpota puolustamista"', *Helsingin Sanomat* (26 May 2018).
9 Niinistö 2017, *op. cit.* See also R Uosokainen, 'Puolustusministeri Niinistö: Demilitarisoituna Ahvenanmaa muodostaa sotilaallisen tyhjiön', *Yle Uutiset* (17 October 2016).

In particular, he cautioned against the possibility that the Åland Islands are turned into a theatre of war in case a foreign State is willing to breach the rules of international law which the Russian Federation had recently demonstrated by the occupation and annexation of Crimea.[10]

Finland drew such conclusions swiftly after the occupation of Crimea. This is demonstrated by the comment of the Finnish defence minister Jussi Niinistö in July 2015 that Finland's armed forces are preparing to counter unidentified soldiers on the Åland Islands.[11] In 2017, Finland amended its national defence law and criminal law to unequivocally prohibit the presence of unidentified soldiers in its territory and sanctioned the breach of this rule with a fine or a maximum of one year of imprisonment.[12] This legislative approach may serve as a deterrence against any border crossings by (an) unidentified soldier(s), including by combat divers (so-called frogmen). In recent years, Finland has repeatedly conducted military exercises in its Archipelago Sea, e.g., "Vilma" in 2018, "Silja" in 2019, "Lotta" in May 2020 and "Kaisla 20" in November and December 2020, complemented with two joint naval exercises with, respectively, Sweden and Estonia in October 2020.[13]

13.2 Legal Regime of the Åland Strait

Passage through the Åland Strait is regulated by the 1921 Convention. Pursuant to the 1921 Convention, the Åland Strait is subject to a specific passage regime. In terms of Article 35(c) of LOSC, the Åland Strait is a strait in which passage is regulated by a long-standing international convention, i.e. the 1921 Convention, in force specifically relating to this strait.[14] This means that, although the strait

10 Ibid.

11 L Viirand, 'Kaitseminister Niinistö: Soome valmistub Ahvenamaa kaitsmiseks "roheliste mehikeste" eest', *ERR Uudised* (30 July 2015).

12 See further, Spiliopoulou Åkermark, Hyttinen and Kleemola-Juntunen, *op. cit.*, 151–152.

13 Finnish Navy Press Release, '"VILMA" meritaisteluharjoitus valtaa Saaristomeren', *Merivoimat* (21 May 2018). Finnish Navy Press Release, 'Meritaisteluharjoitus Siljan soveltava vaihe alkaa 3.6. - Sota-aluksia ja rannikkojoukkoja liikkeellä Suomenlahdella ja Saaristomerellä', *Merivoimat* (2 June 2019). E Tuominen, 'Meritaisteluharjoitus Lotta mittaa Merivoimien taistelukykyä', *Ruotuväki* (27 May 2020). Finnish Navy Press Release, 'Baltic Shield 2020 toteutetaan Rannikkolaivaston ammuntojen yhteydessä', *Merivoimat* (2 October 2020). Finnish Navy Press Release, 'Merioperaatiot tähtäimessä Kaisla 20 -harjoituksessa', *Merivoimat* (20 November 2020). Finnish Navy Press Release, 'Suomi–Ruotsi-yhteistyö jatkuu miinantorjuntaharjoituksessa', *Merivoimat* (9 October 2020).

14 See further on the passage regime of the Åland Strait, in P Kleemola-Juntunen, *The Åland Strait* (Brill, Leiden/Boston, 2018), 122–145.

connects Swedish and Finnish EEZs in the Gulf of Bothnia and the Baltic Sea proper, the right of transit passage (Art 38 of LOSC) does not apply to ships and aircraft in the Åland Strait. Finland and Sweden would have minimal control over the influx of foreign ships and aircraft to the Åland region and the Gulf of Bothnia if the regime of transit passage would apply to the Åland Strait.

Under Article 5 of the 1921 Convention, foreign ships are entitled to the right of innocent passage in the Åland Strait. Finland has maintained that "the legal regime of innocent passage in the strait has remained unchanged after the entry into force of the Convention."[15] Where historically a specific passage regime has been in force in a strait for a long time, as in the case of the Åland Strait, the LOSC gives priority under Article 35(c) to the relevant long-standing international convention. It is generally agreed that the criteria of Article 35(c) of LOSC are met in the instances of the Danish Straits,[16] the Åland Strait,[17] the Strait of Magellan,[18] and the Turkish Straits.[19]

The United States have never recognised the Åland Strait as an international strait regulated by a long-standing convention in terms of Article 35(c) of LOSC.[20] In 1992, the United States pointed out that it is not a party to the 1921 Convention and "*has never recognized this international strait as falling within*

15 Permanent Mission of Finland to the United Nations, 22 August 1997, No. YKEC032-46, 2, available https://www.un.org/Depts/los/LEGISLATIONANDTREATIES/PDFFILES/communications/fin_due_publicity_22aug1997.pdf; accessed 18 March 2021.

16 Division for Ocean Affairs and the Law of the Sea, *op. cit.*, Denmark's declaration upon the ratification of LOSC on 16 November 2004. Sweden's declaration upon signing the LOSC on 10 December 1982 and ratifying it on 25 June 1996.

17 Ibid., Sweden's declaration. Ibid., Finland's declaration upon signing the LOSC on 10 December 1982 and ratifying it on 21 June 1996. In drafting the LOSC, its Article 35(c) was commonly understood to also include the Åland Strait. See also Denmark's Counter-Memorial in the Passage through the Great Belt Case (Finland v. Denmark) Copenhagen: Government of the Kingdom of Denmark 1992, 238–239. Nevertheless, the US has not recognised the Åland Strait as an international strait regulated by a long-standing convention in terms of Article 35(c) of LOSC. See RW Smith, J Ashley Roach, *Limits in the Seas, No. 112: United States Responses to Excessive National Maritime Claims* (US Department of State, Washington D.C., 1992) 67. See also P Kleemola-Juntunen, *Passage Rights in International Law: A Case Study of the Territorial Waters of the Åland Islands* (Lapland University Press, Rovaniemi, 2014) 256.

18 Division for Ocean Affairs and the Law of the Sea, *op. cit.*, Chile's declaration upon ratifying the LOSC on 25 August 1997. Ibid., Argentina's declaration upon ratifying the LOSC on 1 December 1995.

19 Ünlü, *op. cit.*, 54.

20 See Smith and Ashley Roach 1992, *op. cit.*, 67. Ashley Roach, Smith 2012, *op. cit.*, 284. See also R Platzöder, 'Bridges and Straits in the Baltic Sea', in R Platzöder, P Verlaan (eds), *The Baltic Sea: New Developments in National Policies and International Cooperation* (Martinus Nijhoff, The Hague/London/Boston, 1996) 148.

the Article 35(c) exception."[21] On the other hand, the United States does not any longer uphold this protest in its Navy's collection of coastal States' claims and the United States responses in respect of them.[22] Furthermore, Kraska and Pedrozo who both have a strong background in working for the United States Navy and Department of Defence, have found that the Åland Strait is subject to the Article 35(c)-exception.[23] It would, arguably, contribute to the demilitarisation efforts of the Åland region if States would unequivocally agree on the applicability of the regime of innocent passage to the Åland Strait. Otherwise, warships and military aircraft would enjoy under the regime of transit passage principally the high seas freedoms of navigation and overflight in the Åland Strait which would result in an increase of warships and military aircraft in and over the Gulf of Bothnia.

Pursuant to Article 4 of the 1921 Convention, any military, naval or air force cannot enter or remain in the demilitarised zone of the Åland Islands.[24] In respect of foreign warships, the right to enter the archipelago and to anchor there temporarily is subject to strict requirements as such permission can be granted by Finland to only one warship of any State at a time (Art 4(b)). For example, in 2017, Finland denied access for the Russian Navy's training ship *Kruzenstern* with 164 cadets onboard to the main port of the Åland Islands, Maarianhamina.[25]

The 1921 Convention provides Finland with certain means for responding to attacks in the Åland region by, among others, unidentified soldiers. The Finnish defence minister has commented that when the situation requires, Finland has the troops and means ready to deploy them to the Åland region, but also warned that if an attack occurs, then Finland would have to undertake a "considerable race to the Åland Islands".[26] The 1921 Convention does not permit Finland to fortify the Åland Islands for deterring such attacks. Nevertheless, the 1921 Convention allows Finland to react proportionally to any attempts aimed at occupying the Åland Islands or parts of the region. This follows from Article 4(a) of the 1921 Convention, according to which, in time of

21 Smith and Ashley Roach 1992, *op. cit.*, 67.

22 United States Navy Judge Advocate General's Corps, 'Finland. Summary of Claims', November 2017, available https://www.jag.navy.mil/organization/documents/mcrm/Finland2017.pdf; accessed 18 March 2021.

23 Kraska and Pedrozo, *op. cit.*, 226.

24 This is subject to exceptions provided in Article 7 of the 1921 Convention.

25 Anonymous, 'HBL: Pääesikunta kieltää venäläisen purjealuksen pääsyn Ahvenanmaalle', *Yle Uutiset* (28 August 2017). See also M Gestrin-Hagner, 'Huvudstaben förbjöd ryskt skolfartyg att besöka Åland', *Hufvudstadsbladet* (28 August 2017).

26 Räisänen, *op. cit.*

peace, Finland may, if exceptional circumstances demand, send into the zone and keep there temporarily such other armed forces, in addition to the regular police force, as shall be strictly necessary for the maintenance of order.

In addition, if the Åland Islands would be made the object of hybrid conflict which does not amount to an armed conflict, then Finland can make use of the right to send one or two of its light surface warships to visit the islands, as well as send into the waters of the zone and keep there temporarily other surface ships, which cannot exceed a total displacement of 6.000 tons. This follows from Article 4(b) of the 1921 Convention which also allows Finland to grant a permit for entering the archipelago and to anchor there temporarily for one warship of another State at a time.

CHAPTER 14

Threats of Piracy in the Straits of Malacca, Sunda, Lombok

The previous chapters centred around maritime hybrid warfare and hybrid conflicts in or near the Strait of Hormuz, the Bab el-Mandeb, the Viro Strait, the Taiwan Strait, and the Kerch Strait. This chapter focuses on the Straits of Malacca and Singapore that together with the Straits of Sunda and Lombok serve as the main gateways to the South China Sea. The Straits of Malacca and Singapore have not been a theatre of hybrid warfare or hybrid conflict, but similarly to the Åland Strait this waterway appears particularly vulnerable to hybrid threats.

14.1 Legal and Geopolitical Characteristics

The main passage to the South China Sea traverses the Straits of Malacca and Singapore, which, if combined, are commonly referred to as the most densely navigated straits globally and constituting the second-largest oil chokepoint after the Strait of Hormuz.[1] However, as examined above (Chapter 9 of Part 3), in geographical terms, the Strait of Singapore is not the busiest strait based on the density of ship traffic, albeit it remains by far the busiest strait that is subject to the legal regime of straits under Part III of LOSC.

The Straits of Malacca and Singapore comprises a continuous waterway connecting the Indian Ocean with the South China Sea. Thus, from the perspective of international shipping, the Straits of Malacca and Singapore constitute an integral whole. Geographically, the two straits are different from one another. The narrow and relatively short Strait of Singapore is located rather within the South China Sea, while the Strait of Malacca spans a large maritime area on the western side of the Malay Peninsula.

1 N McCarthy, 'Global Oil Shipments Depend on Major Chokepoints', Statista (25 March 2021). L Villar, M Hamilton, 'The Strait of Malacca, a key oil trade chokepoint, links the Indian and Pacific Oceans', US Energy Information Administration (11 August 2017).

MAP 12 The Strait of Malacca
SOURCE: OPENSTREETMAP.ORG, 'STRAIT OF MALACCA', 2021, AVAILABLE WWW.OPENSTREETMAP.ORG; ACCESSED 30 AUGUST 2021. THE MAP IS MODIFIED BY THE AUTHOR SO AS TO DEPICT THE LIMITS OF THE STRAIT OF MALACCA TO THE EXTENT THAT IT IS UP TO 24 NM WIDE.

Geographically, the Strait of Malacca is nearly 1000 km (540 NM) long.[2] Legally speaking, however, the Strait of Malacca is approximately 320 km (173 NM) long, as measured based on its southern limit (Indonesia's Karimunbesar Island) and an imaginary line connecting a coastal point near Malaysia's capital Kuala Lumpur with the Indonesian coast on Sumatra Island (northern limit). In that area, the Strait of Malacca is less than 24 NM wide as measured from the relevant baselines and thus falls under the sovereignty of its coastal States, i.e. Malaysia's territorial sea and Indonesia's archipelagic waters and territorial sea.[3] Consequently, Part III of LOSC is applicable to the Strait of Malacca only in approximately one third of the strait's geographical limits (see Map 12). The

2 Measurement is based on the geographical points constituting the limits of the Strait of Malacca, as defined in *Limits of Oceans and Seas* (3rd ed., International Hydrographic Organization, Monte Carlo 1953), 23.

3 See 'Malaysia' and 'Indonesia', MarineRegions.org, available https://www.marineregions.org/eezdetails.php?mrgid=8483&zone=eez_12nm; accessed 30 August 2021. See also the maps and legislation included in Malaysia, 'Legislation', Division for Ocean Affairs and the Law of the Sea, available https://www.un.org/depts/los/LEGISLATIONANDTREATIES/STATEFILES/MYS.htm; accessed 30 August 2021. See also Indonesia, Ibid., available https://www.un.org/depts/los/LEGISLATIONANDTREATIES/STATEFILES/IDN.htm; accessed 30 August 2021.

Strait of Malacca connects the Malaysian and Indonesian EEZs in the west[4] and the EEZs in the South China Sea. Hence, the approx. 320-km-long part of the Strait of Malacca is subject to the right of transit passage (Art 38 of LOSC).

The right of transit passage also applies in the Strait of Singapore that joins the Strait of Malacca near Indonesia's Karimunbesar Island. Unlike the Strait of Malacca, the geographical and legal limits of the Strait of Singapore are identical as the entire Strait of Singapore falls under the sovereignty of its coastal States. It is located between, on the one hand, Singapore and Malaysia and, on the other hand, Indonesia. It is approximately 100-km-long and very narrow strait as its width mostly stays around 10 NM, while at its narrowest point between St John Island (Singapore) and Pulau Senang (Indonesia) the strait is only 2 NM wide.[5] The Johor Strait separates Singapore Island from mainland Malaysia. It is even narrower than the Strait of Singapore and not used for international navigation. Since 1924, the Johor Strait is closed for ship crossings between the Strait of Malacca and South China Sea due to the construction of the 1-km-long Johor-Singapore Causeway.[6]

The Straits of Malacca and Singapore are subject to a complex set of navigational safety measures, including a TSS,[7] mandatory ship reporting system 'STRAITREP',[8] Vessel Traffic and Information System,[9] and an under keel clearance[10] (of at least 3.5 metres). These measures reduce the threat of shipping accidents in the long and narrow sea route. Yet the accident risk in the Strait of Singapore is still significant as its narrowest point is only approximately 2

---

4 These EEZs are located, *inter alia*, in the area that is commonly identified by geographers as the Strait of Malacca, but where navigation and overflight does not need to be safeguarded under Part III of the LOSC as the high seas freedoms are guaranteed in the relevant EEZs.

5 Navionics ChartViewer, *op. cit.*, the Strait of Singapore.

6 'Singapore-Johor Causeway Opens, 28th Jun 1924', *HistorySG* (Government of Singapore 2021), available https://eresources.nlb.gov.sg/history/events/4aee3cb2-e472-4fa6-987a-2aeedf0d101f (accessed 17 August 2021).

7 Inter-Governmental Maritime Consultative Organization, Resolution A.375(X) 'Navigation through the Straits of Malacca and Singapore', adopted on 14 November 1977, available https://wwwcdn.imo.org/localresources/en/KnowledgeCentre/IndexofIMOResolutions/AssemblyDocuments/A.375(10).pdf (accessed 30 August 2021).

8 See Maritime and Port Authority Singapore, 'Vessel Traffic Information System', available https://www.mpa.gov.sg/web/portal/home/port-of-singapore/operations/vessel-traffic-information-system-vtis (accessed 30 August 2021). The International Register of Shipping, 'IMO Navigation Rules at Straits of Malacca and Singapore', 7 December 2019, available https://intlreg.org/2019/12/07/imo-navigation-rules-at-straits-of-malacca-and-singapore/ (accessed 30 August 2021).

9 Caminos, Cogliati-Bantz, *op. cit.*, 393.

10 Molenaar 1998, *op. cit.*, 316–318.

NM wide.[11] This implies that it is in principle possible that a major accident causes the blockage of international navigation through the Straits of Malacca and Singapore. Such incident may be accidental or deliberately caused, e.g., by launching a cyber-attack, by an entity that considers that the disruption of commerce in one of the main arteries of global commerce would serve its interests.

Such blockage would have a significant impact on the world economy, as illustrated by the above-discussed six-days-long blockage of the Suez Canal in March 2021.[12] However, these risks are to some extent mitigated by the fact that ship traffic between the Indian Ocean and the South China Sea could be redirected from the Straits of Malacca and Singapore into the Indonesian straits of Sunda or Lombok.

Sunda and Lombok straits connect the Indian Ocean with the Java Sea that is located between some of the world's largest islands: Sumatra, Java, and Borneo. The small Sangian Island separates the Sunda Strait, located between the Indonesian islands Sumatra and Java, into two short channels. The eastern channel is slightly wider (5.5 NM) than the western channel (4 NM).[13] The Lombok Strait is situated between Bali Island and Lombok Island approximately 1000 km east of the Sunda Strait. It is approximately 11.5 NM wide and 30 NM long.[14] Distinct from the Sunda Strait that includes numerous islets and shoals in its northern end in the Java Sea, the Lombok Strait does not present significant navigational hazards and due to its great depth (mostly 400–1200 metres) is suitable for submerged transit.[15]

Both the Sunda Strait and the Lombok Strait are located in the Indonesian archipelagic waters,[16] rendering the right of archipelagic sea lanes passage applicable to ships and aircraft crossing the straits (Art 53 of LOSC). Prior to the entry into force of the LOSC, Indonesia temporarily closed the Sunda and Lombok Straits for international traffic in the course of its 1988 naval exercises.[17]

11 Navionics ChartViewer, *op. cit.,* the Singapore Strait. Notably, according to other accounts, the narrowest breadth of the Singapore Strait is 3.2 NM. See Ashley Roach and Smith 2012, *op. cit.*, 305.

12 See *supra* Chapter 6.2 of Part 2.

13 Navionics ChartViewer, *op. cit.,* the Sunda Strait. Notably, according to other accounts, the two channels of the Sunda Strait are at their narrowest respectively 3.7 NM and 2.4 NM wide. See Ashley Roach and Smith 2012, *op. cit.*, 332.

14 Ibid., the Lombok Strait.

15 Ibid., the Sunda Strait, the Lombok Strait.

16 M.Z.N.67.2009.LOS (Maritime Zone Notification), Deposit by the Republic of Indonesia of a list of geographical coordinates of points, pursuant to article 47, paragraph 9, of the Convention, 25 March 2009.

17 Ashley Roach and Smith 2012, *op. cit.*, 332–333.

The archipelagic sea lanes passage, as guaranteed under the Convention, now prevents the closure of the straits. The archipelagic sea lanes passage is functionally equivalent to the right of transit passage as they are both based on the freedoms of navigation and overflight. The two legal regimes safeguard expeditious, unobstructed, and non-suspendable transit between two parts of the high seas/EEZ, while allowing aircraft and ships to navigate in their normal mode (incl., e.g., submerged). The main distinction between the rights of transit and archipelagic sea lanes passage is that while the former applies to all foreign ships and aircraft in a strait from coast to coast, the latter applies only in the designated sea lanes and air routes or in normal routes used for navigation if archipelagic sea lanes are not designated (see Arts 38 and 53 of LOSC). In 2002, Indonesia designated archipelagic sea lanes in the Sunda Strait and the Lombok Strait.[18]

Notably, the risk of occurrence of a complete blockage in the Strait of Singapore similar to that of the Suez Canal in 2021 is reduced by geographical factors. The minimal width of the Suez Canal is about 200 metres, while the narrowest (2 NM) part of the sea route in the Strait of Singapore is approximately 20 times wider. On the other hand, the density of ship traffic in the Strait of Singapore is also significantly greater. While on average, nearly 50 vessels sail through the Suez Canal daily,[19] the daily ship crossings of the Strait of Singapore (ships over 300 GT) amount on average to slightly over 230.[20] Furthermore, in contrast to the Suez Canal, the Strait of Singapore has been for centuries, and still is, a global hotspot for piracy and armed robbery.

14.2 Threats of Piracy in Indonesia and the Straits of Malacca and Singapore

Article 101(1) of LOSC defines piracy as any illegal acts of violence or detention, or any act of depredation, committed for private ends by the crew or the passengers of a private ship or a private aircraft, and directed on the high seas, against another ship or aircraft, or against persons or property on board such ship or aircraft, or against a ship, aircraft, persons or property in a place outside

18 Article 11(1)-(3) of the Indonesian Government Regulation No. 37 on the Rights and Obligations of Foreign Ships and Aircraft Exercising the Right of Archipelagic Sea Lane Passage through Designated Archipelagic Sea Lanes, adopted 28 June 2002, entered into force 28 June 2002.

19 BBC News 24 March 2021, *op. cit.*

20 Hand, *op. cit.*

the jurisdiction of any State. Thus, it sets a spatial criterion according to which for an armed robbery to be categorized as piracy it needs to occur outside the jurisdiction of any State. In this legal framework, piracy may occur on the high seas as well as in the EEZ,[21] but outside its scope fall in any case attacks against ships in waters that fall under the sovereignty of the relevant coastal State. The distinction between piracy and armed robbery[22] is particularly relevant in the case of Indonesian archipelagic waters and territorial sea, and the Straits of Malacca and Singapore that fall under the sovereignty of Indonesia, Malaysia, and Singapore.

Reportedly, at least since 1990s, Southeast Asia has been the most affected region globally from piracy and armed robbery that has brought about also the highest number of fatalities among the crews of targeted ships (see also Figure 5).[23] In 2020, the incidents of piracy and armed robbery almost doubled in Asia, particularly in the Straits of Malacca and Singapore, and the South China Sea.[24] However, these absolute numbers should be interpreted in the light of the fact that the sea routes in and around the Straits of Malacca and Singapore are the busiest globally. Thus, from an individual seafarer's perspective, the likelihood of falling the victim of a pirate attack or armed robbery is not greater than in, e.g., West Africa or West Indian Ocean.[25]

The number of attacks against ships navigating in the Strait of Singapore has increased from 3 in 2018 to 23 in 2020.[26] At the same time, the recent successful counter-piracy operations in the Strait of Malacca and around the Horn of Africa demonstrate that it is possible to suppress newly emerged waves of attacks against ships relatively quickly. In 1998, the IMO characterised piracy and armed robbery in the Strait of Malacca as having an endemic character[27] and, in 2000, the Strait of Malacca reported over 70 incidents of piracy or armed robbery that was overshadowed only by the number of attacks in

21 D Guilfoyle, 'The Legal Challenges in Fighting Piracy' in B van Ginkel, FP van der Putten (eds), *The International Response to Somali Piracy: Challenges and Opportunities* (Brill, Leiden/Boston, 2010), 128.

22 See further on the distinction between the two legal concepts, in RC Beckmann, 'Combatting Piracy and Armed Robbery Against Ships in Southeast Asia: The Way Forward' (2002) 33(3–4) *Ocean Development & International Law*, 319–320.

23 A McCauley, 'The Most Dangerous Waters in the World', *Time* (22 September 2014).

24 Viotti, *op. cit.*

25 D Rosenberg, C Chung, 'Maritime Security in the South China Sea: Coordinating Coastal and User State Priorities' (2008) 39(1) *Ocean Development & International Law*, 60.

26 See *supra* Figure 5.

27 IMO, 'Report of the Maritime Safety Committee on its Sixty-Ninth Session', MSC 69/22, 1998, 62.

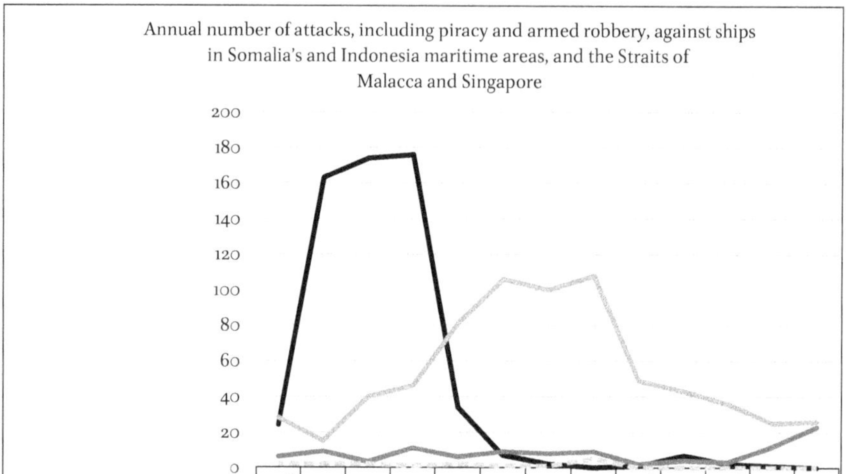

	2008	2009	2010	2011	2012	2013	2014	2015	2016	2017	2018	2019	2020
Somalia	24	163	174	176	34	7	2	0	1	7	2	1	0
Strait of Singapore	6	9	3	11	6	9	8	9	2	4	3	12	23
Indonesia	28	15	40	46	81	106	100	108	49	43	36	25	26
Strait of Malacca	2	2	2	1	2	1	1	5	0	0	0	0	0

FIGURE 5 Piracy and armed robbery in Somalia, Indonesia, and the Straits of Malacca and Singapore
Note: Figure is based on data collected from EU Naval Force – Somalia, *op. cit.* ICC-IMB Piracy and Armed Robbery Against Ships: Report for the Period 1 January – 31 March 2021 (ICC International Maritime Bureau, London, 2021), 18. ICC-IMB Piracy and Armed Robbery Against Ships: Report for the Period 1 January – 31 December 2020 (ICC International Maritime Bureau, London, 2021), 6, 21. ICC-IMB Piracy and Armed Robbery Against Ships: Report for the Period 1 January – 31 December 2015 (ICC International Maritime Bureau, London, 2016), 5. ICC-IMB Piracy and Armed Robbery Against Ships: Report for the Period 1 January – 31 December 2011 (ICC International Maritime Bureau, London, 2012), 5.

Indonesia.[28] After Indonesia and Malaysia decided in 2005 to increase their efforts in patrolling their long coasts and adjacent waters in the Strait of Malacca,[29] the incidents of piracy and armed robbery were reduced to only a couple per year.[30]

28 Beckmann, *op. cit.*, 324.

29 ICC-IMB 2020 Report, *op. cit.*, 21. On the regulatory framework stipulated in bilateral treaties concluded between Indonesia and Malaysia and applicable to the patrols in the Strait of Malacca, see Beckmann, *op. cit.*, 330–331. See also Caminos, Cogliati-Bantz, *op. cit.*, 401.

30 See *supra* Figure 5.

Since 2016, attacks on ships have not been reported in the Strait of Malacca.[31] Similarly, the surge of pirate attacks in Somalia's maritime area around the Horn of Africa in 2009–2011 was effectively suppressed by the intervention of international coalition forces, the NATO, and the EU.[32] This intervention followed the aim of Article 100 of LOSC that stipulates the obligation of all States to cooperate fully in the repression of piracy on the high seas or in any other place outside the jurisdiction of any State. Due to reasons discussed above, such international intervention absent of the prior permission of the relevant coastal State(s) is not possible in the Strait of Singapore or in the up to 24-NM-wide part of the Strait of Malacca as well as in straits situated in the archipelagic waters of Indonesia, e.g., the straits of Sunda and Lombok.

31 Ibid.

32 Ibid. See *supra* Chapter 6.3 of Part 2.

PART 5

Concluding Observations on the Implications of Hybrid Threats for Maritime Security Law

CHAPTER 15

A Need for a New Legal Framework on Hybrid Naval Warfare?

Based on the incidents in the Black Sea, the Strait of Hormuz, the Baltic Sea, and the South China Sea in the past decade, one may reasonably argue that State practice demonstrates the increasing use of hybrid naval warfare techniques. Historians have pointed out that hybrid warfare is not a distinctly new phenomenon and, instead, simply constitutes a novel term for a centuries-old concept.[1] For example, in the second half of the 20th century, armed coercion at sea falling just below the threshold of an armed conflict was often referred to as 'gunboat diplomacy'.[2] This term may as well be used for characterising the nature of recent inter-State conflicts at sea that form the object of this study, including the 2018 Kerch Strait incident, the 2019 *Stena Impero* incident, Israel-Iran 'shadow war', and maritime incidents in the disputed areas in the South China Sea.

In the negotiations and drafting of the treaties on the law of the sea and armed conflict, States did not consider it necessary to establish a separate legal framework for hybrid warfare. When drafting the relevant treaties, they instead proceeded from traditional concepts of laws of peace and war. Although rapid developments in technology have made it now possible to adopt more sophisticated means of hybrid warfare, including cyber warfare that has now become part of modern warfare, States should still principally be able to classify any incidents of hybrid warfare under either the ramifications of armed conflict or peacetime law enforcement operations.

A new legal framework for hybrid naval warfare that falls between the laws of peace and war would risk creating additional ambiguities in assessing the legality of the aggressor's actions in the so-called grey zone. Hence, it might contribute to the aims of States that employ practices of maritime hybrid warfare and seek to create legal uncertainty to advance their geopolitical interests. A distinct legal framework for hybrid naval warfare would thus arguably create

1 PR Mansoor, 'Introduction: Hybrid Warfare in History', in W Murray, PR Mansoor (eds.), *Hybrid Warfare: Fighting Complex Opponents from the Ancient World to the Present* (Cambridge University Press, New York, 2012), 1.

2 J Cable, *Gunboat Diplomacy 1919–1991: Political Applications of Limited Naval Force* (Palgrave Macmillan, London, 1994). See also Patalano, *op. cit.*, 814, 817.

further legal ambiguity, rather than help solving current problems in distinguishing the law of peace from the laws of naval warfare.

Instead, legally speaking, it might be reasonable to wait for international judicial bodies to establish solid case law on differences between military and law enforcement operations. However, this approach entails a risk that international courts and tribunals might not meet the expectations in their proceedings to address the phenomenon of grey zone conflict. Arguably, this may happen if the international courts and tribunals, for example, uphold the rather strict thresholds of an armed attack and State responsibility which aggressor States currently can make use of in waging hybrid naval conflicts. This was debated above with a focus on the *Oil Platforms Case* (*supra* Chapter 5.2 of Part 2).

René Värk has noted that "hybrid warfare relies on the ambiguities, loopholes and thresholds in international law".[3] Broadly speaking, ambiguities and loopholes are inherent in the field of law and it is common that interested parties take advantage of them to benefit their interests. Such behaviour is as characteristic in geopolitics as it is in, for example, financial sector and investment law. However, where such practices emerge that take advantage of so-called grey zones, law gradually adapts to such developments. In general, where disputes arise over the interpretation of the applicable laws in situations concerning grey zones in whatever field of law, recourse is made to courts for justice and legal certainty. Similarly, one may expect that the current ambiguities regarding the classification of incidents which have occurred in grey zones will gradually dissolve in judicial proceedings on a case-by-case basis.

The case law of international courts and tribunals demonstrates that numerous ambiguous questions that at the time could easily have been referred to as grey zones, were effectively settled by judicial bodies. The first case brought before the ICJ in 1947 concerned the passage of warships through a strait, the coastal State of which deemed such passage prejudicial to its security interests and used force against these warships, consequently damaging the warships and causing casualties among the servicemen. The circumstances of the *Corfu Channel Case*, as summarized in Chapter 2.3 of Part 1 of this book, are strikingly similar to the case which was brought before the Annex VII Arbitral Tribunal over 70 years later in the *Dispute Concerning the Detention of Ukrainian Naval Vessels and Servicemen* concerning the 2018 Kerch Strait incident.[4]

---

3 Värk 2020, *op. cit.*, 33.

4 See *supra* Chapter 4.1 of Part 2.

The 1946 Corfu Channel incident can be as well categorized in modern terminology as a grey zone conflict similar to the 2018 Kerch Strait incident. Yet, as a result of the ICJ's judgment in the *Corfu Channel Case* it became settled that neutral States have a right to send their ships, including warships, through international straits without the previous authorisation of the strait State. The ICJ provided much needed clarity on the thresholds and limits of the right of innocent passage through straits and the legal concept of strait.

Similarly, the on-going arbitration proceedings between Ukraine and the Russian Federation over passage rights through the Kerch Strait can potentially significantly contribute to confining the legal scope of grey zone conflicts by clarifying the thresholds subject to which the passage of sovereign immune vessels through a disputed maritime area is governed by the rules of naval warfare and in which cases such passage remains regulated by peacetime rules of the law of the sea.

By contrast, the 2007 *Vironia* incident in the Gulf of Finland that concerned the Russian Federation's discriminatory restrictions against the innocent passage of a commercial ferry line as well as the 2019 arrest of the United Kingdom-flagged tanker *Stena Impero* by Iran clearly do not cross the threshold for the applicability of the laws of naval warfare. Instead, these two incidents may be characterised as unlawful and discriminatory peacetime navigational restrictions under the LOSC, as discussed next.

CHAPTER 16

Discriminatory Navigational Restrictions in the Context of Hybrid Conflicts

The implications of peacetime discriminatory navigational restrictions in the context of hybrid conflicts are illustrated by the *Vironia* and *Stena Impero* incidents that were examined above (*supra* Chapters 8 and 11 of Part 3). Both incidents involved a coastal State's economic and socio-political coercion against the flag State. Outside the confines of a purely doctrinal framework the two incidents can be categorised as falling under the concept of hybrid conflict.

The *Vironia* incident occurred in the wake of the 2007 mass riots of Russian-speaking minority in Tallinn. It can be seen as part of a larger campaign of intimidating measures, such as widescale cyber-attacks. The incident involved a regular ferry line that operated between Estonia and Finland for which she had to cross the Russian Federation's territorial sea in the centre of the Gulf of Finland proper. All ships entering the Russian Federation's maritime area in the Gulf of Finland from the west, including by crossing the Estonian-Russian maritime boundary, are required to obtain prior authorisation from the Russian VTS centre. The Russian Federation refused to grant its permit for *Vironia* which caused the closure of the commercial ferry line. The incident shows that States can use discriminatory navigational restrictions relatively effectively for achieving their political goals without triggering any diplomatic protest from the States affected.

As analysed above,[1] the Russian Federation's restrictive approach to the passage rights and freedoms of foreign ships in the Gulf of Finland contradicts the terms of LOSC. It lacks the legal basis for denying the right of innocent passage through its whole maritime area in the Gulf of Finland proper for ships that do not seek to enter its ports. Foreign ships, including commercial vessels, were obliged to request prior permission for navigating through the Soviet Union's territorial sea since at least the 1940s. The 2007 *Vironia* incident illustrates that the Russian Federation has partially returned to such a practice by hampering the establishment and operation of regular ferry lines that seek to operate between the ports of eastern Estonia and eastern Finland. They have been unable to launch or continue their business due to the Russian

1 See *supra* Chapter 11 of Part 3.

 | DOI:10.1163/9789004509368_018

Federation's permit-based passage regime. This has a direct negative impact on commerce, regional development and international relations in the Gulf of Finland region. This practice also appears to be discriminatory, since there have been no reports about similar refusals to the exercise of the right of innocent passage by other non-governmental ships that have sailed between eastern Estonia and eastern Finland via the Russian Federation's territorial sea.

The Russian Federation has not presented a public explanation on why and on what legal basis it requires prior permission from a foreign ship that seeks to traverse its territorial sea in the Gulf of Finland proper. Thus, the *Vironia* incident raises the question of whether or not Estonia and Finland should protest or otherwise object to the Russian Federation's permit-based passage regime in the Gulf of Finland.

In 2017, the Estonian Ministry of Foreign Affairs commented that it has not deemed it necessary to establish a position on the legality of the Russian Federation's practice in setting restrictions to navigation of foreign ships in the Gulf of Finland as the operators at that time had not shown any interest in relaunching the ferry line between Sillamäe and Kotka ports.[2] The ministry reiterated this position in 2020.[3] On the other hand, one should acknowledge that, as explained above,[4] local governments, port authorities, and potential operators have actively sought to relaunch a ferry line between eastern Estonia and eastern Finland throughout the past ten years and, according to media reports, such efforts are also presently underway.

The Russian Federation tends to restrict navigational rights and freedoms not only in its maritime areas in the Baltic Sea, but also in the Arctic and the Black Sea, resorting occasionally to discriminatory practices. This behaviour appears to have its roots in the Soviet Union's practice of applying the doctrine of *mare clausum* to its adjacent maritime areas prior to the 1989 Jackson Hole statement. The main reason for this appears to be shifts in its security and policy-related interests.

Unlike the *Vironia* incident in the Baltic Sea and the Kerch Strait incident in the Black Sea,[5] the restriction of navigation rights and freedoms in the

2 Comment obtained from the Director General of the Legal Department of the Ministry of Foreign Affairs of Estonia, Ms Kerli Veski on 15 February 2017 in response to the author's information request no. 4–4/813–1.

3 Comment obtained from the advisor of the Legal Department of the Ministry of Foreign Affairs of Estonia, Mr Jaanus Kirikmäe on 13 October 2020 in response to the author's information request no. 4–4/5063.

4 See *supra* Chapter 11.3 of Part 3.

5 For a description of the Kerch Strait incident, see, e.g., ITLOS *Order of 25 May 2019, op. cit.*, paras. 30–32.

Northern Sea Route is not rooted in a reactionary policy, but rather on a conceptually different interpretation of LOSC, especially Article 234, as compared with other States, and its ramifications for the passage of foreign ships in ice-covered areas. This has not called for any hybrid conflicts between the coastal and user States of the Northern Sea Route. Yet the impediments to navigation that the Russian Federation has set in respect of the Northern Sea Route in the Arctic have triggered protests from States that consider such requirements to breach the passage regime of the Russian Arctic straits under the LOSC.[6]

The *Vironia* incident bears resemblance to the 2018 Kerch Strait incident in that they both appear to have been provoked by the Russian Federation to serve as a policy instrument in response to a specific development that the Russian Federation perceives as strongly contradicting its geopolitical interests. The *Vironia* incident was partly caused by the relocation of a Soviet Union's war memorial and the following unrest among the Russian-speaking minority in Tallinn,[7] while the general ramification of the Kerch Strait incident is intertwined with the change of government in Ukraine. The epicentre of both incidents may have been temporally limited (the *Vironia* incident in 2007 and the Kerch Strait incident in 2018), but they have had a long-lasting effect on international navigation in the relevant maritime area. Estonia and Finland have downplayed the *Vironia* incident by not using publicly any diplomatic measures to resolve the apparently still continuing deadlock regarding impediments that the Russian Federation has set to the north-south passage of a commercial ferry line through its territorial sea. Ukraine, on the other hand, initiated two arbitration proceedings to challenge the legality of the Russian Federation's restrictions on the passage of ships to and from the Sea of Azov.[8]

In the Black Sea region, the Russian Federation has hampered not only the access of Ukrainian-flagged ships, but also third State commercial ships to the Sea of Azov. The EU Parliament has condemned the situation in the Sea of Azov, noting "the excessive stopping and inspection of commercial vessels, including ... ships under flags of various EU Member States".[9] Thus, the EU has reacted before when ships sailing under the flags of its Member States have

6 See, e.g., the protest of the United States: 'Russia – Northern Sea Route' in CD Guymon (ed), *Digest of United States Practice in International Law* (United States Department of State, Washington DC, 2015), 526–528; see further on the Russian Federation's claims in, e.g., Solski, *op. cit.*, 192–197.

7 See, e.g., Anonymous, 'Tallinn tense after deadly riots', *BBC News* (28 April 2007). Ellam, *op. cit.*

8 See *supra* Chapter 4.1 of Part 2.

9 European Parliament 2018 resolution on the situation in the Sea of Azov, *op. cit.*

been negatively impacted by the Russian Federation's practice of setting navigation restrictions that contradict the interests of the EU. In view of ensuring navigational rights and freedoms also in other maritime regions, the EU should not hesitate in protesting against a coastal State's discriminatory restrictions against international shipping.

In that context, Finland, Estonia, and the EU should consider submitting a protest if the Russian Federation again refuses to grant to a commercial ferry line the right of innocent passage for making a north-south crossing of the Gulf of Finland proper, since a permit-based passage regime appears to lack a legal basis under the LOSC. The *Vironia* incident demonstrates that if restrictions on the passage rights of foreign ships render it practically impossible to operate a commercial ferry line between the ports of the EU Member States, then this has dire implications also to the EU free movement of persons and goods, and thereby to the EU single market.

For the smooth operation of global transport of goods and passengers, it is important that coastal States do not apply any illegal restraints on the exercise of the right of innocent passage. From the perspective of global supply chain and international trade, the Viro Strait, the Kerch Strait and other European straits do not have as much significance as the straits of Hormuz and Bab el-Mandeb that are bordering, respectively, the eastern and western coasts of the Arabian Peninsula. Global maritime trade is reliant on the safe and unobstructed passage through these two straits as they constitute by volume of cargo the world's most important and third-largest maritime oil chokepoints (the Strait of Malacca is the second-largest chokepoint).[10] The strategic significance of these two geographic bottlenecks for the contemporary oil-based world economy is stressed by the fact that unlike the straits of Hormuz and Bab el-Mandeb, the Strait of Malacca has many relatively short round-about routes, e.g., via the straits of Lombok and Makassar.

Yet in recent years, international vessel traffic through the straits of Hormuz and Bab el-Mandeb has been destabilized by the imposition of discriminatory navigational restrictions against foreign ships passing through these waterways. This was discussed above based on a case study of the arrest of the United Kingdom-flagged tanker *Stena Impero* by Iran in the Strait of Hormuz in 2019 (*supra* Chapter 8.3 of Part 3).

The greatest threat to international shipping in waters around the Arabian Peninsula stems from the Yemeni armed conflict and the Iran-Israel 'shadow war' in the maritime domain. Incidents in and around the straits of Hormuz

10 McCarthy, *op. cit.*

and Bab el-Mandeb raise questions about the thresholds of an armed conflict and State responsibility. As discussed next, the means for tackling the phenomenon of hybrid naval warfare within the existing legal framework include adherence to the strict definition of an armed conflict that was coined by the ICTY in the *Tadić Case* and which is recognised by the ICRC (see also *supra* Chapter 5.2 of Part 2) and, potentially, the lowering of the currently rather strict threshold of State responsibility for direct support to non-State actors that conduct attacks against other States (see *supra* Chapter 6.6 of Part 2).

CHAPTER 17

Low-Intensity Use of Force (Hybrid Warfare) through the Prism of Law Enforcement and an Armed Attack

Based on the previous analysis (*supra* Chapter 5 of Part 2), it appears that under the current legal framework and case law a State might be somewhat paradoxically obliged to comply with Article 2(4) of the UN Charter in its response to such unlawful use of force in hybrid naval conflicts that does not meet the gravity threshold under the ICJ's case law for it falling within the ambit of an armed attack. Clearly, the targeted State may employ force to protect itself against aggression by making use of law enforcement measures. However, this entails that its use of arms bears the risk of exceeding the limits of proportionality, the limits of which are significantly narrower in the law enforcement domain as compared to armed conflicts.

It would be desirable that international judicial bodies openly address this problem in their future case law. For example, if the Annex VII Arbitral Tribunal interprets the applicable law from the perspective of whether or not the Kerch Strait incident constituted (part of) an armed conflict between the two States or a law enforcement operation (possibly within an armed conflict), it would significantly contribute to increasing legal certainty over the legal categorisation of naval incidents that currently are often deemed as falling in a grey zone between the laws of peace and war.

Yet such expectations were also prevalent in relation to the ICJ's proceedings in the *Oil Platforms Case*. As examined above, the ICJ's judgment in the *Oil Platforms Case* is not particularly encouraging in confirming the hypothesis that the unclarity in the legal categorisation of incidents that have occurred in grey zones will gradually dissolve in the proceedings before international judicial bodies on a case-by-case basis. One may even wonder if the reason why we are debating the need for a legal framework of hybrid naval warfare is partly due to the ICJ's judgment in the *Oil Platforms Case*.

In its judgment, the ICJ appears to have opened the door for hybrid naval warfare by, on the one hand, setting the threshold of an armed attack to a high level, while, on the other hand, narrowly interpreting the law of State responsibility. In this context, the Annex VII Arbitral Tribunal will hopefully provide its contribution to developing the jurisprudence on the legal framework applicable to the use of force in the maritime domain. Its on-going proceedings

DOI:10.1163/9789004509368_019

pertaining to the Kerch Strait incident provide a fertile ground for reflecting on the limits of *jus ad bellum* in the modern conflicts that often occur in so-called grey zones.

Instead of debating about the need for creating a new legal framework that would govern incidents falling in the grey zone, it is rather desirable that effort is made to codify and develop the rules applicable to maritime law enforcement and naval warfare. In addition, international courts and tribunals can use the cases brought before them to try closing the door for hybrid warfare. One possibility for international courts and tribunals for achieving this is by way of shifting its practice on international security law away from the ICJ's concept of the *most grave form of the use of force* for categorising a military conflict between States as an armed conflict triggering the applicability of humanitarian law. This approach would follow, *inter alia*, the guidance offered by the ICRC:

> If minor clashes between States are not considered to be an international armed conflict or if the very beginning of hostilities is not regulated by humanitarian law, one would have to identify an alternative in terms of the applicable law. Human rights law and domestic law do not seem to be equipped to deal fully with inter-State violence. For its part, the *jus ad bellum* provides a general framework on the lawfulness of the recourse to the use of force but contains only very general rules on the way force may be used. Once force is actually being used by one State against another, humanitarian law provides detailed rules that are well tailored to inter-State armed confrontations. It is therefore logical and in conformity with the humanitarian purpose of the Conventions that there be no requirement of a specific level of intensity of violence to trigger an international armed conflict.[1]

The concept of the *most grave form of the use of force*, as established in the jurisprudence of the ICJ, currently limits the right of self-defence in response to low-intensity warfare. This results in legal uncertainty, especially for the victim States, on how to respond to the low-intensity use of force by another State (e.g., the Kerch Strait incident). It contradicts with the aim that, as expressed by Gill and Fleck, "in order to be realistic and fair for combatants who need to make split-second decisions, the rules regulating the use of force must be clear and simple."[2]

1 ICRC 2016 commentary, *op. cit.*, on Common Article 2, para 243.

2 Gill and Fleck, *op. cit.*, 82.

Alternatively, it is possible to uphold the strict threshold of an armed attack and the right of self-defence and assess the legality of hybrid naval conflicts *prima facie* from the perspective of law enforcement operations. For example, Klein has argued that:

> It seems that any proposal to enhance maritime security will have its drawbacks and its opponents. An incremental change in perspective is proposed here in relation to law enforcement powers rather than relying on expansive interpretations of the law on the use of force and the law of armed conflict. The latter raises legal conundra that extend well beyond questions of maritime security.[3]

This view predates the rapid rise of inter-State conflicts in the maritime domain in the past years. It was made in the context of the so-called 'war on terror' when the maritime security law was mainly challenged by non-State actors, in respect of whom the application of the law enforcement paradigm is well-founded. At the time, the legal challenges in maritime security were predominantly associated with terrorism and, to a somewhat lesser extent, with piracy.[4] By contrast, in recent years, the main threats to maritime security have shifted away from terrorism and piracy. Instead, the world has returned to a so-called great power competition between major maritime powers and the accompanying inter-State naval conflicts.

This study has shown that in the past couple of years alone, there have been numerous inter-State conflicts (including the Yemeni armed conflict and the escalation of the Russia-Ukraine War in 2022) that have spread to the maritime domain. This is demonstrated by the 2018 Kerch Strait incident, 2019 limpet mine attacks in the Strait of Hormuz, attacks against international shipping in and around the Bab el-Mandeb in the broader framework of the Yemeni armed conflict, the recent hybrid naval warfare ('shadow war') between Iran and Israel, as well as the blockade of the Sea of Azov and attacks against neutral commercial ships in the Black Sea (both in 2022). In addition, 2021 marked growing tensions between the militaries and coast guards of China and Taiwan in the Taiwan Strait.

In the light of these developments, one may argue that instead of shifting the legal governance of such incidents to the purview of law enforcement that

3 Klein, *op. cit.*, 300.

4 See for example the various contributions to the collection of conference presentations, in MH Nordquist, R Wolfrum, JN Moore, R Long (eds.), *Legal Challenges in Maritime Security* (Brill, Leiden, Boston, 2008), 1–592.

traditionally falls under the framework of peacetime administrative law, it is rather desirable that the use of armed force between States and against States remains regulated under the *jus ad bellum* and *jus in bello*.[5] After all, attacks carried out by States against States by means of using firearms, explosive devices and sabotage traditionally fall under the legal framework of international humanitarian law.[6]

5 Notably, the applicability of the law of naval warfare to non-international armed conflicts "is a contentious issue". Heintschel von Heinegg 2016, *op. cit.*, 211ff.

6 Gill and Fleck, *op. cit.*, 73.

CHAPTER 18

Guidelines for Distinguishing between the Rules of Armed Conflict and Law Enforcement in Grey Zone Naval Incidents

This chapter aims to provide guidance for parties to hybrid naval warfare for determining whether the rules of armed conflict or law enforcement are applicable to various situations where force has been used against ships. This roadmap draws from the observations of the case studies of parts II and III of this book. The guidelines are based on the relevant case law and systemized into three categories: first, a commercial ship v. government ship/warship (State vessel) scenario; second, a State vessel v. commercial ship scenario; third, a State v. State scenario. The following analysis focuses on the use of force against ships, but the rules apply *mutatis mutandis* also in relation to aircraft and installations and structures at sea.

18.1 Use of Force by State Vessels against Attacks Launched from Commercial Ships

Force may be used to defend a government ship or warship against an attack that has been launched by private persons on-board a commercial ship or structure (e.g., a platform). For example, the use of force may be necessary to counter a terrorist attack launched by explosive-laden boats,[1] or in response to irregulars who use a commercial oil platform as their base.[2] Notably, if the government ship or warship was attacked by such private persons that were not acting on behalf of a foreign State and nor was a foreign State substantially involved in such attack by non-State actors, then the victim State cannot invoke the right of self-defence under Article 51 of the UN Charter.[3] The ICJ has found that: "Article 51 of the Charter thus recognizes the existence of an inherent right of self-defence in the case of armed attack by one State against

1 See *supra* Chapters 6.3–6.4 of Part 2.
2 See *supra* Chapter 5.2 of Part 2.
3 *Military and Paramilitary Activities in and against Nicaragua, op. cit.,* para 195. Armed Activities on the Territory of the Congo, *op. cit.,* para 146. Definition of Aggression, *op. cit.*, Art 3(g).

DOI:10.1163/9789004509368_020

another State."[4] The ICJ has not recognised that Article 51 would encompass actions by non-State actors which are not attributable to any State. Notably, the ICJ's strict position on that issue has been criticized in the relevant legal literature, since Article 51 of the UN Charter does not *expressis verbis* limit the scope of perpetrators of an 'armed attack' to States.[5] The ICJ's high threshold of an armed attack that triggers the right of self-defence under Article 51 raises questions of the range of available measures for a conflicting side against whom force has been unlawfully used.

If a private person uses force against government ship or warship, then its crew has the right to employ defensive measures to the degree necessary for deterring the attack. Depending on the situation, this may involve counterfire and deliberate sinking or destruction of the commercial ship or structure from where the attack was launched even if it means, in extreme circumstances, a potential loss of human life. Recourse to administrative law-based framework of law enforcement measures and criminal law-based concept of self-defence is available for the crew of the targeted government ship or warship. The criminal law-based concept of self-defence also applies in cases where a commercial vessel uses force against another commercial vessel, e.g. in a context where there is an armed security team onboard (for example, for counter-piracy purposes).

Under its case law, the ICJ has introduced an innovative concept of countermeasures.[6] In the legal literature, it has been characterised as a "very controversial and contested concept".[7] It is unclear if States may employ proportionate countermeasures involving force as suggested by some authors in the legal literature.[8] The ICJ has not addressed the question if States are allowed to use firearms under the concept of countermeasures for deterring unlawful use of force. Yet it is doubtful that the use of force falls within the scope of the legal concept of countermeasures. Rather, the victim State cannot make use of the law of countermeasures as a legal basis for its use of force against an attack launched from commercial ships. The Annex VII Arbitral Tribunal has found that: "It is a well established principle of international law that

4 *Legal Consequences of the Construction of a Wall in the Occupied Palestinian Territory, op. cit.*, para 139.
5 See *supra* Chapter 6 of Part 2.
6 *United States Diplomatic and Consular Staff in Tehran, op. cit.*, para 53. *Military and Paramilitary Activities in and against Nicaragua, op. cit.*, para 248. *Gabčikovo-Nagymaros Project, op. cit.*, para 82.
7 Ruys and Verhoeven, *op. cit.*, 309.
8 See, e.g., Klein, *op. cit.*, 267, 270.

countermeasures may not involve the use of force."[9] This was examined in more detail in Chapter 6.7 of Part 2 of this book.

The victim State needs to comply with Article 2(4) of the UN Charter when employing law enforcement or criminal law-based measures to counter such attacks of non-State actors that fall below the 'gravity threshold' of an armed attack, as set by the ICJ. Consequently, the victim State's use of arms needs to strictly stay within the confines of the limits of proportionality that are narrower in the law enforcement and criminal law paradigms as compared to the right of self-defence under Article 51 of the UN Charter. Hence, the measures employed by the victim State in response to an unlawful attack against a ship flying its flag may give rise to potential breaches of human rights law if it cannot rely on the derogation clauses of human rights law that apply in emergency situations or international humanitarian law as *lex specialis*. These legal complexities are discussed in Chapters 5.2–5.3 and 6.7 of Part 2 of this book.

Nonetheless, the victim State may invoke the right of self-defence under Article 51 of the UN Charter if it can prove another State's substantial involvement in the attack that was carried out by non-State actors. For this, the victim State needs to show that:

- The State suspected of sponsoring non-State actors meets the characteristics of "sending by or on behalf of a state of armed bands, groups, irregulars or mercenaries, which carry out acts of armed force against another state".[10]
- "[S]uch an operation [of non-State actors], because of its scale and effects, would have been classified as an armed attack rather than as a mere frontier incident had it been carried out by regular armed forces."[11]

If the victim State is successful in claiming that it has the right of self-defence against attacks launched by non-State actors, then its use of force under *jus in bello* must still comply with the limitations of necessity and proportionality.[12] Yet, as explained by Gill and Fleck in the Handbook of the International Law of Military Operations, the main difference here is that in law enforcement operations these principles imply that the destruction of life is prohibited except for extreme situations, whereas in an armed conflict enemy combatants are

9 Annex VII Arbitral Tribunal, *Guyana v. Suriname Award, op. cit.*, para 446.

10 Definition of Aggression, *op. cit.*, Art 3(g).

11 *Military and Paramilitary Activities in and against Nicaragua, op. cit.*, para 195.

12 San Remo Manual, Rules 3–5 that reflect customary international law; in the context of *jus ad bellum*, see also *Military and Paramilitary Activities in and against Nicaragua, op. cit.*, para 176; *Legality of the Threat or Use of Nuclear Weapons, op. cit.*, paras 41–42.

legitimate targets.[13] Thus, the limits of necessity and proportionality in relation to the use of force are more flexible in an armed conflict.

18.2 Use of Force against a Commercial Ship in a Law Enforcement Operation

Law enforcement officials, particularly Navy's high-ranking military officers in cases where they are performing law enforcement in geopolitically sensitive situations, e.g., in disputed areas, must take caution that they issue clear orders to private persons against whom they are enforcing the coastal State's law. This is important for avoiding the law enforcement actions falling in the domain of *jus ad bellum*. This is exemplified by the *Guyana v. Suriname arbitration* that concerned an order issued from a warship that Suriname had tasked to perform law enforcement in a geopolitically sensitive context. Its order for a commercial ship and a private structure to leave the disputed area in 12 hours left too much room for interpretation about the consequences that would follow in case it is not complied with ("the consequences will be yours").[14]

The *Guyana v. Suriname arbitration* illustrates the risk that accompanies the issuing of ambivalent orders. Such vaguely worded orders may be interpreted by private persons on-board a ship and its flag State or any other State involved in the relevant actions in a disputed area as a threat of the use of force in breach of Article 2(4) of the UN Charter, the LOSC, and general international law. This may suffice for bringing the actions under the *jus ad bellum* paradigm even though the officials that issued the order might not have had any actual intention (from their subjective point of view) to consider undertaking military activities in a disputed area against a commercial ship and private property (an oil rig, a submarine pipeline/cable, etc).

Where force is used for stopping a ship, it needs to follow the principle of proportionality. Law enforcement officials or Navy servicemen onboard State-owned ships need to exercise self-restraint when they are using force against commercial ships; use of force "must be avoided as far as possible".[15] Thus, in maritime enforcement, for the use of force to be lawful, it needs to be employed as a last resort. This means that it needs to be clearly shown that other, less-intrusive options for stopping a commercial ship had been

13 Gill and Fleck, *op. cit.*, 70, 77.
14 Annex VII Arbitral Tribunal, *Guyana v. Suriname Award, op. cit.*, para 433.
15 M/V "SAIGA" (No. 2), *op. cit.*, para 155.

exhausted. In normal circumstances, such means include the following practices (also referred to as the *Saiga* principles):

- First, giving an internationally recognized auditory or visual signal to stop.
- If the order to stop is not complied with, the pursuing ship may proceed in its gradual response to use warning shots, including where necessary, the firing of shots across the bow of the ship.
- If the order to stop and warning shots fail, the pursuing vessel may use force as a last resort and provided that appropriate warnings are first issued. The use of force may include the ramming of the ship as well as targeted shots against the ship.[16] Recourse to force must have a basis in international law and needs to be unavoidable, reasonable, and necessary.[17]
- When, as a last resort, force is used, the crew needs to avoid intentional sinking of a ship and must take all efforts to ensure that life is not endangered.[18]
- However, in exceptional cases, the principle of proportionality does not exclude the possibility of intentionally sinking a commercial ship if it is unmanned and poses an imminent threat to the coastal State or the marine environment.[19]

Provided that these rules are complied with, the use of force against a commercial ship in a law enforcement operation in principle meets the proportionality and necessity conditions. As discussed in the next section, a single episode of the use of force by a government ship or warship against a commercial ship usually does not exceed the threshold of an armed attack in terms of Article 51 of the UN Charter in response to which the flag State of the targeted commercial ship could claim the right of self-defence. Thus, as a rule, the use of force in maritime law enforcement operation against a commercial ship does not give rise to the application of the rules of armed conflict. However, in exceptional cases, attacks against commercial ships may amount to an armed conflict. Such instances are discussed next in the State v. State scenario.

16 Ibid., para 156.

17 Annex VII Arbitral Tribunal, *Guyana v. Suriname Award, op. cit.*, para 445. Arctic Sunrise Award, *op. cit.*, para 222.

18 Ibid. *I'm Alone* case, *op. cit.*, 330. *Red Crusader* case, *op. cit.*, 538.

19 E.g., the *MV Torrey Canyon* incident, see *supra* Chapter 3.2 of Part 1.

18.3 State vs State Scenario

Determining whether the rules of armed conflict or law enforcement apply in situations where one State has used force against ships of another flag State can be difficult. On this question, there are contradictory views and considerable amount of ambiguity in the relevant case law and legal literature. The following sections summarize the findings of this study based on a differentiation between so-called tanker war scenario and clashes between warships or government ships of conflicting States.

18.3.1 *'Tanker war' Scenario*

Based on State practice and case law, it is unclear if the use of force outside the law enforcement paradigm against a single commercial ship can amount to an armed attack under Article 51 of the UN Charter if it causes significant damage to the ship, its crew, or cargo. This matter was at the heart of judicial proceedings before the ICJ in the *Oil Platforms Case*. The United States claimed that an attack against a single commercial ship amounted to an armed attack,[20] while Iran maintained the opposite and substantiated its position with extensive references to views of well-known legal scholars supporting that view.[21] The ICJ did not rule out the plausibility of either position but disregarded the United States' claim based on the lack of evidence of Iran's responsibility and the conclusion that the missile was not specifically aimed at that particular commercial ship, "but simply programmed to hit some target in Kuwaiti waters."[22] Similarly, the ICRC abstains from giving a definite answer on whether an attack against a single commercial ship can amount to an armed attack under Article 51 of the UN Charter.[23] Yet the ICJ has found that cases of low-intensity use of force against ships can amount to an armed attack when assessed cumulatively.[24]

Albeit the use of force against a single commercial ship might not trigger an armed conflict, the right to exercise self-defence under Article 51 of the UN Charter is certainly not excluded in cases where attacks against commercial

20 ICJ, *Oil Platforms Case*, Counter-Memorial and Counter-Claim Submitted by the United States of America, 23 June 1997, para 4.10. ICJ, *Oil Platforms Case*, Rejoinder Submitted by the United States of America, 23 March 2001, para 5.22.

21 ICJ, *Oil Platforms Case*, Reply and Defence to Counter-Claim Submitted by the Islamic Republic of Iran, Vol. 1, 10 March 1999, paras. 7.37–7.41.

22 *Oil Platforms Case*, Judgment, *op. cit.*, para 64.

23 ICRC 2016 commentary, *op. cit.*, on Common Article 2, para 227. ICRC 2017 commentary, *op. cit.*, on Common Article 2, para 249.

24 *Oil Platforms Case*, Judgment, *op. cit.*, para 64.

ships of a specific flag State are systemic and cause significant damage.[25] For example, of the cases studied above, the episodes of alleged Iranian limpet mine attacks against foreign tankers in the Strait of Hormuz in 2019 and the systemic attacks against the commercial ships flying either Israeli or Irani flag in the recent Israel-Iran 'shadow war' on the long waterway from the Strait of Hormuz to the Mediterranean can potentially fall under the so-called 'tanker war' scenario. Yet there is not sufficient evidence of the suspected States' direct involvement in these attacks.

For invoking the right of self-defence under Article 51 of the UN Charter in response to attacks against commercial ships, it is necessary for a State to show, *inter alia*, that:

- There is persuasive evidence that the suspected State bears responsibility for carrying out such attacks.[26]
- The State responsible for the attack intentionally and systemically targeted ships flying the flag of the State that invokes the right of self-defence and that the attacks were not indiscriminate (e.g., a mine or missile was simply aimed to hit some target).[27]
- The attack caused significant damage, either to ships, their crew, or goods. According to Article (d) of the UN General Assembly Resolution 3314 *Definition of Aggression*, an act of aggression includes "[a]n attack by the armed forces of a State on the land, sea or air forces, or marine and air fleets of another State". It is not certain how many attacks on a single flag State would suffice. Notably, the ICJ has found that cases of low-intensity use of force against ships can amount to an armed attack when assessed cumulatively.[28]
- The attacked commercial ships, whatever their ownership, were flying the flag of the State that claims the right of self-defence so that the attacks on the commercial ships can be equated with an attack on that State.[29]

Provided that these conditions are satisfied, the State acting in self-defence can use measures against the State that is responsible for the attacks. Its use of force under the law of self-defence must comply with the principles of necessity and proportionality and the rules of armed conflict, including, first and foremost, the principles and rules of humanitarian law.[30] This implies, for

25 See below on the Definition of Aggression, *op. cit.*, Art 3(d).

26 *Oil Platforms Case*, Judgment, *op. cit.*, para 64.

27 Ibid.

28 Ibid.

29 Ibid.

30 *Military and Paramilitary Activities in and against Nicaragua, op. cit.*, para 176. *Legality of the Threat or Use of Nuclear Weapons, op. cit.*, paras 41-42.

example, that the use of force under the right of self-defence must be aimed against an appropriate military target, not against a "target of opportunity".[31]

18.3.2 *Warship/Government Ship vs Warship/Government Ship Scenario*

Under the LOSC, both warships and government ships (e.g., Coast Guard vessels) are entitled to perform law enforcement operations and may use force in that capacity.[32] The ITLOS has noted that: "[T]he traditional distinction between naval vessels and law enforcement vessels in terms of their roles has become considerably blurred … and it is not uncommon today for States to employ the two types of vessels collaboratively for diverse maritime tasks."[33] Thus, as explained by the Annex VII Arbitral Tribunal, "the mere involvement of military vessels or personnel in an activity does not *ipso facto* render the activity military in nature."[34] It follows that the status of the State-owned ship that uses force against another State's warship or government ship is not determinative for the legal classification of the incident.

Nonetheless, it is of great relevance whether the use of force is targeted against a foreign warship or not, since, as stated by the ITLOS, "a warship is an expression of the sovereignty of the State whose flag it flies."[35] Where the aggression is directed against a warship, the following criteria can be distilled from the relevant case law for determining the applicable legal framework:

- The classification of the use of force is based on the actual merits of the incident, not its form. In the view of the ITLOS, "the distinction between military and law enforcement activities must be based primarily on an objective evaluation of the nature of the activities in question, taking into account the relevant circumstances in each case."[36] For example, the coastal State's use of potentially lethal measures, e.g. depth charges, to counter an unlawful incursion of a foreign submarine into its territorial sea can be viewed potentially from the perspective of either the law enforcement or *jus in bello* framework. In case the suspected vessel is a private submarine or unmanned submersible used for, e.g., drug smuggling, then the incident falls under the law enforcement paradigm. By contrast, where the coastal State's Navy is engaged in a standoff with a foreign State's submarine that has invaded the

31 *Oil Platforms Case*, Judgment, *op. cit.*, para 76.
32 See, e.g., Articles 107, 111(5), and 224 of LOSC.
33 ITLOS Order of 25 May 2019, *op. cit.*, para 64.
34 *Dispute Concerning Coastal State Rights*, 2020 Award on Preliminary Objections, *op. cit.*, para 340.
35 "ARA Libertad" 2012 Provisional Measures Order, *op. cit.*, para 94.
36 ITLOS Order of 25 May 2019, *op. cit.*, para 66.

coastal State's territory and resists orders to leave, then the incident is *prima facie* governed by the rules of *jus in bello* (international humanitarian law).[37]

- The distinction between military and law enforcement activities and the legality of acting in self-defence under Article 51 of the UN Charter is based primarily on the objective assessment of the use of force, not by the subjective assessment of the situation by the State invoking the right of self-defence.[38]
- The use of force against "a single military vessel might be sufficient to bring into play the "inherent right of self-defence"".[39] Consequently, this entitles the victim State to use force against the aggressor State and invoke the applicability of the rules of *jus in bello*.
- According to the ICJ, for the right of self-defence to apply, there needs to be:
  - Conclusive evidence that the State suspected of carrying out the attack is responsible for it.[40]
  - Evidence that the use of force against a foreign warship "was aimed specifically at" that flag State (vs an indiscriminate attack).[41] In other words, there needs to be clarity that the State that used force against a foreign warship had the "specific intention of harming that ship, or other … vessels" flying the same flag.[42]
- Other factors that indicate that a naval incident might be governed by the rules of armed conflict rather than maritime law enforcement include, *inter alia*:
  - Recognition of state of war by the parties to the conflict, although nowadays such declarations of war are rare, and it does not constitute a precondition for the classification of the use of force as an armed conflict (Common Article 2 of the Geneva Conventions).[43]
  - The existence of a stand-off "involving the military forces of one side and a combination of military and paramilitary forces on the other, arrayed in opposition to one another".[44]

37 See *supra* Chapter 7.3 of Part 2.
38 ITLOS Order of 25 May 2019, *op. cit.*, para 65.
39 *Oil Platforms Case*, Judgment, *op. cit.*, para 72.
40 Ibid.
41 Ibid., para 64.
42 Ibid.
43 According to Heintschel von Heinegg, "[t]he characterization of a given situation by governments is irrelevant." Ibid., 451.
44 *South China Sea Arbitration*, Award of 12 July 2016, *op. cit.*, para 1161.

- Reciprocity in fighting, although it is not a precondition for the aggressor State's use of force to be qualified as an armed attack triggering the right of self-defence of the targeted State that the latter 'fights back'.[45] For example, if a tactical nuclear weapon is used in a surprise attack against a foreign warship, then it would meet the level of an intensity of fighting (see next) to constitute an armed attack triggering an international armed conflict between the two States even if the attack has such an effect on the targeted State that it does not respond militarily.
- Intensity of fighting, but for the use of force to be categorized as an armed conflict it is not necessarily a precondition that the use of force reaches a high level of intensity, as examined next.

The criteria for the determination of the existence of an armed conflict are not uniform under the current case law of international courts and tribunals. The divergence appears to be caused, among other factors, by the somewhat different approaches of the ICJ and the ICTY on this matter. According to the ICTY, "an armed conflict exists whenever there is a resort to armed force between States or protracted armed violence between governmental authorities and organized armed groups or between such groups within a State."[46] The ICTY has distanced itself from the 'gravity threshold' as it found that:

> [T]he existence of armed force between States is sufficient of itself to trigger the application of international humanitarian law. … In its adjudication of the nature of the armed conflict with which it is concerned, the Trial Chamber is guided by the Commentary to the Fourth Geneva Convention, which considers that "[a]ny difference arising between two States and leading to the intervention of members of the armed forces" is an international armed conflict and "[i]t makes no difference how long the conflict lasts, or how much slaughter takes place.[47]

This view is shared by the International Criminal Court.[48] By contrast, according to the ICJ's position, the resort to use of force between States also needs to reach a level of sufficient gravity for it being legally categorized as an armed

45 See Heintschel von Heinegg 2016, *op. cit.*, 452.

46 ICTY, *Prosecutor v Tadić*, Decision of 2 October 1995, *op. cit.*, para 70.

47 ICTY, *Prosecutor v. Delalić* and others, Judgment of 16 November 1998, *op. cit.*, paras 184, 208.

48 ICC, *Prosecutor v. Lubanga*, Decision of 29 January 2007, *op. cit.*, para 207.

attack under *jus ad bellum*.[49] Only such use of force that qualifies as a "most grave form of the use of force" can qualify as an armed attack under the ICJ's case law.[50]

The ICJ's 'gravity threshold' for triggering the right of self-defence under Article 51 of the UN Charter leaves a significant room of manoeuvre for States to employ low-intensity use of force against adversaries. Legally speaking, this facilitates the ambiguous domain of hybrid naval warfare that exceeds the level of maritime law enforcement but falls below the threshold of an armed attack under Article 51 of the UN Charter. The victim State will likely be seen as falling under the *de minimis* threshold and needs to comply with Article 2(4) of the UN Charter when employing law enforcement or criminal law-based measures to counter such attacks that fall below the 'gravity threshold' of an armed attack, as set by the ICJ. Consequently, the victim State's use of arms needs to strictly stay within the confines of the limits of proportionality that are narrower in the law enforcement and criminal law paradigms as compared to the right of self-defence under Article 51 of the UN Charter.[51]

In such border-line cases that even international judicial bodies are unable to definitely classify in their *ex post* assessments as either falling to the law enforcement or military operations category, the Annex VII Arbitral Tribunal's approach in the *Guyana v. Suriname Case* to favour the 'stronger' categorisation, i.e. military activity over a law enforcement one, and relying on the subjective assessment of the situation by the targeted persons or State essentially supports the victim State in grey zone incidents. The different approach adopted by the ICJ in the *Oil Platforms Case* entails that a victim State in a low-intensity hybrid naval warfare risks the possibility of being eventually dubbed as an aggressor State if it has subjectively deemed itself entitled to the right of self-defence, whereas the objective *ex post* assessment reaches the opposite conclusion that the initial aggression did not meet the threshold of *most grave form of the use of force*.

49 *Oil Platforms Case*, Judgment, *op. cit.*, para 64. *Military and Paramilitary Activities in and against Nicaragua*, *op. cit.*, para 191.

50 Ibid.

51 See *supra* Chapter 5.3.1 of Part 2.

Bibliography

Monographs, Research Articles, Etc.

Alexander, LM 'International Straits', in HB Robertson, Jr. (ed), The Law of Naval Operations (Naval War College Press, Newport, 1991).

Allen, JR, FB Hodges, J Lindley-French, Future War and the Defence of Europe (Oxford University Press, Oxford, 2021).

Ashley Roach, J, JT Oliver, RW Smith, Limits in the Seas, No. 114: Iran's Maritime Claims (United States Department of State, Washington DC, 1994).

Ashley Roach, J, RW Smith, *Excessive Maritime Claims* (Martinus Nijhoff, Leiden/Boston 2012, 3rd Edition).

Beckmann, RC 'Combatting Piracy and Armed Robbery Against Ships in Southeast Asia: The Way Forward' (2002) 33(3–4) Ocean Development & International Law.

Brüel, E International Straits. A Treatise on International Law, vol. II. Straits Comprised by Positive Regulations (Sweet & Maxwell, London, 1947).

Butler, WE The Soviet Union and the Law of the Sea (The Johns Hopkins Press, Baltimore/London, 1971).

Cable, J Gunboat Diplomacy 1919–1991: Political Applications of Limited Naval Force (Palgrave Macmillan, London, 1994).

Caminos, H 'The Legal Regime of Straits in the 1982 United Nations Convention on the Law of the Sea', in Recueil des cours de l'Académie de droit international de la Haye 1987 (Martinus Nijhoff, Dordrecht/Boston/Lancaster, 1989).

Caminos, H, VP Cogliati-Bantz, The Legal Regime of Straits: Contemporary Challenges and Solutions (Cambridge University Press, Cambridge, 2014).

Cannizaro, E 'The Role of Proportionality in the Law of International Countermeasures' (2001) 12 European Journal of International Law.

Cassese, A 'Terrorism is Also Disrupting Some Crucial Legal Categories in International Law' (2001) 12 European Journal of International Law.

Chai, T, H Xue, 'A study on ship collision conflict prediction in the Taiwan Strait using the EMD-based LSSVM method' (2021) 16(5) PLoS ONE.

Chang, Y-C 'The use of force during law enforcement in disputed maritime areas' (2021) 124 Marine Policy.

Churchill, RR, AV Lowe, The Law of the Sea (Manchester University Press, Manchester, 1999).

Churchill, RR, AV Lowe, The Law of the Sea (Manchester University Press, Manchester, 1992).

Dinstein, Y War, Aggression and Self-Defence (6th Ed, Cambridge University Press, Cambridge, 2017).

'Methods and means of warfare at sea', in L Doswald-Beck (ed.), *San Remo Manual on International Law Applicable to Armed Conflicts at Sea* (Cambridge University Press, Cambridge, 1995).

Dunlap, Jr, CJ Law and Military Interventions: Preserving Humanitarian Values in 21st Conflicts (Harvard University, Washington DC, 2001).

Eesti Mereala Planeering. Seletuskiri (The Explanatory Note to the Estonian Maritime Spatial Plan, Rahandusministeerium/Hendrikson&Ko, Tallinn, 2020).

Estonian Foreign Intelligence Service, International Security and Estonia 2019 (Tallinn, 2019).

Fink, M Maritime Interception and the Law of Naval Operations: A Study of Legal Bases and Legal Regimes in Maritime Interception Operations (TMC Asser Press, The Hague, 2018).

Franckx, E 'The U.S.S.R. position on the innocent passage of warships through foreign territorial waters' (1987) 18(1) Journal of Maritime Law and Commerce.

Frostad, M 'Naval Blockade' (2018) 9 Arctic Review on Law and Politics.

Gaggioli, G The Use of Force in Armed Conflicts: Interplay between the Conduct of Hostilities and Law Enforcement Paradigms (ICRC, Geneva, 2013).

Gardner, H Hybrid Warfare: Iranian and Russian Versions of „Little Green Men" and Contemporary Conflict (NATO, Rome 2015).

A Garwood-Gowers, 'Case concerning Oil Platforms (Islamic Republic of Iran v. United States of America) - Did the ICJ Miss the Boat on the Law on the Use of Force' (2004) 5(1) Melbourne Journal of International Law.

Gazzini, T 'A Response to Amos Guiora: Pre-Emptive Self-Defence Against Non-State Actors?' (2008) 13 Journal of Conflict & Security Law.

Gill, TD 'The Law of Armed Attack in the Context of the Nicaragua Case' (1988) 1 Hague Yearbook of International Law.

Gill, T 'The Temporal Dimension of Self-Defence: Anticipation, Pre-emption, Prevention and Immediacy' (2006) Journal of Conflict & Security Law.

Gill, TD, D Fleck, 'Conceptual Distinction and Overlaps between Law Enforcement and the Conduct of Hostilities', in TD Gill, D Fleck (eds), The Handbook of the International Law of Military Operations (Oxford University Press, Oxford 2015), 63.

Glenn, G 'Notes and comments: The Swedish-Soviet territorial sea controversy in the Baltic' (1956) 50(4) American Journal of International Law.

Gorenburg, D The Kerch Strait skirmish: a Law of the Sea perspective (Hybrid CoE, Helsinki, 2018).

Gorina-Ysern, M An International Regime for Marine Scientific Research (Transnational Publishers, Ardsley, 2004).

Greenwood, C 'Scope of Application of Humanitarian Law', in D Fleck (ed.), The Handbook of International Humanitarian Law (2nd Ed, Oxford University Press, Oxford, 2009).

Guilfoyle, D 'The Legal Challenges in Fighting Piracy' in B van Ginkel, FP van der Putten (eds), The International Response to Somali Piracy: Challenges and Opportunities (Brill, Leiden/Boston, 2010).
Guymon, CD (ed), Digest of United States Practice in International Law (United States Department of State, Washington DC, 2015).
Haines, S 'War at sea: Nineteenth-century laws for twenty-first century wars?' 2016 98(2) International Review of the Red Cross.
Hakapää, K, EJ Molenaar, 'Innocent Passage – past and present' (1999) 23 Marine Policy.
Heintschel von Heinegg, W 'The Law of Naval Warfare and International Straits' (1998) 71 International Law Studies.
Heintschel von Heinegg, W 'Naval Blockade' (2000) 75 International Law Studies.
Heintschel von Heinegg, W 'The Law of Armed Conflict at Sea', in D Fleck (ed.), The Handbook of International Humanitarian Law (2nd Ed, Oxford University Press, Oxford, 2009).
Heintschel von Heinegg, W 'Methods and Means of Naval Warfare in Non-International Armed Conflicts' (2012) 88 International Law Studies.
Heintschel von Heinegg, W 'The difficulties of conflict classification at sea: Distinguishing incidents at sea from hostilities' (2016) 98(2) International Review of the Red Cross.
Hoffman, FG Conflict in the 21st Century: The Rise of Hybrid Wars (Potomac Institute for Policy Studies, Arlington 2007).
ICRC, Commentary on the First Geneva Convention: Convention (I) for the Amelioration of the Condition of the Wounded and Sick in Armed Forces in the Field, 2nd edition, 2016.
ICRC, Commentary on the Second Geneva Convention: Convention (II) for the Amelioration of the Condition of Wounded, Sick and Shipwrecked Members of Armed Forces at Sea, 2nd edition, 2017.
Ishii, Y Japanese Maritime Security and Law of the Sea (Brill, Leiden/Boston, 2022).
Jia, BB The Regime of Straits in International Law (Clarendon Press, Oxford, 1998).
Jonson, ER 'The Hydra and the Leviathan: Unmanned Maritime Vehicles and the Militarized Seaspace', in I Braverman, ER Jonson (eds.), Blue Legalities: The Life and Laws of the Sea (Duke University Press, Durham 2019), 186–191.
Kanehara, A 'Reassessment of the Acts of the State in the Law of State Responsibility – A Proposal of an Integrative Theoretical Framework of the Law of State Responsibility to Effectively Cope with the Internationally Harmful Acts of Non-state Actors' (2019) 399 Collected Courses of the Hague Academy of International Law.
Kanehara, A 'The Use of Force in Maritime Security and the Use of Arms in Law Enforcement under the Current Wide Understanding of Maritime Security' (2019) 3(2) Japan Review.

Kempton, SB 'Ship Routing Measures in International Straits' (2000) 14 Ocean Yearbook.

Kleemola-Juntunen, P Passage Rights in International Law: A Case Study of the Territorial Waters of the Åland Islands (Lapland University Press, Rovaniemi, 2014).

Kleemola-Juntunen, P The Åland Strait (Brill, Leiden/Boston, 2018).

Klein, N Maritime Security and the Law of the Sea (Oxford University Press, Oxford 2011).

Koivurova, T, I Pölönen, Transboundary Environmental Impact Assessment in the Case of the Baltic Sea Gas Pipeline (2009) 52 German Yearbook of International Law.

Koskenniemi, M 'Case Concerning Passage Through the Great Belt' (1996) 27 Ocean Development & International Law.

Kraska, J 'The Law of the Sea Convention and the Northwest Passage' (2007) 22(2) The International Journal of Marine and Coastal Law.

Kraska, J 'Legal Vortex in the Strait of Hormuz' (2013) 54(2) Virginia Journal of International Law.

Kraska, J, R Pedrozo, International Maritime Security Law (Martinus Nijhoff, Leiden/Boston, 2013).

Kwast, PJ 'Maritime Law Enforcement and the Use of Force: Reflections on the Categorisation of Forcible Action at Sea in the Light of the Guyana/Suriname Award' (2008) 13(1) *Journal of Conflict & Security Law*.

Lapidoth-Eschelbacher, R The Red Sea and the Gulf of Aden (Martinus Nijhoff, The Hague/Boston/London, 1982).

Lesaffre, H 'Circumstances Precluding Wrongfulness in the ILC Articles on State Responsibility: Countermeasures', in J Crawford, A Pellet, S Olleson (eds), The Law of International Responsibility (Oxford University Press, Oxford, 2010).

Liu, C-H, Z Xu, Y-C Chang, 'Coast Guard Law of the People's Republic of China and Its Implications in International Law' (2021) 36(3) The International Journal of Marine and Coastal Law.

Van Logchem, Y The Rights and Obligations of States in Disputed Maritime Areas (Cambridge University Press, Cambridge, 2021).

López Martín, AG International Straits: Concept, Classification and Rules of Passage (Springer, Heidelberg/Dordrecht/London/New York, 2010).

Lott, A The Estonian Straits: Exceptions to the Strait Regime of Innocent or Transit Passage (Brill, Leiden/Boston, 2018).

Lynch, HF 'Freedom of Navigation in the Persian Gulf and Strait of Hormuz', in MH Nordquist, JN Moore (eds), Security Flashpoints: Oil, Islands, Sea Access and Military Confrontation (Martinus Nijhoff, The Hague/Boston/London, 1998).

Mahmoudi, S 'Passage of warships through the Strait of Hormuz' (1991) Marine Policy.

Mahmoudi, S 'Use of Armed Force against Suspected Foreign Submarines in the Swedish Internal Waters and Territorial Sea' (2018) 33(3) The International Journal of Marine and Coastal Law.

Mansoor, PR 'Introduction: Hybrid Warfare in History', in W Murray, PR Mansoor (eds.), Hybrid Warfare: Fighting Complex Opponents from the Ancient World to the Present (Cambridge University Press, New York, 2012).

Mazarr, MJ, N Beauchamp-Mustafaga, TR Heath, D Eaton, 'What Deters and Why? The State of Deterrence in Korea and the Taiwan Strait', RAND, 2021.

McDorman, TD 'Sovereign Immune Vessels: Immunities, Responsibilities and Exemptions', in H Ringbom (ed), Jurisdiction over Ships: Post-UNCLOS Developments in the Law of the Sea (Brill, Leiden/Boston, 2015).

McLaughlin, R 'Authorizations for maritime law enforcement operations' 2016 98(2) International Review of the Red Cross.

Molenaar, EJ Coastal State Jurisdiction over Vessel-source Pollution (Kluwer Law, The Hague, 1998).

Moore, C 'The Use of Force', in R Warner, S Kaye (eds.), *Routledge Handbook of Maritime Regulation and Enforcement* (Routledge, New York/Abingdon, 2018).

Müllerson, R 'Jus Ad Bellum: Plus Ca Change (Le Monde) Plus C'est La Même Chose (Le Droit)?' (2002) 7 Journal of Conflict & Security Law.

Munoz Mosquera, AB, SD Bachmann, JA Munoz Bravo, 'Hybrid Warfare and the Legal Domain' (2019) 31(1) Terrorism and Political Violence.

Murphy, M, G Schaub Jr, '"Sea of Peace" or Sea of War – Russian Maritime Hybrid Warfare in the Baltic Sea' (2018) 71(2) Naval War College Review.

Murphy, M, FG Hoffman, G Schaub, Jr, Hybrid Maritime Warfare and the Baltic Sea Region (University of Copenhagen, Copenhagen, 2016).

Myjer, EPJ, ND White, 'The Twin Towers Attack: An Unlimited Right to Self-Defence?' (2002) 7 Journal of Conflict & Security Law.

Nandan, SN, DH Anderson, 'Straits Used for International Navigation: A Commentary on Part III of the United Nations Convention on the Law of the Sea 1982' (1989) 60 The British Yearbook of International Law.

Nordquist, MH, R Wolfrum, JN Moore, R Long (eds.), Legal Challenges in Maritime Security (Brill, Leiden, Boston, 2008).

Noyes, JE 'The Territorial Sea and Contiguous Zone', in DR Rothwell, AG Oude Elferink, KN Scott, T Stephens (eds), The Oxford Handbook of the Law of the Sea (Oxford University Press, Oxford, 2015).

O'Connell ME *et al.*, Final Report on the Meaning of Armed Conflict in International Law (International Law Association, The Hague Conference, 2010).

O'Keefe, R 'Proportionality', in J Crawford, A Pellet, S Olleson (eds), The Law of International Responsibility (Oxford University Press, Oxford, 2010).

Oellers-Frahm, K 'The International Court of Justice and Article 51 of the UN Charter', in K Dicke et al. (eds), Weltinnenrecht: Liber amicorum Jost Delbrück (Duncker&Humblot, Berlin, 2005).

Office for Ocean Affairs and the Law of the Sea, The Law of the Sea Baselines: National Legislation With Illustrative Maps (United Nations, New York, 1989).
Oğuz, Ş 'Russian Hybrid Warfare and Its Implications in The Black Sea' (2017) 1(1) Bölgesel Araştırmalar Dergisi.
Orakhelashvili, A 'Legal Consequences of the Construction of a Wall in the Occupied Palestinian Territory: Opinion and Reaction' (2006) 11 Journal of Conflict & Security Law.
Oral, N 'Ukraine v. The Russian Federation: Navigating Conflict over Sovereignty under UNCLOS' (2021) 91 International Law Studies.
Oude Elferink, AG The Law of Maritime Boundary Delimitation: A Case Study of the Russian Federation (Martinus Nijhoff, Dordrecht, 1994).
Oude Elferink, AG 'The Regime of Passage Through the Danish Straits' (2000) 15 The International Journal of Marine and Coastal Law.
Õun, M Juminda miinilahing 1941 – maailmasündmus meie koduvetes (Juminda Sentinel, Juminda, 2006).
Paleri, P Coast Guards of the World and Emerging Maritime Threats (Ocean Policy Studies, Tokyo, 2009).
Papatulica, M 'Black Sea area at the crossroad of the biggest global energy players' interests. The impact on Romania' (2015) 22 Procedia Economics and Finance.
Patalano, A 'When strategy is 'hybrid' and not 'grey': reviewing Chinese military and constabulary coercion at sea' (2019) 31(6) The Pacific Review.
Pedrozo, R 'Close Encounters at Sea: The USNS *Impeccable* Incident' (2009) 62(3) Naval War College Review.
Pedrozo, R 'China's Revised Maritime Traffic Safety Law' (2021) 97 International Law Studies.
Platzöder, R 'Bridges and Straits in the Baltic Sea', in R Platzöder, P Verlaan (eds), The Baltic Sea: New Developments in National Policies and International Cooperation (Martinus Nijhoff, The Hague/London/Boston, 1996).
Qureshi, WA 'The Crisis in Yemen: Armed Conflict and International Law' (2020) 45 North Carolina Journal of International Law.
Raab, D 'Armed Attack after the *Oil Platforms Case*' (2004) 17(4) Leiden Journal of International Law.
Radin, A Hybrid Warfare in the Baltics: Threats and Potential Responses (RAND Corporation, Santa Monica, 2017).
Rahman, C, M Tsamenyi, 'A Strategic Perspective on Security and Naval Issues in the South China Sea', in NA Hu, TL McDorman (eds), Maritime Issues in the South China Sea: Troubled Waters or A Sea of Opportunity (Routledge, New York 2013).
Ramazani, RK The Persian Gulf and the Strait of Hormuz (Sijthoff & Noordhoff, Alphen aan den Rijn, 1979).

Randy Milton, G, T Salathe, Report: Ramsar Advisory Mission N°93 Kurgalsky Peninsula, Russian Federation Wetland of International Importance N°690 (Ramsar Secretariat, Gland, 2020).

Rosenberg, D, C Chung, 'Maritime Security in the South China Sea: Coordinating Coastal and User State Priorities' (2008) 39(1) Ocean Development & International Law.

Ruys, T, S Verhoeven, 'Attacks by Private Actors and the Right of Self-defence' (2005) 10 Journal of Conflict & Security Law.

Ruys, T 'The Meaning of 'Force' and The Boundaries of The Jus Ad Bellum: Are 'Minimal' Uses of Force Excluded from UN Charter Article 2(4)?' (2014) 108(2) The American Journal of International Law.

San Remo Manual on International Law Applicable to Armed Conflicts at Sea, 12 June 1994.

Savolainen, J, T Gill et al., Handbook on Maritime Hybrid Threats – 10 Scenarios and Legal Scans (The European Centre of Excellence for Countering Hybrid Threats, Helsinki, 2019).

Schapiro, LB 'The limits of Russian territorial waters in the Baltic' (1950) 27 The British Yearbook of International Law.

Schatz, VJ, D Koval, 'Russia's Annexation of Crimea and the Passage of Ships Through Kerch Strait: A Law of the Sea Perspective' (2019) 50(2–3) Ocean Development & International Law.

Schofield, C 'Securing the World's Most Dangerous Strait? The Bab-Al Mandeb and Gulf of Aden', in DD Caron and N Oral (eds), Navigating Straits: Challenges for International Law (Martinus Nijhoff, Leiden/Boston, 2014).

Schrijver, N 'Challenges to the Prohibition to Use Force: Does the Straitjacket of Artice 2(4) UN Charter Begin to Gall Too Much?', In N Blokker, N Schrijver (eds), The Security Council and the Use of Force: Theory and Reality – a Need for Change? (Martinus Nijhoff, Leiden/Boston, 2005).

Schwebel, SM Justice in International Law (Cambridge University Press, Cambridge, 1994).

Shah, NA 'Self-defence, Anticipatory Self-defence and Pre-emption: International Law's Response to Terrorism' (2007) 12 Journal of Conflict & Security Law.

Skaridov, A 'The Sea of Azov and the Kerch Straits' in DD Caron and N Oral (eds), Navigating Straits: Challenges for International Law (Martinus Nijhoff, Leiden/Boston, 2014).

Smith, RW, J Ashley Roach, Limits in the Seas, No. 112: United States Responses to Excessive National Maritime Claims (US Department of State, Washington D.C, 1992).

Smith RW et al., Limits in the Seas, No. 120. Straight Baseline and Territorial Sea Claims: Japan (US Department of State, Washington D.C., 1998).

Sohn, L, JE Noyes, E Franckx, K Juras, (eds) Cases and Materials on the Law of the Sea (Brill, Leiden, Boston, 2014).

Solski, JJ 'Russia', in RC Beckman, T Henriksen, KD Kraabel, EJ Molenaar, JA Roach (eds), Governance of Arctic Shipping Balancing Rights and Interests of Arctic States and User States (Brill, Leiden/Boston, 2017).

Soons, AHA Marine Scietific Research and the Law of the Sea (Kluwer, Deventer, 1982).

Spiliopoulou Åkermark, S, T Hyttinen, P Kleemola-Juntunen, 'Life on the Border: Dealing with Territorial Violations of the Demilitarised and Neutralised Zone of the Åland Islands' (2019) 88(2) Nordic Journal of International Law.

Stavridis, J 'Maritime Hybrid Warfare is Coming' (2016) 142(12) US Naval Institute Proceedings.

Stephens, T, DR Rothwell 'Marine Scientific Research', in DR Rothwell, AG Oude Elferink, KN Scott, T Stephens (eds), The Oxford Handbook of the Law of the Sea (Oxford University Press, Oxford, 2015).

Su, J 'The Practice of States on Air Defense Identification Zones: Geographical Scope, Object of Identification, and Identification Measures' (2020) 18(4) Chinese Journal of International Law.

Symmons, CR Historic Waters in the Law of the Sea: A Modern Re-Appraisal (Martinus Nijhoff, Leiden/Boston, 2008).

Taft, WH IV 'Self-Defense and the Oil Platforms Decision' (2004) 29(2) Yale Journal of International Law.

Talmon, S Recognition of Governments in International Law (Clarendon Press, Oxford, 1998).

Tanaka, Y 'Release of a Detained Warship and Its Crew through Provisional Measures: A Comparative Analysis of the ARA Libertad and Ukraine v. Russia Cases' (2020) 96 International Law Studies.

Tanca, A Foreign Armed Intervention in Internal Conflict (Martinus Nijhoff, Dordrecht/Boston/London, 1993).

Twining, W Jurist in Context: A Memoir (Cambridge University Press, Cambridge, 2019).

United Kingdom Foreign, Commonwealth and Development Office, 'Written evidence (UNC0028). UNCLOS: fit for purpose in the 21st century?', UK Parliament, 26 November 2021.

Ünlü, N The Legal Regime of the Turkish Straits (Martinus Nijhoff, Dordrecht, 2002).

Uustal, A Международно-правовой режим территориальных вод (Tartu State University Press, Tartu, 1958).

Uustal, A Rahvusvaheline õigus V: rahvusvaheline mere- ja ilmaruumiõigus (Tartu State University Press, Tartu, 1977).

Uustal, A Rahvusvaheline õigus (Eesti Raamat, Tallinn, 1984).

Värk, R 'Legal element of Russia's hybrid warfare' (2017) 6 ENDC Occasional Papers.

Värk, R 'Legal Complexities in the Service of Hybrid Warfare' (2020) 6 Kyiv-Mohyla Law and Politics Journal.

Vinogradov, S 'Challenges of Nord Stream: Streamlining International Legal Frameworks and Regimes for Submarine Pipelines' (2009) 52 German Yearbook of International Law.

Zou, K 'Navigation in the South China Sea: Why Still an Issue?' (2017) 32(2) The International Journal of Marine and Coastal Law.

Zou, K 'Redefining the Legal Status of the Taiwan Strait' (2000)15(2) The International Journal of Marine and Coastal Law.

United Nations Publications

Annex to the letter dated 25 November 2018 from the Permanent Representative of Ukraine to the United Nations, UN Doc A/73/601–S/2018/1052, 28 November 2018.

Annex to the letter dated 27 November 2018 from the Permanent Representative of Ukraine to the United Nations, UN Doc. A/73/605–S/2018/1053, 30 November 2018.

Annex to the letter dated 29 November 2018 from the Permanent Representative of Ukraine to the United Nations, UN Doc A/73/619–S/2018/1079, 5 December 2018.

Annex to the letter dated 10 December 2018 from the Permanent Representative of Ukraine to the United Nations, UN Doc A/73/659–S/2018/1112, 14 December 2018.

Annex to the letter dated 7 March 2019 from the Permanent Representative of the Russian Federation to the United Nations, Position of the Russian Federation in connection with the adoption of the Contiguous Zone of Ukraine Act, UN Doc A/73/802, 20 March 2019.

Annex to the letter dated 18 April 2019 from the Permanent Representative of Ukraine to the United Nations, UN Doc A/73/844–S/2019/334, 23 April 2019.

Code of Conduct for Law Enforcement Officials, Adopted by General Assembly resolution 34/169 of 17 December 1979.

General Assembly, Report of the Secretary-General: Implementing the Responsibility to Protect (2009, UN Doc. A/2211).

Letter dated 3 December 1971 from the Permanent Representatives of Algeria, Iraq, Libyan Arab Republic and People's Democratic Republic of Yemen to the United Nations Addressed to the President of the Security Council, UN Doc. S/10409, 3 December 1971.

Letter dated 5 January 2017 from the Chargé d'affaires a.i. of the Permanent Mission of the United Arab Emirates to the United Nations addressed to the President of the Security Council, UN Doc. S/2017/17, 6 January 2017.

Letter dated 20 July 2019 from the Chargé d'affaires a.i. of the Permanent Mission of the United Kingdom of Great Britain and Northern Ireland to the United Nations addressed to the President of the Security Council, UN Doc. S/2019/589, 22 July 2019.

Letter dated 23 July 2019 from the Chargé d' affaires a.i. of the Permanent Mission of the Islamic Republic of Iran to the United Nations addressed to the Secretary-General and the President of the Security Council, UN Doc. S/2019/593, 23 July 2019.

Letter dated 23 July 2019 from the Chargé d' affaires a.i. of the Permanent Mission of the Islamic Republic of Iran to the United Nations addressed to the Secretary-General and the President of the Security Council, UN Doc. S/2019/593, 23 July 2019.

Maria Luiza Ribeiro Viotti, 'Remarks at Security Council high-level open debate on 'Enhancing Maritime Security: A case for international cooperation'', United Nations, 9 August 2021.

Permanent Mission of Finland to the United Nations, 22 August 1997, No. YKEC032-46.

Ukraine's 'List of geographical coordinates of points defining the baselines for measuring the breadth of the territorial sea, exclusive economic zone and the continental shelf in the Sea of Azov', UN Division for Ocean Affairs and the Law of the Sea, Law of the Sea Bulletin, No. 36, (UN, 1998).

UN Conference on Trade and Development, '2019 e-Handbook of Statistics', Geneva, 2019.

UN Conference on Trade and Development, 'Review of Maritime Transport 2020', Geneva, 2020.

UN Treaty Collection, Convention on the Territorial Sea and the Contiguous Zone, status at 10 February 2021.

UN Treaty Collection, United Nations Convention on the Law of the Sea, status at 10 February 2021.

Submissions in Court Cases

Annex VII Arbitral Tribunal, *Dispute Concerning Coastal State Rights,* Written Observations and Submissions of Ukraine on Jurisdiction, 27 November 2018.

Annex VII Arbitral Tribunal, *Dispute Concerning the Detention of Ukrainian Naval Vessels and Servicemen,* Preliminary Objections of the Russian Federation, 24 August 2020.

Annex VII Arbitral Tribunal, *Dispute Concerning the Detention of Ukrainian Naval Vessels and Servicemen,* Observations of Ukraine on the Question of Bifurcation, 7 September 2020.

Annex VII Arbitral Tribunal, *Dispute Concerning the Detention of Ukrainian Naval Vessels and Servicemen,* Response of the Russian Federation to the Observations of Ukraine on the Question of Bifurcation, 21 September 2020.

Annex VII Arbitral Tribunal, *Dispute Concerning the Detention of Ukrainian Naval Vessels and Servicemen,* Written Observations and Submissions of Ukraine on the Preliminary Objections of the Russian Federation, 27 January 2021.

ICJ, *Oil Platforms Case,* Counter-Memorial and Counter-Claim Submitted by the United States of America, 23 June 1997.

ICJ, *Oil Platforms Case,* Rejoinder Submitted by the United States of America, 23 March 2001.

ICJ, *Oil Platforms Case,* Reply and Defence to Counter-Claim Submitted by the Islamic Republic of Iran, Vol. I, 10 March 1999.

ICJ, Denmark's Counter-Memorial in the Passage through the Great Belt Case (Finland v. Denmark) Copenhagen: Government of the Kingdom of Denmark 1992.

European Union Publications

Council of the European Union, 'European Union Maritime Security Strategy', Brussels 2014.

European Parliament Research Service, 'At a glance – Understanding hybrid Threats', Brussels 2015.

European Parliament, 'At a glance: The Nord Stream 2 pipeline project', 2016.

Responses to Information Requests

Comment obtained from the Director General of the Legal Department of the Ministry of Foreign Affairs of Estonia, Ms Kerli Veski on 15 February 2017 in response to the author's information request no. 4–4/813–1.

Comment obtained from the advisor of the Legal Department of the Ministry of Foreign Affairs of Estonia, Mr Jaanus Kirikmäe on 13 October 2020 in response to the author's information request no. 4–4/5063.

Maritime Authorities' Publications

The Commander's Handbook on the Law of Naval Operations (US Navy, US Marine Corps, US Coast Guard, Norfolk, 2017).

EU Naval Force – Somalia, Operation ATALANTA, 'Key Facts and Figures', 2021.

HELCOM, Annual report on shipping accidents in the Baltic Sea area during 2007, Helsinki 2007.

HELCOM, Annual report on shipping accidents in the Baltic Sea area during 2008, Helsinki 2008.

HELCOM, Annual report on shipping accidents in the Baltic Sea area during 2009, Helsinki 2009.

HELCOM, Annual report on shipping accidents in the Baltic Sea area during 2010, Helsinki 2010.

HELCOM, Annual report on shipping accidents in the Baltic Sea area during 2011, Helsinki 2011.

HELCOM, Annual report on shipping accidents in the Baltic Sea area during 2012, Helsinki 2012.

HELCOM, Annual report on shipping accidents in the Baltic Sea area during 2013, Helsinki 2014.

HELCOM, Shipping accidents in the Baltic Sea from 2014 to 2017, Helsinki 2018.

HELCOM, '166, Kurgalsky Peninsula'.

ICC-IMB Piracy and Armed Robbery Against Ships: Report for the Period 1 January – 31 December 2011 (ICC International Maritime Bureau, London, 2012).

ICC-IMB Piracy and Armed Robbery Against Ships: Report for the Period 1 January – 31 December 2015 (ICC International Maritime Bureau, London, 2016).

ICC-IMB Piracy and Armed Robbery Against Ships: Report for the Period 1 January – 31 March 2021 (ICC International Maritime Bureau, London, 2021).

ICC-IMB Piracy and Armed Robbery Against Ships: Report for the Period 1 January – 31 December 2020 (ICC International Maritime Bureau, London, 2021).

IMO, 'Report of the Maritime Safety Committee on its Sixty-Ninth Session', MSC 69/22, 1998.

International Association of Marine Aids to Navigation and Lighthouse Authorities, IALA VTS Manual, (Ed. 6, IALA, Saint Germain en Laye, 2016).

International Association of Marine Aids to Navigation and Lighthouse Authorities, IALA Guideline 1071 – Establishment of a Vessel Traffic Service beyond Territorial Seas, (Ed. 1, IALA, Saint Germain en Laye, 2009).

International Register of Shipping, 'IMO Navigation Rules at Straits of Malacca and Singapore', 7 December 2019.

Limits of Oceans and Seas (3rd ed., International Hydrographic Organization, Monte Carlo, 1953).

Maritime and Port Authority Singapore, 'Vessel Traffic Information System'.

M Stankiewicz et al, 'Ensuring safe shipping in the Baltic' HELCOM, Helsinki 2009.

Rosmorport, Azovo-Chernomorsky Basin Branch, VTS Services, 'Statistics', 2020.

Rosmorport, 'General Information/VTS Coverage Areas', 'VTS services', 2021.

Rosmorport, North-Western Basin Branch, 'VTS coverage areas', 2021.

Rosmorport, North-Western Basin Branch, 'Terms and conditions of navigation VTS services', 2021.

Rosmorport, North-Western Basin Branch, 'Terms and conditions of navigation VTS services with the use of Saint Petersburg VTS', 2021.
Shipping accidents in the Baltic Sea 2018, HELCOM, 2019.
Suez Canal Traffic Statistics: Annual Report 2017, Suez Canal Authority 2018.
Traffic Management Finland, Helsinki VTS Master's Guide, 2020.
'VTS certificate of the Kerch Strait, highest category', Rosmorport 2017.
VTS services, 'General Information', 'Terms and conditions of navigation services in the VTS of the Kerch Strait', Rosmorport 2020.

Newspaper Articles and Press Releases

Abdallah, N, D Nehme et al., 'Saudi-led coalition says it foiled Red Sea attack by Yemen's Houthis', Reuters (23 February 2020).
Ahlander, J 'Foreign submarine sighted in Sweden last year: Dagens Nyheter', Reuters (26 February 2016).
Al-Khalidi, S 'Syria says U.S. sanctions behind acute fuel crisis', Reuters (17 September 2020).
American Institute in Taiwan, 'U.S.-Taiwan Coast Guard Working Group Advances Joint Maritime Cooperation Goals', Press Release, 11 August 2021.
Anischchuk, A 'Putin admits Russian forces were deployed to Crimea', Reuters (17 April 2014).
Anonymous, 'New submarine search off Porvoo', Helsingin Sanomat (15 August 2001).
Anonymous, 'Yemen says tanker blast was terrorism', BBC News (16 October 2002).
Anonymous, 'Vene uurimislaev Pjotr Kotsov eiras Eesti piirivalve korraldusi', Eesti Päevaleht (19 November 2005).
Anonymous, 'Sillamäe-Kotka laevaliin teeb avareisi 17. veebruaril', Postimees (12 January 2006).
Anonymous, 'Sillamäe-Kotka laevaliin on Ida-Viru tänavune turismitegu', Logistikauudised (8 December 2006).
Anonymous, 'Tallinn tense after deadly riots', *BBC News* (28 April 2007).
Anonymous, 'Päivittäinen laivaliikenne Kotkan ja Sillamäen välillä päättyy', Yle Uutiset (17 October 2007).
Anonymous, 'Kotkan ja Viron välistä laivaliikennettä viritellään taas', Yle Uutiset (1 February 2011).
Anonymous, 'Guantanamo prisoner al-Darbi admits MV Limburg attack', BBC News (20 February 2014).
Anonymous, 'Russian plane has near-miss with passenger aircraft over Sweden', The Guardian (13 December 2014).

Anonymous, 'Finland drops depth charges in 'submarine' alert', BBC News (28 April 2015).

Anonymous, 'Missile Attack Destroys Ex-Navy Ship off Yemen', The Maritime Executive (3 October 2016).

Anonymous, 'U.S. Navy Sends Warships to Secure Bab el-Mandeb', The Maritime Executive (4 October 2016).

Anonymous, 'Pirates attack oil tanker near Bab al-Mandab', Al Arabiya News (27 October 2016).

Anonymous, 'Hormuz and Malacca Remain Top Oil Chokepoints', Maritime Executive (8 April 2017).

Anonymous, 'HBL: Pääesikunta kieltää venäläisen purjealuksen pääsyn Ahvenanmaalle', Yle Uutiset (28 August 2017).

Anonymous, 'Sweden to re-establish military unit on Baltic Sea island', The Associated Press (13 December 2017).

Anonymous, 'Explosion damages vessel carrying wheat to Yemen', Reuters (11 May 2018).

Anonymous, 'Arab coalition destroys 86 Houthi-planted naval mines in Red Sea', Arab News (25 November 2018).

Anonymous, 'Ukraine-Russia sea clash: Who controls the territorial waters around Crimea?', BBC News (27 November 2018).

Anonymous, 'Estonia, Poland deny entry to Russian ship over Crimea cadets', RTL Today (12 April 2019).

Anonymous, 'Ka Poola keelas Vene purjelaeval oma vetesse sisenemise', Postimees (12 April 2019).

Anonymous, 'Strait of Hormuz: US confirms drone shot down by Iran', BBC News (20 June 2019).

Anonymous, 'Gulf tanker attacks: Iran releases photos of 'attacked' ship', BBC News (14 October 2019).

Anonymous, 'Passenger Port of St. Petersburg summed up 2019 navigation results', PortNews (2 December 2019).

Anonymous, 'EDF: No improvement in Russian military flight practices, despite claims', ERR News (27 December 2019).

Anonymous, 'USS Cole bombing: Sudan agrees to compensate families', BBC News (13 February 2020).

Anonymous, '2 Russian aircraft suspected of violating Finland's airspace', The Washington Post (28 July 2020).

Anonymous, 'Russian fighter jets suspected of violating Finnish airspace', Yle Uutiset (28 July 2020).

Anonymous, 'South Korea to send delegation after Iran seizes tanker', BBC News (5 January 2021).

Anonymous, 'Netanyahu accuses Iran of attacking Israeli-owned ship in Gulf', The Guardian (1 March 2021).
Anonymous, 'Egypt's Suez Canal blocked by huge container ship', BBC News (24 March 2021).
Anonymous, 'Iranian ship thought to be used as military base attacked, says Tehran', The Guardian (7 April 2021).
Anonymous, 'Three killed in attack on Iran fuel tanker off Syria after suspected drone attack', Al Arabiya (24 April 2021).
Anonymous, 'Ship owner says Suez Canal was at fault over Ever Given grounding- lawyer', Reuters (22 May 2021).
Anonymous, 'No end to Yemen civil war on the horizon, senior UN official briefs Security Council', UN News (23 August 2021).
Anonymous, 'Taiwan says 19 Chinese warplanes entered air defence zone', BBC News (6 September 2021).
Anonymous, 'Nord Stream 2: German minister warns Russia over Ukraine', Deutsche Welle (18 December 2021).
Anonymous, 'Российские военные проведут учения с корабельными группами в Черном море', Interfax (10 February 2022).
Anonymous, 'Russia confirms suspension of movement of commercial vessels in the Azov sea – Interfax', Reuters (24 February 2022).
Anonymous, 'Navigation in Kerch Strait not suspended - Russian agency', Interfax (24 February 2022).
Anonymous, 'Rosmorrechflot confirms suspended navigation in Sea of Azov', Interfax (24 February 2022).
Anonymous, 'Full text: Putin's declaration of war on Ukraine', The Spectator (24 February 2022).
Anonymous, 'Ukraine: AOAV's data on harm to civilians by explosive weapons', Action on Armed Violence (1 March 2022).
Anonymous, 'Turkey warns against passing of warships from its straits', Al Jazeera (1 March 2022).
Anonymous, 'Bangladeshi Ship Hit in Attack Near Mykolaiv, Killing One Engineer', The Maritime Executive (2 March 2022).
Anonymous, 'Estonian-owned cargo ship sinks off Odesa after Russian action', ERR News (3 March 2022).
Anonymous, 'Ukraine: Estonian cargo ship sinks after blast in Black Sea', BBC News (4 March 2022).
Anonymous, 'Ukraine: Safe passage for civilians from Mariupol halted for a second day; ICRC calls on parties to agree to specific terms', ICRC (6 March 2022).
Balmforth, T 'U.S denies it carried out operations in Russian territorial waters', Reuters (15 February 2022).

Barden, J 'The Strait of Hormuz is the world's most important oil transit chokepoint', US Energy Information Administration (20 June 2019).

Bayoumy, Y, P Stewart, 'Exclusive: Iran steps up weapons supply to Yemen's Houthis via Oman – officials', Reuters (20 October 2016).

Blair, E 'Latest on tanker attacks south of the Strait of Hormuz', Reuters (14 June 2019).

Blanchard, B 'Taiwan reports largest incursion yet by Chinese air force', Reuters (15 June 2021).

Blinken, AJ Secretary of State 'Nord Stream 2 and Potential Sanctionable Activity', Press Statement, 18 March 2021.

Bowman, B, K Zimmerman, 'Biden Can't Bring Peace to Yemen While Iran Keeps Sending Weapons', Foreign Policy (4 March 2021).

Buck, T, R Olearchyk, 'Merkel warns Nord Stream 2 must protect Ukraine role', Financial Times (10 April 2018).

Burns, S, S Carswell, 'Russia moves naval exercises outside Ireland's Exclusive Economic Zone', The Irish Times (29 January 2022).

Bush, D 'Turkish bulker hit by bomb off Odessa', Lloyd's List (24 February 2022).

Cavas, CP 'New Houthi weapon emerges: a drone boat', Defense News (19 February 2017).

Cavegn, D 'Defense minister: No reason to worry about Russian heliport on Gogland', ERR News (10 August 2019).

Cavegn, D 'UK planning landing operations exercise in Estonia in summer 2019', ERR News (9 December 2018).

Chulov, M 'Officials investigating why Iran warship caught fire and sank in Gulf of Oman', The Guardian (2 June 2021).

Cooper, H, E Schmitt, 'Biden Weighs Deploying Thousands of Troops to Eastern Europe and Baltics', *The New York Times* (23 January 2022).

Council of the EU, 'Syria: EU renews sanctions against the regime by one year', Press Release (17 May 2019).

Devitt, P, G Stolyarov, N Zinets, 'Ukraine shuts ports as conflict threatens grain supplies', Reuters (24 February 2022).

Dickerman, K, L d`Aki, 'Inside the Swedish military presence on Gotland, the most strategic island for defense against Russian aggression', The Washington Post (30 August 2018).

Eelmets, J 'Sillamäe-Kotka laevaliini taastamine sõltub kokkuleppest Venemaaga', ERR Uudised (20 November 2015).

Egozi, A 'Houthis Lay Sea Mines In Red Sea; Coalition Boasts Few Minesweepers', Breaking Defense (14 June 2021).

Elagina, D 'Volume of cargo handled in Russia in 2019, by largest port', Statista (16 January 2020).

Ellam, H 'Pronksiöö tulemus: Sillamäe-Kotka laevaliin suletakse', Äripäev (17 October 2007).

Erkoyun, E, T Gumrukcu, 'Turkey says Russia cancelled Black Sea passage bid upon its request', Reuters (2 March 2022).
Erkoyun, E, T Gumrukcu, 'Turkey to implement pact limiting Russian warships to Black Sea', Reuters (27 February 2022).
The Estonian Government Office, 'Valitsus otsustas kabinetinõupidamisel mitte rahuldada Nord Stream AG taotlust mereuuringuteks Eesti majandusvööndis', Press Release (6 December 2012).
Fassihi, F, E Schmitt, R Bergman, 'Israel-Iran Sea Skirmishes Escalate as Mine Damages Iranian Military Ship', The New York Times (7 April 2021).
Finnish Navy Press Release, '"VILMA" -meritaisteluharjoitus valtaa Saaristomeren', Merivoimat (21 May 2018).
Finnish Navy Press Release, 'Meritaisteluharjoitus Siljan soveltava vaihe alkaa 3.6. - Sota-aluksia ja rannikkojoukkoja liikkeellä Suomenlahdella ja Saaristomerellä', Merivoimat (2 June 2019).
Finnish Navy Press Release, 'Baltic Shield 2020 toteutetaan Rannikkolaivaston ammuntojen yhteydessä', Merivoimat (2 October 2020).
Finnish Navy Press Release, 'Suomi–Ruotsi-yhteistyö jatkuu miinantorjuntaharjoituksessa', Merivoimat (9 October 2020).
Finnish Navy Press Release, 'Merioperaatiot tähtäimessä Kaisla 20 -harjoituksessa', Merivoimat (20 November 2020).
Foy, H, N Astrasheuskaya, 'Why Nord Stream 2 is at heart of US warnings to Putin over Ukraine', Financial Times (9 December 2021).
Francis, M 'Aid workers describe 'apocalyptic' scenes in Mariupol, a Ukrainian city under siege', Yahoo News (9 March 2022).
Gardner, F 'China warns UK as carrier strike group approaches', BBC News (30 July 2021).
Gestrin-Hagner, M 'Huvudstaben förbjöd tyskt skolfartyg att besöka Åland', Hufvudstadsbladet (28 August 2017).
Ghobari, M, A Abdelaty et al., 'Yemen's Houthis attack Saudi ship, launch ballistic missile', Reuters (30 January 2017).
Government of Canada, 'Government of Canada prohibits Russian ships and fishing vessels from entering Canadian ports and internal waters', Press Release (1 March 2022).
Graham-Harrison, E 'Iran's top diplomat in UK summoned over seizure of Stena Impero tanker', The Guardian (20 July 2019).
Granlund, J 'Ökad beredskap på Gotland – försvaret kallar in reservofficerare', Aftonbladet (13 January 2022).
Gunter, J 'Mariupol under siege: 'We are being completely cut off'', BBC (3 March 2022).
Halminen, L 'Viron yleisradio: Venäjän ulkoministeri Sergei Lavrovin kone loukkasi Viron ilmatilaa matkallaan Suomeen', Helsingin Sanomat (5 May 2017).

Hand, M 'Malacca Straits VLCC traffic doubles in a decade as shipping traffic hits all time high in 2017', SeaTrade Maritime News (19 February 2018).

Harding, L, J Borger, J Henley, 'Russian bombing of maternity hospital 'genocide', says Zelenskiy', The Guardian (9 March 2022).

Harris, S, P Sonne, 'Russia planning massive military offensive against Ukraine involving 175,000 troops, U.S. intelligence warns', The Washington Post (3 December 2021).

Harris, M 'Phantom Warships Are Courting Chaos in Conflict Zones', *Wired* (27 July 2021).

Johnson, J 'U.S. warship conducts Sea of Japan operation in challenge to Russia's 'excessive maritime claims'', The Japan Times (6 December 2018).

Johnson, S 'Sweden to boost Gotland air defense amid Russia tensions', Reuters (1 July 2019).

Juliano, M 'Bulkers Cluster Off Bosphorus And Kerch Straits Amid Russia-Ukraine Conflict', TradeWinds (1 March 2022).

Kagge, R, T Sildam, 'Vene laev tabati Eesti vetest uurimistöölt', Postimees (11 November 2005).

Kavi, A 'Biden Warns U.S. Won't Send Troops to Rescue Americans in Ukraine', The New York Times (10 February 2022).

Kivil, K 'Odessa lähedal läks põhja Eesti firmale kuuluv kaubalaev', ERR Uudised (3 March 2022).

Korobtsova, K, L King, 'Putin vs. the web: Russia tries to hide casualties and searing war images', Los Angeles Times (4 March 2022).

Krjukov, A 'Lennuliiklusteeninduse AS: Vene õhuvägi teeb Eesti neutraalvete kohal umbes 400 lendu aastas', ERR Uudised (12 February 2017).

Kuus, I 'Kunda sadam kaalub laevaliini Loviisasse', ERR Uudised (11 May 2019).

LaGrone, S 'CNO Richardson: USS Mason 'Appears to Have Come Under Attack'', USNI News (15 October 2016).

Lauri, V 'Salmistul toimub brittide meredessant', ERR Uudised (29 June 2019).

Lee, Y, D Lague, B Blanchard, 'China launches 'gray-zone' warfare to subdue Taiwan', Reuters (10 December 2020).

Lendon, B 'Why Russian and Chinese warships teaming up to circle Japan is a big deal', CNN News (25 October 2021).

Lied, H, M Gundersen, 'Norske marineskip ble manipulert inn i russisk farvann', *NRK-beta* (25 September 2021).

Liptak, K 'Biden vows to protect Taiwan in event of Chinese attack', CNN News (22 October 2021).

Loiko, SI 'Russians sink a boat off Ukraine coast - their own', Los Angeles Times (5 March 2014).

Lubold, G, B Faucon, F Schwartz, 'Israeli Strikes Target Iranian Oil Bound for Syria', The Wall Street Journal (11 March 2021).

Lysberg, M, HC Ekroll, 'Russisk forskningsskip arrestert i dansk havn - danske myndigheter avviser meldinger om russisk krigsskip i området', *Aftenposten* (4 November 2021).

MacAskill, E 'Russian troops removing ID markings 'gross violation'', The Guardian (6 March 2014).

Männi, M 'Mereväelane: Eestil ei ole täielikku ülevaadet, mis meie vetes toimub', Postimees (19 October 2014).

Marrow, A, M Trevelyan, 'Russia ready to fire if foreign subs and ships intrude, military official says', Reuters (14 February 2022).

Marcus, J 'Iran tanker row: US requests detention of Grace 1 in Gibraltar', BBC News (15 August 2019).

Marcus, J 'Stena Impero: Seized British tanker leaves Iran's waters', BBC News (27 September 2019).

Martina, M, I Ali, 'U.S. warship transits Taiwan Strait after Chinese assault drills', Reuters (28 August 2021).

McCarthy, N 'Global Oil Shipments Depend on Major Chokepoints', Statista (25 March 2021).

McCauley, A 'The Most Dangerous Waters in the World', Time (22 September 2014).

McGuinness, D 'How a cyber attack transformed Estonia', BBC News (27 April 2017).

Michaelson, R 'Kyiv piles pressure on Ankara to close straits to Russia's warships', The Guardian (26 February 2022).

Michaelson, R 'Ever Given released from Suez canal after compensation agreed', The Guardian (7 July 2021).

Nakayama, Y 'China's claims on the South China Sea are a warning to Europe', Financial Times (8 April 2019).

Nardelli, A, G Arnett, 'NATO reports surge in jet interceptions as Russia tensions increase', The Guardian (3 August 2015).

Nebehay, S 'Civilian death toll in Ukraine now 474 but more casualties reported -U.N.', Reuters (8 March 2022).

Niemeläinen, J 'Kotkan ja Sillamäen välinen laivalinja lopettaa', Helsingin Sanomat (18 October 2007).

Niinistö, J 'Itämeren geostrateginen merkitys kasvussa', Centrum Balticum (2 March 2017).

Nilsen, T 'Norway intelligence warns about new nuclear weapons technology developed by Russia', The Barents Observer (8 February 2021).

Nobakht, P 'Why Does the Strait of Hormuz Matter?', BBC News (11 June 2019).

Nord Stream AG, 'Nord Stream to Assess Options to Further Increase Gas Import Capacities Through the Baltic Sea', Press Release (11 May 2012).

Nord Stream AG, 'Nord Stream to Further Develop Finnish Route Alternative After Estonia Rejects Survey Application', Press Release (6 December 2012).

Nord Stream 2, 'Approved Danish Route Stretches South-East of Bornholm', Press Release (2019).
Nord Stream, 'Last Nord Stream 2 Pipe Has Been Welded in the Baltic Sea', Press Release (6 September 2021).
Ozberk, T 'Turkey Closes The Dardanelles And Bosphorus To Warships', Naval News (28 February 2022).
Payne, J 'Ukraine says two commercial ships hit by Russian missiles near Odessa port', Reuters (26 February 2022).
Prentice, A 'Aid convoy to Ukraine's Mariupol turns back due to fighting - deputy PM', Reuters (10 March 2022).
Punamäe, S 'Eestisse mittelastud purjelaev pani Vene meedia kihama', Postimees (11 April 2019).
Püss, F 'Lennuamet: sagedased õhupiiri rikkumised on tingitud asjaolust, et Vaindloo saare kohal osutab lennuliiklusteenuseid Venemaa', Delfi (21 July 2018).
Räisänen, K 'Jussi Niinistön mukaan Ahvenanmaalla on "herätty todellisuuteen", kun turvallisuusuhat ovat muuttuneet: "Ei se demilitarisointi ainakaan helpota puolustamista"', Helsingin Sanomat (26 May 2018).
Ratcliffe, V, J Lee, A Shahla, 'British Marines Seize Supertanker Carrying Iranian Oil to Syria, Causing Diplomatic Row', Time (4 July 2019).
Raun, A 'Paet tõi uuringust keeldumiseks kolm põhjendust', Postimees (20 September 2007).
Reimer, A 'Vähi ja Vallbaum ristasid laevaliini nimel mõõgad', Virumaa Teataja (17 January 2018).
Rettman, A 'Russia threatens to cut Ukraine gas over Donbas war', EU Observer (7 June 2021).
Romanovitš, G 'Soome ja Eesti otsisid mereühenduse võimalusi', Põhjarannik (30 June 2016).
Romanovitš, G 'Laevaliin vajab tasuvusanalüüsi', Põhjarannik (3 November 2016).
Rosendahl, J 'Finnish military fires depth charges at suspected submarine', Reuters (28 April 2015).
The Russian Federation's Ministry of Foreign Affairs, 'Comment by the Information and Press Department on Ukraine filing an arbitration memorandum regarding the Kerch Strait incident', 26 May 2020.
Russon, MA 'The cost of the Suez Canal blockage', BBC News (29 March 2021).
Salomaa, M 'Ulkoministeriö kutsui Venäjän suurlähettilään puhutteluun – "Suomi ottaa alueloukkaukset aina vakavasti"', Helsingin Sanomat (7 October 2016).
Santora, M 'What Happened on Day 6 of Russia's Invasion of Ukraine', The New York Times (2 March 2022).
Saul, J 'Boat that attacked gas tanker off Yemen carried explosives: shipowner', Reuters (3 November 2016).

Saul, J 'Cargo ship sinks off Odessa after explosion, crew members missing -ship manager', Reuters (3 March 2022).

Starr, M 'Russian navy using civilian ships as human shields, Ukraine claims', The Jerusalem Post (3 March 2022).

Sildam, T, K Kaas, 'Vene hävituslennukid tungisid Eesti taevasse', Postimees (5 March 2004).

Sildam, T 'Venemaa tunnistas Eesti majandusvetes uurimist', Postimees (28 November 2005).

Slavin, E 'Navy strikes radar sites in Yemen in response to missile attacks on ships', Stars and Stripes (13 October 2016).

Smith, HL 'US sends warship into Ukraine's Black Sea crisis', The Times (6 December 2018).

Sorensen, MS 'Sweden Reinstates Conscription, With an Eye on Russia', The New York Times (2 March 2017).

Staalesen, A 'A major oil exploration is going on in Russia's East Arctic waters', The Barents Observer (24 August 2021).

State Department's Press Statement, 'Russia's Harassment of International Shipping Transiting the Kerch Strait and Sea of Azov', Washington DC, 30 August 2018.

Suciu, P 'French Flagship to Support NATO Mission as Tensions Rise in Europe', The National Interest (2 March 2022).

Tian, YL, Y Lee, 'China holds assault drills near Taiwan after 'provocations', Reuters (17 August 2021).

Traufetter, G 'Bundesregierung stoppt umstrittene Gaspipeline Nord Stream 2', Der Spiegel (22 February 2022).

Tuominen, E 'Meritaisteluharjoitus Lotta mittaa Merivoimien taistelukykyä', Ruotuväki (27 May 2020).

The United States Energy Information Administration, 'The Bab el-Mandeb Strait is a strategic route for oil and natural gas shipments', 27 August 2019.

The United States Department of the Treasury, 'Treasury Sanctions Key Military Leaders of the Ansarallah Militia in Yemen', Press Release, 2 March 2021.

Uosokainen, R 'Puolustusministeri Niinistö: Demilitarisoituna Ahvenanmaa muodostaa sotilaallisen tyhjiön', Yle Uutiset (17 October 2016).

Viirand, L 'Kaitseminister Niinistö: Soome valmistub Ahvenamaa kaitsmiseks "roheliste mehikeste" eest', ERR Uudised (30 July 2015).

Villar, L, M Hamilton, 'The Strait of Malacca, a key oil trade chokepoint, links the Indian and Pacific Oceans', US Energy Information Administration (11 August 2017).

Wallace, J 'Ukraine / Russia - Port update', Standard Club (25 February 2022).

Weiss, C 'Analysis: Houthi naval attacks in the Red Sea', FDD's Long War Journal (17 August 2019).

Whyte, A 'Estonia bars Russian vessel entering waters, on Crimea annexation issue', ERR News (12 April 2019).

Willsher, K 'UK takes part in huge French naval exercise to counter 'emerging threats', The Guardian (5 December 2021).

Wintour, P 'Biden can help end Yemen civil war by backing referendum, say secessionists', The Guardian (1 March 2021).

Wintour, P 'Saudi Arabia proposes ceasefire plan to Yemen's Houthi rebels', The Guardian (22 March 2021).

Wintour, P 'Hopes for Yemen peace deal fade as 'obscene' Marib death toll rises', The Guardian (7 May 2021).

Wintour, P 'New UN envoy to Yemen urged to broaden talks to end civil war', The Guardian (7 October 2021).

Woo, R, B Blanchard, I Ali, 'China condemns U.S., Canada for sending warships through Taiwan Strait', Reuters (17 October 2021).

Wright, H 'Russian ambassador summoned after aircraft breaches Estonian airspace', ERR News (24 September 2019).

Wright, H 'Russian plane flies in Estonian airspace without permission', ERR News (10 June 2020).

Xuanzun, L 'US warships' Taiwan Straits transit, S.China Sea drill futile to contain China: observers', Global Times (29 July 2021).

台湾海峡首艘千吨级海事巡航救助船开工建造 ('Construction of the first 1,000-ton maritime cruise rescue ship in the Taiwan Strait starts'), *Xinhua* (24 May 2019).

Blog Posts

Alghoozi, L 'The Houthi Attacks Against the UAE: Rules of Conflict and International Law of State Responsibility', EJIL: Talk!, 12 March 2022.

Aliano, A, R Spivak, 'Ukraine Symposium – The Montreux Convention and Turkey's Impact on Black Sea Operations', Articles of War of Lieber Institute, West Point, 25 April 2022.

Anonymous, 'Yemen war: Who is the Southern Transitional Council?', Middle East Eye, 30 August 2019.

Callaghan, C, R Schroeder, W Porter, 'Mapping Gray Maritime Networks for Hybrid Warfare', Center for International Maritime Security, 1 July 2020.

Drennan, J 'The Gate of Tears: Interests, Options, and Strategy in the Bab-el-Mandeb Strait', Center for International Maritime Security, 30 January 2018.

Fink, M 'Ukraine Symposium – The War at Sea: Is there a Naval Blockade in the Sea of Azov?', Articles of War of Lieber Institute, West Point, 24 March 2022.

Knights, M, F Nadimi, 'Curbing Houthi Attacks on Civilian Ships in the Bab al-Mandab', The Washington Institute for Near East Policy, 27 July 2018.
Kraska, J 'The Kerch Strait Incident: Law of the Sea or Law of Naval Warfare?' 3 December 2018, EJIL: Talk!.
Kuczyński, G 'Nord Stream 2: A Trap for Ukraine', The Warsaw Institute Review, 10 February 2019.
Overfield, C 'Turkey Must Close the Turkish Straits Only to Russian and Ukrainian Warships', Lawfare (5 March 2022).
Sakamoto, S 'China's New Coast Guard Law and Implications for Maritime Security in the East and South China Seas', Lawfare (16 February 2021).
Urcosta, RB 'Russia's Strategic Considerations on the Sea of Azov', Warsaw Institute (3 December 2018).

Miscellaneous

Black Sea News, Monitoring reports of the on the duration of artificial delays of vessels in the Kerch Strait from 2018 to 2021.
Encyclopaedia Britannica, 'USS Cole attack'.
Encyclopaedia Britannica, 'Bab el-Mandeb Strait'.
Eurostat, 'Maritime ports freight and passenger statistics', 18 March 2020.
Internet Encyclopedia of Ukraine, 'Kerch Strait'.
International Union for Conservation of Nature and Natural Resources, The.
Marine Traffic, 'Gulf of Finland'.
Marine Traffic, 'Sea of Azov'.
Nord Stream 2, 'Shareholder & Financial Investors'.
The Office of the Prosecutor, Report on Preliminary Examination Activities 2016 (International Criminal Court 2016).
The Office of the Prosecutor, Report on Preliminary Examination Activities 2017 (International Criminal Court 2017).
Port of Helsinki, 'The world's busiest passenger port', Press Announcement, 29 May 2018.
Russian Geographical Society, 'Complex Expedition "Hogland", Islands'.
'Singapore-Johor Causeway Opens, 28th Jun 1924', HistorySG (Government of Singapore 2021).
UA-515, Ministry of Foreign Affairs of Ukraine, 'For the attention of the Ministry of Foreign Affairs of the Russian Federation', No. 21/20-410-747, 24 May 2001.
UA-516, Ministry of Foreign Affairs of Ukraine, 'For the attention of the Ministry of Foreign Affairs of the Russian Federation', No. 72/22-446-2110, 15 September 2002.

UN, 'About UNVIM', The United Nations Verification and Inspection Mechanism for Yemen webpage.

The UN Refugee Agency, 'Refugees fleeing Ukraine (since 24 February 2022)'.

UNDOALAS, 'The United Nations Convention on the Law of the Sea of 10 December 1982: Chronological lists of ratifications of, accessions and successions to the Convention and the related Agreements', 28 May 2021.

United States Navy Judge Advocate General's Corps, 'Finland. Summary of Claims', November 2017.

Chronological Table of International Instruments

Treaties

Convention Relating to the Regulation of Aerial Navigation, adopted 13 October 1919, entered into force 1 June 1922, 11 LNTS 173.

Treaty of Peace between Finland and Soviet Government of Russia, adopted 14 October 1920, entered into force 31 December 1920, 3 LNTS 65.

Convention Relating to the Non-fortification and Neutralisation of the Aaland Islands, adopted 20 October 1921, entered into force 6 April 1922, 9 LNTS 211.

Convention and Statute on the International Régime of Maritime Ports, adopted 9 December 1923, entered into force 26 July 1926, 58 LNTS 285.

Convention regarding the Régime of the Straits, adopted 20 July 1936, entered into force 9 November 1936, 173 LNTS 213.

Peace Treaty between the Soviet Union and Finland, adopted 12 March 1940, entered into force 13 March 1940, (1940) 34(3) American Journal of International Law (Supplement: Official Documents) 127–131.

Charter of the United Nations, adopted 26 June 1945, entered into force 24 October 1945, 1 UNTS XVI.

Treaty of Peace with Finland, adopted 10 February 1947, entered into force 16 September 1947, (1948) 42(3) American Journal of International Law (Supplement: Official Documents) 203–223.

The North Atlantic Treaty, adopted 4 April 1949, entered into force 24 August 1949, 34 UNTS 243.

Convention (I) for the Amelioration of the Condition of the Wounded and Sick in Armed Forces in the Field, adopted 12 August 1949, entered into force 21 October 1950.

Convention (II) for the Amelioration of the Condition of Wounded, Sick and Shipwrecked Members of Armed Forces at Sea, adopted 12 August 1949, entered into force 21 October 1950.

Convention (III) relative to the Treatment of Prisoners of War, adopted 12 August 1949, entered into force 21 October 1950.

Convention (IV) relative to the Protection of Civilian Persons in Time of War, adopted 12 August 1949, entered into force 21 October 1950.

Convention on the Territorial Sea and the Contiguous Zone, adopted 29 April 1958, entered into force 10 September 1964, 516 UNTS 205.

Vienna Convention on the Law of Treaties, adopted 23 May 1969, entered into force 27 January 1980, 1155 UNTS 331.

Convention on the International Regulations for Preventing Collisions at Sea, adopted 20 October 1972, entered into force 15 July 1977, 1050 UNTS 16.

International Convention for the Safety of Life at Sea (SOLAS), adopted 1 November 1974, entered into force 25.05.1980, 1184 UNTS 278.

Peace Treaty between Israel and Egypt, adopted 26 March 1979, entered into force 25 April 1979, 1138 UNTS 59.

Exchange of Notes Constituting an Agreement between Denmark and Sweden concerning the Delimitation of the Territorial Waters between Denmark and Sweden, adopted 25 June 1979, entered into force 21 December 1979.

United Nations Convention on the Law of the Sea, adopted 10 December 1982, entered into force 16 November 1994, 1833 UNTS 397.

Exchange of Notes Constituting an Agreement on the Procedure to be followed in the Modification of the Limits of the Territorial Waters in the Gulf of Finland, adopted 4 May 1994, entered into force 31 July 1995, 1887 UNTS 223.

Treaty of Peace between the State of Israel and the Hashemite Kingdom of Jordan, adopted 26 October 1994, entered into force 10 November 1994, 2042 UNTS 351.

Map added to the Agreement between the Republic of Finland and the Republic of Estonia on the Boundary of the Maritime Zones in the Gulf of Finland and the Northern Baltic Sea, adopted 18 October 1996, entered into force 7 January 1997.

Agreement between the Russian Federation and Ukraine on the Russian-Ukrainian State Border, adopted 28 January 2003, entered into force 23 April 2004.

Agreement between the Russian Federation and Ukraine on Cooperation in the Use of the Sea of Azov and the Kerch Strait, adopted 24 December 2003, entered into force 5 May 2004.

Annex 15 to the Convention on International Civil Aviation (16th ed.), International Civil Aviation Organization, Montréal 2018.

International Maritime Organization Instruments

Inter-Governmental Maritime Consultative Organization, Resolution A.284(VIII), "Routeing Systems", adopted on 20 November 1973.

Inter-Governmental Maritime Consultative Organization, Resolution A.375(X) 'Navigation through the Straits of Malacca and Singapore', adopted on 14 November 1977.

Inter-Governmental Maritime Consultative Organization, COLREG.2/Circ.11, 'Amended Traffic Separation Scheme in the Strait of Hormuz', adopted on 7 June 1979.

IMO Resolution A.572(14), as amended, 'General Provisions on Ships' Routeing', adopted on 20 November 1985, entered into force (as amended) 1 January 1997.

IMO, COLREG.2/Circ. 33, Annex to the 'Traffic Separation Scheme "In the Strait of Hormuz" Change of Reference Chart and Chart Datum', adopted on 25 February 1994.

IMO Assembly, Resolution A.857(20), Annex 1, 'Guidelines and Criteria for VTS', adopted on 27 November 1997, entered into force 3 December 1997.

UN and EU Resolutions and Decisions

Council Decision (CFSP) 2022/578 of 8 April 2022 amending Decision 2014/512/CFSP concerning restrictive measures in view of Russia's actions destabilising the situation in Ukraine.
European Parliament resolution (EU) No 2018/2870(RSP), of 25 October 2018, On the situation in the Sea of Azov.
European Parliament resolution (2022/2564(RSP)), of 1 March 2022, On the Russian aggression against Ukraine.
General Assembly Resolution 29/3314, adopted 14 December 1974, Annex 'Definition of Aggression'.
General Assembly Resolution 66/99, adopted 9 December 2011.
General Assembly Resolution 68/262, adopted 27 March 2014.
General Assembly Resolution ES-11/1, adopted 2 March 2022.
Security Council Resolution 1816, adopted 2 June 2008.
Security Council Resolution 2216, adopted 14 April 2015.
Security Council Resolution 2316, adopted 9 November 2016.

International Law Commission Draft Articles

International Law Commission, Draft Articles on Responsibility of States for Internationally Wrongful Acts, November 2001, Supplement No. 10, A/56/10.

Chronological List of Declarations and Statements

Declaration concerning the Laws of Naval War, London, adopted 26 February 1909.
'Declaration by Norway, Denmark and Sweden relative to the Establishment of Uniform Rules of Neutrality. Stockholm, 21.12.1912' (1913) 7(3) American Journal of International Law.
Declaration between Denmark, Finland, Iceland, Norway and Sweden for the Purpose of Establishing Similar Rules of Neutrality, 27 May 1938 Stockholm; 'Denmark-Finland-Iceland-Norway-Sweden: Declaration Regarding Similar Rules of Neutrality' (1938) 32 The American Journal of International Law.
Iran's declaration upon signing LOSC on 10 December 1982.

Finland's declaration upon signing the LOSC on 10 December 1982 and ratifying it on 21 June 1996.

The Russian Federation's declaration upon signing the LOSC on 10 December 1982 and ratifying it on 12 March 1997.

Sweden's declaration upon signing the LOSC on 10 December 1982 and ratifying it on 25 June 1996.

Ukraine's declaration upon signing the LOSC on 10 December 1982 and ratifying it on 26 July 1999.

Oman's declarations made upon ratification of LOSC on 17 August 1989.

Joint Statement by the United States of America and the Union of Soviet Socialist Republics: Uniform Interpretation of Rules of International Law Governing Innocent Passage, 23 September 1989 Jackson Hole; 14 Law of the Sea Bulletin 12.

Argentina's declaration upon ratifying the LOSC on 1 December 1995.

Chile's declaration upon ratifying the LOSC on 25 August 1997.

Denmark's declaration upon the ratification of LOSC on 16 November 2004.

NATO, Wales Summit Declaration: Issued by the Heads of State and Government participating in the meeting of the North Atlantic Council in Wales, 5 September 2014.

NATO, Brussels Summit Declaration: Issued by the Heads of State and Government participating in the meeting of the North Atlantic Council in Brussels, 11–12 July 2018.

Joint Statement of the United States and Germany on Support for Ukraine, European Energy Security, and our Climate Goals, 21 July 2021.

Table of National Legislation

Canada's Legislation

Special Economic Measures (Russia) Regulations, SOR/2014-58, adopted 17 March 2014, last amended 6 March 2022.

Regulations Amending the Special Economic Measures (Russia) Regulations, adopted 6 March 2022, entered into force 6 March 2022.

China's Legislation

Maritime Traffic Safety Law of the People's Republic of China, adopted 2 September 1983 (revised 29 April 2021, entered into force 1 September 2021).

Law on the Territorial Sea and the Contiguous Zone, adopted 25 February 1992, entered into force 25 February 1992.

Exclusive Economic Zone and Continental Shelf Act, adopted 26 June 1998, entered into force 26 June 1998 (promulgated by the Order of the Chairman of the People's Republic of China No. 6 (on the same act) of 26 June 1998).

Coast Guard Law of the People's Republic of China, adopted 22 January 2021, entered into force 1 February 2021.

Djibouti's Legislation

Decree No. 85-048 PR/PM, Defining Maritime Limits and Frontiers of Djibouti, adopted and entered into force on 5 May 1985.

Finland's Legislation

Territorial Surveillance Act (Aluevalvontalaki), adopted 18 August 2000, entered into force 1 January 2001.

Government Decree on Territorial Surveillance (Valtioneuvoston asetus aluevalvonnasta), adopted 16 November 2000, entered into force 1 January 2001.

Germany's Legislation

Proclamation by the Government of the Federal Republic of Germany concerning the extension of the breadth of the German territorial sea, adopted 11 November 1994, entered into force 1 January 1995.

Japan's Legislation

Enforcement Order of the Law on the Territorial Sea and the Contiguous Zone (Cabinet Order No. 210 of 1977, as amended by Cabinet Order No. 383 of 1993, and Cabinet Order No. 206 of 1996), Annexed Schedule 2 (with reference to articles 3 and 4).

Indonesia's Legislation

Government Regulation No. 37 on the Rights and Obligations of Foreign Ships and Aircraft Exercising the Right of Archipelagic Sea Lane Passage through Designated Archipelagic Sea Lanes, adopted 28 June 2002, entered into force 28 June 2002.

M.Z.N.67.2009.LOS (Maritime Zone Notification), Deposit by the Republic of Indonesia of a list of geographical coordinates of points, pursuant to article 47, paragraph 9, of the Convention, 25 March 2009.

Iran's Legislation

Act on the Marine Areas of the Islamic Republic of Iran in the Persian Gulf and the Oman Sea, adopted on 20 April 1993, entered into force on 2 May 1993.

The Russian Federation's/Soviet Union's Legislation

Instructions for the navigation of ships in coastal waters within artillery range of coastal batteries in peacetime ('Инструкции для плавания судов в береговых водах в пределах зоны обстрела береговых батарей в мирное время'), Order no 897 from the Revolutionary Military Council of 5 July 1924.

The Decree no. 4450 of the Council of Ministers of the Soviet Union on the Confirmation of a List of Geographic Coordinates Determining the Position of the Baseline in the Arctic Ocean, the Baltic Sea and Black Sea from which the Width of the Territorial Waters, Economic Zone and Continental Shelf of the U.S.S.R. is Measured, 15 January 1985.

Federal Act on the internal maritime waters, territorial sea and contiguous zone of the Russian Federation, adopted 16 July 1998, entered into force on 31 August 1998.

Sweden's Legislation

Neutrality Act of Sweden ('Innefattande vissa neutralitetsbestämmelser'), No. 187, 27 May 1938.

Regulation on the Intervention of the Swedish Armed Forces in Case of the Violation of the Swedish Territory in Time of Peace and Neutrality (Förordning om Försvarsmaktens ingripanden vid kränkningar av Sveriges territorium under fred och neutralitet), adopted 17 June 1982, as amended SFS 2019: 776.

Taiwan's Legislation

Law of the People's Republic of China on the Exclusive Economic Zone and the Continental Shelf, adopted 26 June 1998, entered into force 26 June 1998.

Law on the Territorial Sea and the Contiguous Zone of the Republic of China, adopted 21 January 1998, entered into force 21 January 1998.

Ukraine's Legislation

ВЕРХОВНА РАДА УКРАЇНИ, Проєкт Закону про внутрішні води, територіальне море та прилеглу зону України (draft law on internal waters, the territorial sea and the contiguous zone of Ukraine), No. 2605, від 30.12.2002 року.

ВЕРХОВНА РАДА УКРАЇНИ, Голова Комітету, До реєстр. No. 0051, від 16.07.2015 року.

Law about adjacent zone of Ukraine of December 6, 2018, No. 2641-VIII, signed by the President of Ukraine on 29 December 2018.

United Kingdom's Legislation

The Russia (Sanctions) (EU Exit) (Amendment) (No. 4) Regulations 2022, adopted 1 March 2022, entered into force 1 March 2022.

Yemen's Legislation

Act No. 45 Concerning the Territorial Sea, Exclusive Economic Zone, Continental Shelf and other Marine Areas, adopted on 17 December 1977, entered into force on 15 January 1978.

Republican Resolution on Law No. 37 of 1991 on the Territorial Sea, Contiguous Zone, Exclusive Economic Zone and Continental Shelf, adopted on 13 April 1991, entered into force on 13 April 1991.

Law establishing the maritime baseline of the Republic of Yemen, adopted and entered into force on 23 November 2014.

M.Z.N.112.2015.LOS of 7 January 2015, 'Deposit of a list of geographical coordinates of points concerning the baselines for measuring the breadth of the territorial sea of the Republic of Yemen'.

Chronological Table of Cases

Claim of the British Ship "I'm Alone" v. United States, 'Reports of the Commissioners' (1935) 29(2) American Journal of International Law, 228.
Corfu Channel Case (United Kingdom v. Albania), Judgment, I.C.J. Reports 1949.
Saudi Arabia v. Arabian American Oil Co. (Aramco), Arbitration Tribunal (1958), 27 International Law Reports 117 (1963), p. 212.
Investigation of certain incidents affecting the British trawler Red Crusader, Denmark v United Kingdom, Report of 23 March 1962 of the Commission of Enquiry established by the Government of the United Kingdom of Great Britain and Northern Ireland and the Government of the Kingdom of Denmark on 15 November 1961, 1962 (24) Reports of International Arbitral Awards, 521.
United States Diplomatic and Consular Staff in Tehran (United States of America v. Iran), ICJ Reports 1980, p. 3.
Case Concerning Military and Paramilitary Activities in and against Nicaragua (Nicaragua v. United States of America), Judgment, ICJ Reports 1986, p. 111.
Land, Island and Maritime Frontier Dispute (El Salvador v. Honduras: Nicaragua intervening), Judgment, ICJ Reports 1992, p. 351.
Case concerning Passage through the Great Belt (Finland v. Denmark), Order of 29 July 1991, Provisional Measures, ICJ Reports 1992, p. 12.
Prosecutor v Tadić, International Criminal Tribunal for the Former Yugoslavia, Jurisdiction, Case No IT-94-1-AR72, 2 October 1995.
Legality of the Threat or Use of Nuclear Weapons, Advisory Opinion, ICJ Reports 1996, p. 226.
Gabčikovo-Nagymaros Project (Hungary v Slovakia) ICJ Reports 1997, p. 7
Prosecutor v Tadić, International Criminal Tribunal for the Former Yugoslavia, Opinion and Judgment, Case No. IT-94-1-T, 7 May 1997.
Award of the Arbitral Tribunal in the first stage of the proceedings between Eritrea and Yemen (territorial sovereignty and scope of the dispute), Decision of 9 October 1998.
ICTY, Prosecutor v. Zejnil Delalić, Zdravko Mucić also known as "Pavo", Hazim Delić Esad Landžo also known as "Zenga", Judgment of 16 November 1998.
M/V "SAIGA" (No. 2) (Saint Vincent and the Grenadines v. Guinea), Judgment, ITLOS Reports 1999, p. 10.
Award of the Arbitral Tribunal in the second stage of the proceedings between Eritrea and Yemen (Maritime Delimitation), Decision of 17 December 1999.
Oil Platforms (Islamic Republic of Iran v. United States of America), Judgment, ICJ Reports 2003, p. 161.
Prosecutor v Kordić and Čerkez, International Criminal Tribunal for the Former Yugoslavia, Judgment, Case No. IT-95-14/2-A, 17 December 2004.

Legal Consequences of the Construction of a Wall in the Occupied Palestinian Territory (Advisory Opinion), ICJ Reports 2004, p. 136.

Armed Activities on the Territory of the Congo (Democratic Republic of the Congo v. Uganda), Judgment, ICJ Reports 2005, p. 168.

International Criminal Court, Prosecutor v. Thomas Lubanga Dyilo, Decision on the confirmation of charges, 29 January 2007.

Annex VII Arbitral Tribunal, Matter of an Arbitration between Guyana and Suriname, Award of 17 September 2007.

Territorial and Maritime Dispute (Nicaragua v. Colombia), Judgment, ICJ Reports 2012, 624.

"ARA Libertad" (Argentina v. Ghana), Provisional Measures, Order of 15 December 2012, ITLOS Reports 2012, p. 332.

Arctic Sunrise Arbitration (the Netherlands v. the Russian Federation), Award of LOSC Annex VII Tribunal, 14 August 2015.

South China Sea Arbitration (the Philippines v. China), Award of LOSC Annex VII Tribunal, 12 July 2016.

Final Award of 29 June 2017 pursuant to the Arbitration Agreement between the Government of the Republic of Croatia and the Government of the Republic of Slovenia, signed on 4 November 2009.

Case concerning the detention of three Ukrainian naval vessels (Ukraine v. Russian Federation), International Tribunal for the Law of the Sea, Provisional Measures, Order of 25 May 2019.

Dispute Concerning the Detention of Ukrainian Naval Vessels and Servicemen, Annex VII Arbitral Tribunal, Procedural Order No. 1, 22 November 2019.

Dispute Concerning Coastal State Rights in the Black Sea, Sea of Azov, and Kerch Strait (Ukraine v. the Russian Federation), Annex VII Arbitral Tribunal, Award Concerning the Preliminary Objections of the Russian Federation, 21 February 2020.

Dispute Concerning the Detention of Ukrainian Naval Vessels and Servicemen, Annex VII Arbitral Tribunal, Procedural Order No. 2, 27 October 2020.

Allegations of Genocide under the Convention on the Prevention and Punishment of the Crime of Genocide (Ukraine v. Russian Federation), Request for the indication of provisional measures, ICJ, Order of 16 March 2022.

Chronological List of Maps

Map of the Gulf of Finland and the Northern Baltic Sea, added to the 1996 Agreement between the Republic of Finland and the Republic of Estonia on the Boundary of the Maritime Zones in the Gulf of Finland and the Northern Baltic Sea.
The Russian Federation's nautical chart 'Восточная часть Финского залива', scale 1:250 000, 19 July 1997.
Map 'The Strait of Hormuz' (The United States Central Intelligence Agency, Washington DC, 2004).
Chart no. 300, 'Soome laht: Paldiskist Narvani' (Estonian Maritime Administration, Tallinn, 2010).
Marineregions.org, 'Europe', 2010.
Wikimedia Commons, 'South China Sea Claims and Boundary Agreements 2012'.
Charts of Estonia, vol 1, 'Gulf of Finland: Suurupi Peninsula to Narva' (Estonian Maritime Administration, Tallinn, 2015).
Map of the maritime zones in the Sea of Azov, in Annex VII Arbitral Tribunal, Dispute Concerning Coastal State Rights, Written Observations and Submissions of Ukraine on Jurisdiction, 27 November 2018, para 73.
Map of the Bab el-Mandeb Strait and maritime areas around the Arabian Peninsula, in 'The Bab el-Mandeb Strait is a strategic route for oil and natural gas shipments', The United States Energy Information Administration, 27 August 2019.
Map of the Gulf of Finland, in Rosmorport, 'General Information/VTS Coverage Areas', 'VTS services'.
Map: The Nord Stream 2 Route, Nord Stream 2 AG, 2019.
HELCOM Map and Data Service, 'The Gulf of Finland', 2020.
Marineregions.org, 'Overlapping claim Ukrainian Exclusive Economic Zone', 2020.
Marineregions.org, 'Djibouti', 2021.
MarineRegions.org, 'Indonesia', 2021.
MarineRegions.org, 'Iran', 2021.
MarineRegions.org, 'Malaysia', 2021.
MarineRegions.org, 'Russia', 2021.
Marineregions.org, 'Yemen', 2021.
Navionics ChartViewer, 'The Bab el-Mandeb', Garmin 2021.
Navionics ChartViewer, 'The Gulf of Finland', Garmin 2021.
Navionics ChartViewer, 'Gulf of Riga', Garmin 2021.
Navionics ChartViewer, 'Hanish Islands', Garmin 2021.
Navionics ChartViewer, 'The Lombok Strait', Garmin 2021.
Navionics ChartViewer, 'The Strait of Singapore', Garmin 2021.
Navionics ChartViewer, 'The Sunda Strait', Garmin 2021.

Navionics ChartViewer, 'The Taiwan Strait', Garmin 2021.
OpenStreetMap.org, 'Strait of Malacca', 2021.
Wikimedia Commons, 'The Bab el-Mandeb', 2021.

Index

www.ingramcontent.com/pod-product-compliance
Lightning Source LLC
Chambersburg PA
CBHW071353220926
51613CB00009B/179
* 9 7 8 9 0 0 4 5 0 9 3 5 1 *